The
Kensington Collection

Kinnaird, Kinnaird Estate, By Dunkeld, Perthshire, Scotland

Front Cover: **Amberley Castle, Amberley, Arundel, West Sussex, England**

Back Cover: **Sheen Falls Lodge, Kenmare, Co. Kerry, Ireland**

KENSINGTON WEST PRODUCTIONS
LONDON
ENGLAND

ACKNOWLEDGEMENTS

We are extremely grateful to the numerous hoteliers who have advised on the compilation of this, the first edition of our new guide, The Kensington Collection. The advice we received varied immensely; some hotels advised on the layout and editorial of the book, others merely ensured that the information was clear and easy for our typesetters to work from. I am especially grateful to Tim Hart for penning our foreword; the standards set at Hambleton Hall are renowned and it is an honour to include such establishments in these pages. Like a newly opened hotel or restaurant we are bound to make some errors but we hope in time, as we re-publish the title, it will mature and flourish along with the hotels it endeavours to proclaim.

We are, as ever, grateful to our realm of production staff from research to editing, to typesetting to origination to print. We are also grateful to the many bookshops who promote and sell our titles; we are equally grateful to the many people who purchase this title. It was of course conceived with you in mind, please don't hesitate to let us know of any errors or omissions. Our abiding intention is to improve, like a fine wine, year on year.

Julian West

Kensington West Productions Ltd.
338 Old York Road, Wandsworth, London, SW18 1SS
Tel: 081 877 9394, Fax: 081 870 4270

Editors
Giles Appleton, Sally Conner, Julian West

Consultant Hotel Editors
Janet Blair, Nova Jayne Heath, David MacLaren, Jason McCreight, Louise Speller

Cartography
Camilla Charnock

Typesetting
Wandsworth Typesetting Ltd., 205a St Johns Hill, London
Bookman Ltd., 2C Merrywood Road, Bristol

Origination
Trinity Graphics (Hong Kong)

Printing
Nordica Printing Co. Ltd. (Hong Kong)

INTRODUCTION

Kensington West Productions have been involved in the publishing of guide books for some ten years. The books have tended to focus on a specific sport or leisure pursuit, for example; racing and Travelling The Turf, golf and Following The Fairways, fishing and Fishing Forays and stately homes and The Heritage of Great Britain and Ireland.

To complement this information we endeavour to recommend the very finest of venues; hotels, restaurants, inns, pubs and bed and breakfasts. This constant desire to select the best means we have included many of Britain's outstanding hotels and inns of character in our new, practical guide to short breaks which offer something different.

This guide has been developed for two reasons. Firstly, hoteliers, when consulted, were keen to be involved with such a project. Secondly, it seems guests now require something a little more special for their leisure time. As a result, we focus on the exceptional, the unusual and the mystical but not necessarily the expensive.

Hoteliers wanted such a guide book for two principal reasons. First and foremost, the market which was so buoyant in the late eighties has fallen away dramatically, leaving an unpleasant 'hole' in their annual takings. Secondly, so many of the hoteliers own wonderful houses and are, by and large, great enthusiasts. As a result, new ideas simply had to be found to satisfy the needs of the guests and the particular quirks of the individual properties and in some cases proprietors!

Golf courses have been designed, leisure centres built, murder weekends organised, cooking classes arranged. Guests have never had so much choice and never before have they demanded such variety and high standards. It is absolutely certain that your pound will go further today than it did five years ago.

Before choosing, take your time and think hard. Do you want to be pampered? Do you want to spoil the children? Would you like to learn how to play golf or clay pigeon shoot? Do you want a ride in the country or a night at the opera?

The book is full of many ideas for your entertainment and pleasure and we hope that, on reading it, you put our hoteliers to the test. We are sure they will welcome it!

The book has been divided into three sections. Firstly, a quick reference directory which is includes all our recommended hotels. A small picture may also be included but not on every occasion. These pages give you a guide to the main facilities offered by each establishment. A price guide is also given together with general details so you know what to expect from your chosen hotel.

You should always, however, make your own additional enquiries and ensure that a brochure and a list of the current tariffs are sent to you prior to booking and remember to ask if there are any special discounts available.

The Key Page will explain fully how the grid works and the maps will give you a guide as to the approximate location of the hotel you are considering. Do ask for detailed directions from the hotel when booking as many are hidden away and are quite difficult to find.

The second section includes a number of general interest articles which we hope will whet your appetite for a few excursions.

The third section of the book includes a series of hotels that have been individually selected to be featured in the Kensington Collection. The features are produced by the hoteliers themselves. They are all unequivocally enthusiastic on the marketing of these short breaks and are particularly recommended.

Esseborne Manor

CONTENTS

Hintlesham Hall

FOREWORD

I am suspicious of new hotel guides. Too many of them select their entries on the basis that all who pay are welcome, which provides little qualitative guidance to the reader.

The Kensington West system is to put in every establishment that the editor likes, and then invite those who wish to emphasise their virtues to take additional advertising space. This ensures a more comprehensive listing of worthwhile establishments nation wide.

Experience with previous publications ensures that the publishers are particularly well informed on the regional sporting and cultural possibilities of our nation.

At Hambleton Hall we are situated in a perfect position to indulge in such sports as windsurfing, trout fishing, fox hunting, golf, swimming and tennis, and we have half-a-dozen top grade 'statelies' within a stones throw; but I have to admit that a minority of my clients throw themselves wholeheartedly into these activities. With us the number one sport remains the pursuit of fine food and wine for which we offer unrivalled facilities.

We wish this new publication the success it deserves in publicising the special qualities of Britain as a holiday destination and the special facilities that are offered at a large number of them.

TIM HART

Hambleton Hall

ENGLAND

Hotel	Co-ordinates
1 Abbey House, Barrow in Furness	13 I
2 Abbey Park, Redditch	8 O
3 Abingworth Hall, Storrington	5 S
4 Alderley Edge, Alderley Edge	10 M
5 Alexander House, Turners Hill	5 T
6 Allt-Yr-Ynys Hotel, Walterstone	7 J
7 Alverton Manor, Truro	3 D
8 Amberley Castle, Amberley	5 S
9 Anchor Hotel, Porlock Harbour	5 H
10 Angel, Bury St Edmunds	8 V
11 Angel, Guildford	5 R
12 Ansty Hall, Ansty	8 O
13 Appleby Manor, Appleby-in-Westmorland	14 K
14 Armathwaite Hall, Bassenthwaite	14 I
15 Arundell Arms, Lifton	4 F
16 Ashwick House, Dulverton	4 H
17 Aydon Grange, Corbridge	15 N
18 Bailiffscourt, Climping	4 S
19 Barnsdale Lodge, Oakham	9 Q
20 Bath Place, Oxford	7 P
21 Bath Spa, Bath	6 K
22 Bay Tree Hotel, Burford	7 N
23 The Beaufort, London SW3	6 T
24 Beechfield House, Beanacre	6 M
25 Beechleas House, Wimborne Minster	4 M
26 Bel Alp House, Haytor	4 H
27 The Belfry, North Wishaw	9 N
28 Bell Inn, Aston Clinton	7 R
29 Bell Inn, Stilton	9 R
30 Belmont House, Leicester	9 P
31 Belton Woods, Belton	10 R
32 The Berkeley, London SW1	6 T
33 Biggin Hall, Biggin	10 N
34 Bilbrough Manor, Bilbrough	12 P
35 Billesley Manor, Alcester	8 O
36 Bishop Field Country House Hotel, Hexham	14 L
37 Bishopstrow House, Warminster	5 L
38 Black Lion, Long Melford	8 V
39 The Black Swan, Kirkby Stephen	13 K
40 Blakeney Hotel, Blakeney	10 W
41 Blakes Hotel, London SW7	6 T
42 Blunsdon House Hotel, Blunsdon	6 N
43 Box House, Nr Bath	6 L
44 Breadsall Priory, Morley	10 O
45 Briggens House, Stanstead Abbots	7 T
46 Brockencote Hall, Chaddesley Corbett	8 K
47 Brookdale House, North Huish	3 G
48 Buckland Manor, Buckland	7 N
49 Buckland Tout Saints, Kingsbridge	3 G
50 Burgh Island, Bigbury-on-Sea	3 F
51 Calcot Manor, Tetbury	6 L
52 Cannizaro House, London SW19	6 T
53 Careys Manor, Brockenhurst	4 O
54 Carlton Hotel, Bournemouth	4 N
55 Carlyon Bay Hotel, St Austell	3 E
56 Carnarvon Arms, Dulverton	5 G
57 The Castle, Taunton	4 J
58 Castletown Golf Links, Derbyhaven	12 E
59 Cavendish Hotel, Baslow	10 N
60 Chateau La Chaire, Rozel	1 M
61 Chedington Court, Chedington	4 J
62 Cheltenham Park Hotel, Cheltenham	7 M
63 Chelwood House, Chelwood	6 K
64 Chester Grosvenor, Chester	10 I
65 Chewton Glen, New Milton	4 O
66 Chilston Park Hotel, Lenham	5 V
67 Claridges, London W1	6 S
68 Clearwell Castle, Royal Forest of Dean	7 K
69 Cliveden, Taplow	6 R
70 Close Hotel, Tetbury	6 L
71 Combe Grove Manor, Monkton Combe	5 L
72 Combe House, Gittisham	4 I
73 Congham Hall, Kings Lynn	9 U
74 Corse Lawn House, Corse Lawn	7 L
75 Cotswold House, Chipping Campden	7 M
76 Cottage in the Wood, Malvern Wells	8 K
77 Crabwall Manor, Mollington	10 J
78 Crathorne Hall, Crathorne	14 O
79 Crosby Lodge, Crosby-on-Eden	15 J
80 The Crown, Boroughbridge	13 O
81 Crown Inn, Chiddingfolds	5 R
82 Dale Hill, Ticehurst	5 U
83 Danescombe Valley, Calstock	3 F
84 Danesfield House, Medmenham	6 R
85 Daneswood House Hotel, Shipham	5 J
86 Dean Court, York	13 R
87 Devonshire Arms, Bolton Abbey	12 N
88 Dormy House, Broadway	7 N
89 Dormy House, Ferndown	4 N
90 Dorset Square Hotel, London NW1	6 T
91 Dower House Hotel, Knaresborough	13 O
92 Down Hall, Hatfield Heath	7 S
93 Downrew House, Bishops Tawton	5 F
94 Dukes Hotel, London SW1	6 T
95 Eastwell Manor, Boughton Lees	5 V
96 Elcot Park, Elcot	6 P
97 Elms Hotel, Abberley	8 K
98 Esseborne Manor, Hurstbourne Tarrant	5 P
99 Ettington Park, Alderminster	7 O
100 Evesham Hotel, Evesham	8 K
101 Farlam Hall, Brampton	15 J
102 The Feathers, Ludlow	8 J
103 The Feathers, Woodstock	7 P
104 Feversham Arms, Helmsley	13 P
105 Fifehead Manor, Middle Wallop	5 O
106 Findon Manor, Findon	4 S
107 Fingals at Old Coombe Manor, Dittisham	3 H
108 Fischer's at Baslow Hall, Baslow	10 O
109 Flitwick Manor, Flitwick	7 R
110 Foley Arms Hotel, Great Malvern	7 K
111 Forest of Arden Hotel, Meriden	8 O
112 47 Park Street, London W1	6 S
113 Fosse Manor, Stow On The Wold	7 N
114 Four Seasons Inn on the Park, London W1	6 T
115 Fredrick's Hotel, Maidenhead	6 Q
116 Gara Rock, East Portlemouth	3 G

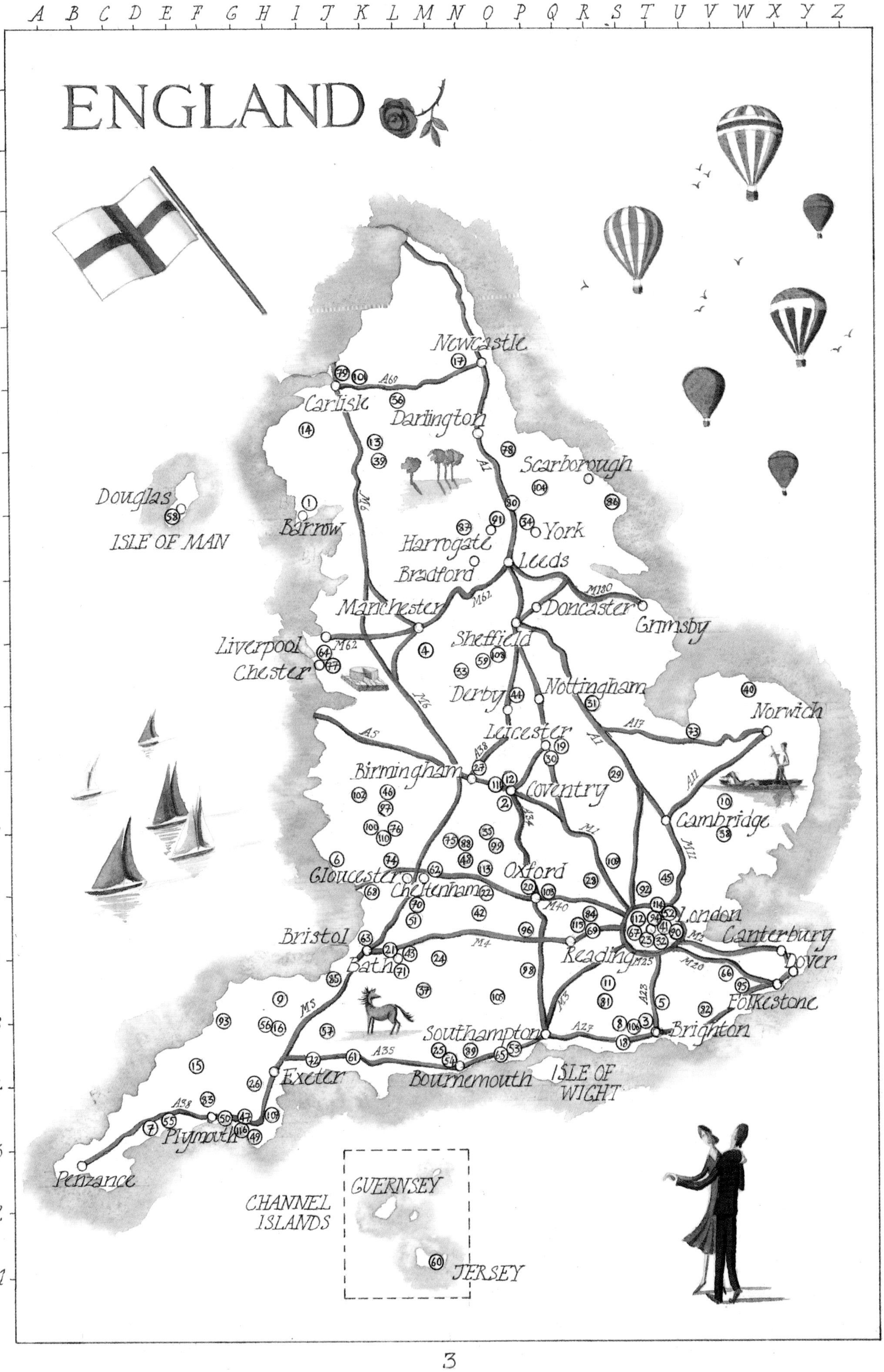

ENGLAND
Newcastle
Carlisle
Darlington
Scarborough
Douglas
ISLE OF MAN
Barrow
York
Harrogate
Leeds
Bradford
Manchester
Doncaster
Grimsby
Liverpool
Chester
Sheffield
Nottingham
Derby
Leicester
Norwich
Birmingham
Coventry
Cambridge
Gloucester
Cheltenham
Oxford
London
Canterbury
Bristol
Bath
Reading
Dover
Folkestone
Southampton
Brighton
Exeter
Bournemouth
ISLE OF WIGHT
Plymouth
Penzance
CHANNEL ISLANDS
GUERNSEY
JERSEY
A69
M6
A1
M62
M180
A5
A38
A17
A11
M1
A34
M11
M40
M4
M2
M25
M20
M5
M3
A23
A27
A35
A38

ENGLAND

Hotel	Co-ordinates	Hotel	Co-ordinates
117 The George, Stamford	8 R	180 Lygon Arms, Broadway	7 N
118 Gidleigh Park, Chagford	3 F	181 Lythe Hill, Haslemere	5 Q
119 Gilpin Lodge, Windermere	13 J	182 Maison Talbooth, Dedham	7 V
120 Goodwood Park Hotel, Chichester	4 Q	183 Mallory Court, Leamington Spa	8 N
121 Gordleton Mill, Lymington	4 O	184 Le Manoir Aux Quat' Saisons, Great Milton	6 P
122 The Goring, London SW1	6 S	185 The Manor, Chadlington	7 N
123 Grafton Manor, Bromsgrove	8 M	186 Manor House, Castle Combe	6 L
124 The Grand, Brighton	4 T	187 Manor House, Walkington	12 R
125 The Grand, Eastbourne	4 J	188 Manor of Groves, Sawbridgeworth	6 T
126 Grapevine, Stow-on-the-Wold	7 N	189 McCoy's, Staddle Bridge	14 N
127 Gravetye Manor, East Grinstead	5 T	190 Meon Valley Hotel, Shedfield	4 P
128 Great Tree Hotel, Chagford	4 G	191 Meudon Hotel, Mawnan Smith	2 C
129 Greenway, Cheltenham	7 L	192 Michael's Nook, Grasmere	13 I
130 Halewell Close, Withington	6 M	193 Middlethorpe Hall, York	12 O
131 Hall Garth, Coatham Mundeville	14 N	194 Mill End, Chagford	3 F
132 Halmpstone Manor, Bishop's Tawton	4 F	195 Mill House, Kingham	7 N
133 Hambleton Hall, Hambleton	8 P	196 Miller Howe, Windermere	13 J
134 Hanbury Manor, Thundridge	6 S	197 Millers House, Middleham	13 M
135 Hartwell House, Aylesbury	6 Q	198 Monkey Island Hotel, Bray-on-Thames	6 Q
136 Hassop Hall, Great Longstone	10 O	199 Moore Place, Aspley Guise	7 Q
137 Hatton Court, Upton St Leonards	6 K	200 Moorland Hotel, Haytor	4 G
138 Hawkstone Park, Weston-under-Redcastle	9 J	201 Mortons House Hotel, Corfe Castle	4 M
139 The Haycock, Wansford	8 R	202 Mottram Hall, Prestbury	10 M
140 Hayton Hall, Wetheral	15 J	203 Mount Royale, York	12 P
141 Highbullen, Chittlehamholt	4 G	204 Nansidwell, Mawnan Smith	2 C
142 Hintlesham Hall, Ipswich	7 V	205 Nare Hotel, Veryan	2 C
143 Hipping Hall, Kirkby Lonsdale	13 K	206 Netherfield Place, Battle	4 U
144 Hoar Cross Hall Health Spa, Hoar Cross	9 N	207 New Hall, Sutton Coldfield	8 N
145 Hob Green, Markington	13 N	208 New Park Manor, Brockenhurst	4 O
146 Holbeck Ghyll, Windermere	13 I	209 Nidd Hall, Nidd	12 O
147 Holbrook House, Holbrook	4 K	210 Normanton Park, Rutland Water	8 Q
148 Holne Chase, Ashburton	4 G	211 Nunsmere Hall, Sandiway	10 J
149 Hope End, Ledbury	7 K	212 Nutfield Priory, Nutfield	5 S
150 Horn of Plenty, Tavistock	3 F	213 Nuthurst Grange, Hockley Heath	8 N
151 Hornby Hall, Culgaith	14 K	214 Oakley Court, Windsor	5 Q
152 Horsted Place, Little Horsted	4 T	215 Ockenden Manor, Cuckfield	4 S
153 Hotel l'Horizon, St Brelade's Bay	1 L	216 Old Bell Hotel, Malmesbury	6 L
154 Hunstrete House, Hunstrete	5 K	217 Old Bridge, Huntingdon	8 S
155 Huntsham Court, Bampton	4 H	218 Old Rectory, Great Snoring	10 V
156 Hutton Court, Hutton	5 J	219 Old Swan & Mill, Minster Lovell	6 O
157 Hythe Imperial, Hythe	5 V	220 Park Farm, Hethersett	9 V
158 Inn at Whitewell, Whitewell	12 K	221 Park House, Bepton	4 Q
159 Jervaulx Hall, Jervaulx	13 N	222 Passford House, Lymington	4 O
160 Knoll House, Studland Bay	4 N	223 Pear Tree, Purton	6 M
161 Lainston House, Sparsholt	4 O	224 Pengethley Manor Hotel, Ross-on-Wye	7 J
162 Lamb Inn, Burford	6 N	225 Pennyhill Park, Bagshot	5 Q
163 Langar Hall, Langar	9 P	226 Penrhos Court, Kington	7 I
164 Langdale Hotel, Great Langdale	13 I	227 Petersham Hotel, Richmond	5 S
165 Langley House Hotel, Wiveliscombe	5 I	228 Petty France, Dunkirk	5 K
166 Lee Park, Romsey	4 O	229 Petwood House, Woodhall Spa	10 S
167 Leeming House, Ullswater	14 J	230 The Pheasant, Seavington St Mary	4 I
168 Lewtrenchard Manor, Lewdown	3 E	231 Pheasant Hotel, Harome	13 P
169 Linden Hall, Longhorsley	15 M		
170 Linthwaite House, Windermere	13 J		
171 Little Grove, St Lawrence	1 L		
172 Little Hemingfold, Battle	4 U		
173 Little Thakeham, Storrington	4 R		
174 Lodore Swiss, Borrowdale	14 H		
175 Longueville Manor, St Saviour	1 L		
176 Lords Of The Manor, Upper Slaughter	7 M		
177 Lostwithiel , Lower Polscoe	3 D		
178 Lower Slaughter Manor, Lower Slaughter	7 N		
179 Lucknam Park, Colerne	5 L		

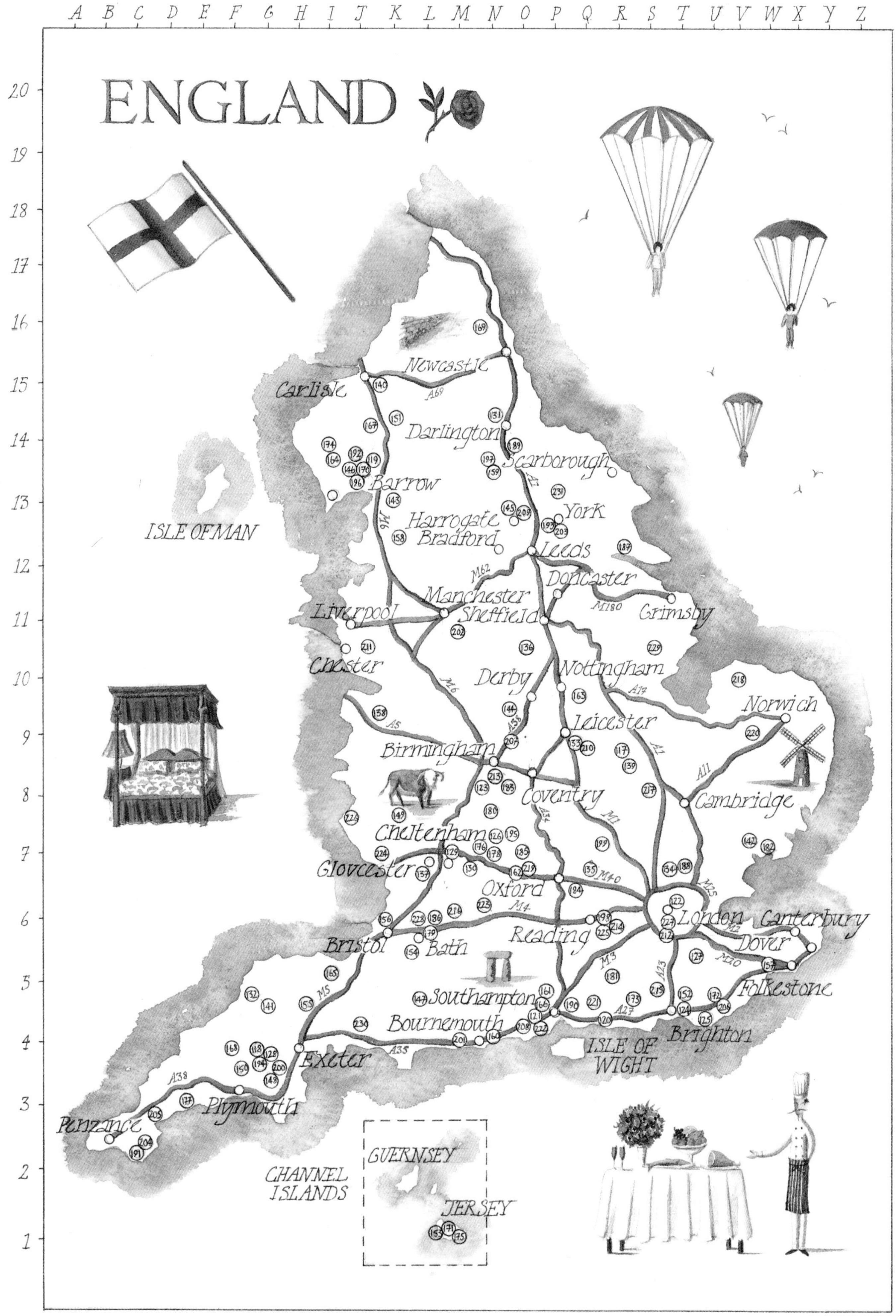

ENGLAND

Top coordinate markers: A B C D E F G H I J K L M N O P Q R S T U V W X Y Z

Left coordinate markers: 20 19 18 17 16 15 14 13 12 11 10 9 8 7 6 5 4 3 2 1

ISLE OF MAN

Carlisle
Newcastle
A69
140
151
167
Darlington
131
174
192
119
189
Scarborough
164
146
170
197
159
196
Barrow
231
143
York
Harrogate
145
209
193
Bradford
158
203
187
Leeds
M62
Doncaster
Manchester
Grimsby
Liverpool
Sheffield
202
M180
211
229
Chester
136
218
Derby
Nottingham
138
A5
144
163
Norwich
207
Leicester
220
Birmingham
133
210
17
A11
139
213
217
Cambridge
123
185
Coventry
224
149
186
A1
Cheltenham
126
195
193
176
178
185
34
88
Gloucester
129
130
213
M40
142
182
157
62
135
156
228
186
214
223
M4
122
Oxford
124
24
79
Reading
199
London
Canterbury
Bristol
154
Bath
228
214
212
Dover
M3
127
157
165
181
215
152
172
209
Folkestone
132
161
173
Southampton
147
24
125
141
153
M5
166
190
221
A27
Brighton
234
Bournemouth
12
120
208
232
163
118
128
201
164
ISLE OF
156
194
200
WIGHT
143
Exeter
A35
177
Plymouth
205
Penzance
204
191

A38

GUERNSEY

CHANNEL
ISLANDS

JERSEY
155
171
175

5

ENGLAND

Hotel	Co-ordinates
232 The Plough, Clanfield	6 O
233 Plumber Manor, Sturminster Newton	4 K
234 Pontlands Park, Great Baddow	7 U
235 Pool Court, Pool-in-Wharfedale	12 N
236 Priory Hotel, Bath	6 K
237 Priory Hotel, Wareham	4 L
238 Puckrup Hall, Puckrup	7 L
239 Raven Hall, Ravenscar	13 Q
240 Ravenswood Hall, Bury St Edmunds	8 U
241 Redwood Lodge, Failand	6 J
242 Riber Hall, Matlock	10 N
243 The Ritz, London W1	6 S
244 Riverside Hotel, Ashford-in-the-Water	10 M
245 Romans Hotel, Silchester	6 P
246 Rookery Hall, Worleston	10 J
247 Rookhurst Georgian, Hawes	13 K
248 Rose & Crown Inn, Bainbridge	13 K
249 Royal Beacon, Exmouth	4 G
250 Royal Berkshire, Ascot	6 Q
251 Royal Crescent, Bath	5 K
252 Runnymede Hotel, Egham	6 R
253 Ryedale Lodge, Nunnington	13 P
254 La Sablonnerie, Sark	1 L
255 Salford Hall Hotel, Abbots Salford	8 M
256 Saunton Sands Hotel, Saunton	5 F
257 The Savoy, London WC2	6 S
258 Selsdon Park, Sanderstead	6 T
259 Sharrow Bay, Ullswater	14 J
260 Ship Hotel, Shepperton	6 S
261 Shrigley Hall, Pott Shrigley	11 L
262 Sign of The Angel, Lacock	6 L
263 Snooty Fox, Tetbury	6 L
264 Sopwell House, St Albans	7 S
265 South Lodge, Lower Beeding	5 S
266 Spa Hotel, Tunbridge Wells	5 U
267 Spread Eagle, Midhurst	5 Q
268 Springs Hotel, North Stoke	6 P
269 Sprowston Manor, Norwich	9 W
270 St Mellion Golf & Country Club, Saltash	3 E
271 St Michael's Hotel, Falmouth	2 C
272 The Stafford, London SW1	6 S
273 Stanneylands, Wilmslow	11 L
274 Stapleford Park, Melton Mowbray	10 O
275 Stock Hill Country House Hotel, Gillingham	5 K
276 Stocks Country House Hotel, Aldbury	7 R
277 Ston Easton Park, Ston Easton	5 J
278 Stonehouse Court, Stonehouse	6 K
279 String of Horses, Faugh	14 J
280 Studley Priory, Horton-Cum-Studley	7 P
281 Summer Lodge, Evershot	4 J
282 Swan Diplomat, Streatley-on-Thames	6 P
283 Tanyard Hotel, Boughton Monchelsea	5 U
284 Tewkesbury Park Hotel, Tewkesbury	7 L
285 Thornbury Castle, Thornbury	6 J
286 Three Swans Hotel, Market Harborough	9 P
287 Thurlestone Hotel, Thurlestone	3 G
288 Tillmouth Park, Cornhill-on-Tweed	16 L
289 Tower, Sway	4 O
290 Tudor Park Hotel & Country Club, Bearsted	6 U
291 Tufton Arms, Appleby-in-Westmorland	14 K
292 Tylney Hall, Rotherwick	6 Q
293 Ufford Park, Ufford	8 X
294 Victoria Hotel, Sidmouth	4 H

Hotel	Co-ordinates
295 Waren House Hotel, Belford	13 M
296 Wateredge Hotel, Ambleside	13 I
297 Welcombe Hotel, Stratford-on-Avon	8 N
298 Well House, Liskeard	3 E
299 Wentbridge House Hotel, Wentbridge	11 O
300 Weston Manor, Weston-on-the-Green	7 P
301 Wharton Lodge, Weston under Pentyard	7 J
302 Whatley Manor, Easton Grey	6 K
303 Whipper-In Hotel, Oakham	9 Q
304 Whitechapel Manor, South Molton	4 G
305 Whitehall, Broxted	7 T
306 Whitwell Hall, Whitwell-on-the-Hill	13 P
307 Willington Hall, Willington	10 J
308 Wood Hall, Linton	12 O
309 Woodhayes Hotel, Whimple	4 H
310 Woodhouse, Princethorpe	8 D
311 Woolacombe Bay Hotel, Woolacombe	5 S
312 Woolley Grange, Woolley Green	5 L
313 Wordsworth Hotel, Grasmere	13 I
314 Worsley Arms, Hovingham	13 P
315 Wyck Hill House, Stow-on-the-Wold	7 N
316 Yarlbury Cottage, Dorchester	5 J
317 Ye Olde Bell, Hurley	6 Q

Petty France

6

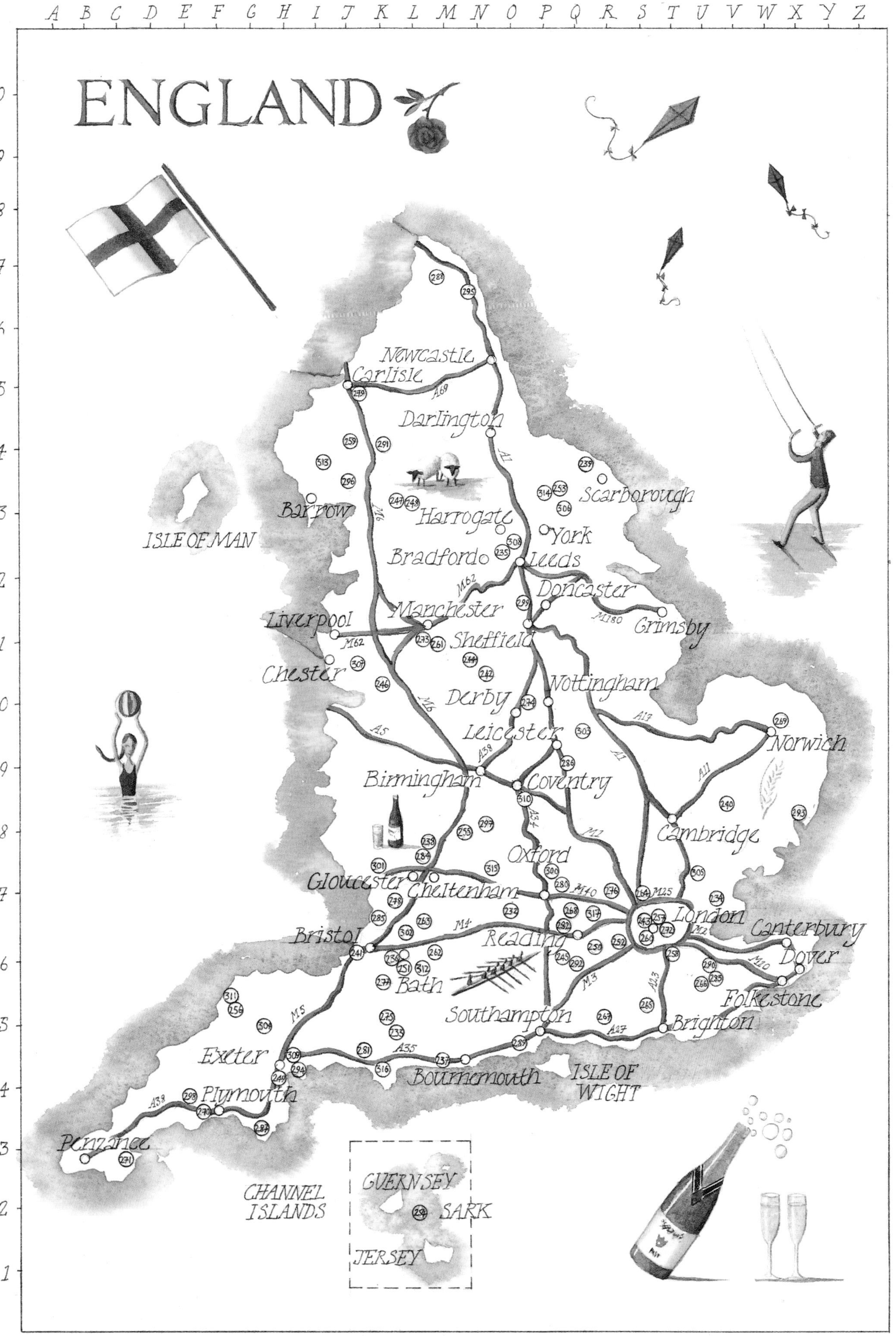

A B C D E F G H I J K L M N O P Q R S T U V W X Y Z

20
19
18
17
16
15
14
13
12
11
10
9
8
7
6
5
4
3
2
1

ENGLAND

ISLE OF MAN

Newcastle
Carlisle
279
A69
Darlington
259 291
513
296
A1
M6
247 248
Barrow
Harrogate
239
514 253
Scarborough
506
Bradford
235
509
York
Leeds
M62
299
Doncaster
M180
Grimsby
Liverpool
233 261
Manchester
Sheffield
M62
307
244
Chester
246
242
Derby
Nottingham
234
A1
M6
303
Leicester
A19
269
Norwich
A5
A38
Birmingham
239
Coventry
A11
510
240
293
258
255 293
A34
M6
Cambridge
284
Oxford
M11
301
515
306
505
Gloucester Cheltenham
248
280 M40 276
M1 M25
234
285
263
232
268 317
245 252
263 225 232
London
Canterbury
Bristol
302
M4
Reading
258 264
M2
290
Dover
241
238 262
245 292
253
266 235
Folkestone
251 312
Bath
277
M3
265
Brighton
311
273
A3
259
50
M5
233
Southampton
267 A27
281
A35
287
Exeter
309
516
237
ISLE OF
WIGHT
249 294
Bournemouth
299
Plymouth
270
282
Penzance
291

CHANNEL
ISLANDS

GUERNSEY
232
SARK

JERSEY

7

SCOTLAND

Hotel	Co-ordinates	Hotel	Co-ordinates
1 Airds Hotel, Port Appin	9 I	64 Kinnaird, Dunkeld	9 P
2 Altnaharra Hotel, Altnaharra	15 M	65 Kirroughtree Hotel, Newton Stewart	2 L
3 Alton Burn, Nairn	13 O	66 Knipoch Hotel, Oban	8 H
4 Ardanaiseig, Kilchrenan	8 J	67 Knockie Lodge, Whitebridge	11 L
5 Ardfillayne, Dunoon	7 J	68 Knockinaam Lodge, Portpatrick	2 I
6 Ardsheal House, Kentallen of Appin	9 J	69 Knockomie Hotel, Forres	13 Q
7 Argyll Hotel, Isle of Iona	8 C	70 Ladyburn , Maybole	4 K
8 Arisaig House, Arisaig	10 G	71 Letham Grange, Colliston	9 T
9 Auchendean Lodge, Dulnain Bridge	11 P	72 Lockerbie Manor, Lockerbie	7 T
10 Auchterarder House, Auchterarder	7 P	73 Lodge on the Loch, Onich	10 J
11 Balbirnie House, Markinch	11 R	74 Lomond Hills, Freuchie	8 R
12 Balgonie Country House, Ballater	10 R	75 Mansion House Hotel, Elgin	13 R
13 Ballathie House Hotel, Kinclaven by Stanley	9 P	76 Minmore House, Glenlivet	12 Q
14 Banchory Lodge, Banchory	11 U	77 Moffat House Hotel, Moffat	4 Q
15 Baron's Craig Hotel, Rockcliffe	2 P	78 Muckrach Lodge, Grantown-on-Spey	11 P
16 Borthwick Castle, Gorebridge	5 R	79 Murrayshall, Scone	7 Q
17 Bunchrew House, Bunchrew	12 M	80 Nivingston House Hotel, Cleish Hills	7 P
18 Burghfield House, Dornoch	14 M	81 One Devonshire Gardens, Glasgow	6 L
19 The Caledonian Hotel, Edinburgh	6 Q	82 Peat Inn, Peat Inn	8 S
20 Cameron House, Alexandria	7 L	83 Pittodrie House, Inverurie	11 T
21 Castle Hotel, Huntly	12 T	84 Polmaily House, Drumnadrochit	12 L
22 Channings, Edinburgh	6 Q	85 Raemoir House Hotel, Raemoir	11 T
23 Chapeltoun House, Stewarton	5 L	86 Rescobie, Leslie	7 R
24 Clifton House, Nairn	13 O	87 Roman Camp, Callander	8 P
25 Comlongon Castle, Clarencefield	2 Q	88 Rufflets, St Andrews	7 T
26 Contin House, Strathpeffer	13 L	89 Seafield Lodge, Grantown-on-Spey	11 P
27 Corsemalzie House Hotel, Newton Stewart	2 L	90 St Andrews Golf Hotel, St Andrews	8 S
28 Coul House Hotel, Strathpeffer	13 L	91 St Andrews Old Course Hotel, St Andrews	8 S
29 Craigdarroch Lodge, Strathpeffer	13 M	92 Stotfield House, Lossiemouth	13 Q
30 Craigellachie Hotel, Craigellachie	12 R	93 Summer Isles, Achiltibuie	15 I
31 Craigendarroch, Ballater	11 R	94 Sunlaws House Hotel, Kelso	5 T
32 Creebridge House, Newton Stewart	2 L	95 Torwood House, Glenluce	2 K
33 Crinan Hotel, Crinan	7 H	96 Tullich Lodge, Ballater	11 R
34 Cringletie House, Peebles	5 Q	97 Turnberry Hotel, Turnberry	4 J
35 Cromlix House, Dunblane	7 O	98 Ulbster Arms, Halkirk	16 P
36 Cross Keys, Kelso	5 T	99 Westerwood, Cumbernauld	6 M
37 Culcreuch Castle, Fintry	6 O		
38 Cullen Bay Hotel, Buckie	13 T		
39 Culloden House Hotel, Inverness	12 N		
40 Dalmahoy Hotel, Golf & Country Club, Kirknewton	6 P		
41 Dalmunzie House Hotel, Blairgowrie	9 R		
42 Dryburgh Abbey, Dryburgh	4 T		
43 Dunkeld House, Dunkeld	9 P		
44 Ednam House, Kelso	5 U		
45 Farleyer House, Aberfeldy	9 O		
46 Fernie Castle, Letham	8 R		
47 Gean House, Alloa	7 P		
48 Gleddoch House, Langbank	6 L		
49 Glenborrodale Castle, Glenborrodale	10 F		
50 Gleneagles, Auchterarder	8 P		
51 Glenfeochan House, Oban	8 H		
52 Greywalls, Muirfield	7 T		
53 Inver Lodge, Lochinver	15 J		
54 Invercreran, Appin	9 H		
55 Inverlochy Castle, Torlundy	10 J		
56 Invery House, Banchory	11 U		
57 Isle of Eriska, Oban	9 H		
58 Johnstounburn House, Humbie	6 S		
59 Kenmore Hotel, Kenmore	9 O		
60 Kildrummy Castle Hotel, Kildrummy	11 S		
61 Kilfinan Hotel, Nr Tighnabruaich	6 I		
62 Kinloch Castle, Isle of Rhum	11 E		
63 Kinloch House Hotel, Blairgowrie	10 P		

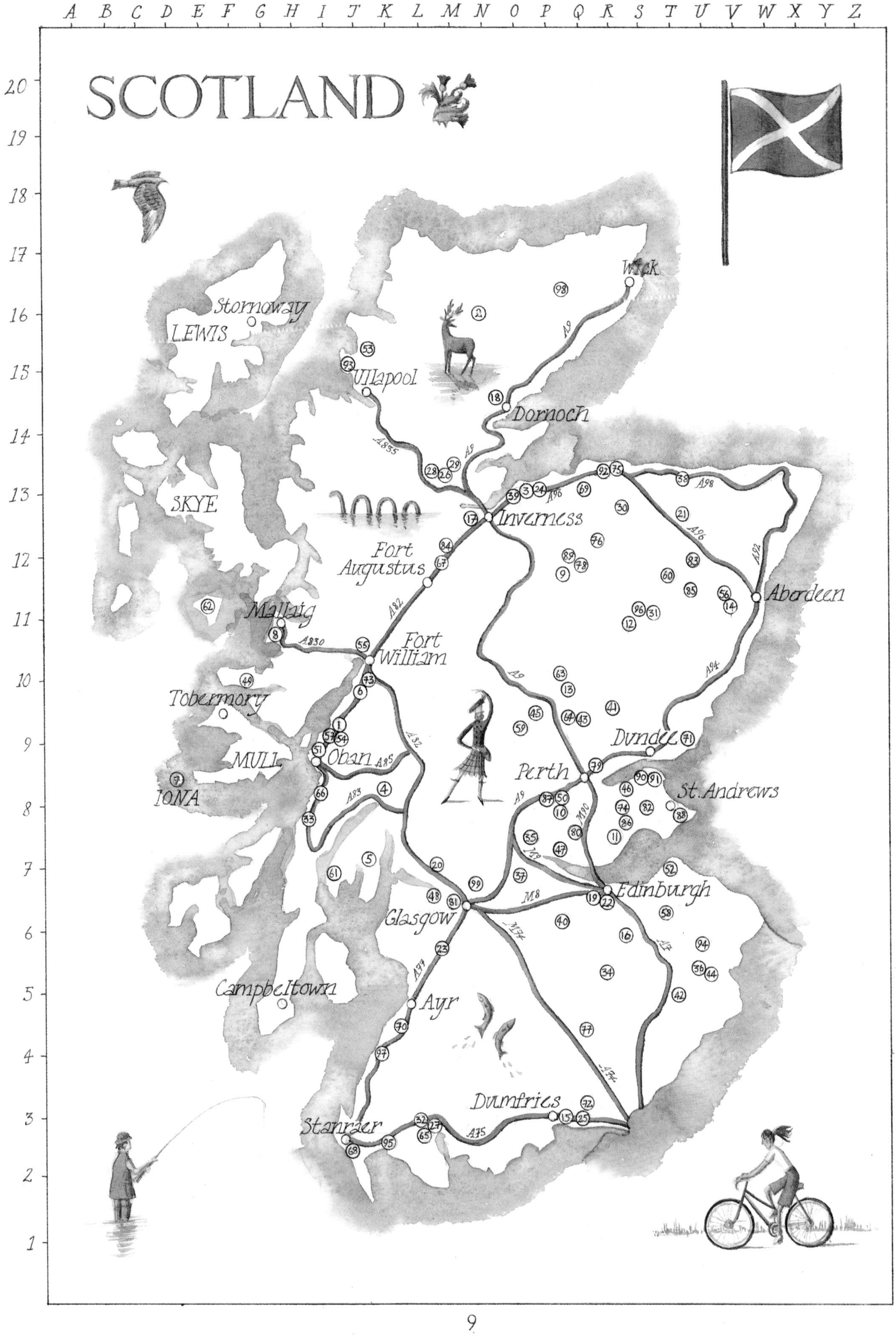

SCOTLAND

Wick

Stornoway

LEWIS

Ullapool

Dornoch

SKYE

Inverness

Fort Augustus

Mallaig

Aberdeen

Fort William

Tobermory

Dundee

Oban

MULL

Perth

St.Andrews

IONA

Edinburgh

Glasgow

Campbeltown

Ayr

Dumfries

Stranraer

IRELAND (including Northern Ireland)

Hotel	Co-ordinates
1 Adare Manor, Adare	6 I
2 Aghadoe Heights, Killarney	5 G
3 Ashford Castle, Cong	10 H
4 Ballylickey Manor House, Bantry Bay	3 G
5 Ballymaloe House, Midleton	4 M
6 Ballynahinch Castle, Ballynahinch	10 E
7 Bantry House, Bantry	3 G
8 Berkeley Court, Dublin	10 T
9 Black Heath, Coleraine	16 R
10 Blackwater Lodge, Upper Ballyduff	4 M
11 Caragh Lodge, Caragh Lake	4 E
12 Cashel House, Cashel	9 E
13 Coopershill House, Riverstown	12 K
14 Culloden Hotel, Holywood	14 V
15 Currarevagh House, Oughterard	9 G
16 Downhill, Ballina	12 I
17 Dromoland Castle, Newmarket-on-Fergus	7 H
18 Enniscoe House, Castlehill	12 G
19 Glassdrumman House, Annalong	12 U
20 Gregans Castle, Ballyvaughan	8 H
21 Gurthalougha House, Balinderry	7 M
22 Innishannon Hotel, Innishannon	3 K
23 International Hotel, Killarney	4 G
24 Kildare House Hotel, Straffan	9 R
25 Longueville House, Mallow	4 K
26 Magherabuoy House, Portrush	16 R
27 Marlfield House, Gorey	7 U
28 Mount Falcon Castle, Ballina	12 H
29 Mount Juliet, Thomastown	6 Q
30 Moyglare Manor, Moyglare	10 S
31 Newport House, Newport	11 G
32 Nuremore Hotel, Carrickmacross	12 R
33 Park Hotel, Kenmare	4 F
34 Rathmullan House, Rathmullan	16 N
35 Rathsallagh House, Dunlavin	8 S
36 Rock Glen, Clifden	10 E
37 Rosleague Manor, Letterfrack	10 E
38 Sheen Falls Lodge, Kenmare	4 G
39 Slieve Donard, Newcastle	13 U
40 Slieve Russell, Ballyconnell	12 N
41 St Ernans House Hotel, Donegal	14 L
42 Tinakilly House, Rathnew	8 V
43 Towers, Glenbeigh	4 E
44 Waterford Castle, Ballinakill	5 Q
45 The Westbury, Dublin	9 U

Ashford Castle

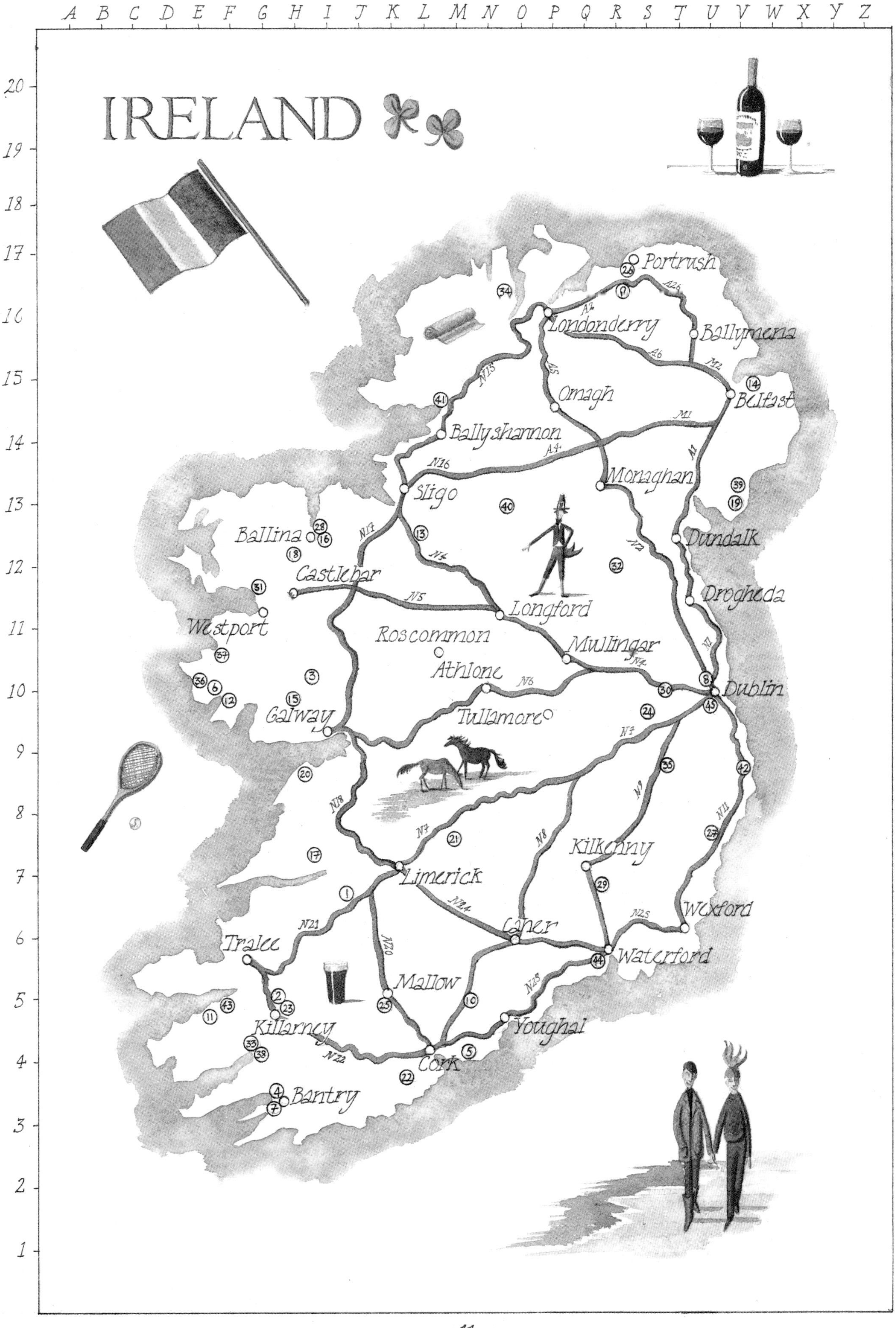

20 19 18 17 16 15 14 13 12 11 10 9 8 7 6 5 4 3 2 1

IRELAND

Portrush
Londonderry
Ballymena
Omagh
Belfast
Ballyshannon
Monaghan
Sligo
Dundalk
Ballina
Castlebar
Drogheda
Westport
Roscommon
Mullingar
Athlone
Longford
Galway
Tullamore
Dublin
Limerick
Kilkenny
Wexford
Tralee
Mallow
Cahir
Waterford
Killarney
Cork
Youghal
Bantry

N15, A2, A24, A5, A6, M2, M1, A4, A1, N16, N17, N4, N2, N5, N6, N3, N8, N7, N9, N8, N24, N25, N21, N20, N22, N25, M7, M11, M50

WALES

Hotel	Co-ordinates	Hotel	Co-ordinates
1 Bodidris Hall, Llandegla	14 T	21 Pale Hall, Llandderfel	13 Q
2 Bodysgallen Hall, Llandudno	16 O	22 Pen-y-gwrd, Nantgwynant	14 M
3 Borthwnog Hall, Bontddu	12 M	23 Penally Abbey, Penally	5 G
4 Castle Hotel, Trecastle	7 O	24 Penhelig Arms, Aberdovey	11 M
5 Coed-y-Mwstwr, Coychurch	4 Q	25 Plas Bodegroes, Pwllheli	13 J
6 Conrah Country Hotel, Chancery	9 L	26 Plas Penhelig, Aberdovey	11 M
7 Cwrt Bleddyn, Tredunnock	4 U	27 Portmeirion Hotel, Portmeirion	13 M
8 Dolmelynllyn Hall, Dolgellau	12 N	28 Seiont Manor, Llanrug	14 L
9 Egerton Grey, Porthkerry	3 R	29 Soughton Hall, Northop	15 T
10 Glanrannell Park, Crugybar	7 M	30 St Pierre Hotel, Chepstow	4 W
11 Gliffaes, Crickhowell	6 S	31 St Tudno Hotel, Llandudno	16 N
12 Glyn Isa, Rowen	15 N	32 Tan-y-Foel, Betws-y-Coed	14 P
13 Griffin Inn, Llyswen	7 S	33 Tre-Ysgawen Hall, Llangefni	15 K
14 Gwesty Fferm Penbontbren Farm Hotel, Glynarthen	7 J	34 Trearddur Bay, Holyhead	16 H
15 Lake Hotel, Llangammarch Wells	7 P	35 Ty Newydd, Hirwaun	5 Q
16 Lake Vyrnwy Hotel, Llanwddyn	12 Q	36 Ty'n-y-Cornel, Talyllyn	11 M
17 Llangoed Hall, Llyswen	7 S	37 Tyddyn Llan, Llandrillo	13 R
18 Llyndir Hall, Rossett	14 U	38 West Arms, Llanarmon Dyffryn Ceiriog	13 S
19 Maes-y-Neuadd, Talsarnau	13 M	39 Ynyshir Hall, Eglwysfach	10 M
20 Old Rectory, Llansantffraid	15 O		

Hotel Maes-y-Neuadd

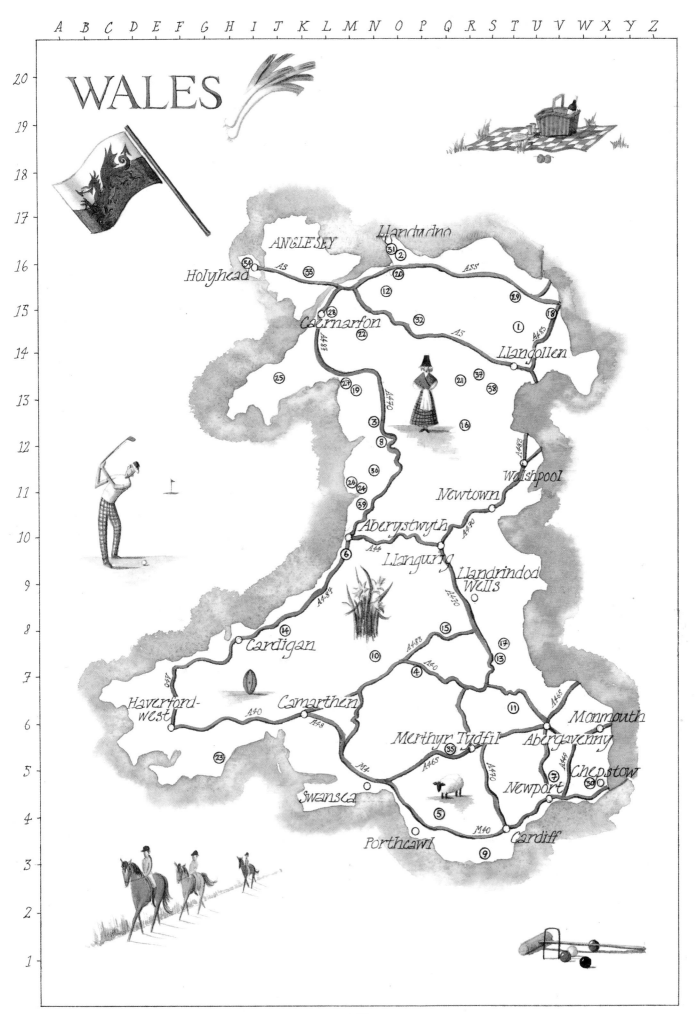

WALES

A B C D E F G H I J K L M N O P Q R S T U V W X Y Z

ANGLESEY

Llandudno

Holyhead

Caernarfon

Llangollen

Welshpool

Newtown

Aberystwyth

Llangurig

Llandrindod Wells

Cardigan

Haverford-west

Carmarthen

Merthyr Tydfil

Monmouth

Abergavenny

Chepstow

Newport

Swansea

Porthcawl

Cardiff

A SELECTION OF HOTEL CHAINS AND CONSORTIA

As I intimated in the introduction to this guide, a little spare cash in the kitty can go a long way. What is more, as hotel facilities are improved and new breaks introduced many of the tariffs remain fairly flexible. Seasonal discounts are usually available so take a little extra time to search around for your ideal break in line with your own budget. In these particularly difficult times it is always worth asking your chosen hotel if they have a package deal of some description available. Perhaps a second or third night could be half price or some of your meals included in the price. What you must do is ensure that all the so called 'extras' are included in the quoted price and if not, then ask what additional charges you could expect. Of course, you may be terribly rich and can 'damn the expense,' or perhaps just unwilling to ask. Well, good luck to you. Whatever your circumstances, there are plenty of places willing to take your hard earned cash, and some, plenty of it!

It is fair to say that the majority of this collection of hotels are part of small groups or are independently run establishments. However, that is not to say that the larger chains are not flexible and it is worthwhile considering these groups and a number of consortia who represent groups of hotels.

In my view, the trend of discounting will continue long after the recession officially ends and it may develop more subtly to become an accepted part of hotel reservations; although the more cut throat discounting arising from the recession will probably end. Regulars who are paying the going rate will soon become very disillusioned if they are aware of fellow guests who are enjoying cheaper accommodation. Even the bigger chains, ever protective of their image, are seeing this as a problem. There is perhaps one notable exception to this; London. Dealings in the capital, with its huge influx of business travellers and 'package deal' tourists, are more flexible, if more impersonal.

A number of the middle of the range hotels now offer excellent weekend packages and sometimes these have to be booked through an agent. Although this involves a little extra hassle, the added discounts can be quite remarkable. Monday to Thursday 'expense account' trade keeps mid week prices buoyant but if you can take a mini break, to include a Saturday, you may net a good deal.

Many of these hotels can also arrange some excellent breaks with theatre trips and shopping excursions being two obvious ideas. At The Berkeley (0800) 181123, one of London's leading hotels, there was an outstanding deal for golfers with a round of golf at Wentworth included in an already substantially reduced room rate. This was offered during 1992 and was possible by virtue of The Savoy Group owning shares in the course. Nevertheless, it shows good initiative and offers tremendous value to the golfer.

I feel that more and more hotels will move towards weekends with 'added value'. Free dinners, flowers, champagne, golf and even presents such as bathrobes will become the norm.

Traditionally, high summer in the capital has been hectic for the hotels, but over the last few years the tourist industry has suffered for many reasons and discount rates on rooms are now better than ever during the summer. You could also ask for a corporate rate to procure a discount. The fact that you are not a corporation does not usually matter and you may be offered a discount of 10% or more.

So what of the various chains and consortia? Superbreak Mini Holidays 071-278 0383 have a brochure which features in excess of 500 hotels in the three to five star category throughout Britain. Best Western (0800) 515535 have in excess of 200 independently owned hotels under their marketing umbrellas. Their members range dramatically in what they have to offer and prices are similarly variable. Discounts, however, are often generous and the brochure is very helpful in that it grades each hotel according to its facilities. Consort Hotels (0904) 620137 are slightly less opulent than Best Western but the prices are competitive and will have great appeal to those touring the country. This is not to say that the facilities are in any way poor, far from it.

Crystal Holidays 081-930 8513 have a very rounded, comprehensive brochure which represents some of Britain's finest hotels in a slightly 'package deal' way. This has the benefit of having mass appeal but by the same token it deflects from the exclusivity of some of the distinguished hotels within the brochure.

The bigger groups are increasingly offering a room by room charge rather than a levy per person, particularly beneficial to families. Indeed, some hotels are offering to accommodate children free of charge to encourage families to book a break.

The Forte Group is Britain's largest hotel chain and offers something for just about everyone. It has Travelodges, Post Houses and Crest Business Hotels under its banner as well as the collection of Heritage Hotels which includes traditional inns and historic properties from the characterful to the luxurious. All manner of seasonal breaks are available in these hotels and in the past the Group has provided some excellent activity weekends with the focus on ideas varying from sport to the arts. The advantage of booking with such a group is that you do have a wide choice, however, as with all large chains the hotels are run on fairly strict guidelines and the price for this is sometimes a lack of atmosphere. More often that not, the food too is rather plain, lacking in flair.

Other leading hotel groups include: Mount Charlotte Thistle, a recently merged group who offer a good selection of three to four star establishments. A similar description could be applied to Queens Moat House and Hilton Hotels.

I suppose I have always been a fan of the independents, but it would be crass not to recognise the strengths of the groups, the greatest of which is to maintain a steady standard.

Other hotel groups include Resort Hotels (0345) 313213, De Vere, Country Club Hotels, Swallow, Jarvis, Holiday Inns, Stakis and Rank. It strikes me from the feedback we receive that the hotels within these groups vary dramatically. The manager is the key to a well run hotel but you can make some general observations about the groups themselves.

De Vere Hotels are well served with leisure facilities, as are Country Club Hotels and Swallow Hotels. All three chains offer excellent packages with activity breaks taking centrestage. Stakis and Holiday Inns vary considerably. The Dunkeld House, a Stakis concern, could not be more effectively managed – an encouraging sign in these recession bitten times. Some Holiday Inns are built in true seventies style and are quite horrendous to look at. The facilities within are, however, often extremely good. Furthermore, at the

A SELECTION OF HOTEL CHAINS AND CONSORTIA

weekend, when the business trade dries up, the hotels are keen to attract guests and some excellent discounts are available. Jarvis Hotels are essentially the former Embassy hotels. The figurehead who governs the group and lends his name too, is well thought of within the trade and the hotels are predominantly well run, offering a variety of weekend breaks.

By and large hotel chains are owned by multi-nationals and these groups should not be confused with the consortia who market the groups, representing independent and often very exclusive hotels. These groups, more often than not, have produced outstanding brochures which will leave you in no doubt as to what luxuries to expect on your weekend away.

Many of these hotels are marvellously situated with beautiful grounds. The restaurants too are often quite outstanding in their own right. Some such hotels have been particularly badly hit by the recession and as a result are offering some unusually spectacular deals. The facilities on offer vary dramatically as do the types of breaks on offer. Many of these hotels are featured in our collection but some additional information may be helpful.

Relais et Chateaux 071-491 2516 offer an exquisite collection of delightful hotels, the founding fathers of this inspired group, have cuisine close to the gourmet's heart and the guide helpfully illustrates the various strengths of the individual hotels. If the restaurant is starred it will be outstanding.

The guide covers many good Irish hotels plus a selection from around the globe. The rather pompously named Leading Hotels of the World (0800) 181123 certainly provides some excellent choices, but by no means does it include all the finest hotels. Its somewhat misleading title should not put off those seeking a selection of first class hotels. An altogether more appropriate title is given to a guide which includes a number of Britain's distinguished hotels; Small Luxury Hotels of the World (0800) 282124. This wonderful guide offers true temptation in the face of economic adversity. Another appropriately named group is The Pride of Britain. A group of 30 fine hotels, these establishments tend to be houses of character run as hotels by their proud owners. Their pride shows through in the running of the hotels and whilst they may not be the grandest in the country they are well worth looking out for, particularly if you enjoy that 'home from home' feeling. It should be pointed out that each hotel chips in to the production of the brochure which is of a high quality.

Other groups congregate in a particular region with local hoteliers combining to maximise their collective strengths, attracting the prospective visitor to a particular area or region. I sometimes wonder whether this works as quite clearly the hotel is promoting the competition nearby. However, for the prospective guest these brochures offer a valuable insight into a specific area.

Three of the best selections focus on a particular country. The Blue Book, which features Irish Country House Hotels and restaurants is very helpful. It can be obtained, free of charge, from any Irish Tourist Board or from the Association (010 353 46) 23416. The selection is not large but the majority of the better hotels are featured.

Another popular and established group comes under the Welsh Rarebit banner. Once again, their list is impressive

but by no means exhaustive. The standard of members is generally high and the restaurants of a good standard too. The hotels invariably have a country location and for those seeking to explore the heart of Wales this brochure will be an invaluable companion.

A similar statement can be made about Scotland's Country Hotels and Inns Guide (0349) 64040. This guide is pocket size and clearly laid out. It features a number of fine establishments but unfortunately some of the country's finest hotels are not included. Nevertheless it is a useful companion when exploring the delights of bonnie Scotland.

The focus of The Kensington Collection is by and large on the better, independent and usually larger hotels of Great Britain and Ireland. There are, however, a number of organisations which represent the smaller bed and breakfast type of establishment. These houses are often run by the resident proprietor with dinner hosted by him or her in a house party style. Not to the taste of some but often very entertaining indeed. If this is the kind of hospitality that appeals to you then contact Wolsey Lodges (0449) 745297. They have in the region of 170 members all who have been carefully selected.

The Hidden Ireland (010 353 1) 686463 is another delightful collection of houses of architectural interest combined with a warm Irish welcome. Prices vary considerably but the standard is first rate. It would, however, be misleading to classify these two organisations as hotel chains. Their intrinsic charm and genuine appeal lies in the unique qualities of each individual property and proprietor.

One last thought when considering any break is to consult with the various national tourist offices. They are able to provide listings of the local tourist boards where you will find up to date information on accommodation. Some are even able to make reservations on your behalf.

As we continually seek more for our money and even more out of life, so the various leisure groups have had to reappraise their businesses. In the hotel industry the results have been by and large, impressive. Times may be hard, but I feel confident that there is something to suit everyone's budget.

Don't forget to look for a bargain. Plan ahead and whether its parachuting or putting your feet up take yourself away and spoil yourself. Happy hunting!

Sunlaws

A SELECTION OF HOTEL CHAINS AND CONSORTIA

Best Western
Tel: 081-547 1515
Fax: 081-546 1638

Clipper Hotels
Tel: (0202) 687777
Fax: (0202) 683404

Consort Hotels
Tel: (0904) 620137
Fax: (0904) 611320

Copthorne Hotels
Tel: (0342) 714971
Fax: (0342) 717353

Country Club Hotels
Tel: (0582) 396969
Fax: (0582) 400024

Crystal Holidays
Tel: 081-390 8513
Fax: 081-390 6378

De Vere Hotels
Tel: (0925) 265050
Fax: (0925) 601264

Doyle Group
Tel: (010 353 1) 605222
Fax: (010 353 1) 608496

Edwardian Hotels
Tel: 081-564 8888
Fax: 081-759 8422

Elegant Ireland
Tel: (010 353 1) 751665
Fax: (010 353 1) 751012

Forte
Tel: (0345) 404040

H H Group Ltd
Tel: (0342) 844400
Fax: (0342) 844566

Hamdden:
Tel: (0222) 813322
Fax: (0222) 811329

Hastings Hotels
Tel: (0232) 745251
Fax: (0232) 748152

Hilton International (UK)
Tel: (0923) 246464
Fax: (0923) 815519

Holiday Inn
Tel: 071-586 7551
Fax: 071-722 5483

Hospitality Hotels Of Cornwall
Tel: (0872) 553655
Fax: (0872) 553774

Irish Country Houses & Restaurants
  Association
Tel: (010 353 46) 23416
Fax: (010 353 46) 23292

Jarvis
Tel: 071-225 1831
Fax: 071-589 8193

Lansbury Hotels
Tel: (0582) 400158
Fax: (0582) 400024

Leading Hotels Of The World
Tel: 071-936 5000
Fax: 071-353 1904

Marriot Hotels
Tel: 071-434 2299
Fax: 071-287 0271

Mount Charlotte Thistle Hotels
Tel: 071-937 8033
Fax: 071-938 3658

Novotel
Tel: 071-724 1000
Fax: 081-748 9116

Poste Hotels
Tel: (0780) 782223
Fax: (0780) 783031

Premier House
Tel: (0925) 413416
Fax: (0925) 52501

Pride Of Britain
Tel: (0264) 76444
Fax: (0264) 76473

Queens Moat Houses Plc
Tel: (0708) 730522
Fax: (0708) 762691

Rank Hotels
Tel: 081-569 7211
Fax: 081-569 7109

Relais et Chateaux
Tel: 071-491 2516
Fax: 071-409 2557

Resort Hotels
Tel: (0273) 676717
Fax: (0273) 606675

Sarova Hotels
Tel: 071-589 6000
Fax: 071-225 3476

Scotland's Commended Country
  Hotels & Inns
Tel: (0349) 64040
Fax: (0349) 64044

Sheraton Hotels
Tel: 071-731 0315
Fax: 071-731 0532

Shire Inns
Tel: (0282) 414141
Fax: (0282) 415322

Small Luxury Hotels Of The World
Tel: 081-877 9477
Fax: 081-877 9500

Stakis Hotels
Tel: 041-221 0000
Fax: 041-304 1111

Swallow Hotels
Tel: 091-5294666
Fax: 091-5295062

Thames Valley Hotels
Tel: (0452) 611233
Fax: (0452) 612945

The Hidden Ireland
Tel: (010 353 1) 686463
Fax: (010 353 1) 686578

Welsh Rarebits
Tel: (0686) 668030
Fax: (0686) 668029

Wolsey Lodges
Tel: (0449) 741771

KEY

We should emphasise strongly that our quick reference pages are based on information compiled with the help of hoteliers and their staff. While all the information was accurate at the time of going to press, various changes will inevitably have taken place. We would therefore advise you to check with the hotels to ensure that what you require is still available at the time of your visit. Naturally, most facilities are unlikely to have 'disappeared' but you may find that the fishing, for instance, is not as good as in previous seasons for example, in Kent where serious water shortages are affecting some of the rivers. Prices also vary from season to season and if the economy continues to languish in recession, it is fair to say that prices will have to remain very competitive.

What follows is a brief resume of how to get the most out of The Kensington Collection.

Map
Each hotel has been placed in its appropriate geographical location. The key refers to each country:

E = The map of England (includes the Channel Islands)
S = The map of Scotland
W = The map of Wales
I = The map of Ireland (includes Northern Ireland)

England has been split into three separate maps and the hotels included by name, in alphabetical order. Each hotel has specific coordinates to enable you to locate it easily on the map.

Key
We have tried to indicate when particular facilities are available either at the hotel, or by arrangement nearby. The following key has been used:

◆ = on site
★ = can be organised

Number of rooms
In the main, the hotels included in The Kensington Collection are fairly small although some do have in excess of 100 rooms. These hotels are identified with a (✝). All other hotels have the exact number of rooms marked.

Price range
Prices are quoted per person per night
A: £20- £60, **B**: £60- £80, **C**: £80- £100, **D**: £100 plus, **S** = special breaks available.
It is important to emphasise here that prices can vary dramatically from season to season. Where an **S** is shown, hotels have short breaks available at special prices this, however, does not mean that other hotels will not arrange a bargain break.

Disabled
Naturally, all hoteliers are delighted to welcome disabled people wherever possible. However, some hotels are simply better prepared and equipped to look after those with special needs and where this is the case it has been indicated (◆).

Children
Some hoteliers welcome them (◆). Others prefer not to have children among their guests in which case, the column has been left blank. Where children are accepted over a certain age, the age is marked (**10**). Some hotels require prior warning (**P**).
Where special breaks are available for children they are marked with a (**C**).

Meeting facilities
This is an essential part of the business world and many hotels are very adept at combining business with pleasure. Conference and meeting facilities are marked and we have indicated the maximum number of persons accommodated. If this is over 100 then the column is marked (✝).

Credit cards
At least two major credit cards are accepted.

TV
Televisions in all the rooms.

Parking
Where there is ample parking for guests.

Restaurants
By and large hotel restaurants are open to non-residents. Where this is not the case it is marked with an (**R**).

Direct dial telephones
Telephones in each room.

Helicopter landing
You may be surprised to see so many hotels able to accept helicopter landings. In some instances this may only be a local field. Clearly hoteliers are keen to welcome this type of guest, presumably as they have large amounts of loot.

Pets
To some, a break from their pet would be sheer misery. Some hoteliers are pleased to welcome pets and these are marked (◆). Some will take pets by prior arrangement (**P**) and some, guide dogs only (**G**).

Leisure centre
These facilities vary dramatically from the gym to sauna, pools, massage and whirlpool etc. More and more hotels are expanding their facilities in this area but some are clearly better than others. Please examine all brochures carefully.

Snooker
Usually this means a snooker table. Some hotels only have a billiard table.
If you are an aspiring Steve Davis, please telephone in advance.

Croquet
Often available and definitely increasing in popularity. A good game if you have not already discovered it. Lawns often in idyllic setting, the perfect place to clobber the ball of your nearest and dearest.

Squash
This relates to the game, not the drink. Surprisingly few hotels have this facility.

KEY

Tennis

Many hotels have a court(s). Most are outdoor and the standard of upkeep will vary dramatically.

Indoor swimming pool

These may vary in size from plunge pool to reasonable length pool. Please check.

Outdoor swimming pool

Check the temperature!

Golf

Golf is an infuriating but addictive sport. Today, several hotels have their own courses which can vary dramatically in standard and upkeep. Some are almost championship standard, others a casual nine holes.

Many hotels now have good relationships with nearby courses and can arrange tee times and reduced fees. Please bring a handicap certificate with you and check times are available, especially at weekends.

◆ = on site.

★ = can be organised

Fishing

Some hotels are fortunate enough to own their own stretch of water. Others can arrange rods elsewhere. As the quality of the fishing can vary please check with the hotel in advance as to the running.

◆ = on site

★ = can be organised

Cycling

Bicycles can be hired from some hotels and these have been marked. countryside.

◆ = on site

★ = can be organised

Horseracing

We have indicated where there is a racecourse within 20 miles of the hotel.

Horse riding

A few hotels have stables but many can arrange horse riding nearby. Please take suitable clothing or enquire into hiring.

◆ = on site

★ = can be organised

Eastwell Manor

KEY

Shooting

Many hotels will arrange clay pigeon shooting and some do have rough or driven shooting available on their land. We have marked those with clays (**C**). Those with other types are marked ◆ or ★ as appropriate. Archery is marked (**A**).

Walking

We have tried to pinpoint hotels in particularly pleasant settings or with walks mapped out.

Airborne

As a man with little or no head for heights, I fail to understand the attraction of such pursuits as parachuting, hang-gliding and ballooning. However, these pastimes are popular and several hotels are able to organise such activities.

◆ = on site
★ = can be organised

Sailing

A life on the ocean wave may not appeal to everyone but several hotels have moorings, others are very willing to arrange sailing or boat trips for the enthusiast

◆ = on site
★ = can be organised

Seaside

Hotels which overlook the sea are marked (**S**). Those within ten miles are marked with the mileage (**10**).

Theatre

This category includes not all, but two major artforms, Opera trips (**O**) Theatre (**T**). Many hotels are able to organise trips to these cultural events if you give them prior warning.

Gourmet

Now this is a tricky one! The majority of our recommended hotels offer fine cuisine, some however take pleasure in organising Wine Tastings (**W**), Culinary weekends or Cookery Classes (**C**) and Banquets (**B**). The fact that a ◆ is not indicated does not imply that the cuisine is lacking in some way.

Diet and health

From pampering to skin care to work out to taking it very gently. This category covers hotels that can arrange 'product weekends' or short breaks for pure pampering. This need not necessaily mean rabbit food but clearly the cuisine will be tempered with the spirit of the occasion.

Bridge and cards

Many hotels organise special card weekends which can be instructive or competitive and these have been marked for the card sharks amongst you. Bridge is especially popular.

Literary

For those who enjoy 'wandering lonely as a cloud' and waxing lyrical. The special breaks vary from literary lectures to poetry reading.

Painting and crafts

This can be instructional or participatory or both, Painting (**P**), Flower Arranging (**F**), Weaving (**W**).

Romantic

Champagne, four posters, candlelight dinners, dancing, that sort of idea. Some hotels can arrange special touches with a little warning for that anniversary, birthday or even wedding night!

Murder and fantasy

Not for the shy, silly games, fancy dress dinners and whodunit weekends are becoming increasingly popular. An excellent idea for those wishing to organise a large group break.

Heritage

Britain and Ireland are so rich in heritage that the vast majority of hotels are in close proximity to some or all of the following; stately homes, castles, museums, gardens and galleries. We have used a ten mile radius to give you some guide.

Shopping

We have tried to identify hotels with interesting or excellent shopping facilities nearby. London is one very obvious example others include the Cotswolds for antiques, Bath for boutiques and many more.

Outward bound

This category caters for those who enjoy more strenuous pursuits; long walks, hiking, abseiling, back packing, mountain biking etc. Many such enthusiasts prefer to rough it, but for those who seek to slumber in style, a number of hotels can accommodate them.

Peace and quiet

Many hotels enjoy delightful locations but we have tried to indicate where a hotel has a particularly picturesque and peaceful setting. Where a (**B**) is marked, the area is good for birdwatching.

In town

Where the hotel is in a city or a busy location

In the country

A rural or village setting, or even perhaps in a small market town.

Telephone and Fax machines

British Telecom endeavour to make all publisher's lives a nightmare by changing numbers as frequently as possible. This is an extremely up to date list but please forgive us if numbers have changed since publication.

Calls to Ireland

All calls to Ireland should be prefixed with 010 353. Exclude the 0 from the next group of digits if dialling from mainland Britain.

THE KENSINGTON COLLECTION - BY COUNTY

This list is designed to help those who are going to visit an area or perhaps those who wish to plan a tour of certain hotel's in a region of the British Isles.

ENGLAND

Avon
Bath Spa, Bath
Chelwood House, Chelwood
Combe Grove Manor, Monkton Combe
Hunstrete House, Hunstrete
Hutton Court, Hutton
Petty France, Dunkirk
Priory Hotel, Bath
Redwood Lodge, Failand
Royal Crescent, Bath
Thornbury Castle, Thornbury

Bedfordshire
Flitwick Manor, Flitwick
Moore Place, Aspley Guise

Berkshire
Cliveden, Taplow
Elcot Park, Elcot
Fredrick's Hotel, Maidenhead
Monkey Island Hotel, Bray-on-Thames
Oakley Court, Windsor
Royal Berkshire, Ascot
Swan Diplomat, Streatley-on-Thames
Ye Olde Bell, Hurley

Buckinghamshire
Bell Inn, Aston Clinton
Danesfield House, Medmenham
Hartwell House, Aylesbury

Cambridgeshire
Bell Inn, Stilton
The Haycock , Wansford
Old Bridge, Huntingdon

Channel Isles
Chateau La Chaire, Rozel
Hotel l'Horizon, St Brelade's Bay
Little Grove, St Lawrence
Longueville Manor, St Saviour
La Sablonnerie, Sark

Cheshire
Alderley Edge, Alderley Edge
Chester Grosvenor, Chester
Crabwall Manor, Mollington
Mottram Hall, Prestbury
Nunsmere Hall, Sandiway
Rookery Hall, Worleston
Shrigley Hall, Pott Shrigley
Stanneylands, Wilmslow
Willington Hall, Willington

Cornwall
Alverton Manor, Truro
Carlyon Bay Hotel, St Austell
Danescombe Valley, Calstock
Lostwithiel , Lower Polscoe
Meudon Hotel, Mawnan Smith
Nansidwell, Mawnan Smith
Nare Hotel, Veryan
St Mellion Golf & Country Club, Saltash
St Michael's Hotel, Falmouth
Well House, Liskeard

Cumbria
Abbey House, Barrow in Furness
Appleby Manor, Appleby-in-
   Westmorland
Armathwaite Hall, Bassenthwaite
The Black Swan, Kirkby Stephen
Crosby Lodge, Crosby-on-Eden
Farlam Hall, Brampton
Gilpin Lodge, Windermere
Hayton Hall, Wetheral
Hipping Hall, Kirkby Lonsdale
Holbeck Ghyll, Windermere
Hornby Hall, Culgaith
Langdale Hotel, Great Langdale
Leeming House, Ullswater
Linthwaite House, Windermere
Lodore Swiss, Borrowdale
Michael's Nook, Grasmere
Miller Howe, Windermere
Sharrow Bay, Ullswater
String of Horses, Faugh
Tufton Arms, Appleby-in-Westmorland
Wateredge Hotel, Ambleside
Wordsworth Hotel, Grasmere

Derbyshire
Biggin Hall, Biggin
Breadsall Priory, Morley
Cavendish Hotel, Baslow
Fischer's at Baslow Hall, Baslow
Hassop Hall, Great Longstone
Riber Hall, Matlock
Riverside Hotel, Ashford-in-the-Water

Devon
Arundell Arms, Lifton
Bel Alp House, Haytor
Brookdale House, North Huish
Buckland Tout Saints, Kingsbridge
Burgh Island, Bigbury-on-Sea
Combe House, Gittisham
Downrew House, Bishops Tawton
Fingals at Old Coombe Manor,
   Dittisham
Gara Rock, East Portlemouth
Gidleigh Park, Chagford
Great Tree Hotel, Chagford
Halmpstone Manor, Bishop's Tawton
Highbullen, Chittlehamholt
Holne Chase, Ashburton
Horn of Plenty, Tavistock
Huntsham Court, Bampton
Lewtrenchard Manor, Lewdown
Mill End, Chagford
Moorland Hotel, Haytor
Royal Beacon, Exmouth
Saunton Sands Hotel, Saunton
Thurlestone Hotel, Thurlestone
Victoria Hotel, Sidmouth
Whitechapel Manor, South Molton
Woodhayes Hotel, Whimple
Woolacombe Bay Hotel, Woolacombe

Dorset
Beechleas House, Wimborne Minster
Carlton Hotel, Bournemouth
Chedington Court, Chedington
Dormy House, Ferndown
Knoll House, Studland Bay
Mortons House Hotel, Corfe Castle
Plumber Manor, Sturminster Newton
Priory Hotel, Wareham
Stock Hill Country House Hotel,
   Gillingham
Summer Lodge, Evershot
Yarlbury Cottage, Dorchester

Durham
Hall Garth, Coatham Mundeville

Essex
Maison Talbooth, Dedham
Pontlands Park, Great Baddow
Whitehall, Broxted

Gloucestershire
Calcot Manor, Tetbury
Cheltenham Park Hotel, Cheltenham
Close Hotel, Tetbury
Corse Lawn House, Corse Lawn
Cotswold House, Chipping Campden
Fosse Manor, Stow-on-the-Wold
Grapevine, Stow-on-the-Wold
Greenway, Cheltenham
Halewell Close, Withington
Hatton Court, Upton St Leonards
Lords Of The Manor, Upper Slaughter
Lower Slaughter Manor, Lower Slaughter
Puckrup Hall, Puckrup
Snooty Fox, Tetbury
Stonehouse Court, Stonehouse
Tewkesbury Park Hotel, Tewkesbury
Wyck Hill House, Stow-on-the-Wold
Clearwell Castle, Royal Forest of Dean

Hampshire
Careys Manor, Brockenhurst
Chewton Glen, New Milton
Esseborne Manor, Hurstbourne Tarrant
Fifehead Manor, Middle Wallop
Gordleton Mill, Lymington
Lainston House, Sparsholt
Lee Park, Romsey
Meon Valley Hotel, Shedfield
New Park Manor, Brockenhurst
Passford House, Lymington
Romans Hotel, Silchester
Tower, Sway
Tylney Hall, Rotherwick

THE KENSINGTON COLLECTION - BY COUNTY

Hereford & Worcester
Abbey Park, Redditch
Allt-Yr-Ynys Hotel, Walterstone
Brockencote Hall, Chaddesley Corbett
Buckland Manor, Buckland
Cottage in the Wood, Malvern Wells
Dormy House, Broadway
Elms Hotel, Abberley
Evesham Hotel, Evesham
Foley Arms Hotel, Great Malvern
Grafton Manor, Bromsgrove
Hope End, Ledbury
Lygon Arms, Broadway
Pengethley Manor Hotel, Ross-on-Wye
Penrhos Court, Kington
Salford Hall Hotel, Abbots Salford
Wharton Lodge, Weston under
    Pentyard

Hertfordshire
Briggens House, Stanstead Abbots
Down Hall, Hatfield Heath
Hanbury Manor, Thundridge
Manor of Groves, Sawbridgeworth
Sopwell House, St Albans
Stocks Country House Hotel, Aldbury

Humberside
Manor House, Walkington

Isle of Man
Castletown Golf Links, Derbyhaven

Kent
Chilston Park Hotel, Lenham
Eastwell Manor, Boughton Lees
Hythe Imperial, Hythe
Spa Hotel, Tunbridge Wells
Tanyard Hotel, Boughton Monchelsea
Tudor Park Hotel & Country Club,
    Bearsted

Lancashire
Inn at Whitewell, Whitewell

Leicestershire
Barnsdale Lodge, Oakham
Belmont House, Leicester
Normanton Park, Rutland Water
Stapleford Park, Melton Mowbray
Three Swans Hotel, Market Harborough
Whipper-In Hotel, Oakham

Lincolnshire
Belton Woods, Belton
The George, Stamford
Hambleton Hall, Hambleton
Petwood House, Woodhall Spa

London
The Beaufort, London SW3
The Berkeley, London SW1
Blakes Hotel, London SW7
Cannizaro House, London SW19

Claridges, London W1
Dorset Square Hotel, London NW1
Dukes Hotel, London SW1
47 Park Street, London W1
Four Seasons Inn on the Park,
    London W1
The Goring, London SW1
The Ritz, London W1
The Savoy, London WC2
The Stafford, London SW1

Middlesex
Ship Hotel, Shepperton

Norfolk
Blakeney Hotel, Blakeney
Congham Hall, Kings Lynn
Old Rectory, Great Snoring
Park Farm, Hethersett
Sprowston Manor, Norwich

Northumberland
Aydon Grange, Corbridge
Bishop Field Country House Hotel,
    Hexham
Linden Hall, Longhorsley
Tillmouth Park, Cornhill-on-Tweed
Waren House Hotel, Belford

Nottinghamshire
Langar Hall, Langar

Oxfordshire
Bath Place, Oxford
Bay Tree Hotel, Burford
The Feathers, Woodstock
Lamb Inn, Burford
Le Manoir Aux Quat' Saisons,
    Great Milton
The Manor, Chadlington
Mill House, Kingham
Old Swan & Mill, Minster Lovell
The Plough, Clanfield
Springs Hotel, North Stoke
Studley Priory, Horton-Cum-Studley
Weston Manor, Weston-on-the-Green

Shropshire
The Feathers, Ludlow
Hawkstone Park, Weston-under-
    Redcastle

Somerset
Anchor Hotel, Porlock Harbour
Ashwick House, Dulverton
Carnarvon Arms, Dulverton
The Castle, Taunton
Daneswood House Hotel, Shipham
Holbrook House, Holbrook
Langley House Hotel, Wiveliscombe
The Pheasant, Seavington St Mary
Ston Easton Park, Ston Easton

Staffordshire
Hoar Cross Hall Health Spa, Hoar Cross

Suffolk
Angel, Bury St Edmunds
Black Lion, Long Melford
Hintlesham Hall, Ipswich
Ravenswood Hall, Bury St Edmunds
Ufford Park, Ufford

Surrey
Angel, Guildford
Crown Inn, Chiddingfolds
Lythe Hill, Haslemere
Nutfield Priory, Nutfield
Pennyhill Park, Bagshot
Petersham Hotel, Richmond
Runnymede Hotel, Egham
Selsdon Park, Sanderstead

Sussex
Abingworth Hall, Storrington
Alexander House, Turners Hill
Amberley Castle, Amberley
Bailiffscourt, Climping
Dale Hill, Ticehurst
Findon Manor, Findon
Goodwood Park Hotel, Chichester
The Grand, Brighton
The Grand, Eastbourne
Gravetye Manor, East Grinstead
Horsted Place, Little Horsted
Little Hemingfold, Battle
Little Thakeham, Storrington
Netherfield Place, Battle
Ockenden Manor, Cuckfield
Park House, Bepton
South Lodge, Lower Beeding
Spread Eagle, Midhurst

Warwickshire
Ansty Hall, Ansty
The Belfry, Wishaw
Billesley Manor, Alcester
Ettington Park, Alderminster
Forest of Arden Hotel, Meriden
Mallory Court, Leamington Spa
Welcombe Hotel, Stratford-on-Avon
Woodhouse, Princethorpe

West Midlands
New Hall, Sutton Coldfield
Nuthurst Grange, Hockley Heath

Wiltshire
Beechfield House, Beanacre
Bishopstrow House, Warminster
Blunsdon House Hotel, Blunsdon
Box House, Nr Bath
Lucknam Park, Colerne
Manor House, Castle Combe
Old Bell Hotel, Malmesbury
Pear Tree, Purton
Sign of the Angel, Lacock

THE KENSINGTON COLLECTION - BY COUNTY

Whatley Manor, Easton Grey
Woolley Grange, Woolley Green

Yorkshire
Bilbrough Manor, Bilbrough
Crathorne Hall, Crathorne
The Crown, Boroughbridge
Dean Court, York
Devonshire Arms, Bolton Abbey
Dower House Hotel, Knaresborough-
Feversham Arms, Helmsley
Hob Green, Markington
Jervaulx Hall, Jervaulx
McCoy's, Staddle Bridge
Middlethorpe Hall, York
Millers House, Middleham
Mount Royale, York
Nidd Hall, Nidd
Pheasant Hotel, Harome
Pool Court, Pool-in-Wharfedale
Raven Hall, Ravenscar
Rookhurst Georgian, Hawes
Rose & Crown Inn, Bainbridge
Ryedale Lodge, Nunnington
Wentbridge House Hotel, Wentbridge
Whitwell Hall, Whitwell-on-the-Hill
Wood Hall, Linton
Worsley Arms, Hovingham

SCOTLAND

Aberdeenshire
Castle Hotel, Huntly
Craigendarroch, Ballater
Kildrummy Castle Hotel, Kildrummy
Pittodrie House, Inverurie
Tullich Lodge, Ballater

Argyll
Airds Hotel, Port Appin
Ardanaiseig, Kilchrenan
Ardfillayne, Dunoon

Ardsheal House, Kentallen of Appin
Argyll Hotel, Isle of Iona
Chapeltoun House, Stewarton
Crinan Hotel, Crinan
Glenborrodale Castle, Glenborrodale
Glenfeochan House, Oban
Invercreran, Appin
Isle of Eriska, Oban
Kilfinan Hotel, Nr Tighnabruaich
Knipoch Hotel, Oban
One Devonshire Gardens, Glasgow
Westerwood, Cumbernauld

Ayrshire
Ladyburn , Maybole
Turnberry Hotel, Turnberry

Banffshire
Craigellachie Hotel, Craigellachie
Cullen Bay Hotel, Buckie
Minmore House, Glenlivet

Dumfries & Galloway
Baron's Craig Hotel, Rockcliffe
Comlongon Castle, Clarencefield
Kirroughtree Hotel, Newton Stewart
Knockinaam Lodge, Portpatrick
Lockerbie Manor, Lockerbie
Moffat House Hotel, Moffat
Torwood House, Glenluce

Dunbartonshire
Cameron House, Alexandria

Fife
Balbirnie House, Markinch
Fernie Castle, Letham
Gean House, Alloa
Lomond Hills, Freuchie
Peat Inn, Peat Inn
Rescobie, Leslie
Rufflets, St Andrews
St Andrews Golf Hotel, St Andrews

St Andrews Old Course Hotel,
   St Andrews

Grampian
Balgonie Country House, Ballater
Mansion House Hotel, Elgin

Inverness-shire
Alton Burn, Nairn
Arisaig House, Arisaig
Auchendean Lodge, Dulnain Bridge
Bunchrew House, Bunchrew
Clifton House, Nairn
Culloden House Hotel, Inverness
Inverlochy Castle, Torlundy
Kinloch Castle, Isle of Rhum
Knockie Lodge, Whitebridge
Lodge on the Loch, Onich
Polmaily House, Drumnadrochit
Ulbster Arms, Halkirk

Kincardineshire
Banchory Lodge, Banchory
Invery House, Banchory
Raemoir House Hotel, Raemoir

Kinross-shire
Nivingston House Hotel, Cleish Hills

Lothian
Borthwick Castle, Gorebridge
The Caledonian Hotel, Edinburgh
Channings, Edinburgh
Dalmahoy Hotel, Golf & Country Club,
   Kirknewton
Greywalls, Muirfield
Johnstounburn House, Humbie

Morayshire
Knockomie Hotel, Forres
Muckrach Lodge, Grantown-on-Spey
Seafield Lodge, Grantown-on-Spey
Stotfield House, Lossiemouth

Egerton Grey Country House Hotel

THE KENSINGTON COLLECTION - BY COUNTY

Peebleshire
Cringletie House, Peebles

Perthshire
Auchterarder House, Auchterarder
Ballathie House Hotel, Kinclaven
   by Stanley
Cromlix House, Dunblane
Dalmunzie House Hotel, Blairgowrie
Dunkeld House, Dunkeld
Farleyer House, Aberfeldy
Gleneagles, Auchterarder
Kenmore Hotel, Kenmore
Kinloch House Hotel, Blairgowrie
Kinnaird, Dunkeld
Letham Grange, Colliston
Murrayshall, Scone
Roman Camp, Callander

Renfrewshire
Gleddoch House, Langbank

Ross-shire
Contin House, Strathpeffer
Coul House Hotel, Strathpeffer
Craigdarroch Lodge, Strathpeffer
Summer Isles, Achiltibuie

Roxburghshire
Cross Keys, Kelso
Dryburgh Abbey, Dryburgh
Ednam House, Kelso
Sunlaws House Hotel, Kelso

Stirlingshire
Culcreuch Castle, Fintry

Sutherland
Altnaharra Hotel, Altnaharra
Burghfield House, Dornoch
Inver Lodge, Lochinver

Wigtownshire
Corsemalzie House Hotel,
   Newton Stewart
Creebridge House, Newton Stewart

IRELAND

Co Antrim
Magherabuoy House, Portrush

Co Cavan
Slieve Russell, Ballyconnell

Co Clare
Dromoland Castle, Newmarket-
   on-Fergus
Gregans Castle, Ballyvaughan

Co Cork
Ballylickey Manor House, Bantry Bay
Ballymaloe House, Midleton

Bantry House, Bantry
Innishannon Hotel, Innishannon
Longueville House, Mallow

Co Donegal
Rathmullan House, Rathmullan
St Ernans House Hotel, Donegal

Co Down
Culloden Hotel, Holywood
Glassdrumman House, Annalong
Slieve Donard, Newcastle

Co Dublin
Berkeley Court, Dublin
The Westbury, Dublin

Co Galway
Ballynahinch Castle, Ballynahinch
Cashel House, Cashel
Currarevagh House, Oughterard
Rock Glen, Clifden
Rosleague Manor, Letterfrack

Co Kerry
Aghadoe Heights, Killarney
Caragh Lodge, Caragh Lake
International Hotel, Killarney
Park Hotel, Kenmare
Sheen Falls Lodge, Kenmare
Towers, Glenbeigh

Co Kildare
Kildare House Hotel, Straffan
Moyglare Manor, Moyglare

Co Kilkenny
Mount Juliet, Thomastown

Co Limerick
Adare Manor, Adare

Co Londonderry
Black Heath, Coleraine

Co Mayo
Ashford Castle, Cong
Downhill, Ballina
Enniscoe House, Castlehill
Mount Falcon Castle, Ballina
Newport House, Newport

Co Monaghan
Nuremore Hotel, Carrickmacross

Co Sligo
Coopershill House, Riverstown

Co Tipperary
Gurthalougha House, Balinderry

Co Waterford
Blackwater Lodge, Upper Ballyduff
Waterford Castle, Ballinakill

Co Wexford
Marlfield House, Gorey

Co Wicklow
Rathsallagh House, Dunlavin
Tinakilly House, Rathnew

WALES

Anglesey
Tre-Ysgawen Hall, Llangefni

Clwyd
Bodidris Hall, Llandegla
Llyndir Hall, Rossett
Soughton Hall, Northop
Tyddyn Llan, Llandrillo
West Arms, Llanarmon Dyffryn Ceiriog

Dyfed
Conrah Country Hotel, Chancery
Glanrannell Park, Crugybar
Gwesty Fferm Penbontbren Farm
   Hotel, Glynarthen
Penally Abbey, Penally

Glamorgan
Coed-y-Mwstwr, Coychurch
Egerton Grey, Porthkerry
Ty Newydd, Hirwaun

Gwent
Cwrt Bleddyn, Tredunnock
St Pierre Hotel, Chepstow

Gwynedd
Bodysgallen Hall, Llandudno
Borthwnog Hall, Bontddu
Dolmelynllyn Hall, Dolgellau
Glyn Isa, Rowen
Maes-y-Neuadd, Talsarnau
Old Rectory, Llansantffraid
Pale Hall, Llandderfel
Pen-y-gwrd, Nantgwynant
Penhelig Arms, Aberdovey
Plas Bodegroes, Pwllheli
Plas Penhelig, Aberdovey
Portmeirion Hotel, Portmeirion
Seiont Manor, Llanrug
St Tudno Hotel, Llandudno
Tan-y-Foel, Betws-y-Coed
Trearddur Bay, Holyhead
Ty'n-y-Cornel, Talyllyn

Powys
Castle Hotel, Trecastle
Gliffaes, Crickhowell
Griffin Inn, Llyswen
Lake Hotel, Llangammarch Wells
Lake Vyrnwy Hotel, Llanwddyn
Llangoed Hall, Llyswen
Ynyshir Hall, Eglwysfach

THE KENSINGTON COLLECTION - BY TOWN

This is a reference guide to the 500 hotel's in the Kensington Collection with the nearest landmark, village, town or city. The place listed may not always be the exact location of the hotel, but is the preferential landmark. After all, some of our recommendations are fairly remotely located - so do always ask for good directions in advance of your journey.

ENGLAND (including the Channel Isles)
Abberley, Elms Hotel
Abbots Salford, Salford Hall Hotel
Alcester, Billesley Manor
Aldbury, Stocks Country House Hotel
Alderley Edge, Alderley Edge
Alderminster, Ettington Park
Amberley, Amberley Castle
Ambleside, Wateredge Hotel
Ansty, Ansty Hall
Appleby-in-Westmorland, Appleby Manor
Appleby-in-Westmorland, Tufton Arms
Ascot, Royal Berkshire
Ashburton, Holne Chase
Ashford-in-the-Water, Riverside Hotel
Aspley Guise, Moore Place
Aston Clinton, Bell Inn
Aylesbury, Hartwell House
Bagshot, Pennyhill Park
Bainbridge, Rose & Crown Inn
Bampton, Huntsham Court
Barrow in Furness, Abbey House
Baslow, Cavendish Hotel
Baslow, Fischer's at Baslow Hall
Bassenthwaite, Armathwaite Hall
Bath, Bath Spa
Bath, Priory Hotel
Bath, Royal Crescent
Battle, Little Hemingfold
Battle, Netherfield Place
Beanacre, Beechfield House
Bearsted, Tudor Park Hotel & Country Club
Belford, Waren House Hotel
Belton, Belton Woods
Bepton, Park House
Bigbury-on-Sea, Burgh Island
Biggin, Biggin Hall
Bilbrough, Bilbrough Manor
Bishops Tawton, Downrew House
Bishop's Tawton, Halmpstone Manor
Blakeney, Blakeney Hotel
Blunsdon, Blunsdon House Hotel
Bolton Abbey, Devonshire Arms
Boroughbridge, The Crown
Borrowdale, Lodore Swiss
Boughton Lees, Eastwell Manor
Boughton Monchelsea, Tanyard Hotel
Bournemouth, Carlton Hotel
Brampton, Farlam Hall
Bray-on-Thames, Monkey Island Hotel
Brighton, The Grand
Broadway, Dormy House
Broadway, Lygon Arms
Brockenhurst, Careys Manor
Brockenhurst, New Park Manor
Bromsgrove, Grafton Manor
Broxted, Whitehall
Buckland, Buckland Manor
Burford, Bay Tree Hotel
Burford, Lamb Inn
Bury St Edmunds, Angel
Bury St Edmunds, Ravenswood Hall
Calstock, Danescombe Valley

Castle Combe, Manor House
Chaddesley Corbett, Brockencote Hall
Chadlington, The Manor
Chagford, Gidleigh Park
Chagford, Great Tree Hotel
Chagford, Mill End
Chedington, Chedington Court
Cheltenham, Cheltenham Park Hotel
Cheltenham, Greenway
Chelwood, Chelwood House
Chester, Chester Grosvenor
Chichester, Goodwood Park Hotel
Chiddingfolds, Crown Inn
Chipping Campden, Cotswold House
Chittlehamholt, Highbullen
Clanfield, The Plough
Climping, Bailiffscourt
Coatham Mundeville, Hall Garth
Colerne, Lucknam Park
Corbridge, Aydon Grange
Corfe Castle, Mortons House Hotel
Cornhill-on-Tweed, Tillmouth Park
Corse Lawn, Corse Lawn House
Crathorne, Crathorne Hall
Crosby-on-Eden, Crosby Lodge
Cuckfield, Ockenden Manor
Culgaith, Hornby Hall
Dedham, Maison Talbooth
Derbyhaven, Castletown Golf Links
Dittisham, Fingals at Old Coombe Manor
Dorchester, Yarlbury Cottage
Dulverton, Ashwick House
Dulverton, Carnarvon Arms
Dunkirk, Petty France
East Grinstead, Gravetye Manor
East Portlemouth, Gara Rock
Eastbourne, The Grand
Easton Grey, Whatley Manor
Egham, Runnymede Hotel
Elcot, Elcot Park
Evershot, Summer Lodge
Evesham, Evesham Hotel
Exmouth, Royal Beacon
Failand, Redwood Lodge
Falmouth, St Michael's Hotel
Faugh, String Of Horses
Ferndown, Dormy House
Findon, Findon Manor
Flitwick, Flitwick Manor
Gillingham, Stock Hill Country House Hotel
Gittisham, Combe House
Grasmere, Michael's Nook
Grasmere, Wordsworth Hotel
Great Baddow, Pontlands Park
Great Langdale, Langdale Hotel
Great Longstone, Hassop Hall
Great Malvern, Foley Arms Hotel
Great Milton, Le Manoir Aux Quat' Saisons
Great Snoring, Old Rectory
Guildford, Angel
Hambleton, Hambleton Hall
Harome, Pheasant Hotel
Haslemere, Lythe Hill
Hatfield Heath, Down Hall
Hawes, Rookhurst Georgian
Haytor, Bel Alp House
Haytor, Moorland Hotel
Helmsley, Feversham Arms
Hethersett, Park Farm
Hexham, Bishop Field Country House Hotel
Hoar Cross, Hoar Cross Hall Health Spa

THE KENSINGTON COLLECTION - BY TOWN

Hockley Heath, Nuthurst Grange
Holbrook, Holbrook House
Horton-Cum-Studley, Studley Priory
Hovingham, Worsley Arms
Hunstrete, Hunstrete House
Huntingdon, Old Bridge
Hurley, Ye Olde Bell
Hurstbourne Tarrant, Esseborne Manor
Hutton, Hutton Court
Hythe , Hythe Imperial
Ipswich, Hintlesham Hall
Jervaulx, Jervaulx Hall
Kingham, Mill House
Kings Lynn, Congham Hall
Kingsbridge, Buckland Tout Saints
Kington, Penrhos Court
Kirkby Lonsdale, Hipping Hall
Kirkby Stephen, The Black Swan
Knaresborough, Dower House Hotel
Lacock, Sign of the Angel
Langar, Langar Hall
Leamington Spa, Mallory Court
Ledbury, Hope End
Leicester, Belmont House
Lenham , Chilston Park Hotel
Lewdown, Lewtrenchard Manor
Lifton, Arundell Arms
Linton, Wood Hall
Liskeard, Well House
Little Horsted, Horsted Place
London SW3, The Beaufort
London SW1, The Berkeley
London SW7, Blakes Hotel
London W1, 47 Park Street
London SW19, Cannizaro House
London W1, Claridges
London NW1, Dorset Square Hotel
London SW1, Dukes Hotel
London W1, Four Seasons Inn on the Park
London SW1, The Goring
London W1, The Ritz
London WC2, The Savoy
London SW1, The Stafford
Long Melford, Black Lion
Longhorsley, Linden Hall
Lower Beeding, South Lodge
Lower Polscoe, Lostwithiel
Lower Slaughter, Lower Slaughter Manor
Ludlow, The Feathers
Lymington, Gordleton Mill
Lymington, Passford House
Maidenhead, Fredrick's Hotel
Malmesbury, Old Bell Hotel
Malvern Wells, Cottage in the Wood
Market Harborough, Three Swans Hotel
Markington, Hob Green
Matlock, Riber Hall
Mawnan Smith, Meudon Hotel
Mawnan Smith, Nansidwell
Medmenham, Danesfield House
Melton Mowbray, Stapleford Park
Meriden, Forest of Arden Hotel
Middle Wallop, Fifehead Manor
Middleham, Millers House
Midhurst, Spread Eagle
Minster Lovell, Old Swan & Mill
Mollington, Crabwall Manor
Monkton Combe, Combe Grove Manor
Morley, Breadsall Priory
New Milton, Chewton Glen
Nidd, Nidd Hall

North Huish, Brookdale House
North Stoke, Springs Hotel
North Wishaw, The Belfry
Norwich, Sprowston Manor
Nr Bath, Box House
Nunnington, Ryedale Lodge
Nutfield, Nutfield Priory
Oakham, Barnsdale Lodge
Oakham, Whipper-In Hotel
Oxford, Bath Place
Pool-in-Wharfedale, Pool Court
Porlock Harbour, Anchor Hotel
Pott Shrigley, Shrigley Hall
Prestbury, Mottram Hall
Princethorpe, Woodhouse
Puckrup, Puckrup Hall
Purton, Pear TreeRavenscar, Raven Hall
Redditch, Abbey Park
Richmond, Petersham Hotel
Romsey, Lee Park
Ross-on-Wye, Pengethley Manor Hotel
Rotherwick, Tylney Hall
Royal Forest of Dean, Clearwell Castle
Rozel, Chateau La Chaire
Rutland Water, Normanton Park
Saltash, St Mellion Golf & Country Club
Sanderstead, Selsdon Park
Sandiway, Nunsmere Hall
Sark, La Sablonnerie
Saunton, Saunton Sands Hotel
Sawbridgeworth, Manor of Groves
Seavington St Mary, The Pheasant
Shedfield, Meon Valley Hotel
Shepperton, Ship Hotel
Shipham, Daneswood House Hotel
Sidmouth, Victoria Hotel
Silchester, Romans Hotel
South Molton, Whitechapel Manor
Sparsholt, Lainston House
St Albans, Sopwell House
St Austell, Carlyon Bay Hotel
St Brelade's Bay, Hotel l'Horizon
St Lawrence, Little Grove
St Saviour, Longueville Manor
Staddle Bridge, McCoy's
Stamford, The George
Stanstead Abbots, Briggens House
Stilton, Bell Inn
Ston Easton, Ston Easton Park
Stonehouse, Stonehouse Court
Storrington, Abingworth Hall
Storrington, Little Thakeham
Stow on the Wold, Fosse Manor
Stow-on-the-Wold, Grapevine
Stow-on-the-Wold, Wyck Hill House
Stratford-on-Avon, Welcombe Hotel
Streatley-on-Thames, Swan Diplomat
Studland Bay, Knoll House
Sturminster Newton, Plumber Manor
Sutton Coldfield, New Hall
Sway, Tower
Taplow, Cliveden
Taunton, The Castle
Tavistock, Horn of Plenty
Tetbury, Calcot Manor
Tetbury, Close Hotel
Tetbury, Snooty Fox
Tewkesbury, Tewkesbury Park Hotel
Thornbury, Thornbury Castle
Thundridge, Hanbury Manor
Thurlestone, Thurlestone Hotel

THE KENSINGTON COLLECTION - BY TOWN

Ticehurst, Dale Hill
Truro, Alverton Manor
Tunbridge Wells, Spa Hotel
Turners Hill, Alexander House
Ufford, Ufford Park
Ullswater, Leeming House
Ullswater, Sharrow Bay
Upper Slaughter, Lords of the Manor
Upton St Leonards, Hatton Court
Veryan , Nare Hotel
Walkington, Manor House
Walterstone, Allt-Yr-Ynys Hotel
Wansford, The Haycock
Wareham, Priory Hotel
Warminster, Bishopstrow House
Wentbridge, Wentbridge House Hotel
Weston under Pentyard, Wharton Lodge
Weston-on-the-Green, Weston Manor
Weston-under-Redcastle, Hawkstone Park
Wetheral, Hayton Hall
Whimple, Woodhayes Hotel
Whitewell, Inn at Whitewell
Whitwell-on-the-Hill, Whitwell Hall
Willington, Willington Hall
Wilmslow, Stanneylands
Wimborne Minster, Beechleas House
Windermere, Gilpin Lodge
Windermere, Holbeck Ghyll
Windermere, Linthwaite House
Windermere, Miller Howe
Windsor, Oakley Court
Withington, Halewell Close
Wiveliscombe, Langley House Hotel
Woodhall Spa, Petwood House
Woodstock, The Feathers
Woolacombe, Woolacombe Bay Hotel
Woolley Green, Woolley Grange
Worleston, Rookery Hall
York, Dean Court
York, Middlethorpe Hall
York, Mount Royale

SCOTLAND
Aberfeldy, Farleyer House

Achiltibuie, Summer Isles
Alexandria, Cameron House
Alloa, Gean House
Altnaharra, Altnaharra Hotel
Appin, Invercreran
Arisaig, Arisaig House
Auchterarder, Auchterarder House
Auchterarder, Gleneagles
Ballater, Balgonie Country House
Ballater, Craigendarroch
Ballater, Tullich Lodge
Banchory, Banchory Lodge
Banchory, Invery House
Blairgowrie, Dalmunzie House Hotel
Blairgowrie, Kinloch House Hotel
Buckie, Cullen Bay Hotel
Bunchrew, Bunchrew House
Callander, Roman Camp
Clarencefield, Comlongon Castle
Cleish Hills , Nivingston House Hotel
Colliston, Letham Grange
Craigellachie, Craigellachie Hotel
Crinan, Crinan Hotel
Cumbernauld, Westerwood
Dornoch, Burghfield House
Drumnadrochit, Polmaily House
Dryburgh, Dryburgh Abbey
Dulnain Bridge , Auchendean Lodge
Dunblane, Cromlix House
Dunkeld, Dunkeld House
Dunkeld, Kinnaird
Dunoon, Ardfillayne
Edinburgh, The Caledonian Hotel
Edinburgh, Channings
Elgin, Mansion House Hotel
Fintry, Culcreuch Castle
Forres, Knockomie Hotel
Freuchie, Lomond Hills
Glasgow, One Devonshire Gardens
Glenborrodale, Glenborrodale Castle
Glenlivet, Minmore House
Glenluce, Torwood House
Gorebridge, Borthwick Castle
Grantown-on-Spey, Muckrach Lodge

Halewell Close

THE KENSINGTON COLLECTION - BY TOWN

Grantown-on-Spey, Seafield Lodge
Halkirk, Ulbster Arms
Humbie, Johnstounburn House
Huntly, Castle Hotel
Inverness, Culloden House Hotel
Inverurie, Pittodrie House
Isle of Iona, Argyll Hotel
Isle of Rhum, Kinloch Castle
Kelso, Cross Keys
Kelso, Ednam House
Kelso, Sunlaws House Hotel
Kenmore, Kenmore Hotel
Kentallen of Appin, Ardsheal House
Kilchrenan, Ardanaiseig
Kildrummy , Kildrummy Castle Hotel
Kinclaven by Stanley, Ballathie House Hotel
Kirknewton , Dalmahoy Hotel, Golf & Country Club
Langbank, Gleddoch House
Leslie, Rescobie
Letham , Fernie Castle
Lochinver, Inver Lodge
Lockerbie, Lockerbie Manor
Lossiemouth, Stotfield House
Markinch, Balbirnie House
Maybole, Ladyburn
Moffat, Moffat House Hotel
Muirfield, Greywalls
Nairn, Alton Burn
Nairn, Clifton House
Newton Stewart, Corsemalzie House Hotel
Newton Stewart, Creebridge House
Newton Stewart, Kirroughtree Hotel
Nr Tighnabruaich, Kilfinan Hotel
Oban, Glenfeochan House
Oban, Isle of Eriska
Oban, Knipoch Hotel
Onich, Lodge on the Loch
Peat Inn, Peat Inn
Peebles, Cringletie House
Port Appin, Airds Hotel
Portpatrick, Knockinaam Lodge
Raemoir , Raemoir House Hotel
Rockcliffe , Baron's Craig Hotel
Scone, Murrayshall
St Andrews, Rufflets
St Andrews, St Andrews Golf Hotel
St Andrews, St Andrews Old Course Hotel
Stewarton, Chapeltoun House
Strathpeffer, Contin House
Strathpeffer, Coul House Hotel
Strathpeffer, Craigdarroch Lodge
Torlundy, Inverlochy Castle
Turnberry, Turnberry Hotel
Whitebridge, Knockie Lodge

IRELAND

Adare, Adare Manor
Annalong, Glassdrumman House
Balinderry, Gurthalougha House
Ballina, Downhill
Ballina, Mount Falcon Castle
Ballinakill, Waterford Castle
Ballyconnell, Slieve Russell
Ballynahinch, Ballynahinch Castle
Ballyvaughan, Gregans Castle
Bantry, Bantry House
Bantry Bay, Ballylickey Manor House
Caragh Lake, Caragh Lodge
Carrickmacross, Nuremore Hotel
Cashel, Cashel House
Castlehill, Enniscoe House

Clifden, Rock Glen
Coleraine, Black Heath
Cong, Ashford Castle
Donegal, St Ernans House Hotel
Dublin, Berkeley Court
Dublin, The Westbury
Dunlavin, Rathsallagh House
Glenbeigh, Towers
Gorey, Marlfield House
Holywood, Culloden Hotel
Innishannon, Innishannon Hotel
Kenmare, Park Hotel
Kenmare, Sheen Falls Lodge
Killarney, Aghadoe Heights
Killarney, International Hotel
Letterfrack, Rosleague Manor
Mallow, Longueville House
Midleton, Ballymaloe House
Moyglare, Moyglare Manor
Newcastle, Slieve Donard
Newmarket-on-Fergus, Dromoland Castle
Newport, Newport House
Oughterard, Currarevagh House
Portrush, Magherabuoy House
Rathmullan, Rathmullan House
Rathnew, Tinakilly House
Riverstown, Coopershill House
Straffan, Kildare House Hotel
Thomastown, Mount Juliet
Upper Ballyduff, Blackwater Lodge

WALES

Aberdovey, Penhelig Arms
Aberdovey, Plas Penhelig
Betws-y-Coed, Tan-y-Foel
Bontddu, Borthwnog Hall
Chancery, Conrah Country Hotel
Chepstow, St Pierre Hotel
Coychurch, Coed-y-Mwstwr
Crickhowell, Gliffaes
Crugybar, Glanrannell Park
Dolgellau, Dolmelynllyn Hall
Eglwysfach, Ynyshir Hall
Glynarthen, Gwesty Fferm Penbontbren Farm Hotel
Hirwaun, Ty Newydd
Holyhead, Trearddur Bay
Llanarmon Dyffryn Ceiriog, West Arms
Llandderfel, Pale Hall
Llandegla, Bodidris Hall
Llandrillo, Tyddyn Llan
Llandudno, Bodysgallen Hall
Llandudno, St Tudno Hotel
Llangammarch Wells, Lake Hotel
Llangefni, Tre-Ysgawen Hall
Llanrug, Seiont Manor
Llansantffraid, Old Rectory
Llanwddyn, Lake Vyrnwy Hotel
Llyswen, Griffin Inn
Llyswen, Llangoed Hall
Nantgwynant, Pen-y-gwrd
Northop, Soughton Hall
Penally, Penally Abbey
Porthkerry, Egerton Grey
Portmeirion, Portmeirion Hotel
Pwllheli, Plas Bodegroes
Rossett, Llyndir Hall
Rowen, Glyn Isa
Talsarnau, Maes-y-Neuadd
Talyllyn, Ty'n-y-Cornel
Trecastle, Castle Hotel
Tredunnock, Cwrt Bleddyn

Ardanaiseig

Amberley Castle

	Map	Number of rooms	Price range	Disabled	Children	Meeting facilities	Credit cards	TV	Parking	Restaurants	Direct dial telephones	Helicopter landing	Pets	Leisure centre	Snooker	Croquet	Squash	Tennis	Indoor swimming pool	Outdoor swimming pool	Golf	Fishing
Abbey House Barrow in Furness Cumbria	E	32	B	◆	◆	†	◆	◆	◆	◆	◆	◆	◆			◆					★	★
Abbey Park Redditch Hereford & Worcester	E	32	BS	◆	◆	60	◆	◆	◆	◆	◆	◆	◆	◆						◆	◆	◆
Abingworth Hall Storrington Sussex	E	21	B		10	40	◆	◆	◆	◆	◆	◆				◆		◆		◆		
Adare Manor Adare Co Limerick	I	64	SD			†	◆	◆	◆	◆	◆		◆			◆	◆				◆	◆
Aghadoe Heights Killarney Co Kerry	I	60	BS		◆	90	◆	◆	◆	◆	◆		◆			◆	◆				★	★
Airds Hotel Port Appin Argyll	S	12	CD	◆			◆	◆	◆	◆											★	
Alderley Edge Alderley Edge Cheshire	E	32	C		◆	†	◆	◆	◆	◆	◆		P									★	
Alexander House Turners Hill Sussex	E	14	SD			†	◆	◆	◆	◆	◆	◆			◆	◆		◆				★	
Allt-Yr-Ynys Hotel Walterstone Hereford & Worcester	E	12	AS		◆	25	◆	◆	◆	◆	◆		P							◆		★	◆
Altnaharra House Altnaharra Highland	S	21	AS	◆			◆		◆	◆			◆									★	◆
Alton Burn Nairn Highland	S	25	A		◆	50	◆	◆	◆	◆		◆	◆			◆		◆		◆		★	★
Alverton Manor Truro Cornwall	E	25	C	◆	◆	†	◆	◆	◆	◆	◆				◆							★	★
Amberley Castle Amberley Sussex	E	14	D		◆	40	◆	◆	◆	◆	◆	◆	◆			◆						★	★
Anchor Hotel Porlock Harbour Somerset	E	19	BS		◆	◆	◆		◆	◆	◆		◆									★	★
Angel Bury St Edmunds Suffolk	E	42	BD	◆	◆	◆	◆	◆	◆	◆	◆		◆									★	
Angel Guildford Surrey	E	11	SD			†	◆		◆	◆			◆										
Ansty Hall Ansty Warwickshire	E	31	C	◆	◆	70	◆	◆	◆	◆	◆	◆	P									★	
Appleby Manor Appleby-in-Westmorland Cumbria	E	30	A	◆	◆	26	◆	◆	◆	◆			P	◆	◆	◆			◆		★	★
Ardanaiseig Kilchrenan Strathclyde	S	14	C	◆			◆	◆	◆	◆	◆				◆	◆		◆			★	◆
Ardfillayne Dunoon Argyll	S	7	AS				◆	◆	◆	◆	◆		◆								★	★

Airds Hotel

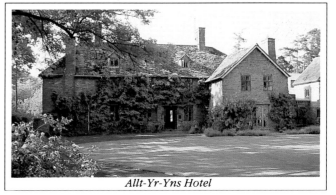

Allt-Yr-Yns Hotel

Cycling	Horseracing	Horse riding	Shooting	Walking	Airborne	Sailing	Seaside	Theatre	Gourmet	Diet and health	Bridge and cards	Literary	Painting and crafts	Romantic	Murder and fantasy	Heritage	Shopping	Outward bound	Peace and quiet	In town	In country	Contact
	◆	★	★	◆	★	★		T					◆	◆		◆	◆	◆	◆		◆	TEL: (0229) 838282 / FAX: (0229) 820403
			C	◆				T	◆					◆		◆	◆	◆	◆		◆	TEL: (0527) 63918 / FAX: (0527) 65872
	◆		C	◆					◆					◆		◆			◆		◆	TEL: (0798) 813636 / FAX: (0798) 813914
		★	C	◆					◆					◆		◆			◆		◆	TEL: (061) 396566 / FAX: (061) 396124
	◆	★	★	◆												◆	◆		◆		◆	TEL: (064) 31766 / FAX: (064) 31345
		★		◆		★		W						◆				◆	◆		◆	TEL: (063 173) 236 / FAX: (063 173) 535
	◆			◆			OT	W						◆		◆	◆		◆		◆	TEL: (0625) 583033 / FAX: (0625) 586343
	◆			◆					◆					◆							◆	TEL: (0342) 714914 / FAX: (0342) 717328
★	◆	★	C	◆				B			◆	◆		◆		◆	◆	◆	◆		◆	TEL: (0873) 890307 / FAX: (0873) 890539
◆		★	◆	◆					◆		◆	◆		◆				◆	B		◆	TEL: (054 981) 222 / FAX:
★	◆		◆		◆		S	T						◆		◆	◆	◆	◆		◆	TEL: (0667) 53325 / FAX:
★	◆	★		◆					◆				◆						◆		◆	TEL: (0872) 76633 / FAX: (0872) 222989
★	◆	★	★	◆	★	★		◆						◆		◆	◆	◆	◆		◆	TEL: (0798) 831992 / FAX: (0798) 831998
		★	★	◆	★	◆									◆	◆		◆	◆		◆	TEL: (0643) 862753 / FAX: (0643) 862843
	◆	★															◆			◆		TEL: (0284) 753926 / FAX: (0284) 750092
								T	◆					◆		◆	◆			◆		TEL: (0483) 64555 / FAX: (0483) 33770
★		★	★	◆				T	◆		◆		◆	◆	◆	◆	◆		◆		◆	TEL: (0203) 612222 / FAX: (0203) 602155
★		★	C	◆		★			◆					◆				◆	◆		◆	TEL: (07683) 51571 / FAX: (07683) 52888
		★	C	◆	★				◆					◆		◆		◆	◆		◆	TEL: (08663) 333 / FAX: (08663) 222
★		★		◆		★	S		◆					◆		◆		◆	◆		◆	TEL: (0369) 2267 / FAX: (0369) 2501

Airds Hotel

Ardfillayne

Aghadoe Heights

Angel Hotel, Bury St Edmunds

Iona Abbey

	Map	Number of rooms	Price range	Disabled	Children	Meeting facilities	Credit cards	TV	Parking	Restaurants	Direct dial telephones	Helicopter landing	Pets	Leisure centre	Snooker	Croquet	Squash	Tennis	Indoor swimming pool	Outdoor swimming pool	Golf	Fishing
Ardsheal House Kentallin of Appin Argyll	S	13	C		♦	10	♦		♦	♦	♦	♦	♦		♦			♦			★	★
Argyll Hotel Isle of Iona Argyll	S	19	A		♦	12	♦	N/A	♦		♦	♦			♦			♦			★	★
Arisaig House Arisaig Inverness-shire	S	15	A		♦					♦												
Armathwaite Hall Bassenthwaite near Kiswick Cumbria	E	42	C			♦	♦	♦	♦	♦			♦	♦	♦			♦			★	♦
Arundell Arms Lifton Devon	E	29	C		♦	80	♦	♦	♦	♦	♦	♦	♦		♦						★	♦
Ashford Castle Cong Co Mayo	I	83	D	♦		†	♦	♦	♦	♦	♦	♦	♦					♦	♦		♦	♦
Ashwick House Dulverton Somerset	E	6	B		♦	10		♦	♦	♦	♦	♦	G								★	★
Auchendean Lodge Dulnain Bridge Invernessshire	S	8	SA	♦	♦		♦	♦	♦	♦			P								♦	★
Auchterarder House Auchterarder Perthshire	S	15	SD			75	♦	♦	♦	♦	♦		♦								★	★
Aydon Grange Corbridge Northumberland	E	3	A				♦		♦	R					♦			♦			★	★
Bailiffscourt Climping, Littlehampton Sussex	E	20			8	36	♦	♦		♦	♦	♦	♦		♦			♦		♦	★	★
Balbirnie House Markinch by Glenrothes Fife	S	30	BD	♦	♦	♦	♦	♦	♦	♦		♦	♦	♦							★	★
Balgonie Country House Ballater Grampian	S	9	A		♦		♦	♦	♦		♦		♦		♦						★	★
Ballathie House Hotel Kinclaven, by Stanley Perthshire	S	36	A	♦		20	♦	♦	♦	♦	♦			♦	♦						★	♦
Ballylickey Manor House Bantry Bay Co Cork	I	6	D		♦		♦	♦	♦	♦	♦									♦	★	♦
Ballymaloe House Shanagarry, Middleton Co Cork	I	30	CS	♦	♦	♦	♦	♦	♦	♦	♦						♦		♦	♦	★
Ballynahinch Castle Ballynahinch, Connemara Co Galway	I	28	C		♦	40	♦	♦		♦	♦			♦			♦			★	♦
Banchory Lodge Banchory Kincardineshire	S	22	B		♦		♦	♦	♦	♦	♦	♦		♦						★	♦
Bantry House Bantry Co Cork	I	9	B		♦	♦	♦		♦	♦					♦	♦					★	★
Barnsdale Lodge Oakham Leicestershire	E	17	AS	♦	♦	†	♦	♦	♦	♦	♦	♦	G								♦	♦

Barnsdale Lodge

Aydon Grange

Iona, Argyll Hotel

Cycling	Horseracing	Horse riding	Shooting	Walking	Airborne	Sailing	Seaside	Theatre	Gourmet	Diet and health	Bridge and cards	Literary	Painting and crafts	Romantic	Murder and fantasy	Heritage	Shopping	Outward bound	Peace and quiet	In town	In country	Contact
★		◆	◆			◆			◆		◆			◆		◆		◆	◆		◆	TEL: (063 174) 227 FAX:
★			◆				S									◆			◆		◆	TEL: (06817) 334 FAX:
			◆			★										◆		◆	◆		◆	TEL: (06875) 210 FAX: (06875) 310
◆	◆	◆	C	◆		★			◆					◆		◆			◆		◆	TEL: (07687) 76551 FAX: (07687) 76220
★		◆	★	◆					◆	★	◆					◆		◆	◆		◆	TEL: (0566) 784666 FAX: (0566) 84494
	◆	◆	★	◆		◆		★	◆					◆		◆			◆		◆	TEL: (092) 46003 FAX: (092) 46260
	◆	★	★	◆					◆					◆		◆		◆	◆		◆	TEL: (0398) 23868 FAX:
★		★	★	◆		★		W		◆	◆	◆	◆	◆		◆	◆	◆	◆		◆	TEL: (047985) 347 FAX:
			★	◆					◆							◆			◆		◆	TEL: (0764) 63646 FAX: (0764) 62939
		★	◆													◆	◆		◆		◆	TEL: (0434) 632169 FAX:
	◆	★	★	◆	★	★	OT							◆	◆	◆	◆		◆		◆	TEL: (0903) 723511 FAX: (0903) 723107
	◆	★					◆	◆								◆	◆		◆		◆	TEL: (0592) 610066 FAX: (0592) 610529
★		★		◆	★									◆		◆		◆	◆		◆	TEL: (03397) 55482 FAX: (03397) 55482
		C							◆							◆			◆		◆	TEL: (025 083) 268 FAX: (025 083) 396
							S		◆					◆					◆		◆	TEL: (027) 50071 FAX: (027) 50124
		★					2	C								◆		◆	◆		◆	TEL: (021) 652531 FAX: (021) 652021
◆		◆	R	◆		★		B						◆		◆			◆		◆	TEL: (095) 31006 FAX: (095) 31085
		★	★	◆	★	★								◆		◆	◆	◆	◆		◆	TEL: (03302) 2625 FAX: (03302) 5019
		★										◆				◆	◆		◆		◆	TEL: (027) 50047 FAX: (027) 51417
◆		◆	C	◆	F	◆		T	B				F	◆	◆	◆	◆	◆	◆		◆	TEL: (0572) 724678 FAX: (0572) 724961

Arundell Arms

Bantry House

Ballylickey Manor House

Ashford Castle

Beachleas House

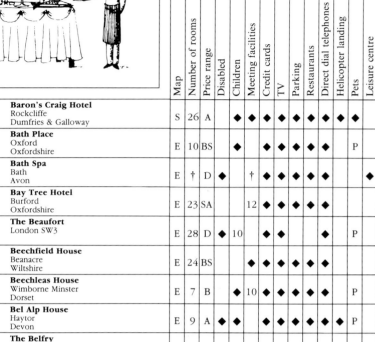

Hotel	Map	Number of rooms	Price range	Disabled	Children	Meeting facilities	Credit cards	TV	Parking	Restaurants	Direct dial telephones	Helicopter landing	Pets	Leisure centre	Snooker	Croquet	Squash	Tennis	Indoor swimming pool	Outdoor swimming pool	Golf	Fishing
Baron's Craig Hotel Rockcliffe Dumfries & Galloway	S	26	A		◆	◆	◆	◆	◆	◆	◆	◆	◆								★	★
Bath Place Oxford Oxfordshire	E	10	BS		◆		◆	◆	◆	◆	◆		P								★	
Bath Spa Bath Avon	E	†	D	◆		†	◆	◆	◆	◆	◆			◆		◆			◆	◆	★	
Bay Tree Hotel Burford Oxfordshire	E	23	SA		12		◆	◆	◆	◆	◆					◆						
The Beaufort London SW3	E	28	D	◆	10		◆	◆			◆		P									
Beechfield House Beanacre Wiltshire	E	24	BS		◆	◆	◆	◆	◆	◆	◆					◆		◆		◆	★	★
Beechleas House Wimborne Minster Dorset	E	7	B	◆	10		◆	◆	◆	◆	◆		P								★	★
Bel Alp House Haytor Devon	E	9	A	◆	◆		◆	◆	◆	◆	◆	◆	P		◆	◆					★	★
The Belfry Wishaw Warwickshire	E	†	BS			◆	◆	◆	◆	◆	◆			◆	◆		◆	◆	◆		◆	
Bell Inn Aston Clinton Buckinghamshire	E	21	B	◆		◆	◆	◆	◆	◆	◆		◆		◆						★	
Bell Inn Stilton Cambridgeshire	E	19	AS			†	◆	◆	◆	◆	◆										★	
Belmont House Leicester Leicestershire	E	68	B		◆	†	◆	◆	◆	◆	◆		P								★	★
Belton Woods Belton Lincolnshire	E	96	BS	◆	◆	†	◆	◆	◆	◆	◆	◆	◆	◆	◆	◆	◆	◆	◆	◆	◆	
The Berkeley London SW1	E	†	DS			◆	◆	◆	◆	◆	◆		◆						◆	◆		
Berkeley Court Dublin Co Dublin	I	†	C	◆		◆	◆	◆	◆	◆	◆		◆					◆			★	
Biggin Hall Biggin, Buxton Derbyshire	E	14	A		12	20	◆		◆	◆		◆	◆								★	★
Bilbrough Manor Bilbrough Yorkshire	E	12	A		10	30	◆	◆	◆	◆	◆	◆	G			◆					★	★
Billesley Manor Alcester Warwickshire	E	41	S		◆	†	◆	◆	◆	◆	◆					◆		◆	◆		★	★
Bishop Field Country House Hotel Allendale, Hexham Northumberland	E	11	AS	◆	◆	20	◆		◆	◆			◆								★	★
Bishopstrow House Warminster Wiltshire	E	32	D			60	◆	◆	◆	◆	◆					◆		◆	◆			◆

Biggin Hall

Bilbrough Manor

Bishop Field Country House

Cycling	Horseracing	Horse riding	Shooting	Walking	Airborne	Sailing	Seaside	Theatre	Gourmet	Diet and health	Bridge and cards	Literary	Painting and crafts	Romantic	Murder and fantasy	Heritage	Shopping	Outward bound	Peace and quiet	In town	In country	TEL / FAX
		★	◆			★	S		◆							◆			◆		◆	TEL: (055663) 225 FAX:
★		★	◆					T						◆		◆	◆		◆			TEL: (0865) 791812 FAX: (0865) 791834
	◆				★			T	◆	◆				◆		◆	◆		◆	◆		TEL: (0225) 444424 FAX: (0225) 444006
									◆					◆		◆	◆		◆		◆	TEL: (0993) 822791 FAX: (0993) 823008
	◆	★					OT			◆				◆		◆			◆			TEL: 071-584 5252 FAX: 071-589 2834
	◆	★												◆		◆			◆		◆	TEL: (0225) 703700 FAX: (0225) 790118
		★	◆			★	8							◆		◆	◆		◆			TEL: (0202) 841684 FAX:
	◆	★	◆					◆						◆		◆		◆	◆		◆	TEL: (0364) 661217 FAX: (0364) 661292
	◆	★	C					T						◆		◆	◆		◆			TEL: (0675) 470301 FAX: (0675) 470178
								◆						◆		◆			◆		◆	TEL: (0296) 630252 FAX: (0296) 631250
★	◆	★	★		★	★		T	◆					◆		◆	◆		◆		◆	TEL: (0733) 241066 FAX: (0733) 245173
★	◆							T						◆					◆			TEL: (0533) 544773 FAX: (0533) 470804
★	◆	★	★	◆	B			B	◆							◆	◆				◆	TEL: (0476) 593200 FAX: (0476) 74547
	◆						◆	B	◆					◆		◆	◆		◆	◆		TEL: (071) 235 6000 FAX: (071) 235 4330
	◆						5	◆						◆		◆			◆			TEL: ((01) 601 711 FAX: (01) 617 238
★		★												◆		◆			◆		◆	TEL: (0298) 84451 FAX:
	◆	★	C	◆	B			W	◆					◆		◆			◆		◆	TEL: (0937) 834002 FAX: (0937) 834724
★	◆	★	C	◆	GB	◆		B						◆		◆	◆	◆	◆		◆	TEL: (0789) 400888 FAX: (0789) 764145
★	◆	★	★	◆													◆	◆	◆		◆	TEL: (0434) 683248 FAX: (0434) 683830
	◆		◆	◆				◆						◆		◆	◆		◆		◆	TEL: (0985) 212312 FAX: (0985) 216769

Beechfield House

Bay Tree

The Belfry

Billesley Manor

Blunsdon House

Bodysgallen Hall

Name	Map	Number of rooms	Price range	Disabled	Children	Meeting facilities	Credit cards	TV	Parking	Restaurants	Direct dial telephones	Helicopter landing	Pets	Leisure centre	Snooker	Croquet	Squash	Tennis	Indoor swimming pool	Outdoor swimming pool	Golf	Fishing
Black Heath Coleraine Co Londonderry	I	5	A		12	♦	♦	♦	♦	♦											★	★
Black Lion Long Melford Suffolk	E	9	A		♦	30	♦	♦	♦	♦	♦		♦			♦					★	★
The Black Swan Kirkby Stephen Cumbria	E	16	AS	♦	♦	10	♦	♦	♦	♦	♦		♦					♦			★	★
Blackwater Lodge Upper Ballyduff Co Waterford	I	20	B	♦	♦		♦		♦	♦	♦	♦	♦		♦						★	♦
Blakeney Hotel Blakeney Norfolk	E	60	B	♦	♦	†	♦	♦	♦	♦			♦	♦	♦					♦		
Blakes Hotel London SW7	E	52	D		♦	25	♦	♦	♦	♦			P	♦					♦		★	
Blunsdon House Hotel Blunsdon Wiltshire	E	88	SB		♦	†	♦	♦	♦	♦	♦		G	♦	♦		♦	♦	♦		♦	★
Bodidris Hall Llandegla Clwyd	I	12	BS		♦	40	♦	♦	♦	♦	♦		G								★	★
Bodysgallen Hall Llandudno Gwynedd	I	28	CD		♦	50	♦	♦	♦	♦					♦		♦				★	★
Borthwick Castle Gorebridge Lothian	S	9	A		♦	30		♦	♦	♦		★	P								★	★
Borthwnog Hall Bontddu Gwynedd	S	3	AS		♦	5	♦	♦	♦				G									★
Box House Box, Nr Bath Wiltshire	E	9	9		♦	35	♦	♦	♦	♦	♦		♦							♦	★	★
Breadsall Priory Morley Derbyshire	E	91	C	♦	♦	†	♦	♦	♦	♦	♦		G	♦	♦		♦	♦	♦		♦	★
Briggens House Stanstead Abbots Hertfordshire	E	54	B	♦	♦	†	♦	♦	♦	♦	♦		G		♦			♦			★	★
Brockencote Hall Chaddesley Corbett Hereford & Worcester	E	8	C	♦	♦	20	♦	♦	♦	♦	♦				♦						★	
Brookdale House North Huish Devon	C	8	SA			10	♦	♦	♦	♦	♦				♦						★	★
Buckland Manor Buckland Hereford & Worcester	E	10	D				♦		♦	♦	♦				♦			♦		♦		
Buckland Tout Saints Kingsbridge Devon	E	12	B		8	20	♦	♦	♦	♦	♦				♦						★	★
Bunchrew Houser Bunchrew Inverness-shire	S	11	BS	♦	♦		♦	♦	♦	♦	♦		P								★	♦
Burgh Island Bigbury-on-Sea Devon	E	14	B		♦	60	♦	♦	♦	♦	♦		G		♦	♦		♦		♦	★	★

Black Lion

Blakeney Hotel

Cycling	Horseracing	Horse riding	Shooting	Walking	Airborne	Sailing	Seaside	Theatre	Gourmet	Diet and health	Bridge and cards	Literary	Painting and crafts	Romantic	Murder and fantasy	Heritage	Shopping	Outward bound	Peace and quiet	In town	In country	TEL / FAX
		★	◆		P		10										◆		◆		◆	TEL: (0265) 868433 / FAX:
★	◆	★	C	◆	◆			◆	◆					◆	◆	◆	◆		◆		◆	TEL: (0787) 312356 / FAX:
		★		◆					◆					◆					◆		◆	TEL: (05396) 23204 / FAX:
★		★	★	◆					◆							◆		◆	◆		◆	TEL: (058) 60235 / FAX: (058) 60162
◆		★		◆		★	S							◆	◆				◆	◆		TEL: (0263) 740797 / FAX: (0263) 740795
★	◆	★	◆	◆				T	◆	◆	◆			◆			◆		◆	◆		TEL: 071-370 6701 / FAX: 071-373 0442
	◆	★	★	◆		★		T	◆			◆			◆	◆					◆	TEL: (0793) 721701 / FAX: (0793) 721056
		★	CR	◆				W	◆					◆					◆		◆	TEL: (097888) 434 / FAX: (097888) 335
				◆			S		◆					◆		◆			◆		◆	TEL: (0492) 584466 / FAX: (0492) 582519
		★	CR	◆								◆		◆		◆			◆		◆	TEL: (0875) 20514 / FAX: (0875) 21702
		★		◆	◆		S							◆		◆			◆		◆	TEL: (034149) 271 / FAX:
★	◆	★	C	◆	FBG		OT	◆	◆					◆		◆	◆	◆			◆	TEL: (0225) 744447 / FAX: (0225) 743971
	◆	★	★	◆				T	◆	◆	◆	◆	◆	◆	◆	◆	◆		◆		◆	TEL: (0332) 832235 / FAX: (0332) 833509
		★	C					◆						◆		◆			◆		◆	TEL: (0279) 792416 / FAX: (0279) 793685
		★	C	◆				W						◆		◆			◆		◆	TEL: (0562) 777876 / FAX: (0562) 777872
★	◆	★	★	◆	B		8	T	◆					◆		◆	◆		◆		◆	TEL: (0548) 82402 / FAX: (0548) 82698
	◆	◆	★	◆				◆	◆	◆	◆	◆	◆	◆		◆	◆		◆		◆	TEL: (0386) 852626 / FAX: (0386) 853557
★	◆	★	★	◆	◆	★	5	T	◆				◆	◆	◆	◆	◆		◆		◆	TEL: (0548) 853055 / FAX: (0548) 856261
◆		★	★	◆	★	◆	S	T	◆					◆		◆	◆		◆		◆	TEL: (0463) 234917 / FAX:
	◆	◆	C	◆		◆	S	◆											◆		◆	TEL: (0548) 810514 / FAX: (0548) 810243

Buckland Tout Saints

Blackwater Lodge

Black Swan

Black Heath House

Caledonian Hotel

Calcot Manor

	Map	Number of rooms	Price range	Disabled	Children	Meeting facilities	Credit cards	TV	Parking	Restaurants	Direct dial telephones	Helicopter landing	Pets	Leisure centre	Snooker	Croquet	Squash	Tennis	Indoor swimming pool	Outdoor swimming pool	Golf	Fishing
Burghfield House Dornoch Highland	S	37	BS	◆	◆	†	◆	◆	◆	◆	◆		◆		◆						◆	
Calcot Manor Tetbury Gloucestershire	E	15	AS	◆	8	22	◆	◆	◆	◆	◆	◆			◆					◆	★	★
The Caledonian Hotel Edinburgh Lothian	S	†	D	◆		†	◆	◆	◆	◆	◆										★	★
Cameron House Loch Lomond, Alexandria Dunbartonshire	S	68	D	◆	◆	†	◆	◆	◆	◆	◆	◆	◆	◆	◆	◆	◆	◆			◆	◆
Cannizaro House London SW19	E	46	DS		10	50	◆	◆	◆	◆	◆		P								★	
Caragh Lodge Caragh Lake Co Kerry	I	10	A	P			◆	◆	◆	◆				◆				◆			★	◆
Careys Manor Brockenhurst Hampshire	E	†	BS		8	40	◆	◆	◆	◆	◆		P	◆	◆			◆			★	★
Carlton Hotel Bournemouth Dorset	E	71	SD	◆	◆		◆	◆	◆	◆	◆			◆	◆					◆	★	
Carlyon Bay Hotel St Austell Cornwall	E	73	BS	◆	◆		◆	◆	◆	◆	◆	◆	P	◆	◆		◆		◆	◆	◆	◆	★
Carnarvon Arms Dulverton Somerset	E	25	AS	◆	◆	◆	◆	◆	◆	◆			◆	◆	◆	◆		◆				◆
Cashel House Cashel Co Galway	I	32	B		5		◆	◆	◆	◆						◆					★	★
Castle Hotel Huntly Aberdeenshire	E	21	SA	◆	◆	70	◆	◆	◆		◆	◆			◆						★	★
The Castle Taunton Somerset	E	35	C	◆		90	◆	◆	◆	◆	◆	◆	◆								★	★
Castle Hotel Trecastle, Brecon Powys	W	10	A		◆	10	◆	◆	◆	◆			P								★	★
Castletown Golf Links Derbyhaven Isle Of Man	E	57	SB	◆	◆	†	◆	◆	◆	◆	◆	◆	◆	◆	◆			◆	◆		◆	★
Cavendish Hotel Baslow Derbyshire	E	23	B		◆	16	◆	◆	◆	◆	◆	◆										◆
Channings Edinburgh Lothian	S	48	B	◆	◆		◆	◆	◆	◆	◆											
Chapeltoun House Stewarton Argyll	S	8	AS		12		◆	◆		◆	◆	◆									★	◆
Chateau La Chaire Rozel Channel Isles (Jersey)	E	14	C		7	12	◆	◆	◆	◆	◆		G								★	
Chedington Court Chedington, Nr Beaminster Dorset	E	10	B		◆	14	◆	◆	◆	◆	◆	◆	◆		◆	◆					◆	★

Cavendish Hotel

Cannizaro House

→ CHEDINGTON COURT

Channings

Castle Hotel, Taunton

Cycling	Horseracing	Horse riding	Shooting	Walking	Airborne	Sailing	Seaside	Theatre	Gourmet	Diet and health	Bridge and cards	Literary	Painting and crafts	Romantic	Murder and fantasy	Heritage	Shopping	Outward bound	Peace and quiet	In town	In country	Contact
★		◆	◆	◆		★	S				◆					◆	◆					TEL: (0862) 810212 FAX: (0862) 8102434
★	◆	★	◆	C	◆	★		OT	◆	◆				◆		◆	◆	◆	◆		◆	TEL: (0666) 890391 FAX: (0666) 890394
	◆	◆					G		◆							◆	◆		◆			TEL: 031-225 2433 FAX: 031-225 6632
◆		★	◆	◆	★	◆		OT	◆	◆				◆		◆		◆	◆		◆	TEL: (0389) 55625 FAX: (0389) 59906
★	◆	★		◆	◆			◆	◆					◆		◆	◆		◆	◆		TEL: 081-879 1464 FAX: 081-879 7338
◆		★		◆		★	10							◆					◆		◆	TEL: (066) 69115 FAX: (066) 69136
◆		★	★	◆	★	★	4	OT	W	◆				◆		◆	◆	◆	◆		◆	TEL: (0590) 23551 FAX: (0590) 22799
		★				★	S	◆	◆	◆				◆					◆	◆		TEL: (0202) 552011 FAX: (0202) 299573
◆		★	★	◆		★	S							◆		◆			◆		◆	TEL: (0726) 812304 FAX: (0726) 814938
◆		◆	◆	◆										◆		◆	◆		◆		◆	TEL: (0398) 23302 FAX: (0398) 24022
		◆		◆		◆	S		◆					◆		◆			◆		◆	TEL: (095) 31001 FAX: (095) 31077
★		★	★	◆				T						◆		◆		◆	◆		◆	TEL: (0466) 792696 FAX: (0466) 792641
★	◆		★	◆				◆	◆					◆		◆	◆		◆	◆		TEL: (0823) 272671 FAX: (0823) 336066
		★	★	◆														◆	◆		◆	TEL: (0874) 636354 FAX:
★		★	★	◆		★	S							◆		◆	◆		◆		◆	TEL: (0624) 822201 FAX: (0624) 824633
				◆										◆		◆	◆	◆	◆		◆	TEL: (0246) 582311 FAX: (0246) 582312
				◆				T						◆		◆	◆	◆	◆	◆		TEL: 031-315 2226 FAX: 031-332 9631
				◆			10	T	◆					◆		◆			◆		◆	TEL: (0560) 82696 FAX: (0560) 85100
		★		◆			1	T	◆					◆			◆		◆		◆	TEL: (0534) 863354 FAX: (0534) 865137
		★	★	◆				◆	◆					◆		◆			◆		◆	TEL: (0935) 891265 FAX: (0935) 891442

Chedington Court

Cameron House

Clifton House

Chester Grosvenor

Hotel	Map	Number of rooms	Price range	Disabled	Children	Meeting facilities	Credit cards	TV	Parking	Restaurants	Direct dial telephones	Helicopter landing	Pets	Leisure centre	Snooker	Croquet	Squash	Tennis	Indoor swimming pool	Outdoor swimming pool	Golf	Fishing
Cheltenham Park Hotel Charlton Kings, Cheltenham Gloucestershire	E	†	B	◆	◆	†	◆	◆	◆	◆	◆		P								★	★
Chelwood House Chelwood Avon	E	11	BS		10	25	◆	◆	◆	◆	◆		G			◆					★	★
Chester Grosvenor Chester Cheshire	E	86	D		◆	◆	◆	◆	◆	◆	◆				◆						★	★
Chewton Glen New Milton Hampshire	E	60	DS	◆	7	†	◆	◆	◆	◆	◆	◆		◆	◆	◆	◆	◆	◆	◆	◆	★
Chilston Park Hotel Lenham Kent	E	40	BS	◆	◆	◆	◆	◆	◆	◆	◆	◆	P		◆	◆		◆			★	◆
Claridges London W1	E	†	DS	◆	◆	†	◆	◆		◆	◆		G	★				★			★	
Clearwell Castle Royal Forest of Dean Gloucestershire	E	17	A			†	◆	◆	◆	◆	◆		P								★	★
Clifton House Nairn Highland	S	16	AS			◆		◆	◆	◆			◆								★	★
Cliveden Taplow Berkshire	E	31	D	◆	◆	◆	◆	◆	◆	◆	◆	◆		◆	◆	◆	◆	◆	◆	◆	★	◆
Close Hotel Tetbury Gloucestershire	E	15	A		◆	22	◆	◆	◆	◆	◆		P			◆					★	
Coed-y-Mwstwr Coychurch Glamorgan	W	24	BS	◆	◆	†	◆	◆	◆	◆	◆	◆	P		◆	◆		◆		◆	★	★
Combe Grove Manor Monkton Combe, Bath Avon	E	41	SC		◆	60	◆	◆	◆	◆	◆				◆		◆	◆	◆	◆	★	
Combe House Gittisham Devon	E	15	BS		◆	30	◆			◆	◆		◆			◆					★	◆
Comlongon Castle Clarencefield, Dumfries Dumfries & Galloway	S	11	AB	◆	◆	◆	◆	◆	◆	◆	◆		G								★	★
Congham Hall Grimston, Kings Lynn Norfolk	E	14	B		12	12	◆	◆	◆	◆	◆	◆				◆		◆		◆	★	★
Conrah Country Hotel Chancery, Aberystwyth Dyfed	W	21	A		5	60	◆		◆	◆	◆	◆				◆			◆		★	★
Contin House Contin, Strathpeffer Ross-shire	S	5	A		8	10	◆	◆	◆	◆	◆	◆	◆								★	★
Coopershill House Riverstown Co Sligo	I	7	SA			◆		◆	R	◆	◆					◆					★	★
Corse Lawn House Corse Lawn Gloucestershire	E	19	BC	◆	◆	40	◆	◆	◆	◆	◆	◆				◆		◆		◆	★	★
Corsemalzie House Hotel Newton Stewart Wigtownshire	S	15	AS		◆	70	◆	◆	◆	◆	◆		◆			◆					★	★

Chewton Glen

Chilston Park

Cycling	Horseracing	Horse riding	Shooting	Walking	Airborne	Sailing	Seaside	Theatre	Gourmet	Diet and health	Bridge and cards	Literary	Painting and crafts	Romantic	Murder and fantasy	Heritage	Shopping	Outward bound	Peace and quiet	In town	In country	TEL / FAX
★	◆	★	C	◆	BG			T						◆		◆	◆		◆		◆	TEL: (0242) 222021 / FAX: (0242) 226935
	◆	★	C	◆	B	◆		T	◆					◆		◆	◆		◆		◆	TEL: (0761) 490730 / FAX: (0761) 490730
	◆	★	★	◆			◆	◆			◆	◆		◆	◆	◆	◆	◆	◆	◆		TEL: (0244) 324024 / FAX: (0244) 313246
◆		★	★	B	B	★	2		◆	◆				◆		◆	◆		◆		◆	TEL: (0425) 275341 / FAX: (0425) 272310
	◆	★	★	◆	◆			T	◆		◆			◆		◆	◆		◆		◆	TEL: (0622) 859803 / FAX: (0622) 858588
	◆			◆				OT	B					◆		◆	◆			◆		TEL: 071-499 8860 / FAX: 071-499 2210
		★	C	◆										◆		◆		◆	◆		◆	TEL: (0594) 832320 / FAX: (0594) 835523
		★		◆			S	T						◆					◆	◆		TEL: (0667) 53119 / FAX: (0667) 52836
	◆	★	C	◆		★			◆	◆				◆		◆	◆		◆		◆	TEL: (0628) 668561 / FAX: (0628) 661837
	◆	★	C	◆	BG			T	◆	★				◆	◆	◆			◆		◆	TEL: (0666) 502272 / FAX: (0666) 504401
			C	◆	B		3					◆		◆			◆		◆		◆	TEL: (0656) 860621 / FAX: (0656) 863122
	◆	★	★	◆	★			T	◆	◆				◆		◆	◆		◆		◆	TEL: (0225) 834644 / FAX: (0225) 834961
	◆		★	◆				T						◆		◆	◆		◆		◆	TEL: (0404) 42756 / FAX: (0404) 46004
★		★	★	◆										◆	◆	◆			◆		◆	TEL: (038787) 283 / FAX: (038787) 266
★	◆	★	C	◆	FB		10		◆					◆		◆	◆			B	◆	TEL: (0485) 600250 / FAX: (0485) 601191
★			◆				3	T						◆		◆	◆		◆		◆	TEL: (0970) 617941 / FAX: (0970) 624546
		★	D	◆					◆	◆				◆					◆		◆	TEL: (0997) 421920 / FAX: (0997) 421841
★	◆	★	C	◆			10	T						◆		◆		◆	◆		◆	TEL: (071) 65108 / FAX: (071) 65466
★	◆	★	★	★	◆	★		T	◆	◆	◆	◆	◆	◆		◆	◆		◆		◆	TEL: (0452) 680479 / FAX: (0452) 780840
★		★	★	◆		★	6							◆			◆		◆		◆	TEL: (098) 886 254 / FAX: (098) 886 213

Chester Grosvenor

Contin House

Claridges

Congham Hall

Culcreuch Castle

Cotswold House

	Map	Number of rooms	Price range	Disabled	Children	Meeting facilities	Credit cards	TV	Parking	Restaurants	Direct dial telephones	Helicopter landing	Pets	Leisure centre	Snooker	Croquet	Squash	Tennis	Indoor swimming pool	Outdoor swimming pool	Golf	Fishing
Cotswold House Chipping Campden Gloucestershire	E	15	A		8	20	◆	◆	◆	◆	◆										★	★
Cottage in the Wood Malvern Wells Hereford & Worcester	E	20	CD	◆		14	◆	◆	◆	◆	◆		◆								★	★
Coul House Hotel Strathpeffer Ross-shire	S	21	AS	◆	◆	50	◆	◆	◆	◆	◆		◆								◆	★
Crabwall Manor Mollington Cheshire	E	48	CD	◆	◆	◆	◆	◆	◆	◆	◆	◆			◆	◆					★	★
Craigdarroch Lodge Strathpeffer Ross-shire	S	13	AS	◆		20		◆	◆	◆			◆		◆			◆	◆		★	◆
Craigellachie Hotel Craigellachie Banffshire	S	30	AS			60	◆	◆	◆	◆	◆		P	◆	◆			◆			★	★
Craigendarroch Ballater Aberdeenshire	S	50	D	◆	◆	◆	◆	◆	◆	◆	◆		◆	◆		◆	◆	◆	◆		★	★
Crathorne Hall Crathorne Yorkshire	E	37	SC		◆	†	◆	◆	◆	◆	◆	◆	P			◆					★	★
Creebridge House Newton Stewart Wigtownshire	S	18	A	◆	◆	70	◆	◆	◆	◆	◆	◆	◆		◆	◆					★	★
Crinan Hotel Crinan Argyll	S	22	A					◆	◆	◆													◆
Cringletie House Peebles Borders	S	13	A	◆			◆	◆	◆	◆	◆	◆			◆			◆			★	★
Cromlix House Dunblane Perthshire	S	14	CS		◆	28	◆	◆	◆	◆			P		◆			◆			★	★
Crosby Lodge Crosby-On-Eden, Carlisle Cumbria	E	11	B		P	12	◆		◆	◆	◆		P									★
Cross Keys Kelso Roxburghshire	S	25	A	◆	◆	†	◆	◆		◆	◆		◆	◆	◆						★	★
The Crown Boroughbridge Yorkshire	E	42	A	◆	◆	†	◆	◆	◆	◆	◆		◆								★	★
Crown Inn Chiddingfold Surrey	E	8	A		◆	65	◆	◆		◆	◆		◆								★	★
Culcreuch Castle Fintry Stirlingshire	S	8	A		◆	†	◆	◆	◆	◆	◆	◆	P			◆					★	★
Cullen Bay Hotel Cullen, Buckie Banffshire	S	15	A		◆	50	◆	◆	◆	◆	◆		◆								★	★
Culloden Hotel Holywood Co Down	I	91	A	◆	◆	†	◆	◆	◆	◆	◆		P	◆	◆	◆	◆	◆	◆		★	★
Culloden House Hotel Inverness Inverness-shire	S	25	SD		10	◆	◆	◆	◆	◆	◆	◆	P		◆			◆			★	★

Craigdarroch Lodge

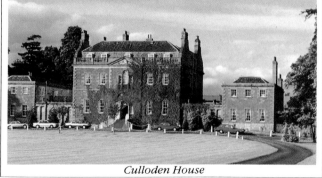

Culloden House

→ CULLODEN HOUSE HOTEL

Cycling	Horseracing	Horse riding	Shooting	Walking	Airborne	Sailing	Seaside	Theatre	Gourmet	Diet and health	Bridge and cards	Literary	Painting and crafts	Romantic	Murder and fantasy	Heritage	Shopping	Outward bound	Peace and quiet	In town	In country	TEL / FAX
★	◆	★		◆				T						◆		◆	◆		◆		◆	TEL: (0386) 840330 / FAX: (0386) 840310
	◆	★		◆				TO						◆		◆	◆		◆		◆	TEL: (0684) 573487 / FAX: (0684) 560662
		★	★	◆		★	6	OT						◆		◆	◆	◆	◆		◆	TEL: (0997) 421487 / FAX: (0997) 421945
	◆	★	★		★	★		T	◆					◆		◆			◆		◆	TEL: (0244) 851666 / FAX: (0244) 851400
★		★	★	◆		★		T									◆	◆			◆	TEL: (0997) 421265 / FAX:
★		★	★	◆					◆	◆				◆	◆	◆	◆	◆	◆		◆	TEL: (0340) 881204 / FAX: (0340) 881253
◆		★	★	◆					◆	◆				◆		◆	◆		◆		◆	TEL: (03397) 55858 / FAX: (03397) 55447
	◆	★	★	★		★	★		◆					◆		◆	◆		◆		◆	TEL: (0642) 700398 / FAX: (0642) 700814
★		★	★	◆		★	◆5							◆		◆	◆	◆	◆			TEL: (0671) 2121 / FAX:
			◆			★	S												◆		◆	TEL: (054683) 261 / FAX: (054683) 292
		★		◆					◆							◆	◆		◆		◆	TEL: (07213) 233 / FAX: (07213) 244
★	◆	★	★	◆					◆		◆			◆		◆			◆		◆	TEL: (0786) 822125 / FAX: (0786) 825450
	◆	★		◆															◆		◆	TEL: (0228) 573 618 / FAX: (0228) 573 428
★	◆	★	★	◆					◆								◆			◆		TEL: (0573) 223303 / FAX: (0573) 225792
	◆	★	★	◆	★	★		T	◆			◆		◆	◆	◆			◆		◆	TEL: (0423) 322328 / FAX: (0423) 324512
	◆		C	◆	★									◆		◆	◆	◆	◆		◆	TEL: (042) 868 2259 / FAX:
◆	◆	★	★	◆				B						◆		◆	◆		◆		◆	TEL: (036086) 228 / FAX: (0532) 390093
★			◆		★	◆	◆									◆	◆		◆		◆	TEL: (0542) 40432 / FAX: (0542) 40900
		★		◆		★	◆5	OT						◆		◆	◆		◆	◆		TEL: (0232) 425223 / FAX: (0232) 426777
★		★	★	◆			2	T						◆		◆	◆		◆		◆	TEL: (0463) 790461 / FAX: (0463) 792181

Crosby Lodge

Cottage in the Wood

Crabwall Manor

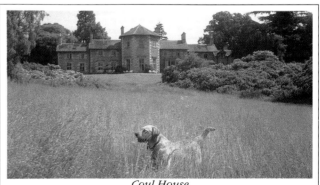

Coul House

	Map	Number of rooms	Price range	Disabled	Children	Meeting facilities	Credit cards	TV	Parking	Restaurants	Direct dial telephones	Helicopter landing	Pets	Leisure centre	Snooker	Croquet	Squash	Tennis	Indoor swimming pool	Outdoor swimming pool	Golf	Fishing
Currarevagh House Oughterard, Connemara Co Galway	I	15	AS		P			◆	◆		◆		P		◆		◆				★	◆
Cwrt Bleddyn Tredunnock Gwent	W	36	BS	◆	†	◆	◆	◆	◆	◆	◆	◆	P	◆	◆	◆	◆	◆	◆		★	★
Dale Hill Ticehurst Sussex	E	25	SA	◆	◆	40	◆	◆	◆	◆	◆		◆	◆	◆		★	★	◆		◆	★
Dalmahoy Hotel, Golf & Country Club Kirknewton Lothian	S	†	DS	◆	◆	†	◆	◆	◆	◆	◆		◆	◆	◆		◆	◆	◆		◆	★
Dalmunzie House Hotel Blairgowrie Perthshire	S	18	A	◆	◆	20	◆		◆	◆		◆	◆		◆		◆				◆	◆
Danescombe Valley Calstock Cornwall	E	S	B		12		◆		◆	◆											★	★
Danesfield House Medmenham Buckinghamshire	E	36	D	◆		◆	◆	◆	◆	◆	◆				◆		◆		◆			★
Daneswood House Hotel Shipham Somerset	E	12	A		◆	20	◆	◆	◆	◆	◆		P								★	★
Dean Court York Yorkshire	E	40	B	◆	◆	15	◆	◆	◆	◆	◆		P								★	
Devonshire Arms Bolton Abbey Yorkshire	E	40	DS	◆	◆	†	◆	◆	◆	◆	◆	◆			◆						★	◆
Dolmelynllyn Hall Dolgellau Gwynedd	W	11	B		10	30	◆	◆	◆	◆	◆		◆								★	◆
The Dormy Hotel Ferndown, nr Bournemouth Dorset	E	†	BS	◆	◆	◆	◆	◆	◆	◆			◆	◆		◆	◆	◆		★	★
Dormy House Broadway Hereford & Worcester	E	49	BS	◆	†	◆	◆	◆	◆	◆	◆	◆	P	◆		◆					★	★
Dorset Square Hotel London NW1	E	37	BC	◆			◆	◆		◆	◆											
Dower House Hotel Knaresborough Yorkshire	E	32	B		◆	50	◆	◆	◆	◆	◆		◆					◆		★	◆
Down Hall Hatfield Heath Hertfordshire	E	†	B			†	◆	◆	◆	◆	◆		◆	◆	◆		◆	◆			
Downhill Ballina Co Mayo	I	56	B	◆	†	◆	◆	◆	◆	◆	◆	G	◆		◆	◆	◆		★	◆
Downrew House Bishops Tawton Devon	E	12	A	◆	◆	24	◆	◆	◆	◆	◆		◆	◆	◆		◆		◆	★	★
Dromoland Castle Newmarket-on-Fergus Co Clare	I	73	D		◆		◆	◆	◆	◆	◆			◆	◆		◆			◆	◆
Dryburgh Abbey Dryburgh, St Boswells Borders	S	28	AB	◆	◆	†	◆	◆	◆	◆	◆	◆	P								★	★

Dolmelynllyn Hall

Dale Hill

Dale Hill

Daneswood House

Cycling	Horseracing	Horse riding	Shooting	Walking	Airborne	Sailing	Seaside	Theatre	Gourmet	Diet and health	Bridge and cards	Literary	Painting and crafts	Romantic	Murder and fantasy	Heritage	Shopping	Outward bound	Peace and quiet	In town	In country	Contact
★		★	◆																★B			TEL: (091) 82312/3 FAX: (091) 82731
◆																						TEL: (063349) 521 FAX: (063349) 220
	◆	★	C	◆	GB			◆						◆		◆	◆		◆		◆	TEL: (0580) 200112 FAX: (0580) 201249
★	◆	★	★	◆		★		◆	◆	◆				◆		◆	◆		◆		◆	TEL: 031-333 1845 FAX: 031-335 3203
◆	◆	◆	★	◆		★		◆								◆	◆	◆	◆		◆	TEL: (0250) 885224 FAX: (0250) 885225
◆		★	◆	◆	H												◆		◆		◆	TEL: (0822) 832414 FAX:
★		★		◆		★		T								◆		◆	◆			TEL: (0628) 891010 FAX: (0628) 890408
	◆	◆	◆					◆						◆		◆	◆				◆	TEL: (0934) 843145 FAX: (0934) 843824
★	◆	★	★	◆		◆	★	12	OT							◆	◆		◆		◆	TEL: (0904) 625082 FAX: (0904) 620305
★	◆	★	C	◆				T	◆						★	◆	◆			◆		TEL: (0756) 710441 FAX: (0756) 710564
★	◆	★	◆	◆	◆									◆		◆	◆	◆	◆		◆	TEL: (0341) 40273 FAX:
◆		★	C	◆				T	◆							◆		◆	◆		◆	TEL: (0202) 872121 FAX: (0202) 895388
◆	◆	◆	C	◆	◆		S	◆	◆					◆		◆			◆		◆	TEL: (0386) 852711 FAX: (0386) 858636
◆	◆	★	C	◆	◆			T	◆				◆		◆	◆	◆		◆		◆	TEL: (071) 723 7874 FAX: (071) 724 3328
	◆							TO						◆		◆	◆		◆			TEL: (0423) 863302 FAX: (0423) 867665
		★	★	◆				T	◆										◆		◆	TEL: (0279) 731441 FAX: (0279) 730416
								◆	◆												◆	TEL: (096) 21033 FAX: (096) 21338
★		★	★	◆			7	T	◆	◆	◆			◆		◆	◆		◆		◆	TEL: (0271) 42497 FAX: (0271) 23947
★		★	★	◆			8	T								◆	◆		◆		◆	TEL: (061) 368144 FAX: (061) 363355
★		★	★	◆			10		◆					◆		◆			◆		◆	TEL: (0835) 22261 FAX: (0835) 23945

Currarevagh House

Devonshire Arms

Dromoland Castle

Dalmunzie House

DUKES HOTEL →

	Map	Number of rooms	Price range	Disabled	Children	Meeting facilities	Credit cards	TV	Parking	Restaurants	Direct dial telephones	Helicopter landing	Pets	Leisure centre	Snooker	Croquet	Squash	Tennis	Indoor swimming pool	Outdoor swimming pool	Golf	Fishing
Dukes Hotel London SW1	E	64	D	◆	◆	◆	◆	◆		◆	◆			★								
Dunkeld House Hotel Dunkeld Perthshire	S	92	C	◆	◆	85	◆	◆	◆	◆	◆	◆	◆	◆	◆	◆			◆	◆	★	◆
Eastwell Manor Boughton Lees Kent	E	23	CS	◆	◆	†	◆	◆	◆	◆	◆	◆	◆		◆	◆		◆			★	★
Ednam House Kelso Borders	S	32	A		◆	†	◆	◆	◆	◆	◆	◆	◆			◆					★	◆
Egerton Grey Porthkerry Glamorgan	W	10	BS		◆	◆	◆	◆	◆	◆	◆		P	◆		◆		◆			★	★
Elcot Park Elcot Berkshire	E	75	A	◆	◆	†	◆	◆	◆	◆	◆	◆	◆		◆	◆		◆			★	★
Elms Hotel Abberley Hereford & Worcester	E	25	C	◆	◆		◆	◆	◆	◆	◆	◆	◆			◆		◆			★	★
Enniscoe House Castlehill Co Mayo	I	6	AS		◆	60	◆		◆	◆											★	◆
Esseborne Manor Hurstbourne Tarrant Hampshire	E	12	BS	◆	12	10	◆	◆	◆	◆	◆				★	◆		◆			★	
Ettington Park Alderminster Warwickshire	E	48	DS	◆	◆	80	◆	◆	◆	◆	◆	◆		◆		◆		◆	◆		★	◆
Evesham Hotel Waterside, Evesham Hereford & Worcester	E	40	A		◆	◆	◆	◆	◆	◆	◆		◆			◆			◆			
Farlam Hall Brampton Cumbria	E	13	CS		5		◆	◆	◆	◆	◆	◆	◆			◆						
Farleyer House Aberfeldy Perthshire	S	11	C		◆		◆		◆	◆	◆		P								◆	★
The Feathers Ludlow Shropshire	E	40	B		◆	◆	◆	◆	◆	◆	◆		◆		◆							
The Feathers Woodstock Oxfordshire	E	17	BS			30	◆	◆	◆	◆	◆		P									
Fernie Castle Letham Fife	S	15	BS	◆		†	◆	◆	◆	◆	◆	◆	G								★	★
Feversham Arms Helmsley Yorkshire	E	18	AS	◆	◆	30	◆	◆	◆	◆	◆	◆	◆					◆		◆	★	★
Fifehead Manor Middle Wallop, Stockbridge Hampshire	E	16	A	◆	◆	20	◆	◆	◆	◆	◆	◆	◆			◆					★	★
Findon Manor Findon Sussex	E	10	AS	◆	◆	35	◆	◆	◆	◆	◆		◆			◆					★	
Fingals at Old Coombe Manor Dittisham Devon	E	9	BC		◆	◆	◆	◆	◆	◆	◆			◆	◆	◆			◆	◆	◆	

Feversham Arms

Dukes Hotel

Eastwell Manor

Esseborne Manor

44

Cycling	Horseracing	Horse riding	Shooting	Walking	Airborne	Sailing	Seaside	Theatre	Gourmet	Diet and health	Bridge and cards	Literary	Painting and crafts	Romantic	Murder and fantasy	Heritage	Shopping	Outward bound	Peace and quiet	In town	In country	TEL / FAX
	♦	★	♦					TO	♦	♦				♦		♦	♦			♦		TEL: 071-491 4840 FAX: 071-493 1264
♦	♦	★	C	♦		♦		♦	♦	♦				♦		♦	♦				♦	TEL: (0350) 737772 FAX: (0350) 728924
		★	★	♦	B			♦						♦	♦	♦	♦		♦		♦	TEL: (0233) 635751 FAX: (0233) 635530
★	♦	★	♦											♦		♦			♦		♦	TEL: (0573) 224168 FAX: (0573) 226319
		★	★	♦		★	♦	♦	♦										♦		♦	TEL: (0446) 711666 FAX: (0446) 711690
★	♦	★	★	♦	♦B			♦	♦	♦				♦	♦	♦	♦				★	TEL: (0488) 58100 FAX: (0488) 58288
	♦	★	C	♦	♦B			T	♦					♦		♦			♦		♦	TEL: (0299) 896 666 FAX: (0299) 896 804
★		★	♦		★			♦						♦		♦			♦		♦	TEL: (096) 31112 FAX: (096) 31773
	♦		C	♦				♦						♦		♦	♦		♦		♦	TEL: (026476) 444 FAX: (026476) 473
		♦	★	♦	B			T	♦					♦	♦	♦	♦		♦		♦	TEL: (0789) 450123 FAX: (0789) 450472
																♦	♦		♦	♦		TEL: (0386) 765566 FAX: (0386) 765443
♦	♦	★	♦														♦		♦		♦	TEL: (06977) 46234 FAX: (06977) 46683
	♦	★	♦					T	♦							♦			♦		♦	TEL: (0887) 820332 FAX: (0887) 829430
	♦	★	♦											♦		♦			♦	♦		TEL: (0584) 875261 FAX: (0584) 876030
			♦					♦						♦		♦	♦		♦		♦	TEL: (0993) 812291 FAX: (0993) 813158
	★	★	♦					W		♦				♦		♦			♦		♦	TEL: (033781) 381 FAX: (033781) 422
	♦	★	D	♦			♦							♦		♦	♦		♦		♦	TEL: (0439) 70766 FAX: (0439) 70346
	♦	★	♦				♦									♦			♦		♦	TEL: (0264) 781565 FAX: (0264) 781400
	♦	★	★	♦										♦		♦	♦		♦		♦	TEL: (0903) 872733 FAX: (0903) 770220
♦	★		♦	★	★			♦	♦				♦						♦		♦	TEL: (080422) 398 FAX: (080422) 408

Elcot Manor

Fingals

Ettington Park

Farlam Hall

	Map	Number of rooms	Price range	Disabled	Children	Meeting facilities	Credit cards	TV	Parking	Restaurants	Direct dial telephones	Helicopter landing	Pets	Leisure centre	Snooker	Croquet	Squash	Tennis	Indoor swimming pool	Outdoor swimming pool	Golf	Fishing
Fischer's at Baslow Hall Baslow Derbyshire	E	6	B		10	♦	♦		♦	♦												★
Flitwick Manor Flitwick Bedfordshire	E	15	B	♦	♦	36	♦	♦	♦	♦	♦	♦	♦			♦		♦			★	
Foley Arms Hotel Great Malvern Hereford & Worcester	E	28	A		♦	†	♦	♦	♦	♦	♦		♦								★	★
Forest of Arden Hotel Meriden Warwickshire	E	†	DS	♦	♦	†	♦	♦	♦	♦	♦	♦	♦	G	♦	♦		♦	♦	♦	♦	♦
47 Park Street Mayfair London W1	E	52	D			20	♦	♦		♦	♦			★					★			
Fosse Manor Stow On The Wold Gloucestershire	E	20	AS	♦	♦	20	♦	♦	♦	♦	♦		♦			♦					★	★
Four Seasons Inn On The Park Park Lane London W1	E	†	D	♦	♦		♦	♦	♦	♦	♦		♦		♦						★	★
Fredrick's Hotel & Restaurant Maidenhead Berkshire	E	37	D		♦	†	♦	♦	♦	♦	♦	♦				♦					★	
Gara Rock East Portlemouth nr Salcombe Devon	E	21	A		♦	60	♦	♦	♦	♦	♦		♦			♦		♦			★	★
Gean House Alloa Fife	S	10	BD	♦		20	♦	♦	♦	♦	♦		♦			♦		♦			★	★
The George Stamford Lincolnshire	E	47	SB		♦		♦	♦	♦	♦	♦					♦		♦				
Gidleigh Park Chagford Devon	E	16	DS		♦	18	♦	♦	♦	♦	♦	♦	♦			♦					★	♦
Gilpin Lodge Windermere Cumbria	E	9	AS		9		♦	♦	♦	♦	♦					♦					★	★
Glanrannell Park Crugybar, Llanwrda Dyfed	W	8	A		♦		♦	♦	♦	♦			P									♦
Glassdrumman House Annalong Co Down	I	9	A		♦	20	♦	♦	♦	♦	♦		♦			♦					★	★
Gleddoch House Langbank Renfrewshire	S	33	D		♦	†	♦	♦	♦	♦	♦	♦	♦				♦				★	★
Glenborrodale Castle Glenborrodale, Acharacle Argyll	S	16	D			10	♦	♦	♦	♦	♦	♦	P	♦	♦	♦		♦			★	★
Gleneagles Auchterarder Perthshire	S	†	DS	♦	♦	♦	♦	♦	♦	♦	♦	♦	♦	♦	♦	♦	♦	♦	♦	♦	♦	★
Glenfeochan House Oban Argyll	S	3	D		10	6		♦	♦	R			♦			♦					★	♦
Gliffaes Crickhowell Powys	W	22	A		♦	25	♦		♦	♦	♦	♦	P		♦	♦		♦			★	♦

The George

Gara Rock

Gliffaes

Glanrannell Park

Cycling	Horseracing	Horse riding	Shooting	Walking	Airborne	Sailing	Seaside	Theatre	Gourmet	Diet and health	Bridge and cards	Literary	Painting and crafts	Romantic	Murder and fantasy	Heritage	Shopping	Outward bound	Peace and quiet	In town	In country	TEL / FAX
			◆					◆						◆		◆			◆		◆	TEL: (0246) 583259 FAX:
		★	C	◆				◆	◆					◆		◆			◆		◆	TEL: (0525) 712242 FAX: (0525) 712242
★	★	★		◆				TO	◆					◆		◆	◆		◆		◆	TEL: (0684) 573397 FAX: (0684) 569665
◆	◆	★	C	◆					◆					◆	◆	◆	◆	◆	◆		◆	TEL: (0676) 22335 FAX: (0676) 23711
		★						TO	◆					◆		◆	◆		◆		◆	TEL: 071-491 7282 FAX: 071-491 7281
	◆	★	C	◆				◆						◆	◆	◆	◆	◆	◆		◆	TEL: (0451) 30354 FAX: (0451) 32486
★			★		★		TO							◆		◆	◆		◆			TEL: 071-499 0888 FAX: 071-493 6629
	◆							◆								◆	◆		◆			TEL: (0628) 35934 FAX: (0628) 771054
◆		★	★	◆		◆	S	T	W	◆				◆					◆		◆	TEL: (054884) 2342 FAX: (054884) 3033
	★	★	◆					◆						◆		◆	◆		◆		◆	TEL: (0259) 219275 FAX: (0259) 213827
						★		T	W							◆	◆					TEL: (0780) 55171 FAX: (0780) 57070
★		★	★	◆				◆						◆					◆		◆	TEL: (0647) 432367 FAX: (0647) 432574
★		★		◆		★								◆		◆	◆	◆	◆		◆	TEL: (05394) 88818 FAX: (05394) 88058
		★		◆															B		◆	TEL: (0558) 685230 FAX: (0558) 685 784
◆		★		◆				◆			◆							◆	◆		◆	TEL: (03967) 68451 FAX: (03967) 67041
	◆		C	◆			S		◆					◆	◆	◆			◆		◆	TEL: (0475) 54711 FAX: (0475) 54201
★		★	C	◆		★	S		◆					◆				◆	B		◆	TEL: (09724) 266 FAX: (09724) 224
◆		◆		◆				◆	◆	◆			◆			◆	◆		◆		◆	TEL: (0764) 62231 FAX: (0764) 62022
★		★	C	◆	FG	★			◆				F	◆		◆			B		◆	TEL: (063177) 273 FAX: (063177) 624
★		★	C	◆	B	★									◆	◆		◆	◆		◆	TEL: (0874) 730371 FAX: (0874) 730463

Gidleigh Park

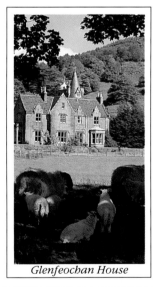

Glenfeochan House

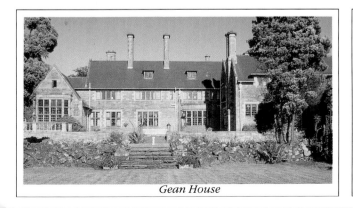

Gean House

Gleneagles

Halewell Close

Griffin Inn

	Map	Number of rooms	Price range	Disabled	Children	Meeting facilities	Credit cards	TV	Parking	Restaurants	Direct dial telephones	Helicopter landing	Pets	Leisure centre	Snooker	Croquet	Squash	Tennis	Indoor swimming pool	Outdoor swimming pool	Golf	Fishing
Glyn Isa Rowen nr Conwy Gwynedd	W	8	SA		◆	70	◆	◆	◆	◆		◆	P			◆					★	◆
Goodwood Park Hotel Chichester, Goodwood Sussex	E	89	SA	◆	◆	†	◆	◆	◆	◆	◆	◆		◆	◆		◆	◆	◆		◆	
Gordleton Mill Lymington Hampshire	E	7	C	◆	7	14	◆	◆	◆	◆	◆										★	★
The Goring London SW1	E	84	C		◆	55	◆	◆		◆	◆										★	
Grafton Manor Bromsgrove Hereford & Worcester	E	9	BS		◆		◆		◆	◆	◆		P			◆					★	
The Grand Brighton Sussex	E	†	BS	◆	◆	◆	◆	◆	◆	◆	◆			◆				◆			★
The Grand Eastbourne Sussex	E	64	CS		◆		◆	◆	◆	◆				◆				◆	◆	★	
Grapevine Stow-on-the-Wold Gloucestershire	E	23	SB		◆	12	◆	◆	◆	◆	◆											
Gravetye Manor East Grinstead Sussex	E	18	D			14	◆	◆	◆	◆		G			◆						★	
Great Tree Hotel Chagford Devon	E	12	AS			30	◆	◆	◆	◆	◆	◆	P								★	★
Greenway Cheltenham Gloucestershire	E	19	AS	◆	7	18	◆	◆	◆	◆	◆				◆						★	
Gregans Castle Ballyvaughan Co Clare	I	22	AB				◆		◆	◆	◆											
Greywalls Muirfield, Gullane Lothian	S	23	BC		◆		◆	◆	◆	◆	◆		P			◆		◆			★	★
Griffin Inn Llyswen, Brecon Powys	W	8	AS		◆	10	◆		◆	◆	◆		◆								★	★
Gurthalougha House Balinderry, Nenagh Co Tipperary	I	8	A		◆		◆		◆	◆											★	◆
Gwesty Fferm Penbontbren Farm Hotel Glynarthen, nr Cardigan, Dyfed	W	10	A	◆	◆	30	◆	◆	◆	◆	◆		P		◆						★	★
Halewell Close Withington, Cheltenham Gloucestershire	E	6	A	◆	◆		◆	◆	◆	R			P							◆		◆
Hall Garth Coatham Mundeville nr Darlington Durham	E	40	SB		◆	†	◆	◆	◆	◆	◆	◆				◆		◆		◆	★	
Halmpstone Manor Bishop's Tawton, Barnstaple Devon	E	6	CS		12	10	◆	◆	◆	◆		◆								★	★
Hambleton Hall Hambleton, Oakham, Leicestershire	E	15	BS	◆	◆	40	◆	◆	◆	◆	◆	◆				◆			◆	★	★

Glyn Isa

Grafton Manor

48

Cycling	Horseracing	Horse riding	Shooting	Walking	Airborne	Sailing	Seaside	Theatre	Gourmet	Diet and health	Bridge and cards	Literary	Painting and crafts	Romantic	Murder and fantasy	Heritage	Shopping	Outward bound	Peace and quiet	In town	In country	TEL / FAX
★		★	C	◆		★	4	T	B					◆		◆	◆	◆	B		◆	TEL: (0492) 650242 FAX: (0492) 650063
	◆							◆		◆	◆					◆	◆		◆		◆	TEL: (0243) 775537 FAX: (0243) 533802
★		★				★	5		◆					◆					◆		◆	TEL: (0590) 682219 FAX: (0590) 683073
	◆							TO	◆							◆	◆			◆		TEL: 071-834 8211 FAX: -071-834 4393
	◆	★		◆				T	◆					◆		◆			◆		◆	TEL: (0527) 579007 FAX: (0527) 575221
	◆					★	S	T		◆						◆	◆		◆			TEL: (0273) 21188 FAX: (0273) 202694
	◆	★		◆			S	OT	◆					◆		◆	◆		◆			TEL: (0323) 412345 FAX: (0323) 412233
★	◆			◆					◆	◆	◆			◆		◆	◆	◆	◆			TEL: (0451) 30344 FAX: (0451) 32278
	◆	★				★								◆					◆		◆	TEL: (0342) 810567 FAX: (0342) 810080
★	◆	★	◆	◆		★		◆						◆		◆	◆		◆		◆	TEL: (0647) 432491 FAX:
	◆		C	◆	★			T	B					◆		◆	◆		◆		◆	TEL: (0242) 862352 FAX: (0242) 862780
				◆			4		◆					◆		◆			◆		◆	TEL: (065) 77005 FAX: (065) 77111
	◆		★	◆			2		◆					◆		◆			B		◆	TEL: (0620) 842144 FAX: (0620) 842241
★		★	★	◆		G			◆					◆				◆	◆		◆	TEL: (0874) 754241 FAX:
		★		◆	★				◆							◆			B		◆	TEL: (067) 22080 FAX: (067) 22154
		★		◆			3		◆							◆			◆		◆	TEL: (0239) 810248 FAX: (0239) 811129
	◆	★		◆				T								◆	◆		◆		◆	TEL: (0242) 890238 FAX:
		★	C	◆	★			TO	B					◆		◆	◆		◆		◆	TEL: (0325) 300400 FAX: (0325) 310083
★		★	★	◆			8							◆		◆			◆		◆	TEL: (0271) 830321 FAX: (0271) 830826
◆	◆	★	★	★	◆	★	★	OT	◆		◆		◆	◆		◆	◆		◆		◆	TEL: (0572) 756991 FAX: (0572) 724721

Great Tree

Halmpstone Manor

Greenway

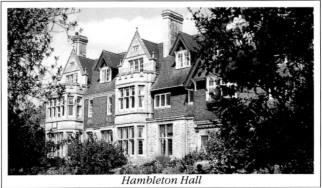

Hambleton Hall

Hatton Court

The Haycock

	Map	Number of rooms	Price range	Disabled	Children	Meeting facilities	Credit cards	TV	Parking	Restaurants	Direct dial telephones	Helicopter landing	Pets	Leisure centre	Snooker	Croquet	Squash	Tennis	Indoor swimming pool	Outdoor swimming pool	Golf	Fishing
Hanbury Manor Thundridge, Hertfordshire	E	86	CD	◆	◆	◆	◆	◆	◆	◆	◆	◆		◆	◆	◆	◆	◆	◆		◆	
Hartwell House Aylesbury, Buckinghamshire	E	32	DS		†	◆	◆	◆	◆	◆	◆			◆		◆			◆		★	◆
Hassop Hall Great Longstone, Derbyshire	E	13	BC	◆		50	◆	◆	◆	◆	◆	◆	P		◆		◆				★	★
Hatton Court Upton St Leonards, Gloucestershire	E	45	AS			60	◆	◆	◆	◆	◆		G	◆		◆				◆	★	★
Hawkstone Park Weston-Under-Redcastle, Shropshire	E	59	BS	◆	◆	†	◆	◆	◆	◆	◆	◆		◆	◆	◆		◆		◆	◆	◆
The Haycock Wansford, Peterborough & Cambridgeshire	E	51	SB	◆	◆	◆		◆	◆	◆	◆	◆									★	★
Hayton Hall Wetheral, Carlisle, Cumbria	E	17	A	◆	◆	†	◆	◆	◆	◆		◆			◆							◆
Highbullen Chittlehamholt, Umberleigh, Devon	E	37	A	◆	8	30	◆	◆	◆	◆	◆	◆	P	◆	◆	◆	◆	◆	◆	◆	◆	◆
Hintlesham Hall Hintlesham, Nr Ipswich, Suffolk	E	33	C		◆	80	◆	◆	◆	◆	◆	◆	P	◆	◆	◆		◆		◆	◆	◆
Hipping Hall Cowan Bridge, Kirkby Lonsdale, Cumbria	E	7	SA		12	20	◆	◆	◆	◆			◆		◆						★	★
Hoar Cross Hall Health Spa Hoar Cross nr Yoxall, Staffordshire	E	80	C		16	†	◆	◆	◆	◆	◆			◆		◆		◆	◆		◆	◆
Hob Green Harrogate, Yorkshire	E	12	B		◆	10	◆	◆	◆	◆		◆			◆							
Holbeck Ghyll Windermere, Cumbria	E	14	AC		◆	16	◆		◆	◆	◆		◆								★	★
Holbrook House Holbrook nr Wincanton, Somerset	E	18	BS			20	◆		◆	◆	◆					◆	◆	◆		◆			
Holne Chase Ashburton, Devon	E	14	A	◆	◆	30	◆	◆	◆	◆	◆	◆	◆		◆						★	◆
Hope End Ledbury, Hereford & Worcester	E		C		12	12	◆		◆	◆	◆										★	
Horn of Plenty Gulworthy, Tavistock, Devon	E	7	A	◆	13	15	◆	◆	◆	◆	◆	◆	◆								★	★
Hornby Hall Culgarith Penrith, Cumbria	E	7	A		◆		◆	◆	◆	R												◆
Horsted Place Little Horsted nr Uckfield, Sussex	E	17	D		7	35	◆	◆	◆	◆	◆	◆			◆		◆	◆		◆	◆	
Hotel l'Horizon St Brelade's Bay, Channel Isles (Jersey)	E	†	BC	◆	◆	†	◆	◆	◆	◆	◆			◆						◆		★

Hoar Cross

Hanbury Manor

Cycling	Horseracing	Horse riding	Shooting	Walking	Airborne	Sailing	Seaside	Theatre	Gourmet	Diet and health	Bridge and cards	Literary	Painting and crafts	Romantic	Murder and fantasy	Heritage	Shopping	Outward bound	Peace and quiet	In town	In country	Contact
			◆					◆	◆										◆		◆	TEL: (0920) 487722 FAX: (0920) 487692
	◆								◆					◆		◆	◆				◆	TEL: (0296) 747444 FAX: (0296) 747450
★	◆	★	C	◆				TO		◆				◆		◆	◆		◆		◆	TEL: (0629) 640488 FAX: (0629) 640577
★	◆	★	★	◆	★			T	◆					◆	◆	◆	◆		◆		◆	TEL: (0452) 617412 FAX: (0452) 612945
			C	◆									◆			◆	◆		◆		◆	TEL: (0939) 200611 FAX: (0939) 200311
★		★		◆	P			T	◆		◆			◆		◆			◆		◆	TEL: (0780) 782223 FAX: (0780) 783031
			★	◆	★				◆					◆		◆			◆		◆	TEL: (0228) 70651 FAX: (0228) 70010
◆		★	★	◆															◆		◆	TEL: (0769) 540561 FAX: (0769) 540492
★	◆	★	★	◆	★	★	15	T	WB	◆	◆		◆	◆	◆	◆	◆	◆	◆		◆	TEL: (047 387) 334 FAX: (047 387) 463
★		★		◆					◆							◆			◆		◆	TEL: (05242) 71187 FAX: (05242) 72452
◆				◆						◆	◆			◆		◆	◆	◆	◆		◆	TEL: (0283) 75671 FAX: (0283) 75652
	◆			◆										◆		◆	◆		◆		◆	TEL: (0423) 770031 FAX: (0423) 771589
		★		◆										◆		◆		◆	◆		◆	TEL: (05394) 32375 FAX: (05394) 34743
	◆	★														◆			◆		◆	TEL: (0963) 32377 FAX:
★		★	C	◆	◆				◆		◆					◆		◆	◆		◆	TEL: (03643) 471 FAX: (03643) 453
	◆	★	C	◆					◆		◆			◆		◆			◆		◆	TEL: (0531) 3613 FAX: (0531) 5697
★	◆	★	★	◆					◆							◆	◆	◆	◆		◆	TEL: (0822) 832528 FAX:
			★	◆												◆			◆		◆	TEL: (0768) 891114 FAX:
				◆					◆					◆		◆			◆		◆	TEL: (0825) 75581 FAX: (0825) 75459
★	◆			◆		★	S		◆	◆				◆		◆			◆		◆	TEL: (0534) 43101 FAX: (0534) 46269

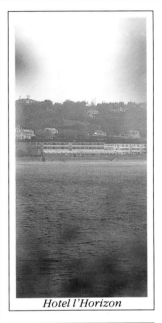

Hotel l'Horizon

Hipping Hall

Horn of Plenty

Hob Green

	Map	Number of rooms	Price range	Disabled	Children	Meeting facilities	Credit cards	TV	Parking	Restaurants	Direct dial telephones	Helicopter landing	Pets	Leisure centre	Snooker	Croquet	Squash	Tennis	Indoor swimming pool	Outdoor swimming pool	Golf	Fishing
Hunstrete House Hunstrete Avon	E	24	C	◆	9	40	◆		◆	◆	◆	◆				◆		◆		◆	★	★
Huntsham Court Huntsham Bampton nr Twerton Devon	E	17	A		◆	25	◆		◆	◆			P	◆	◆			◆			★	★
Hutton Court Hutton Avon	E	8	BC		◆	◆	◆	◆	◆	◆	◆	◆									★	★
Hythe Imperial Hythe Kent	E	†	BS	◆	◆	†	◆	◆	◆	◆	◆	◆		◆	◆	◆	◆	◆	◆		◆	★
Inn at Whitewell Whitewell, Clitheroe Lancashire	E	9	A		◆	50	◆	◆	◆	◆	◆	◆	P	◆							★	◆
Innishannon Hotel Innishannon Co Cork	I	13	BS		◆	†	◆	◆	◆	◆	◆	◆	◆								★	◆
International Hotel Killarney Co Kerry	I	88	A	◆	◆	◆	◆	◆	◆	◆		◆								★	★
Inver Lodge Lochinver Highland	S	20	AB		◆		◆	◆	◆	◆	◆		◆	◆						★	★
Invercreran Appin Argyll	S	9	A	◆	5	20	◆	◆	◆	◆	◆	◆	P								★	★
Inverlochy Castle Torlundy, Fort William Highland	S	16	CD		◆	◆		◆	◆	◆				◆			◆		★	◆
Invery House Banchory Royal Deeside Kincardineshire	S	14	D	◆	◆	◆	◆	◆	◆	◆	◆	◆	◆			◆	◆				★	★
Isle of Eriska Oban Argyll	S	17	C	◆	◆	30	◆	◆	◆	◆	◆	◆	P		◆					★	★
Jervaulx Hall Jervaulx nr Masham Ripon, Yorkshire	E	10	A	◆	◆	20	◆		◆	◆		◆	◆			◆			★	★
Johnstounburn House Humbie nr Edinburgh Lothian	S	20	D		◆	32	◆	◆	◆	◆	◆	◆	◆			◆				◆
Kenmore Hotel Kenmore Perthshire	S	38	B		◆	◆	◆	◆	◆	◆	◆	◆	P			◆			★	◆
Kildare House Hotel Straffan, Kildare Co Kildare	I	45	D	◆	◆	70	◆	◆	◆	◆	◆	◆	◆	◆	◆	◆	◆	◆	◆	◆	◆	◆
Kildrummy Castle Hotel Kildrummy, by Alford Aberdeenshire	S	16	AS		◆		◆	◆	◆	◆	◆		◆		◆					★	◆
Kilfinan Hotel By Tighnabruaich Argyll	S	11	B		◆		◆	◆	◆	◆	◆		P						★	◆
Kinloch Castle Isle of Rhum Highland	S	9	C		7					◆		◆	G	◆						◆
Kinloch House Hotel Blairgowrie Perthshire	S	21	A	◆	◆	12	◆	◆	◆	◆	◆	◆	P						★	★

Invercreran

Invery House

Hutton Court

Kildare House

Cycling	Horseracing	Horse riding	Shooting	Walking	Airborne	Sailing	Seaside	Theatre	Gourmet	Diet and health	Bridge and cards	Literary	Painting and crafts	Romantic	Murder and fantasy	Heritage	Shopping	Outward bound	Peace and quiet	In town	In country	Contact
★	★		C	◆	B		S	T	◆					◆		◆	◆		◆		◆	TEL: (0761) 4909490 / FAX: (0761) 490732
◆		★	C	◆	B			W					◆			◆			◆		◆	TEL: (03986) 210 / FAX:
◆		★	◆			★	3	T	◆					◆	◆	◆	◆		◆		◆	TEL: (0934) 814343 / FAX: (0934) 811018
★	◆	★	C			★	S	◆			◆			◆	◆	◆	◆			◆		TEL: (0303) 267441 / FAX: (0303) 264610
	◆	★	◆	◆				T					◆			◆	◆	◆	◆		◆	TEL: (02008) 222 / FAX:
★	◆	★				★	◆	T	◆		◆			◆		◆	◆	◆	◆		◆	TEL: (021) 775121 / FAX: (021) 775609
★	◆	★	★	◆												◆	◆	◆		◆		TEL: (064) 31816 / FAX: (064) 31837
			◆	◆		★	S											◆			◆	TEL: (0571) 844496 / FAX: (0571) 844395
★		★		◆			½							◆		◆			◆		◆	TEL: (0631) 73414 / FAX: (0631) 73532
	★	★	◆						◆					◆		◆		◆	◆		◆	TEL: (0397) 702177/8 / FAX: (0397) 702953
	★	★	◆						◆	◆							◆		◆		◆	TEL: (03302) 4782 / FAX: (03302) 4712
★		◆	C	◆	G	★	S		W	◆				◆					◆		◆	TEL: (0631 72) 371 / FAX: (0631 72) 531
★	◆	★	★	◆	B			T	◆					◆		◆	◆		◆		◆	TEL: (0677) 60235 / FAX:
◆	◆	★	★	◆			10	T	B					◆		◆	◆	◆	◆		◆	TEL: (087533) 696 / FAX: (087533) 626
★		★	★	◆		★		T	◆							◆		◆	◆		◆	TEL: (0887) 830205 / FAX: (0887) 830262
◆	◆	★	★	◆	◆	★		T	W	C			P	◆		◆	◆		◆		◆	TEL: (1) 627 3333 / FAX: (1) 627 3312
★		★	★	◆					◆							◆		◆	◆		◆	TEL: (09755) 71288 / FAX: (09755) 71345
	★	★	◆		◆		S		◆							◆				B	◆	TEL: (070) 082 201 / FAX: (070) 082 205
			◆				S							◆		◆		◆	◆		◆	TEL: (0687) 2037 / FAX:
★	◆	★	★	◆												◆	◆		◆		◆	TEL: (0250) 884237 / FAX: (0250) 884333

Inn at Whitewell

Johnstounburn House

Kinloch House

Hunstrete House

Ladyburn

Knockomie Hotel

	Map	Number of rooms	Price range	Disabled	Children	Meeting facilities	Credit cards	TV	Parking	Restaurants	Direct dial telephones	Helicopter landing	Pets	Leisure centre	Snooker	Croquet	Squash	Tennis	Indoor swimming pool	Outdoor swimming pool	Golf	Fishing
Kinnaird By Dunkeld Perthshire	S	9	CD	◆	12	25	◆	◆	◆	◆	◆	◆	P		◆	◆		◆			★	◆
Kirroughtree Hotel Newton Stewart Dumfries & Galloway	S	22	C		10	15	◆	◆	◆	◆	◆	◆				◆		◆			★	★
Knipoch Hotel Oban Argyll	S	17	B		◆		◆	◆	◆	◆	◆	◆									★	◆
Knockie Lodge Whitebridge Inverness-shire	S	10	D	◆	10	◆	◆		◆	◆			◆		◆			◆			★	◆
Knockinaam Lodge Portpatrick Dumfries & Galloway	S	10	DS		10	◆	◆	◆	◆	◆	◆	◆	◆			◆					★	★
Knockomie Hotel Forres Morayshire	S	7	A		◆	◆	◆	◆	◆	◆	◆	◆	◆			◆					★	★
Knoll House Studland Bay nr Swanage Dorset	E	80	A		◆		◆	◆	◆	◆	◆		◆		◆			◆		◆	◆	★
Ladyburn Maybole Ayrshire	S	8	B	◆	14	30	◆	◆	◆	◆	◆	◆	P								★	★
Lainston House Sparsholt Hampshire	E	32	D		◆	80	◆	◆	◆	◆	◆	◆	◆		◆	◆		◆			★	◆
Lake Hotel Llangammarch Wells Powys	W	19	B	◆	◆	75	◆	◆	◆	◆	◆	◆	◆		◆	◆					★	◆
Lake Vyrnwy Hotel Llandwddyn Powys	W	38	SB		◆	50	◆	◆	◆	◆	◆	◆	P			◆					★	◆
Lamb Inn Burford Oxfordshire	E	15	SA		◆		◆		◆	◆		◆										★
Langar Hall Langar Nottinghamshire	E	12	A		◆	20	◆	◆	◆	◆	◆	◆	◆			◆					★	
Langdale Hotel Great Langdale nr Ambleside Cumbria	E	65	AS	◆	◆	90	◆	◆	◆	◆	◆	◆	G		◆			◆				◆
Langley House Hotel Wiveliscombe, Taunton Somerset	E	8	AS		◆	20	◆	◆	◆	◆	◆	◆	◆			◆						
Lee Park Romsey Hampshire	E	8	B		◆	12	◆		◆	◆	◆	◆	P			◆					★	
Leeming House Ullswater nr Penrith Cumbria	E	40	C	◆	◆	◆	◆	◆	◆	◆	◆	◆	P			◆					★	
Letham Grange Colliston By Arbroath	S	30	B		◆	†	◆	◆	◆	◆	◆	◆									◆	★
Lewtrenchard Manor Lewtrenchard nr Okehampton Devon	E	8	C		8	50	◆	◆	◆	◆	◆	◆	P			◆					★	◆
Linden Hall Longhorsley, Morpeth Northumberland	E	55	B	◆	◆	†	◆	◆	◆	◆	◆	◆	◆	◆	◆	◆		◆	◆		★	◆

Linden Hall

Langley House

→ LINDEN HALL

Cycling	Horseracing	Horse riding	Shooting	Walking	Airborne	Sailing	Seaside	Theatre	Gourmet	Diet and health	Bridge and cards	Literary	Painting and crafts	Romantic	Murder and fantasy	Heritage	Shopping	Outward bound	Peace and quiet	In town	In country	Contact
★	◆	★	★	◆		★		T	C										◆		◆	TEL: (0796) 482 440 / FAX: (0796) 482 289
		★	R	◆					◆					◆		◆		◆	◆		◆	TEL: (0671) 2141 / FAX: (0671) 2425
		★	★	◆		◆	2		W							◆			◆		◆	TEL: (085) 26 251 / FAX: (085) 26 249
			★	◆		◆			◆							◆			◆		◆	TEL: (04563) 276 / FAX: (04563) 389
	◆	★		◆			S		◆							◆			◆		◆	TEL: (077681) 471 / FAX: (077681) 435
★	★	★	★	★		★	5		WC				P	◆	◆	◆			◆		◆	TEL: (0309) 673146 / FAX: (0309) 673290
		★				◆	S		◆							◆			◆		◆	TEL: (092944) 251 / FAX: (092944) 423
	◆	★	★	◆					◆							◆			◆		◆	TEL: (06554) 585 / FAX: (06554) 580
		★	★						◆							◆	◆		◆		◆	TEL: (0962) 863588 / FAX: (0962) 72672
★		◆	★	◆				T	W				◆	◆		◆			◆		◆	TEL: (05912) 202 / FAX: (05912) 457
◆		★	★	◆		★		T	◆		◆					◆	◆	◆	◆		◆	TEL: (069173) 692 / FAX: (069173) 289
★	◆	★		◆					◆							◆	◆	◆	◆		◆	TEL: (099 382) 3155 / FAX: (099382) 2228
	◆		C	◆	◆				◆	◆	◆	◆	◆	◆	◆	◆	◆		◆		◆	TEL: (0949) 60559 / FAX: (0949) 61045
	◆		C	◆	◆	◆		T	◆	◆				◆		◆		◆	◆		◆	TEL: (09667) 302 / FAX: (09667) 694
	◆			◆	★		10	T											◆		◆	TEL: (0984) 23318 / FAX: (0984) 24573
★	◆	★	◆	◆			BG		W							◆	◆		◆		◆	TEL: (0703) 734087 / FAX: (0703) 740409
★		★	★	◆		★								◆		◆	◆	◆	◆		◆	TEL: (07684) 86622 / FAX: (07684) 86443
★		★	◆	◆		★	◆				◆			◆		◆			◆		◆	TEL: (0241) 89 373 / FAX: (0241) 89 460
★		★	★	◆	PB			T					◆	◆		◆			◆		◆	TEL: (0566) 83256 / FAX: (0566) 83332
◆	◆	★	★	◆	B	★	10	T	◆					◆		◆	◆	◆	◆		◆	TEL: (0670) 516611 / FAX: (0670) 88544

Kinnaird

Knockinaam Lodge

Lainston House

Lake Vyrnwy

Lygon Arms

Little Hemingfold

Lythe Hill

Little Thakeham

	Map	Number of rooms	Price range	Disabled	Children	Meeting facilities	Credit cards	TV	Parking	Restaurants	Direct dial telephones	Helicopter landing	Pets	Leisure centre	Snooker	Croquet	Squash	Tennis	Indoor swimming pool	Outdoor swimming pool	Golf	Fishing
Linthwaite House Windermere Cumbria	E	18	A		◆	22	◆	◆	◆	◆	◆										★	◆
Little Grove St Lawrence Channel Isles (Jersey)	E	13	C		12	20	◆	◆	◆	◆	◆									◆	★	★
Little Hemingfold Hotel Telham, Battle Sussex	E	12	A		◆	20	◆	◆	◆	◆	◆	◆	P			◆		◆			★	◆
Little Thakeham Storrington Sussex	E	9	A		◆	◆	◆	◆	◆	◆	◆					◆		◆		◆	★	
Llangoed Hall Llyswen, Brecon Powys	W	23	D		8	◆	◆	◆	◆	◆	◆			◆	◆		◆				★	◆
Llyndir Hall Rossett, Wrexham, nr Chester Clwyd	W	38	BS	◆	◆	†	◆	◆	◆	◆	◆	◆	G	◆		◆			◆		★	★
Lockerbie Manor Lockerbie Dumfries & Galloway	S	30	A		◆	†	◆	◆	◆	◆	◆	◆		◆							★	★
Lodge on the Loch Onich, nr Fort William Inverness-shire	S	19	C	◆	◆		◆	◆	◆	◆	◆			◆							★	★
Lodore Swiss Hotel Borrowdale, Keswick Cumbria	E	70	B		◆	55	◆	◆	◆	◆	◆	◆	G	◆		◆	◆	◆	◆	◆	★	★
Lomond Hills Freuchie Fife	S	25	A		◆	†	◆	◆	◆	◆	◆			◆	◆				◆		★	★
Longueville House Mallow Co Cork	I	16	AB		10	15	◆	◆	◆	◆	◆			◆	◆						★	★
Longueville Manor St Saviour Channel Isles (Jersey)	E	32	D		7	◆	◆	◆	◆	◆	◆		◆							◆	★	
Lords Of The Manor Upper Slaughter, Cheltenham Gloucestershire	E	29	D		◆	45	◆	◆	◆	◆	◆	◆				◆					★	◆
Lostwithiel Lower Pascoe, Lostwithiel Cornwall	E	18	A		◆	60	◆	◆	◆	◆	◆	◆	P	◆		◆	◆	◆			◆	
Lower Slaughter Manor Lower Slaughter Gloucestershire	E	19	D		10	20	◆	◆	◆	◆	◆	◆	G		◆		◆	◆			★	★
Lucknam Park Colerne Wiltshire	E	42	D		◆	40	◆	◆	◆	◆	◆	◆			◆		◆	◆			★	◆
Lygon Arms Broadway Hereford & Worcester	E	65	CS	◆	◆	80	◆	◆	◆	◆	◆	◆	◆	◆	◆		◆	◆			★	★
Lythe Hill Haslemere Surrey	E	40	BD		◆	70	◆		◆	◆	◆	◆	◆		◆	◆		◆			★	◆
Maes-y-Neuadd Talsarnau, nr Harlech Gwynedd	W	16	BC	◆	◆	◆	◆	◆	◆	◆	◆	◆	P		◆						★	★
Magherabuoy House Portrush Co Antrim	I	38	AS	◆	◆	†	◆	◆	◆	◆	◆		G	◆	◆						★	★

Cycling	Horseracing	Horse riding	Shooting	Walking	Airborne	Sailing	Seaside	Theatre	Gourmet	Diet and health	Bridge and cards	Literary	Painting and crafts	Romantic	Murder and fantasy	Heritage	Shopping	Outward bound	Peace and quiet	In town	In country	TEL / FAX
★		★	★	◆		★								◆		◆	◆	◆	◆		◆	TEL: (05394) 88600 FAX: (05394) 88601
									◆					◆			◆		◆		◆	TEL: (0534) 25321 FAX: (0534) 25325
★	◆	★		◆	★	★	5	T						◆		◆			◆		◆	TEL: (04246) 4338 FAX:
	◆	★	★	◆	★		8		B				◆	◆		◆	◆		◆		◆	TEL: (0903) 744416 FAX: (0903) 745022
		★	C	◆	G				◆					◆		◆			◆		◆	TEL: (0874) 754525 FAX: (0874) 754545
★	◆	★	C	◆	◆			T	W				◆	◆		◆	◆	◆	◆		◆	TEL: (0244) 571648 FAX: (0244) 571258
◆	◆	★	CD	◆			9					◆		◆							◆	TEL: (05762) 2610/3939 FAX: (05762) 3046
		★	C	◆		★			◆				P	◆		◆		◆	◆		◆	TEL: (08553) 237 FAX: (08553) 463
★	◆	★	★	◆	◆	◆			◆	◆	★	◆		◆		◆			◆		◆	TEL: (07687) 77285 FAX: (07687) 77343
★	◆	★	★	◆	★				◆	◆	◆			◆		◆	◆	◆	◆		◆	TEL: (0337) 57329 FAX:
★	◆	★	R	◆		★			◆					◆		◆	◆	◆	◆		◆	TEL: (022) 47156 FAX: (022) 47459
				◆		★			◆					◆					◆		◆	TEL: (0534) 25501 FAX: (0534) 31613
	◆		★					T	W					◆		◆			◆		◆	TEL: (0451) 20243 FAX: (0451) 20696
★		★		◆	B	◆	4		W										◆		◆	TEL: (0208) 873550 FAX: (0208) 873479
★	◆	★	C	◆				T		◆	◆			◆		◆			◆		◆	TEL: (0451) 20456 FAX: (0451) 22150
	◆	★							◆					◆		◆			◆		◆	TEL: (0225) 742777 FAX: (0225) 743536
★		★	★	◆	★			T		◆				◆		◆	◆	◆	◆		◆	TEL: (0386) 852255 FAX: (0386) 858611
	◆	★	★	◆				T	◆					◆		◆	◆				◆	TEL: (0428) 651251 FAX: (0428) 644131
★		★	C	◆			3	OT	W				P	◆	◆	◆		◆	◆		◆	TEL: (0766) 780200 FAX: (0766) 780211
		★		◆			1	T								◆	◆	◆			◆	TEL: (0265) 823507 FAX: (0265) 824687

Maes-y-Neuadd

Linthwaite House

Llangoed Hall

Longueville House

Minmore House

Middlethorpe Hall

	Map	Number of rooms	Price range	Disabled	Children	Meeting facilities	Credit cards	TV	Parking	Restaurants	Direct dial telephones	Helicopter landing	Pets	Leisure centre	Snooker	Croquet	Squash	Tennis	Indoor swimming pool	Outdoor swimming pool	Golf	Fishing
Maison Talbooth Dedham, Colchester Essex	E	10	CS	◆	◆	40	◆	◆	◆	◆	◆	◆	P			◆		★			★	★
Mallory Court Leamington Spa Warwickshire	E	10	B		9	20	◆	◆	◆	◆	◆	◆				◆	◆	◆		◆	★	
Le Manoir Aux Quat' Saisons Great Milton, Oxford Oxfordshire	E	19	D			50	◆	◆	◆	◆	◆	◆	G			◆		◆		◆	★	★
The Manor Chadlington Oxfordshire	E	7	AS			15	◆	◆	◆	◆	◆	◆										
Manor House Castle Combe, Chippenham Wiltshire	E	36	SD	◆	◆	60	◆	◆	◆	◆	◆	◆	P			◆		◆		◆	★	◆
Manor House Walkington, Beverley Humberside	E	5	B		12	15	◆	◆	◆	◆	◆	◆	P								★	
Manor of Groves Sawbridgeworth Hertfordshire	E	35	B	◆	◆	†	◆	◆	◆	◆				◆	◆	◆		◆			◆	★
Mansion House Hotel Elgin Grampian	S		B		◆	†	◆	◆	◆	◆				◆	◆				◆		★	★
Marlfield House Gorey Co Wexford	I	13	D		◆	45	◆	◆	◆	◆						◆		◆			★	◆
McCoy's Staddle Bridge Yorkshire	E	6	B			30	◆	◆	◆	◆	◆	◆									★	★
Meon Valley Hotel Shedfield, Southampton Hampshire	E	83	SB		◆	†	◆	◆	◆	◆	◆	◆		◆	◆		◆	◆	◆		◆	
Meudon Hotel Mawnan Smith nr Falmouth Cornwall	E	32	AS		5		◆	◆	◆	◆	◆		P								★	★
Michael's Nook Grasmere, Ambleside Cumbria	E	14	C			20	◆	◆	◆	◆	◆	◆				◆					★	★
Middlethorpe Hall York Yorkshire	E	29	D		8	50	◆	◆	◆	◆	◆	◆	G			◆					★	★
Mill End Sandy Park, Chagford Devon	E	17	A		◆	6	◆	◆	◆	◆	◆										◆	◆
Mill House Kingham Oxfordshire	E	23	B	◆	5	30	◆	◆	◆	◆	◆					◆					★	◆
Miller Howe Windermere Cumbria	E	13	C		12	15	◆	◆	◆	◆		◆									★	★
Miller's House Middleham nr Wensleydale Yorkshire	E	7	AS		10	14	◆	◆	◆	◆						◆		★			★	★
Minmore House Glenlivet Banffshire	S	A	SA	◆		◆		◆	◆	◆	◆		P			◆		◆		◆	★	★
Moffat House Hotel Moffat Dumfries & Galloway	S	20	A	◆	◆	◆	◆	◆	◆	◆	◆										★	★

Maison Talbooth

Mansion House

Cycling	Horseracing	Horse riding	Shooting	Walking	Airborne	Sailing	Seaside	Theatre	Gourmet	Diet and health	Bridge and cards	Literary	Painting and crafts	Romantic	Murder and fantasy	Heritage	Shopping	Outward bound	Peace and quiet	In town	In country	TEL / FAX
	◆	★	★	◆	FB	★			WB					◆		◆	◆	◆	◆		◆	TEL: (0206) 322367 / FAX: (0206) 322752
	◆	★		◆				◆	◆								◆		◆		◆	TEL: (0926) 330214 / FAX: (0926) 451714
◆	◆	★							◆					◆		◆			◆		◆	TEL: (0844) 278881 / FAX: (0844) 278847
			◆																◆		◆	TEL: (0608) 76711 / FAX:
◆	◆	★	★	◆	★			TO	◆					◆		◆	◆		◆		◆	TEL: (0249) 782206 / FAX: (0249) 782159
	◆	★	C	◆					◆							◆	◆		◆		◆	TEL: (0482) 881645 / FAX: (0482) 866501
		★		◆		★		◆	◆				◆			◆	◆		◆		◆	TEL: (0279) 600777 / FAX: (0279) 600374
★		★	★	◆		★	5							◆		◆	◆	◆		◆		TEL: (0343) 548811 / FAX: (0343) 547916
		★	◆				2							◆		◆			◆		◆	TEL: (055) 21124 / FAX: (055) 21572
★	◆	★	★	◆					◆							◆		◆			◆	TEL: (060982) 671 / FAX:
	◆	★	★	◆		★	8	T	B	◆						◆			◆		◆	TEL: (0329) 833455 / FAX: (0329) 834411
		★		◆		★	S		◆					◆					◆		◆	TEL: (0326) 250541 / FAX: (0326) 250543
★		★	★	◆	★	★		T	W	◆				◆		◆			◆	◆	◆	TEL: (05394) 35496 / FAX: (05394) 35765
★	◆	★	C	◆	B			T	W					◆		◆	◆		◆		◆	TEL: (0904) 641241 / FAX: (0904) 620176
★	◆	◆	★	◆					◆			◆				◆	◆	★	◆		◆	TEL: (0647) 432282 / FAX: (0647) 433106
◆	◆	★	★	◆	★			T	◆	◆				◆		◆	◆		◆		◆	TEL: (0608) 658188 / FAX: (0608) 658492
★		★	C	◆	★			T	◆					◆		◆	◆	◆	◆		◆	TEL: (09662) 42536 / FAX: (09662) 5664
★	◆	★	★	◆	B			T	W				◆	◆	◆	◆	◆	◆	B		◆	TEL: (0969) 22630 / FAX: (0969) 23570
★		★	★	◆					◆					◆		◆		◆	◆		◆	TEL: (08073) 378 / FAX: (08073) 472
		★																	◆	◆		TEL: (0683) 20039 / FAX: (0683) 21288

Michaels Nook

Le Manoir

Manor House, Castle Combe

Le Talbooth

Murrayshall

Moore Place

	Map	Number of rooms	Price range	Disabled	Children	Meeting facilities	Credit cards	TV	Parking	Restaurants	Direct dial telephones	Helicopter landing	Pets	Leisure centre	Snooker	Croquet	Squash	Tennis	Indoor swimming pool	Outdoor swimming pool	Golf	Fishing
Monkey Island Hotel Bray-on-Thames, Maidenhead Berkshire	E	25	AS		◆	†	◆	◆	◆	◆	◆	◆	G			◆					★	◆
Moore Place Aspley Guise, Woburn Bedfordshire	E	54	A	◆	◆	50	◆	◆	◆	◆	◆		◆		◆						★	
Moorland Hotel Haytor Devon	E	23	SA	◆	◆			◆	◆	◆	◆			◆		◆					★★	★
Mortons House Hotel Corfe Castle Dorset	E	17	C		◆	40	◆	◆	◆	◆	◆		◆			◆					★	
Mottram Hall Prestbury Cheshire	E	†	SB	◆	◆	†	◆	◆	◆	◆	◆	◆	P	◆	◆	◆	◆	◆	◆		◆	◆
Mount Falcon Castle Ballina Co Mayo	I	10	A		◆			◆	◆				◆			◆					★	◆
Mount Juliet Thomastown Co Kilkenny	I	32	SD	◆	P		◆	◆	◆	◆	◆	◆	P	◆	◆	◆		◆			◆	◆
Mount Royale York Yorkshire	E	23	SB		◆	20	◆	◆	◆	◆	◆	◆	P	◆	◆					◆	★	
Moyglare Manor Moyglare, Maynooth Co Kildare	I	17	C	◆	P		◆	◆	◆	◆	◆	◆									★	
Muckrach Lodge Dunlain Bridge, Grantown-on-Spey Morayshire	S		A	◆	◆		◆	◆	◆	◆	◆	◆	G								★	◆
Murrayshall Scone, Perth Perthshire	S	19	C		12		◆	◆	◆	◆	◆	◆	P		◆		◆				◆	★
Nansidwell Mawnan Smith, nr Falmouth Cornwall	E	12	B		◆		◆	◆	◆	◆						◆					★★	★
Nare Hotel Veryan, Truro Cornwall	E	36	B	◆	◆	50	◆	◆	◆	◆			◆		◆			◆		◆	★★	★
Netherfield Place Battle Sussex	E	14	SA		P		◆	◆	◆	◆	◆				◆	◆					★★	★
New Hall Sutton Coldfield West Midlands	E	62	D	◆	8	50	◆	◆	◆	◆	◆	◆	G		◆						★	
New Park Manor Brockenhurst, New Forest Hampshire	E	26	B		◆	30	◆	◆	◆	◆	◆	◆	◆		◆		◆			◆		
Newport House Newport Co Mayo	I	19			◆		◆		◆	◆	◆		G		◆						★	◆
Nidd Hall Nidd nr Harrogate Yorkshire	E	59	C	◆	◆	†	◆	◆	◆	◆	◆	◆	G	◆	◆		◆	◆	◆		★	◆
Nivingston House Hotel Cleish Hills nr Kinross Kinross-shire	S	17		◆	◆	40	◆	◆	◆	◆	◆				◆						★★	★
Normanton Park Rutland Water, nr Oakham Leicestershire	E	24	AS	◆	◆	†	◆	◆	◆	◆	◆	◆	G								◆	◆

Monkey Island Hotel

Newport House

Cycling	Horseracing	Horse riding	Shooting	Walking	Airborne	Sailing	Seaside	Theatre	Gourmet	Diet and health	Bridge and cards	Literary	Painting and crafts	Romantic	Murder and fantasy	Heritage	Shopping	Outward bound	Peace and quiet	In town	In country	TEL / FAX
	◆	★	★					T	B					◆		◆	◆		◆		◆	TEL: (0628) 23400 / FAX: (0628) 784732
	◆	★	★	◆	★				◆					◆		◆	◆		◆		◆	TEL: (0908) 282000 / FAX: (0908) 281888
★	◆	★	★	◆	★			T						◆		◆	◆	◆	◆		◆	TEL: (0364) 661407 / FAX:
			◆				4							◆		◆		◆	◆		◆	TEL: (0929) 480988 / FAX: (0929) 480820
	◆	★	C	◆				T	◆	◆				◆	◆	◆	◆		◆		◆	TEL: (0625) 828135 / FAX: (0625) 828950
★		★	◆	★										◆					◆		◆	TEL: (096) 21172 / FAX: (096) 21172
◆	◆	◆	◆	◆				T	◆	◆				◆		◆	◆		◆		◆	TEL: (056) 24455 / FAX: (056) 24522
★	◆	★	◆				◆							◆		◆	◆		◆	◆		TEL: (0904) 628856 / FAX: (0904) 611171
★	◆	★	★	◆				T						◆		◆	◆		◆		◆	TEL: (01) 6286351 / FAX: (01) 6285405
★		★	★	◆										◆		◆	◆	◆	◆		◆	TEL: (047985) 257 / FAX: (047985) 325
	◆	★	◆					T	C					◆		◆		◆			◆	TEL: (0738) 51171 / FAX: (0738) 52595
		★	◆				S	◆						◆		◆			◆		◆	TEL: (0326) 250340 / FAX: (0326) 250440
		★	◆			◆	S	◆			◆			◆					◆		◆	TEL: (0872) 501279 / FAX: (0782) 501856
		C	◆				9	◆						◆		◆			◆		◆	TEL: (0424) 64455 / FAX: (0424) 464024
		★	C	◆				T	W				◆	◆	◆	◆	◆		◆		◆	TEL: 021-378 2442 / FAX: 021-378 4637
◆		◆	◆					◆			◆			◆		◆			◆		◆	TEL: (0590) 23467 / FAX: (0590) 22268
★	◆	★	◆				S	◆						◆		◆			◆		◆	TEL: (098) 41222 / FAX: (098) 41613
	◆	★	C	◆	B	◆		◆					P	◆		◆			◆		◆	TEL: (0423) 771598 / FAX: (0423) 770931
★	◆	★	★	◆				T	W		◆			◆		◆			◆		◆	TEL: (0577) 850216 / FAX: (0577) 850238
◆		◆	C	◆	★	★		T	B				F	◆		◆	◆	◆	◆		◆	TEL: (0780) 720315 / FAX: (0780) 721086

Nare Hotel

Mortons House

Mount Falcon

Mount Juliet

	Map	Number of rooms	Price range	Disabled	Children	Meeting facilities	Credit cards	TV	Parking	Restaurants	Direct dial telephones	Helicopter landing	Pets	Leisure centre	Snooker	Croquet	Squash	Tennis	Indoor swimming pool	Outdoor swimming pool	Golf	Fishing
Nunsmere Hall Sandiway Cheshire	E	32	D	◆	◆	48	◆	◆	◆	◆	◆	◆	G		◆	◆					★	★
Nuremore Hotel Carrickmacross Co Monaghan	I	69	B	◆	◆	†	◆	◆	◆	◆	◆	◆	G	◆	◆		◆	◆	◆			◆	◆
Nutfield Priory Nutfield Surrey	E	46	BS		◆	◆	◆	◆	◆	◆	◆			◆	◆	◆	◆	◆	◆				
Nuthurst Grange Hockley Heath West Midlands	E	15	BD	◆	◆	◆	◆	◆	◆	◆	◆	◆				◆						★	★
Oakley Court Windsor Berkshire	E	92	DS		◆	†	◆	◆	◆	◆	◆	◆			◆	◆						◆	◆
Ockenden Manor Cuckfield Sussex	E	22	SB	◆	◆	22	◆	◆	◆	◆	◆	◆	G									★	★
Old Bell Hotel Malmesbury Wiltshire	E	37	B		◆	40	◆		◆	◆	◆											★	★
Old Bridge Huntingdon Cambridgeshire	E	26	SA		◆	◆	◆		◆	◆											★	◆
Old Rectory Great Snoring Norfolk	E	6	B		12	12	◆	◆	◆	R	◆	◆									★	
Old Rectory Llansantffraid Glan Conwy, nr Conwy Gwynedd	W	6	BC		5		◆		◆	◆	◆		P									★	★
Old Swan & Mill Minster Lovell, nr Witney Oxfordshire	E	60	SC		◆	50	◆	◆	◆	◆	◆		◆		◆	◆		◆			★	★
One Devonshire Gardens Glasgow Strathclyde	S	27	DS		◆	50	◆	◆	◆	◆	◆											★	★
Pale Hall Llanderfel, nr Bala Gwynedd	W	17	B		◆	40	◆	◆	◆	◆	◆	◆	P									★	★
Park Farm Hethersett Norfolk	E	38	A	◆	◆	†	◆	◆	◆	◆	◆		◆		◆		◆	◆				★	
Park Hotel Kenmare Co Kerry	I	50	D	◆	◆	60	◆	◆	◆	◆	◆	◆	G		◆	◆		◆				◆	★
Park House Bepton, Midhurst Sussex	E	11	A	◆	◆		◆	◆	◆	◆	◆	◆				◆		◆		◆		★	
Passford House Lymington Hampshire	E	56	B	◆	◆	60	◆	◆	◆	◆	◆	◆	◆	◆	◆	◆		◆	◆	◆		★	★
Pear Tree Purton nr Swindon Wiltshire	E	18	A	◆	◆	70	◆	◆	◆	◆	◆	◆	P		◆							★	★
Peat Inn Peat Inn by Cupar Fife	S	8	B	◆	◆		◆	◆	◆	◆	◆	◆										★	★
Pen-y-gwryd Nant Gsynant Gwynedd	W	22	A	◆	◆	◆		◆	◆		◆	◆	◆	◆								★	◆

Old Bridge

Oakley Court

Park Farm

Old Rectory, Llansantffraid

Cycling	Horseracing	Horse riding	Shooting	Walking	Airborne	Sailing	Seaside	Theatre	Gourmet	Diet and health	Bridge and cards	Literary	Painting and crafts	Romantic	Murder and fantasy	Heritage	Shopping	Outward bound	Peace and quiet	In town	In country	TEL / FAX
◆	◆	★	C	◆					W					◆		◆			◆		◆	TEL: (0606) 889100 / FAX: (0606) 889055
★	◆		◆		★					◆						◆			◆		◆	TEL: (042) 61438 / FAX: (042) 61853
	◆								◆	◆				◆		◆			◆		◆	TEL: (0737) 822066 / FAX: (0737) 823321
		★	★	★				T	◆							◆			◆		◆	TEL: (0564) 783972 / FAX: (0564) 783919
★	◆	★	AC	◆	★	◆			◆	W				◆	◆	◆	◆		◆		◆	TEL: (0628) 74141 / FAX: (0628) 37011
	◆	★	★	◆	★		◆	◆			◆			◆		◆	◆	◆	◆		◆	TEL: (0444) 416111 / FAX: (0444) 415549
★	◆	◆												◆		◆	◆		◆	◆		TEL: (0666) 822344 / FAX: (0666) 825145
	◆	★	★	◆	★	★		T	W					◆		◆				◆		TEL: (0480) 52681 / FAX: (0480) 411017
★	◆	★		◆			6	◆	◆					◆		◆			◆		◆	TEL: (0328) 820597 / FAX: (0328) 820048
★		★		◆		★	3		◆					◆			◆	◆	◆		◆	TEL: (0492) 580611 / FAX: (0492) 584555
★	◆	★	◆	◆		★			◆	◆				◆	◆	◆	◆		◆		◆	TEL: (0993) 774441 / FAX: (0993) 702002
★	◆	★		◆		★		TO						◆		◆	◆		◆	◆		TEL: (041) 339 2001 / FAX: (041) 337 1663
★		★	◆	◆		★								◆		◆		◆	◆		◆	TEL: (067) 83 285 / FAX:
	◆	★	★	◆				T	B	◆				◆		◆	◆		◆		◆	TEL: (0603) 810264 / FAX: (0603) 812104
★		★	C	◆					◆	◆	◆			◆	◆	◆			◆		◆	TEL: (064) 41200 / FAX: (064) 41402
	◆	★						T								◆	◆	◆	◆		◆	TEL: (0730) 812880 / FAX: (0730) 815643
★		★	★	◆		◆	◆	◆	◆							◆	◆		◆		◆	TEL: (0590) 682398 / FAX: (0590) 682398
		★	★	◆	B			T	◆					◆		◆			◆		◆	TEL: (0793) 772100 / FAX: (0793) 772369
		★	★			★	6	T						◆		◆	◆		◆		◆	TEL: (0334) 84206 / FAX: (0334) 84530
★		★		◆			10	T								◆	◆	◆	◆		◆	TEL: (0286) 870211 / FAX:

Old Rectory, Great Snoring

The Old Bell

Pale Hall

Ockenden Manor

PENALLY ABBEY →

Polmaily House

Petty France

	Map	Number of rooms	Price range	Disabled	Children	Meeting facilities	Credit cards	TV	Parking	Restaurants	Direct dial telephones	Helicopter landing	Pets	Leisure centre	Snooker	Croquet	Squash	Tennis	Indoor swimming pool	Outdoor swimming pool	Golf	Fishing
Penally Abbey Penally nr Tenby Dyfed	W	10	A	◆		12	◆	◆	◆	◆	◆	◆	G		◆	◆				◆	★	★
Pengethley Manor Ross-on-Wye Hereford & Worcester	E	24	AD	◆	◆	◆	◆	◆	◆	◆	◆	◆	◆		◆	◆				◆		
Penhelig Arms Aberdovey Gwynedd	W	11	AS	◆			◆	◆	◆	◆	◆		◆								★	★
Pennyhill Park Bagshot Surrey	E	76	CS	◆		60	◆	◆	◆	◆	◆	◆	P		◆		◆		◆	◆	◆	◆
Penrhos Court Penrhos, Kington Hereford & Worcester	E	19	BD	◆	◆	◆	◆	◆	◆	◆	◆					◆					★	★
Petersham Hotel Richmond Surrey	E	54	D		◆	◆	◆	◆	◆	◆	◆	◆									★	
Petty France Dunkirk, Badminton Avon	E	20	AS	◆	◆	25	◆	◆	◆	◆	◆	◆			◆						★	★
Petwood House Woodhall Spa Lincolnshire	E	46	BS		◆	◆	◆	◆	◆	◆	◆	◆		◆	◆	◆					★	★
Pheasant Hotel Harome, Helmsley Yorkshire	E	12	A	12		6		◆	◆	R	◆		◆						◆		★	★
The Pheasant Seavington St Mary nr Ilminster Somerset	E	10	A	◆	◆		◆	◆	◆	◆	◆	◆									★	★
Pittodrie House Inverurie Aberdeenshire	S	27	AS	◆	◆	†	◆	◆	◆	◆	◆	◆	◆		◆	◆	◆	◆			★	
Plas Badegroes Pwllheli Gwynedd	W	8	A	◆			◆	◆	◆	◆	◆		P		◆						★	
Plas Penhelig Aberdovey Gwynedd	W	11	BS		◆	40	◆	◆	◆	◆	◆	◆	P		◆	★					★	★
The Plough Clanfield Oxfordshire	E	6	AS			15	◆	◆	◆	◆	◆	◆	G								★	★
Plumber Manor Sturminster Newton Dorset	E	16	BS		12		◆	◆	◆	◆	◆				◆						★	★
Polmaily House Drumnadrochit Inverness-shire	S	9	AS	◆			◆		◆	◆	◆		G		◆		◆		◆		★	★
Pontlands Park Great Baddow Essex	E	17	BS	◆		†	◆	◆	◆	◆	◆	◆	◆						◆	◆	★	★
Pool Court Pool-in-Wharfedale Yorkshire	E	6	A		◆	30	◆	◆	◆	◆	◆					★	★				★	★
Portmeirion Hotel Portmeirion Gwynedd	W	90	C		◆	†	◆	◆	◆	◆	◆	◆			◆		◆			◆	★	★
Priory Hotel Bath Avon	E	21	DS	◆		◆	65	◆	◆	◆	◆	◆			◆					◆	★	★

Petersham Hotel

Petwood House

→ PRIORY HOTEL

Cycling	Horseracing	Horse riding	Shooting	Walking	Airborne	Sailing	Seaside	Theatre	Gourmet	Diet and health	Bridge and cards	Literary	Painting and crafts	Romantic	Murder and fantasy	Heritage	Shopping	Outward bound	Peace and quiet	In town	In country	TEL / FAX
◆		★	★	◆	G			W						◆		◆			◆		◆	TEL: (0834) 843033 / FAX: (0834) 844714
																			◆		◆	TEL: (0989) 07211 / FAX: (0989) 87238
		★	★	◆		★	S	W										◆	◆		◆	TEL: (0654) 767215 / FAX: (0654) 767690
	◆	◆	C	◆				T	◆	◆	◆			◆		◆	◆		◆		◆	TEL: (0276) 71774 / FAX: (0276) 73217
◆	◆	★	★	◆	★				◆	◆	◆	◆	◆	◆	◆	◆		◆	◆		◆	TEL: (0544) 230720 / FAX: (0544) 230754
★	◆	★		◆				TO	◆					◆		◆	◆		◆	◆		TEL: 081-940 7471 / FAX: 081-940 9998
◆	◆	★	★	◆	★			T	◆				◆	◆	◆	◆		◆	◆		◆	TEL: (0454) 238361 / FAX: (0454) 238768
◆	◆	★	★	◆				T	◆					◆	◆	◆	◆		◆		◆	TEL: (0526) 352411 / FAX: (0526) 353473
★	◆	★		◆				T								◆	◆	◆	◆		◆	TEL: (0439) 71241 / FAX:
	◆	★		◆	◆			◆	◆					◆		◆	◆		◆		◆	TEL: (0460) 40502 / FAX: (0460) 42388
		★	★	◆					◆					◆	◆	◆			◆		◆	TEL: (0467) 681444 / FAX: (0467) 681648
		★	C	◆		★								◆		◆			◆		◆	TEL: (0758) 612363 / FAX: (0758) 701247
◆		★	★	◆		◆	S							◆		◆		◆	◆		◆	TEL: (0654) 767676 / FAX: (0654) 767783
★	★	★	★	★	★			T						◆		◆	◆		◆		◆	TEL: (036) 781222 / FAX: (036) 781596
		C	◆					◆						◆		◆			◆		◆	TEL: (0258) 72507 / FAX: (0258) 73370
★		★		◆												◆			◆		◆	TEL: (04562) 343 / FAX: (04562) 813
		★	C	◆				T								◆			◆		◆	TEL: (0245) 76444 / FAX: (0245) 478393
	◆	★	★	◆			OT	C						◆		◆	◆	◆			◆	TEL: (0532) 842288 / FAX: (0532) 843115
★		★	★	◆		★	◆ S	◆						◆		◆	◆				◆	TEL: (0766) 770228 / FAX: (0766) 771331
★	◆	★	★	◆	◆			◆	◆			◆	◆		◆	◆	◆	◆		◆	◆	TEL: (0225) 331922 / FAX: (0225) 448276

Pennyhill Park

Pool Court

Priory Hotel

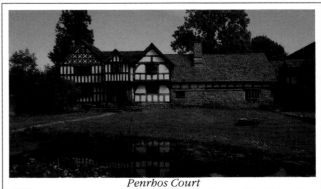

Penrhos Court

PRIORY HOTEL →

	Map	Number of rooms	Price range	Disabled	Children	Meeting facilities	Credit cards	TV	Parking	Restaurants	Direct dial telephones	Helicopter landing	Pets	Leisure centre	Snooker	Croquet	Squash	Tennis	Indoor swimming pool	Outdoor swimming pool	Golf	Fishing
Priory Hotel Wareham Dorset	E	19	B	◆	14	20	◆	◆	◆	◆	◆	◆	G			◆					★	◆
Puckrup Hall Puckrup, Tewkesbury Gloucestershire	E	16	C	◆	◆	†	◆	◆	◆	◆	◆	◆	◆			◆			◆		◆	◆
Raemoir House Hotel Raemoir, Banchory Kincardineshire	S	20	B	◆	◆	50	◆	◆	◆	◆	◆	◆	P			◆		◆			★	★
Rathmullan House Rathmullan Co Donegal	I	23	AS		◆	20	◆		◆	◆	◆	◆		◆		◆		◆	◆		★	★
Rathsallagh House Dunlavin Co Wicklow	I	14	BS	◆	12	40	◆	◆	◆	◆	◆	◆		◆	◆			◆	◆		★	
Raven Hall Ravenscar nr Scarborough Yorkshire	E	53	B	◆	◆	◆	◆	◆	◆	◆	◆	◆		◆	◆		◆		◆			
Ravenswood Hall Bury St Edmunds Suffolk	E	14	A		◆	†	◆	◆	◆	◆	◆	◆	P			◆		◆		◆	★	★
Redwood Lodge Failand nr Bristol Avon	E	†	SB	◆	◆	◆	◆	◆	◆	◆	◆		◆	◆		◆	◆	◆	◆		★	★
Rescobie Leslie Fife	S	10	A		◆	25	◆	◆	◆	◆	◆										★	★
Riber Hall Matlock Derbyshire	E	11	A		10	14	◆	◆	◆	◆	◆					◆					★	★
The Ritz Piccadilly London W1	E	†	D		◆	60	◆	◆		◆	◆		G								★	
Riverside Hotel Ashford-in-the-Water, Bakewell Derbyshire	E	15	AS		4	15	◆		◆	◆	◆		◆			◆					★	★
Rock Glen Clifden Co Galway	I	29	A	◆	◆	10	◆	◆	◆	◆	◆		◆		◆		◆				★	★
Roman Camp Callander, Tayside Perthshire	S	14	B	◆	◆	50	◆	◆	◆	◆	◆		★								◆	◆
Romans Hotel Silchester nr Reading Hampshire	E	25	A	◆	◆	60	◆	◆	◆	◆	◆					◆		◆		◆	◆	★
Rookery Hall Worleston, Nantwich nr Chester Cheshire	E	45	BS	◆	◆	65	◆	◆	◆	◆	◆	◆	G			◆		◆			★	★
Rookhurst Georgian Gayle nr Hawes Yorkshire	E	6	AS		12	10	◆	◆		◆	R		G									
Rose & Crown Inn Bainbridge, Wensleydale Yorkshire	E	12	AS		◆	30	◆	◆	◆	◆		◆	◆									◆
Rosleague Manor Letterfrack, Connemara Co Galway	I	20	A	◆			◆		◆	◆	◆			◆		◆		◆			★	★
Royal Beacon The Beacon, Exmouth Devon	E	38	AS		◆	30	◆	◆	◆	◆	◆		◆		◆						★	★

Riber Hall

Rookhurst Georgian

Raven Hall

Rathmullan House

66

Cycling	Horseracing	Horse riding	Shooting	Walking	Airborne	Sailing	Seaside	Theatre	Gourmet	Diet and health	Bridge and cards	Literary	Painting and crafts	Romantic	Murder and fantasy	Heritage	Shopping	Outward bound	Peace and quiet	In town	In country	Telephone / Fax
★		★	★	◆	★	◆	9				◆			◆		◆			◆		◆	TEL: (09295) 51666 / FAX: (09295) 54519
▲	▲	◆	★	◆	BH			◆	◆					◆	◆	◆	◆		◆		◆	TEL: (0684) 2962000 / FAX: (0684) 850 788
★		◆	◆	◆	★			T	◆					◆		◆			◆		◆	TEL: (03302) 4884 / FAX: (03302) 2171
		★		◆				S						◆					◆		◆	TEL: (074) 58188 / FAX: (074) 58200
★	◆	★	◆	◆					◆					◆	◆	◆	◆	◆	◆			TEL: (045) 53112 / FAX: (045) 53343
	◆		◆					T	◆			◆		◆	◆	◆	◆		◆		◆	TEL: (0723) 870353 / FAX: (0723) 870072
	◆	★	◆	◆				◆	◆					◆		◆			◆		◆	TEL: (0359) 70345 / FAX: (0359) 70788
	◆	★		◆				T	◆		◆			◆		◆	◆				◆	TEL: (0275) 393901 / FAX: (0275) 392104
			◆			◆		◆						◆					◆	◆		TEL: (0592) 742143 / FAX:
	★	C	◆											◆		◆	◆		◆		◆	TEL: (0629) 582795 / FAX: (0629) 580475
	◆	★						T	◆					◆		◆	◆			◆		TEL: (071) 493 8181 / FAX: (071) 493 2687
★	◆	★	★	◆	★			T	◆		◆			◆		◆	◆		◆		◆	TEL: (0629) 814275 / FAX: (0629) 812873
★		★		◆		◆	S		◆		◆		P	◆		◆			◆		◆	TEL: (095) 21035 / FAX: (095) 21737
			◆		★				◆		◆			◆		◆	◆		◆		◆	TEL: (0877) 30003 / FAX: (0877) 31533
	◆	★	C	◆					◆	◆				◆	◆	◆	◆		◆		◆	TEL: (0734) 700421 / FAX: (0734) 700691
★	◆	★	★	◆	★		OT	W						◆		◆	◆		◆		◆	TEL: (0270) 610016 / FAX: (0270) 626027
			◆											◆			◆	◆	◆		◆	TEL: (0969) 667454 / FAX:
														◆		◆			◆		◆	TEL: (0969) 50225 / FAX: (0969) 50735
★		★		◆			S							◆		◆	◆		◆		◆	TEL: (095) 41101 / FAX: (095) 41168
★	◆	★	★	◆		★		◆			◆	◆	◆	◆		◆	◆		◆		◆	TEL: (0395) 264886 / FAX: (0395) 268890

Raemoir House

Riber Hall

Rose and Crown Inn

Puckrup Hall

Shrigley Hall

Sheen Falls

	Map	Number of rooms	Price range	Disabled	Children	Meeting facilities	Credit cards	TV	Parking	Restaurants	Direct dial telephones	Helicopter landing	Pets	Leisure centre	Snooker	Croquet	Squash	Tennis	Indoor swimming pool	Outdoor swimming pool	Golf	Fishing
Royal Berkshire Sunninghill, Ascot Berkshire	E	81	D	◆	◆	75	◆	◆	◆	◆	◆	◆	◆			◆	◆	◆	◆		★	
Royal Crescent Bath Avon	E	42	CD	◆	◆	◆	◆	◆	◆	◆	◆	◆	P			◆				◆	★	★
Rufflets St Andrews Fife	S	27	BS	◆	◆	40	◆	◆	◆	◆	◆	◆									★	★
Runnymede Hotel Egham Surrey	E	†	D	◆	◆	†	◆	◆	◆	◆	◆	◆	◆	◆	◆				◆		★	
Ryedale Lodge Nunnington Yorkshire	E	7	A		◆	◆	◆	◆	◆	◆	◆	◆	G								★	★
La Sablonnerie Little Sark, Sark Channel Islands (Sark)	E	22	A		◆					◆			P			◆						★
Salford Hall Hotel Abbots Salford Hereford & Worcester	E	33	SB			50	◆	◆	◆	◆	◆	◆	G		◆	◆		◆			★	
Saunton Sands Hotel Saunton Devon	E	†	C	◆	◆	†	◆	◆	◆	◆	◆	◆			◆		◆	◆	◆	◆	◆	★
The Savoy The Strand London WC2	E	†	D		◆	†	◆	◆	◆	◆	◆		G								★	
Seafield Lodge Grantown-on-Spey, Moray Morayshire	S	10	SA		◆	50	◆	◆	◆	◆	◆	◆	P								★	★
Seiont Manor Llanrug, Caernarfon Gwynedd	W	28	AB	◆	◆	◆	◆	◆	◆	◆	◆	◆	◆						◆		★	◆
Selsdon Park Sanderstead Surrey	E	†	C		◆	†	◆	◆	◆	◆	◆	◆	◆	◆	◆		◆	◆	◆		◆	
Sharrow Bay Ullswater nr Penrith Cumbria	E	28	DC		13	12	◆	◆	◆	◆	◆										★	★
Sheen Falls Lodge Kenmare Co Kerry	I	40	SD	◆	◆	◆	◆	◆	◆	◆	◆	◆	G	◆	◆	◆		◆			◆	★
Ship Hotel Shepperton Middlesex	E	31	B			60		◆	◆	◆	◆		P									
Shrigley Hall Pott Shrigley nr Macclesfield Cheshire	E	†	SC	◆	◆	†	◆	◆	◆	◆	◆	◆	P	◆	◆		◆	◆	◆		◆	◆
Sign Of The Angel Lacock, Chippenham Wiltshire	E	10	AS	◆	◆	20	◆	◆	◆	◆	◆		◆								★	
Slieve Donard Newcastle Co Down	I	†	SB		◆	◆	◆	◆		◆	◆			◆			◆	◆			★	
Slieve Russell Ballyconnell Co Cavan	I	†	BS	◆	◆	†	◆	◆	◆	◆	◆		◆			◆	◆	◆		◆	★
Snooty Fox Tetbury Gloucestershire	E	12	AS			20	◆	◆		◆	◆		G								★	★

Snooty Fox

Royal Crescent

Cycling	Horseracing	Horse riding	Shooting	Walking	Airborne	Sailing	Seaside	Theatre	Gourmet	Diet and health	Bridge and cards	Literary	Painting and crafts	Romantic	Murder and fantasy	Heritage	Shopping	Outward bound	Peace and quiet	In town	In country	TEL / FAX
★	◆	★	C	◆				T	W	◆				◆	◆	◆	◆		◆		◆	TEL: (0344) 23322 FAX: (0344) 847280
★	◆	★	C	◆				T								◆	◆		◆			TEL: (0225) 319090 FAX: (0225) 339401
★		★	★	◆		★	2	T	W					◆		◆	◆		◆		◆	TEL: (0334) 72594 FAX: (0334) 78703
★	◆	★	★	◆			◆	◆	◆							◆	◆		◆	◆	◆	TEL: (0784) 436171 FAX: (0784) 436340
★	◆	★	★	◆		★			◆					◆		◆			◆		◆	TEL: (0439) 5246 FAX:
	◆	★		◆	★									◆				◆	◆		◆	TEL: (0481) 832061 FAX:
	◆		★	◆	GB			T	B	◆				◆	◆	◆			◆		◆	TEL: (0386) 871300 FAX: (0386) 871301
★		★	★	◆	★	★	◆	◆	◆	◆		◆				◆	◆		◆		◆	TEL: (0271) 890212 FAX: (0271) 890145
	◆	★						OT	◆					◆		◆	◆		◆	◆		TEL: 071-836 4343 FAX: 071-240 6040
★		★	★	◆	★			T					PA	◆		◆	◆	◆	B		◆	TEL: (0479) 2152 FAX: (0479) 2340
◆		◆	★	◆		★	3	◆	◆					◆		◆		◆	◆		◆	TEL: (0286) 673366 FAX: (0286) 2840
	◆	★	C	◆				TO	◆	◆				◆		◆	◆		◆		◆	TEL: 081-657 8811 FAX: 081-651 6171
★		★	◆	FB										◆		◆	◆	◆	◆		◆	TEL: (07684) 86301 FAX: (07684) 86349
◆	◆	◆	C	◆			S		W	◆				◆		◆		◆	◆		◆	TEL: (064) 41600 FAX: (064) 41386
	◆															◆	◆			◆		TEL: (0932) 227320 FAX: (0932) 226668
★		★	C	◆				TO						◆		◆	◆				◆	TEL: (0625) 575757 FAX: (0625) 573323
	◆	★	★	◆				◆						◆		◆	◆		◆		◆	TEL: (0249) 730230 FAX: (0249) 730527
			◆				S		B	◆				◆			◆		◆		◆	TEL: (03967) 23681 FAX: (03967) 24830
★		★	★	◆		★	◆			◆				◆		◆			◆			TEL: (049) 26444 FAX: (049) 26511
★	◆	★	★	◆	★			T						◆		◆	◆			◆		TEL: (0666) 502436 FAX: (0666) 503479

Sheen Falls

Sharrow Bay

La Sablonnerie

Rufflets

Spread Eagle

Sopwell House

	Map	Number of rooms	Price range	Disabled	Children	Meeting facilities	Credit cards	TV	Parking	Restaurants	Direct dial telephones	Helicopter landing	Pets	Leisure centre	Snooker	Croquet	Squash	Tennis	Indoor swimming pool	Outdoor swimming pool	Golf	Fishing
Sopwell House St Albans Hertfordshire	E	84	BD	◆	◆	†	◆	◆	◆	◆	◆		P	◆	◆	◆			◆		★	
Soughton Hall Northop nr Mold Clwyd	W	12	SA		◆	22	◆	◆	◆	◆	◆	◆	P		◆			◆			★	★
South Lodge Lower Beeding Sussex	E	39	DS			85	◆	◆	◆	◆	◆	◆	G		◆	◆		◆			◆	★
Spa Hotel Tunbridge Wells Kent	E	76	SB	◆	◆	◆	◆	◆	◆	◆	◆	◆	P	◆	◆	◆		◆	◆		★	★
Spread Eagle Midhurst Sussex	E	41	B		◆	90	◆	◆	◆	◆	◆		◆								★	★
Springs Hotel North Stoke, Wallingford Oxfordshire	E	38	SC	◆		50	◆	◆	◆	◆	◆	◆	G		◆			◆		◆	★	★
Sprowston Manor Norwich Norfolk	E	†	BS		◆	◆	◆		◆	◆				◆					◆		◆	
St Andrews Golf Hotel St Andrews Fife	S	23	A			†	◆	◆	◆	R	◆		◆								★	★
St Andrews Old Course Hotel St Andrews Fife	S	†	D	◆	◆	†	◆	◆	◆	◆	◆	◆	P	◆				◆			★	★
St Ernans House Hotel Donegal Co Donegal	I	13	A		6		◆	◆	◆	◆	◆	◆									★	★
St Mellion Golf & Country Club St Mellion, Saltash Cornwall	E	24	SC	◆	◆	†	◆	◆	◆	◆	◆	◆		◆	◆		◆	◆	◆		◆	◆
St Michael's Hotel Falmouth Cornwall	E	75	AS	◆	◆	†	◆	◆	◆	◆	◆			◆	◆		◆	◆	◆		★	
St Pierre Hotel Chepstow Gwent	E	†	BS	◆	◆	†	◆	◆	◆	◆	◆	◆	◆	◆	◆	◆	◆	◆	◆		◆	
St Tudno Hotel Llandudno Gwynedd	W	21	BS		◆	40	◆	◆	◆	◆	◆		P						◆		★	★
The Stafford St James's Place London SW1	E	74	D		◆	42	◆	◆	◆	◆	◆		◆								★	
Stanneylands Wilmslow Cheshire	E	33	C	◆	◆	◆	◆	◆	◆	◆	◆										★	
Stapleford Park Melton Mowbray Leicestershire	E	35	BC	◆	10	†	◆	◆	◆	◆	◆	◆	◆		◆			◆				◆
Stock Hill Country House Hotel Gillingham Dorset	E	A	C		7		◆	◆	◆	◆	◆					◆		◆			★	
Stocks Country House Hotel Aldbury nr Tring Hertfordshire	E	18	SB	◆	◆	◆	◆	◆	◆	◆	◆			◆	◆	◆	◆	◆		◆	★	★
Ston Easton Park Ston Easton nr Bath Somerset	E	21	CD		7		◆	◆	◆	◆	◆	◆	P		◆	◆		◆				

Ston Easton Park

Stocks Country House Hotel

Cycling	Horseracing	Horse riding	Shooting	Walking	Airborne	Sailing	Seaside	Theatre	Gourmet	Diet and health	Bridge and cards	Literary	Painting and crafts	Romantic	Murder and fantasy	Heritage	Shopping	Outward bound	Peace and quiet	In town	In country	Contact
		★	★	◆				B	◆					◆		◆	◆		◆		◆	TEL: (0727) 864477 FAX: (0727) 44741
	◆	★	◆				◆				◆			◆	◆	◆	◆		◆		◆	TEL: (035286) 811 FAX: (035286) 382
★	◆	★	★	◆				T	W					◆		◆	◆		◆		◆	TEL: (0403) 891711 FAX: (0403) 891766
	◆	★	★		◆			T	W	◆				◆	◆		◆		◆	◆		TEL: (0892) 520331 FAX: (0892) 510575
	◆	★	★	◆	★	★		◆						◆		◆	◆		◆		◆	TEL: (0730) 816911 FAX: (0730) 815668
◆	◆	★	★	◆	★B		OT	W								◆	◆		◆		◆	TEL: (0491) 36687 FAX: (0491) 36877
			◆			★		B	◆					◆		◆	◆		B		◆	TEL: (0603) 410871 FAX: (0603) 423911
★		★	★	◆			S	T	◆					◆		◆	◆				◆	TEL: (0334) 72611 FAX: (0334) 72188
◆		★	★	◆			◆	TO	W	◆	◆	◆		◆		◆	◆		◆		◆	TEL: (0334) 74371 FAX: (0334) 77668
★	◆	★		◆			S							◆		◆			◆		◆	TEL: (073) 21065 FAX: (073) 22098
★		★	D	◆					◆		◆					◆					◆	TEL: (0579) 50101 FAX: (0579) 50116
		★		◆		★	S		◆					◆		◆	◆	◆			◆	TEL: (0326) 312707 FAX: (0326) 319147
◆	◆		C	◆		★		T	◆					◆		◆	◆				◆	TEL: (0291) 625261 FAX: (0291) 629975
★	◆	★	★	◆		◆	S		◆					◆		◆		◆	◆	◆		TEL: (0492) 874411 FAX: (0492) 860407
	◆							T	◆					◆			◆	◆		◆		TEL: 071-493 0111 FAX: 071-493 7121
★				◆				T	◆					◆					◆		◆	TEL: (0625) 525225 FAX: (0625) 537282
★			◆		★	★		B						◆	◆	◆			◆		◆	TEL: (0572) 84522 FAX: (0572) 84651
	◆	★		◆					◆							◆	◆	◆			◆	TEL: (0747) 823626 FAX: (0747) 825628
★	◆	◆	★	◆	★	★		T	◆	◆				◆		◆	◆		◆		◆	TEL: (0442) 85341 FAX: (0442) 85253
	◆		★	◆	★				◆					◆		◆	◆		◆		◆	TEL: (0761) 241631 FAX: (0761) 241377

St Michaels

South Lodge

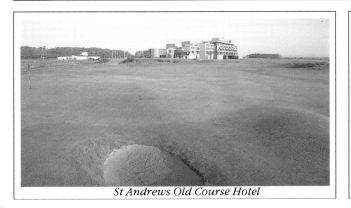

St Andrews Old Course Hotel

Stapleford Park

Tower

Three Swans

	Map	Number of rooms	Price range	Disabled	Children	Meeting facilities	Credit cards	TV	Parking	Restaurants	Direct dial telephones	Helicopter landing	Pets	Leisure centre	Snooker	Croquet	Squash	Tennis	Indoor swimming pool	Outdoor swimming pool	Golf	Fishing
Stonehouse Court Sonehouse Gloucestershire	E	37	B	◆		◆		◆	◆	◆	◆					◆					★	★
Stotfield House Lossiemouth, Moray Highland	S	50	A	◆	†	◆	◆	◆	◆	◆	◆		P								★	★
String of Horses Heaks Hook, Faugh nr Carlisle Cumbria	E	14	B	◆		20	◆	◆	◆	◆	◆		P	◆						◆	★	★
Studley Priory Horton-Cum-Studley Oxfordshire	E	19	DC	◆		50	◆		◆	◆	◆	◆				◆		◆			★	★
Summer Isles Achiltibuie by Ullapool Ross-shire	S	11	A		8			◆	◆				P									◆
Summer Lodge Evershot Dorset	G	17	CD	◆	8	8	◆	◆	◆	◆	◆		P			◆		◆		◆	★	★
Sunlaws House Hotel Heiton Nr Kelso Roxburghshire	S	22	B	◆	◆	40	◆	◆	◆	◆	◆				◆		◆				★	◆
Swan Diplomat Streatley-On-Thames Berkshire	E	46	C	◆	◆	†	◆	◆	◆	◆	◆		◆	◆	◆	◆				◆	★	
Tan-y-Foel Capel Garmon, nr Betws-y-Coed Gwynedd	W	A	BS	◆		◆	◆	◆	◆	◆										◆	★	★
Tanyard Hotel Boughton Monchelsea, Maidstone Kent	E	6	A		6		◆	◆	◆	◆	◆											
Tewkesbury Park Hotel Tewkesbury Gloucestershire	E	78	BS	◆		†	◆	◆	◆	◆	◆	◆	G	◆	◆		◆	◆	◆			◆	
Thornbury Castle Thornbury Avon	E	18	C		12	24	◆	◆	◆	◆	◆				◆						★	★
Three Swans Hotel Market Harborough Leicestershire	E	36	SA	◆	◆	◆	◆	◆	◆	◆	◆		P									★
Thurlestone Hotel Thurlestone, Kingsbridge Devon	E	68	B	◆	◆	†	◆	◆	◆	◆	◆	◆	P	◆	◆		◆	◆	◆	◆	◆	
Tillmouth Park Cornhill-on-Tweed Northumberland	E	13	B	◆		†		◆	◆	◆	◆		◆									★	◆
Tinakilly House Rathnew, Wicklow Co Wicklow	I	29	AC	◆	◆	60	◆	◆	◆	◆	◆						◆				★	★
Torwood House Glenluce, Newton Stewart Dumfries & Galloway	S	9	A	◆	◆	50	◆	◆	◆	◆	◆	◆			◆	◆					★	◆
Tower Sway Hampshire	E	4	A		10		◆	◆	◆	◆							◆	◆			★	★
Towers Glenbeigh Co Kerry	I	35	B	◆		15	◆	◆	◆	◆	◆		P	◆							★	★
Tre-ysgawen Hall Capel Coch nr Llangefni Anglesey	W	19	B	◆	◆	37	◆	◆	◆	◆	◆	◆	P		◆						★	★

Tewkesbury Park

Towers

Cycling	Horseracing	Horse riding	Shooting	Walking	Airborne	Sailing	Seaside	Theatre	Gourmet	Diet and health	Bridge and cards	Literary	Painting and crafts	Romantic	Murder and fantasy	Heritage	Shopping	Outward bound	Peace and quiet	In town	In country	TEL / FAX
★	◆	★		◆	★				◆					◆		◆			◆		◆	TEL: (0453) 825155 FAX: (0453) 824611
★		★	★	◆		★	S		◆					◆		◆		◆	◆		◆	TEL: (0343) 812011 FAX: (0343) 814820
	◆			◆		★								◆		◆	◆		◆		◆	TEL: (022870) 297 FAX: (022870) 675
★	◆	★	★	◆			T		◆		◆			◆	◆	◆	◆		◆		◆	TEL: (0867) 35203 FAX: (0867) 35613
			◆				S		◆		◆								◆		◆	TEL: (085482) 282 FAX: (085482) 251
	◆	★	★	◆		◆													◆		◆	TEL: (0935) 83424 FAX: (0935) 83005
★		★	★	◆				W		◆	◆	◆	◆	◆				◆	◆		◆	TEL: (05735) 331 FAX: (05735) 611
◆	◆	★	★	◆		◆		W	◆					◆	◆	◆			◆		◆	TEL: (0491) 873737 FAX: (0491) 872554
★		★		◆										◆		◆			◆		◆	TEL: (0690) 710507 FAX: (0690) 710681
			◆																◆		◆	TEL: (0622) 744705 FAX: (0622) 741998
◆			◆													◆	◆				◆	TEL: (0684) 295405 FAX: (0684) 292386
	◆	★	★	◆	★		T		◆					◆		◆	◆		◆		◆	TEL: (0454) 281182 FAX: (0454) 416188
	◆	★	★	◆	★		T		◆					◆		◆	◆	◆	◆		◆	TEL: (0858) 466644 FAX: (0858) 433101
★	◆	★	★	◆	★	★	1	T	W							◆			◆		◆	TEL: (0548) 560 382 FAX: (0548) 561069
	◆	★		◆										◆		◆	◆		B		◆	TEL: (0890) 2255 FAX: (0890) 2540
◆	◆	★	★	◆		★	S	O	◆	◆	◆	◆	◆	◆	◆	◆	◆	◆	◆		◆	TEL: (404) 69274 FAX: (404) 67806
◆		★	★	◆	◆			W						◆		◆		◆	◆		◆	TEL: (05813) 469 FAX: (05813) 258
★		★		◆	★	★	3							◆		◆	◆	◆	◆		◆	TEL: (0590) 682117 FAX: (0590) 683785
★	◆	★	★		◆		S		◆					◆		◆			◆		◆	TEL: (066) 68212 FAX:
★		★	★	◆		★		W						◆	◆	◆	◆		◆		◆	TEL: (0248) 750750 FAX: (0248) 750035

Sunlaws

Stonehouse Court

Tillmouth Park

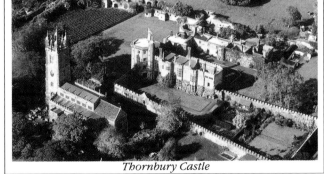

Thornbury Castle

West Arms

	Map	Number of rooms	Price range	Disabled	Children	Meeting facilities	Credit cards	TV	Parking	Restaurants	Direct dial telephones	Helicopter landing	Pets	Leisure centre	Snooker	Croquet	Squash	Tennis	Indoor swimming pool	Outdoor swimming pool	Golf	Fishing
Trearddur Bay Treardour Bay nr Holyhead Gwynedd	W	31	AS			†	◆	◆	◆	◆	◆	◆	P							◆	★	★
Tudor Park Hotel & Country Club Bearsted, Maidstone Kent	E	†	SB	◆	◆	◆	◆	◆	◆	◆	◆	◆	P	◆	◆		◆	◆	◆		◆	
Tufton Arms Appleby-In-Westmorland Cumbria	E	28	B		◆	◆	◆	◆	◆	◆	◆		P								★	◆
Tullich Lodge Ballater Aberdeenshire	S	10	B		◆	◆	◆	◆	◆	◆	◆	◆	◆								★	★
Turnberry Hotel Turnberry Ayrshire	S	†	D	◆	◆	†	◆	◆	◆	◆	◆	◆	P	◆	◆		◆	◆	◆		◆	◆
Ty Newydd Hirwaun Glamorgan	W	26	A	◆	◆	†	◆	◆	◆	◆	◆	◆	P								★	★
Ty'n-y-Cornel Talyllyn Gwynedd	W	15	A	◆		20	◆	◆	◆	◆	◆	◆	◆							◆	★	◆
Tyddyn Llan Llandrillo nr Corwen Clwyd	W	10	SB		◆	50	◆	◆	◆	◆	◆	◆	◆			◆					★	◆
Tylney Hall Rotherwick nr Hook Hampshire	E	91	CD		◆	†	◆	◆	◆	◆	◆	◆	G		◆	◆		◆	◆	◆	◆	★
Ufford Park Ufford, Woodbridge Suffolk	E	25	B	◆	◆	†	◆	◆	◆	◆	◆	◆	G	◆					◆		◆	★
Ulbster Arms Halkirk, Caithness Highland	S	27	AS			◆	◆	◆	◆	◆	◆	◆									★	◆
Victoria Hotel Sidmouth Devon	E	61	C		◆	60	◆	◆	◆	◆	◆	◆	G	◆	◆		◆	◆	◆		★	★
Waren House Waren Mill, Belford Northumberland	E	7	AS		14		◆	◆	◆	◆	◆		P		◆		◆				★	
Watersedge Hotel Ambleside Cumbria	E	23	SB		7		◆	◆	◆	◆	◆											★
Waterford Castle Ballinakill Co Waterford	I	19	D	◆	◆	50	◆	◆	◆	◆	◆	◆	◆		◆		◆	◆			◆	★
Welcombe Hotel Stratford Upon Avon Warwickshire	E	76	D	◆	◆	†	◆	◆	◆	◆	◆	◆	◆			◆		◆			◆	★
Well House St Keyne, Liskeard Cornwall	E	7	SA			◆	◆	◆	◆	◆		◆						◆		◆	★	★
Wentbridge House Hotel Wentbridge, Pontefract Yorkshire	E	12	A	◆		†	◆	◆	◆	◆	◆	◆										
West Arms Llanarmon Dyffryn Ceiriog Clwyd	W	14	AS			30	◆	◆	◆	◆	◆	◆	◆								★	◆
The Westbury Dublin Co Dublin	I	†	SD	◆	◆	◆	◆	◆	◆	◆	◆		G								★	

Trearddur Bay

Ulbster Arms

Tyddyn Llan

→ THE WESTBURY

Cycling	Horseracing	Horse riding	Shooting	Walking	Airborne	Sailing	Seaside	Theatre	Gourmet	Diet and health	Bridge and cards	Literary	Painting and crafts	Romantic	Murder and fantasy	Heritage	Shopping	Outward bound	Peace and quiet	In town	In country	Tel / Fax
		★	★	◆	★	◆	S		B	◆				◆		◆		◆	◆		◆	TEL: (0407) 860 301 / FAX: (0407) 861181
◆		★	★	◆	★			T						◆		◆	◆		◆		◆	TEL: (0622) 34334 / FAX: (0622) 735360
		★	D	◆					◆										◆		◆	TEL: (07683) 51593 / FAX: (07683) 52761
◆		◆	★	◆	★									◆	◆	◆			◆		◆	TEL: (03397) 55406 / FAX: (03397) 55397
★	◆	★	C	◆	★	★	S		B	◆				◆		◆	◆		◆		◆	TEL: (0655) 31000 / FAX: (0655) 31706
		★		◆				W						◆		◆			◆		◆	TEL: (0685) 813433 / FAX: (0685) 813139
◆		★	★	◆					◆		◆							◆	◆		◆	TEL: (0654) 782288 / FAX: (0654) 782679
		★	★	◆		★			◆	◆				◆		◆	◆	◆	◆		◆	TEL: (049084) 264 / FAX: (049084) 264
◆	◆	★	C	◆	BG			T	◆					◆	◆	◆	◆		◆		◆	TEL: (0256) 764881 / FAX: (0256) 768141
★		★	C	◆		★	10	T	W	◆				◆			◆		◆		◆	TEL: (0394) 383555 / FAX: (0394) 383582
		★	★	◆			6									◆			B		◆	TEL: (084783) 206 / FAX: (084783) 206
★	◆	★	C	◆	B	◆	S	T	G	★	◆					◆		◆	◆	◆		TEL: (0395) 512651 / FAX: (0395) 579154
★	◆	★		◆			S		◆					◆		◆		◆	B		◆	TEL: (06684) 581 / FAX: (06684) 484
★		★		◆	★									◆	◆	◆	◆		◆		◆	TEL: (05394) 32332 / FAX: (05394) 32332
★	◆	★	★	◆		★	5		◆	◆				◆		◆	◆		◆		◆	TEL: (051) 78203 / FAX: (051) 79316
★		★	C	◆	B			T	W			◆		◆	◆	◆	◆		◆	◆		TEL: (0789) 295252 / FAX: (0789) 414666
★		★	★	◆		★	4	T	◆							◆			◆		◆	TEL: (0579) 342001 / FAX:
	◆			◆					◆		◆			◆			◆				◆	TEL: (0977) 620444 / FAX: (0977) 620148
★	◆	★	★	◆	★								◆	◆		◆		◆	◆		◆	TEL: (069) 176665 / FAX: (069) 176622
★	◆						6	OT	◆					◆		◆	◆			◆		TEL: (01) 679 1122 / FAX: (01) 679 7078

Waterford Castle

Watersedge

Ty Newydd

Turnberry

Whitwell Hall

Wordsworth Hotel

	Map	Number of rooms	Price range	Disabled	Children	Meeting facilities	Credit cards	TV	Parking	Restaurants	Direct dial telephones	Helicopter landing	Pets	Leisure centre	Snooker	Croquet	Squash	Tennis	Indoor swimming pool	Outdoor swimming pool	Golf	Fishing
Westerwood Cumbernauld Strathclyde	S	47	C		◆	◆	◆	◆	◆	◆	◆	◆		◆	◆			◆	◆		◆	
Weston Manor Weston-on-the-Green Oxfordshire	E	37	CD	◆	◆	◆	◆	◆	◆	◆	◆	◆				◆	◆				◆	★
Wharton Lodge Weston under Penyard, Ross-on-Wye Hereford & Worcester	E	9	CS		7	16	◆	◆	◆	◆	◆	◆	P		◆						★	★
Whatley Manor Easton Grey, Malmesbury Wiltshire	E	29	BS		◆	30	◆	◆	◆	◆	◆	◆	◆	◆	◆	◆		◆		◆		◆
Whipper-In Hotel Oakham, Leicestershire	E	25	SB	◆	◆	75	◆	◆		◆	◆		◆								★	★
Whitechapel Manor South Molton Devon	E	10	AC			22	◆	◆	◆	◆	◆	◆			◆						★	★
Whitehall Broxted Essex	E	25	B		5	†	◆	◆	◆	◆	◆	◆	G					◆		◆	★	★
Whitwell Hall Whitwell-on-the-Hill Yorkshire	E	23	CD		12	20	◆	◆	◆	◆	◆	◆	P		◆			◆	◆			
Willington Hall Willington, Tarporley Cheshire	E	10	A		◆	20	◆	◆	◆	◆	◆		◆		◆						★	★
Wood Hall Linton nr Wetherby Yorkshire	E	44	B	◆	◆	†	◆	◆	◆	◆	◆	◆	◆	◆	◆	◆		◆			★	◆
Wood House Princethorpe nr Rugby Warwickshire	E	17	A		◆	†	◆	◆	◆	◆	◆	◆	G		◆			◆		◆	★	★
Woodhayes Hotel Whimple nr Exeter Devon	E	10	A		12	12	◆	◆	◆	◆	◆		G		◆						★	★
Woolacombe Bay Hotel Woolacombe Devon	E	59	BS		◆	†	◆	◆	◆	◆	◆		◆	◆	◆	◆	◆	◆	◆	◆	★	★
Woolley Grange Woolley Green, Bradford-on-Avon Wiltshire	E	20	CD		◆	◆	◆	◆	◆	◆	◆	◆	◆	◆	◆			◆		◆	★	★
Wordsworth Hotel Grasmere, Ambleside Cumbria	E	37	B	◆	◆	◆	◆	◆	◆	◆	◆	◆		◆				◆		★	★
Worsley Arms Hovingham Yorkshire	E	23	BS		◆	◆	◆	◆	◆	◆	◆	◆				◆	◆			★	★
Wyck Hill House Stow-on-the-Wold Gloucestershire	E	30	SA	◆	◆	◆	◆	◆	◆	◆	◆	◆	◆		◆					★	
Yarlbury Cottage Lower Bockhampton, Dorchester Dorset	E	8	AS		16		◆	◆	◆	◆	◆									★	★
Ye Olde Bell Hurley nr Maidenhead Berkshire	E	41	AC	◆	◆	†	◆	◆	◆	◆	◆	◆	◆		◆					★	★
Ynyshir Hall Eglwysfach, Machynlleth Powys	W	A	C		9	20	◆	◆	◆	◆	◆	◆	P							★	★

Wood Hall

Wharton Lodge

→ YNYSHIR HALL

Cycling	Horseracing	Horse riding	Shooting	Walking	Airborne	Sailing	Seaside	Theatre	Gourmet	Diet and health	Bridge and cards	Literary	Painting and crafts	Romantic	Murder and fantasy	Heritage	Shopping	Outward bound	Peace and quiet	In town	In country	Tel / Fax
								T	◆					◆			◆		◆		◆	TEL: (0236) 457171 / FAX: (0236) 738478
	♠	★	★	◆	✈			T						◆		◆	◆		◆		◆	TEL: (0069) 50621 / FAX: (0869) 50901
★	◆		★	◆	★	★		T	WB	◆	◆	◆	F	◆		◆	◆	◆	◆		◆	TEL: (0989) 81795 / FAX: (0989) 81700
									◆							◆	◆		◆		◆	TEL: (0666) 822 888 / FAX: (0666) 826120
★	★	C	◆		★		◆	◆						◆	◆	◆	◆		◆	◆		TEL: (0572) 756971 / FAX: (0572) 757759
	★			★	★			B						◆		◆	◆	◆	◆		◆	TEL: (0769) 573377 / FAX: (0769) 573797
	★	C	◆						W					◆	◆	◆			◆		◆	TEL: (0279) 850603 / FAX: (0279) 850385
◆	◆	★	D	◆										◆	◆	◆	◆		◆		◆	TEL: (065381) 551 / FAX: (065381) 554
◆	◆	★	★	◆												◆	◆		◆		◆	TEL: (0829) 52321 / FAX: (0829) 52596
	◆	★	★	◆	★		◆									◆	◆		◆		◆	TEL: (0937) 587271 / FAX: (0937) 584353
	◆	★		◆			◆	◆						◆		◆	◆		◆		◆	TEL: (0926) 632303 / FAX: (0926) 632303
◆	★	C	◆			◆		◆						◆		◆			◆		◆	TEL: (0404) 822237 / FAX:
★	★	★	◆				◆ S			◆				◆					◆		◆	TEL: (0271) 870388 / FAX: (0271) 870388
◆	★	★	★	◆	★		◆							◆			◆		◆		◆	TEL: (0225) 864705 / FAX: (0225) 864059
★	★	★	◆		★	★		T	WB					◆		◆		◆	◆		◆	TEL: (05394) 35592 / FAX: (05394) 35765
★	◆	★	★	◆		★			OTWB					◆	◆	◆	◆	◆	◆		◆	TEL: (0653) 628234 / FAX: (0653) 628130
	◆	★	★	◆				◆								◆	◆	◆	◆		◆	TEL: (0451) 831936 / FAX: (0451) 832293
			◆				7									◆	◆	◆	◆		◆	TEL: (0305) 262382 / FAX:
★	◆	★	C	◆	◆			◆		◆				◆		◆	◆		◆		◆	TEL: (0628) 825881 / FAX: (0628) 825939
★	★	★	◆						W				◆	◆					B		◆	TEL: (0654) 781209 / FAX: (0654) 781366

Weston Manor

Westerwood

Whitechapel Manor

Worsley Arms

THE KENSINGTON WEST COLLECTION

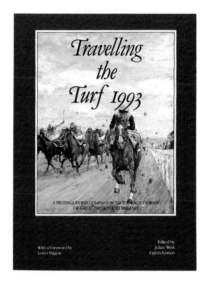

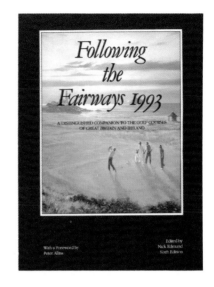

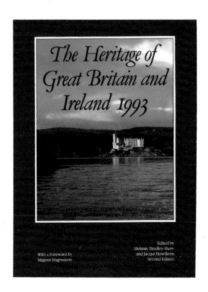

THE KENSINGTON WEST COLLECTION

Kensington West Productions Ltd publish a range of fine sporting and leisure publications, designed to suit the interest and pocket of every leisure enthusiast. Each book is lavishly illustrated and contains extensive and up-to-date information on a range of activities, together with invaluable advice on nearby places of repute (and occasionally of ill-repute!) to eat and stay. Each edition makes a beautiful addition to any library and will provide endless informative pleasure as both a guidebook and an enjoyable reading experience. They also make superb presents. Make your selection from the following titles.

TRAVELLING THE TURF (eighth edition).
The complete guide to the racecourses of Great Britain and Ireland. Travelling the Turf incorporates colour maps, extensive illustrations, many previously unpublished racing scenes with illuminating and witty analysis of every aspect of the racing scene. Comprehensive features on hotels, restaurants, pubs and Bed & Breakfasts are backed up with points and places of interest for the non-racegoer. A powerful resume of the worlds most stylish sport. With a foreword by the sports renowned figure **Lester Piggott**.

FOLLOWING THE FAIRWAYS (sixth edition)
The complete guide to the golf courses of Great Britain and Ireland. Following the Fairways contains an exhaustive directory of over 2,000 golf courses and in-depth features on one hundred of the nations most celebrated tests. The guide is superbly illustrated throughout with many rare examples of golfing art and contemporary golfing landscapes. Some 2,000 practical ideas for places to stay and entertainment off the course make this book a priceless guide for every golfer. An authoritative guide to the worlds fastest growing leisure pursuit. With a foreword by one of the games most respected personalities, **Peter Alliss**.

FISHING FORAYS (second edition)
This latest addition to the Kensington collection embraces in-depth appraisals of famous beats, maps of lochs, lakes and rivers with helpful tips for beginners to the sport on where to fish. Contacts on particular waters make the book a first class investment and provide a short cut to finding how, when and where to fish the celebrated rivers of Britain and Ireland. The usual comprehensive guide to where to stay and eat out combines to make Fishing Forays a treasured addition to any fisherman's library. An engaging summary of one of the worlds most exclusive sports. A jovial foreword by **Chris Tarrant** adds to the originality and vitality of this distinguished guide.

THE HERITAGE OF GREAT BRITAIN AND IRELAND (second edition)
The cream of Britain and Ireland's stately homes, gardens, castles and country houses make this a lavish and not to be missed publication. Over one hundred of our most regal buildings are described in an informative, graphic and lively style, complemented by illustrations and photographs of a variety of paintings and memorabilia from the houses themselves. Additional coverage is given to over 1000 alternative historical sites, with essential recommendations of where to stay and eat out nearby. A beautifully illustrated and practical guide to one of the worlds most enviable collections. A delightfully written foreword by **Magnus Magnusson** adds further weight to this treasured tome.

THE HOLIDAY GOLF GUIDE
Of the plethora of books offering advice on where to golf throughout the world, the Holiday Golf Guide is undoubtedly the most authoritative and the most colourfully presented. An almost unbelievable amount of information is packed into this comprehensive handbook, and lavish photography is sure to make many of the destinations an irresistible attraction. Golfing information is backed up with all manner of enticements for non-golfing companions. The best guide to the best courses all over the world.

THE KENSINGTON COLLECTION (first edition)
As people continue to demand more for their money so hoteliers have created all manner of short breaks to catch the imagination. The Kensington Collection has been produced to reflect this demand. It earmarks all manner of information from prices to what activities each hotel has to offer. Whether you enjoy a stroll in the country or a ride in a hot air balloon, you'll find something to enjoy. Clearly laid out and thoroughly researched the book provides you with umpteen ideas to get away from it all or have a hell of a good time! Midweek breaks and bargain short holidays are listed with authoritative articles on a range of fascinating and original ideas for how to get that little bit more for your money.

ORDER FORM

	Softback	Hardback	Quantity	Value
Travelling the Turf 1993	14.95 1 871 349 01 X	15.95 1 871 349 06 0		
Following the Fairways 1993	14.95 1 871 349 11 7	15.95 1 871 349 16 8		
Fishing Forays 1993	14.95 1 871 349 21 4	15.95 1 871 349 26 5		
The Heritage of Great Britain and Ireland 1993	14.95 1 871 349 31 1	15.95 1 871 349 36 2		
The Kensington Collection 1993	12.95 1 871 349 41 9	14.95 1 871 349 46 X		
The Holiday Golf Guide	12.95 1 871 349 45 1	—		

Please send your order to: Kensington West Productions Ltd., 338 Old York Road, Wandsworth, London SW18 1SS, Tel: 081 877 9394 Fax: 081 870 4270
Cheque (payable to KWP Ltd.) / Access / Visa / AMEX / Diners

Card no. _____ Expiry date _____

Name: _____ Address: _____

_____

TRUE DELIGHT

Worsley Arms Hotel

It is nearly impossible to shortlist establishments that have been emphatically helpful and enthusiastic in the compilation of this book. It is somewhat more straight forward to nominate those hotels which are without doubt the leaders in leisure, although sometimes at a high price. This is a somewhat arbitrary list of those who score highly on one or both of the above criteria, a brief resume is a summary by the editors of their feelings in the matter.

We should emphasize that all the hotels included in this book have been carefully considered before inclusion.

Adare Manor (*outstanding leisure facilities, imposing manor house, fine cooking*)

Amberley Castle (*well run, genuinely historic, intimate hotel with excellent food*)

Ashford Castle (*a fairy tale hotel, fabulous facilities, fantastic food, thoroughly splendid*)

Calcot Manor (*family run, excellent standards in every quarter, a real favourite*)

Chewton Glen (*celebrated hotel, ever improving, fine restaurant – a treat to behold*)

Dromoland Castle (*first class facilities in a wonderful part of Ireland, outstanding cuisine*)

Esseborne Manor (*enthusiasm personified, professionally but personally run – a treat*)

Farlam Hall (*the friendliest hoteliers in Britain, handsome property, homely stay, first class food*)

Gleneagles (*impersonal but outstanding leisure facilities, a catalogue of first class fun*)

Hambleton Hall (*expertly run, excellent restaurant and wines, well located and unpretentious*)

Hanbury Manor (*relative new comer, fine leisure facilities, close to London, friendly staff*)

Hintlesham Hall (*fine food, enterprising new facilities, outstanding edifice, a real winner*)

Horsted Place (*well connected, unobtrusive, pleasant setting, a perfect place*)

Hutton Court (*a first class trier, nothing too much trouble and a pleasant house*)

Kildare House (*Ireland's baby in historic clothing, first class pedigree with infinite promise*)

Lake Hotel (*perfect setting, professionally run, proud of quality and it shows*)

Le Manoir aux Quat' Saisons (*Gourmet's gold mine, wonderful rooms, a marvellous experience*)

Michaels Nook (*friendly staff, tranquillity, delightful country house*)

Murrayshall (*busy, bustling with good golf and gourmet food*)

Newport House (*friendly, professional and well run hotel*)

Park Hotel Kenmare (*a warm friendliness combines with genuine professionalism*)

Puckrup Hall (*not too large not too small, well equipped, just right*)

Sunlaws (*rich in character, fine location, friendly staff, excellent food, thoroughly recommended*)

Turnberry (*outstanding facilities, excellent staff, away from it all – a true delight*)

Worsley Arms Hotel (*handsome, keen to please, a charming hotel to visit*)

GOURMET FOOD IN OUTSTANDING HOTELS

Sharrow Bay

What follows is a list which invariably includes the finest hotel restaurant in Britain and Ireland – which one it is I dare not say! For every day there is a changing mood, a different style, a fickle weather forecast, a tempestuous temper or damn bad luck. What is for sure is that the under mentioned hotels have restaurants of sheer excellence. Perhaps Le Manoir aux Quat' Saisons and Le Gavroche should be seeded one and two, but they would have many rivals who would make a worthy match come the quarter finals. Settings are so important as well, from The Maison Talbooth to Airds Hotel, a refreshing Chablis and a fine evening and I think we'd all be in heaven.

This list is far from complete, but I hope it gives an inkling of the excellence and extravagance that can be found. Our quick reference pages give an even more complete picture with a particular focus on gourmet evenings, cookery classes and wine tastings. I raise my glass to the reader who samples but ten of this list – he may have a heart attack, but he will rest in peace with a smile on his face – pass that Chablis would you?

Adare Manor, Adare, Co Limerick
Airds Hotel, Port Appin, Argyll
Amberley Castle, Amberley, Sussex
Ashford Castle, Cong, Co. Mayo
Auchterarder House, Auchterarder, Perthshire
Bath Spa, Bath, Avon
Briggens House, Stanstead Abbots, Hertfordshire
Calcot Manor, Tetbury, Gloucestershire
Chester Grosvenor, Chester, Cheshire
Chewton Glen, New Milton, Hampshire
Cliveden, Taplow, Berkshire
Corse Lawn House, Corse Lawn, Gloucestershire
Crabwall Manor, Mollington, Cheshire
Culloden House, Holywood, Co Down
Dromoland Castle, Newmarket-on-Fergus, Co Clare
Eastwell Manor, Eastwell Park, Kent
Esseborne Manor, Hurstbourne Tarrant, Hampshire
Farlam Hall, Brampton, Cumbria
Farleyer House, Aberfeldy, Perthshire
Fingals at Old Coombe Manor, Dittisham, Devon

47 Park Streete (Le Gavroche) London
The George, Stamford, Lincolnshire
Gidleigh Park, Chagford, Devon
Gravetye Manor, Gravetye, Sussex
Hambleton Hall, Hambleton, Leicestershire
Hintlesham Hall, Hintlesham, Norfolk
Horsted Place, Little Horsted, East Sussex
Hunstrete House, Hunstrete, Avon
Inverlochy Castle, Torlundy, Highland
Kildare Hotel, Straffan, Co. Kildare
Kinnaird Hotel, By Dunkeld, Perthshire
Knockinaam Lodge, Portpatrick, Dumfries and Galloway
Lake Hotel, Llangammarch Wells, Powys
Le Manoir aux Quat' Saisons, Great Milton, Oxfordshire
Linden Hall, Longhorsley, Northumberland
Longueville House, Longueville, Co Cork
Longueville Manor, St Saviour, Jersey
Lower Slaughter Manor, Lower Slaughter, Gloucestershire
Lucknam Park, Colerne, Wiltshire
Lygon Arms, Broadway, Gloucestershire
Maison Talbooth, Dedham, Essex
Mallory Court, Leamington Spa, Warwickshire
Manor House, Castle Combe, Wiltshire
Marlfield House, Gorey, Co. Wexford
Michaels Nook, Grasmere, Cumbria
Miller Howe, Windermere, Cumbria
Murrayshall, Scone, Perthshire
Nuthurst Grange, Hockley Heath, West Midlands
Oakley Court, Windsor, Berkshire
Park Hotel, Kenmare, Co Kerry
Rookery Hall, Worleston, Cheshire
Savoy, London, WC2
Sharrow Bay, Ullswater, Cumbria
Sheen Falls, Kenmare, Co. Kerry
Ston Easton Park, Ston Easton, Avon
Sunlaws House, Kelso, Roxburghshire
Thornbury Castle, Thornbury, Avon
Waterford Castle, Ballinakill, Co, Waterford
Whitechapel Manor, South Molton, Devon
Wood Hall, Linton, Yorkshire
Wordsworth Hotel, Grasmere, Cumbria

RESTAURANTS WITH ROOMS

The following brief article is a summary of a sample of seasoned establishments to whet the appetite of the most discerning gourmet. They are not just restaurants, however, but a peculiar half breed with rooms available for guests.

These hostelries are special. They are for those who really want to spoil themselves, or a loved one. A not oft' repeated treat.

It is important to remember that the main focus of these establishments is the food, although the proprietors' love of quality is reflected in the rooms where even the smallest of details is never overlooked.

Let us start our adventure at Britain's most renowned eating establishment, Le Manoir Aux Quat' Saisons. Raymond Blanc has created, amidst glorious Oxfordshire countryside, a restaurant of unrivalled excellence. Some may disagree, but no one could doubt the skill and craftsmanship that is quintessentially Le Manoir. The experience begins as you enter the drive. The house, a grand manor, has been carefully restored to create a hotel par excellence. The staff are friendly and courteous, the bedrooms sumptuous and public rooms cosy and characterful.

The food, however, is the main attraction here. An outstanding menu is complemented by the full wine list and discreet service. The meals are faultless, a combination of unusual ingredients artistically presented in perfect surroundings.

The 'experience' does not come cheap but it is one to savour.

From the sophistication of Le Manoir, we take a trip through the vast conurbations of Leeds and Bradford to the countryside beyond. To Wharfedale and Pool Court in Pool-in-Wharfdale. The restaurant may have recently received a deserved Michelin Star but it is only making public what many have known for years. The superbly appointed bedrooms at Pool Court have been tastefully decorated but once again it is the cuisine which takes centre stage. The restaurant service is outstanding and a visit here thoroughly recommended.

Another Yorkshire recommendation is McCoy's at the Tontine. The McCoy brothers run an outstanding restaurant with rooms. The modern British cooking is delightful and the somewhat eccentric decor makes for a talking point and mirrors the cuisine; unique and unusual. Additional bedrooms are under construction here but fear not, this splendid establishment will continue to be a restaurant, first and foremost.

Although there are numerous fine establishments in Scotland I have selected only two here; the Peat Inn near Cupar and Altnaharrie Inn. A night at either would ensure a night to remember. Dedication is the catch word for both proprietors and the standard of cooking, wine and service is a delight. Both kitchens make excellent use of the finest local produce, complemented by wines of the finest quality.

In order to reach Altnaharrie Inn you must take a short boat trip. This quite memorable journey is but the beginning of your voyage of excellence.

Ireland offers a number of fine eating establishments and one favourite is Blair's Cove House, near Bantry in County Cork.

There are stunning views of Bantry Bay and the menu is predictably 'fishy' in emphasis. The restaurant is full of character and a visit is thoroughly recommended. There is only limited accommodation so book well in advance. Another seafood specialist, Doyle's, also has rooms. This restaurant fronts onto John Street in Dingle and is delightfully welcoming, wonderfully Irish and guaranteed to raise the spirits.

Continuing with seafood, this time in England, we would recommend the bright and busy harbourside Seafood Restaurant in Padstow. Bedrooms here are quaint and comfortable and the food of an exemplary standard. Another great favourite, with a different outlook, is the Horn of Plenty in Gulworthy. Sauces are exquisite and the restaurant sets a marvellous standard. The views from the bedrooms over the Tamar Valley are quite stunning.

Creeping ever closer to the metropolis, we find two establishments of true excellence. In Dorchester, Yarlbury Cottage and near to Bath, Box House, Clos du Roy. Both restaurants offer varied menus of excellence and panache with extremely comfortable accommodation. Sauces and only the freshest of ingredients are just two contributing factors to the restaurants' reputations. Similar qualities are found at the redoubtable Redmond's at Malvern View found on Cheltenham's Cleeve Hills. Bedrooms here are functional, not grand, but the cuisine is both stylish and original.

Le Manoir

A somewhat grander establishment is Fischer's at Baslow Hall. The rooms here are stylish and complete with many extra personal touches, a clue to the proprietor's love of originality and perfection. The dining rooms are elegant and the cooking perfection. So perfect in fact, that you will not find any salt or pepper on your table – quite unnecessary. The restaurant is very popular locally so book well in advance.

Another delightful rural setting, this time amidst the lakes of Cumbria, is the location for Uplands. The Miller Howe ethos and quality is a fine hallmark of this excellent establishment.

Our final recommendation is for Plas Bodegroes, Pwllheli. Delicious food and charming rooms make this an excellent place to stay. It may be our only recommendation in Wales but it certainly is a cracker.

Naturally, there are numerous other restaurants we could have included but few which offer the same standard of cuisine combined with the warmth of welcome.

PEACE AND QUIET

Alongside excellent food one of the most popular pastimes is putting the old feet up. Taking it easy, slowing the pace down, having a pleasant evening stroll, these undemanding, stress-free, simple pursuits are at the front of a vast number of peoples' minds. Relaxation, recharging the batteries, unwinding, call it what you will it's simply marvellous to just take stock, breath in the air and think for a while. With this in mind we have listed a number of hotels which have beautiful situations and are just perfect for those of us with troubles on our mind. They are not riddled with leisure facilities, but offer a different charm, peace and quiet.

Ardanaiseig, Kilchrenan
Ardsheal House, Kentallen of Appin
Arisaig House, Arisaig
Ashwick House, Dulverton
Auchterarder House, Auchterarder
Beechfield House, Beanacre
Bel Alp House, Haytor
Bishopstrow House, Warminster
Combe House, Gittisham
Congham Hall, Grimston
Crosby Lodge, Crosby-on-Eden

Farlam Hall, Brampton
Gidleigh Park, Chagford
Hassop Hall, Bakewell
Holbeck Ghyll, Windermere
Hope End, Ledbury
Hunstrete House, Hunstrete
Huntsham Court, Huntsham
Invery House, Banchory
Jervaulx Hall, Jervaulx
Knipoch Hotel, By Oban
Longueville House, Mallow
Lucknam Park, Colerne
Michael's Nook, Grasmere
Nutfield Priory, Nutfield
Old Rectory, Great Snoring
The Pheasant, Harome
Riber Hall, Matlock
Sharrow Bay, Ullswater
South Lodge, Lower Beeding
Tyddyn Llan, Llandrillo
Ulbster Arms, Halkirk
Whitechapel Manor, Whitechapel
Ynyshir Hall, Eglwysfach

Jervaulx Hall

FUN WITH THE FAMILY

It is a general rule that larger groups of hotels tend to consider the family unit more fully and therefore cater better for children. Facilities that are the domain of the business traveller during the week curiously double well for use by the family. As groups are desperate to keep their hotels full at the weekend some outstanding bargain breaks are available. More and more hotels are now specialising in this important area of the market. Couples will continue to have children and it seems we are spending more of our holiday time within the British Isles, so to ignore such a market would appear folly.

There are, of course, a number of hostelries who cringe at the mere thought of toddlers terrorising their dining room but similarly, there are many who are quite used to the unpredictable behaviour of small children.

In our hotel guide we have tried to give some indication as to the accepted age of small guests allowed in the individual hotels. Some have a very clear policy on children, others are less stringent. Where possible, we have marked those hotels which require children to be of a minimum age or those who do not wish to have children as guests at all. As the behaviour of each child varies so much it is rather a difficult subject but whatever your brand of brat, be it angel or little devil, if you are seeking particular facilities for your family these are perhaps some of the features you will wish to consider.

Does the hotel offer a babysitting service or just a listening service? Are cots allowed in your room? What must you pay for taking a small tot with you? Will you be charged extra for a family room? Is there a creche at the hotel? What additional facilities are there for children: swimming pool, games room etc..?

As a rule of thumb, seaside hotels catering specially for the holiday trade tend to be well clued up when it comes to children. The Gara Rock Hotel in East Portlemouth is one excellent example. A special guide is prepared for children's activities; what to do in the event of wet weather, together with a focus on nearby attractions which would appeal to a youngster. All manner of games can be enjoyed, from hunt the thimble to blind man's stick. Two other southern hotels catering effectively for children are Knoll House, Studland Bay and St Michael's Hotel, Falmouth. Two for the bucket-and-spade brigade to consider.

The Langdale Hotel and the Lodore Swiss Hotel are both in Cumbria and both welcome children. Excellent facilities and all manner of local entertainments amidst the glorious Cumbrian scenery set the scene for some first class family fun.

Those of you seeking a quiet weekend away a deux in London, should consider a brilliant concept; Pippa's Pop-Ins 071-385 2458. This is a hotel which doesn't allow adults! Pippa's Pop-Ins is not part of our collection but we do think it to be a marvellous idea. The hotel is the first recognised children's hotel in Britain. It sounds like bags of fun and Mum and Dad can relax at the Ritz while baby finds new friends at his own hotel.

We should end this article with a hotel which focuses on the well being of both parents and children; Woolley Grange. Here Mother and Father can enjoy all the luxuries of a beautiful country house hotel, knowing that the children are also having a marvellous time. Creche and babysitting facilities ensure that a family break can be a relaxing one too. Woolley Grange is also renowned for its excellent cuisine. Fear not, separate dining arrangements are made for the various generations.

In next year's edition we hope to add considerably to our selection of family hotels. Increasingly, both large chains and small private hotels are realising the significance of this market. Children know what they want and woe betide any hotelier who fails to meet the tots' exacting standards.

Charlotte Conner (Age 5)

THE HERITAGE OF GREAT BRITAIN & IRELAND

Britain and Ireland are full of history and rich in character. The countryside is dotted with ruined castles and baronial halls, sites of enormous historical interest where knights fought for their ladies' favour, where medieval jousts were regular events, and where countryman fought countryman in civil war.

Britain is positively alive with 'hand crafted' heritage; Roman Walls and Baths, Iron Age fortifications, Parliamentary buildings and stately homes. All fine examples of Britain's colourful history. Furthermore, in the latter years of this century, we find many a noble family opening the doors of once jealously guarded private houses and grounds. This is often done to raise capital used for vital restoration and running repairs.

We can then find some truly marvellous buildings now open to the public, some of which have been carefully converted into sumptous hotels.

The following list is but a selection of those properties. The accompanying list also includes some of the nation's most celebrated homes and gardens that are open to the public. If you would like an indepth appraisal of these houses our guide 'The Heritage of Great Britain and Ireland' gives details on over 1,200 such places and will prove to be invaluable. Its colour content is a delight and gives an insight to our country's rich and varied history.

LEGENDARY HOTELS

Amberley Castle, Amberley, West Sussex
Ashford Castle, Cong, Co Mayo
Bodidris Hall, Llandegla, Clwyd
Cliveden, Taplow, Berkshire
Comlongon Castle, Clarencefield, Dumfries & Galloway
Crown Inn, Chippingfold, Surrey
Eastwell Manor, Boughton Lees, Kent
Flitwick Manor, Flitwick, Bedfordshire
The George, Stamford, Lincolnshire
Longueville House, Mallow, Co Cork
Lygon Arms, Broadway, Hereford & Worcester
New Hall, Sutton Coldfield, West Midlands
Old Bell, Malmesbury, Wiltshire
Spread Eagle, Midhurst, Sussex
Stapleford Park, Melton Mowbray, Leicestershire
Tanyard Hotel, Boughton Monchelsea, Kent
Thornbury Castle, Thornbury, Avon
Weston Manor, Weston-On-The-Green, Oxford
Whitehall, Broxted, Essex
Ye Olde Bell, Hurley, Berkshire

TWENTY FIVE TO VISIT

Alnwick Castle, Northumberland
Berkeley Castle, Gloucestershire
Birr Castle, Co Offaly
Blenheim Palace, Oxfordshire
Broadlands, Hampshire
Brympton d'Evercy, Somerset
Bunratty Castle, Co Clare
Burghley House, Lincolnshire
Burton Agnes Hall, Humberside
Cardiff Castle, South Glamorgan
Castle Howard, North Yorkshire
Cawdor Castle, Highlands
Chatsworth, Derbyshire
Floors Castle, Borders
Forde Abbey, Somerset
Glamis Castle, Tayside
Holkham Hall, Norfolk
Leeds Castle, Kent
Levens Hall, Cumbria
Malahide Castle, Co Dublin
Royal Pavilion, East Sussex
Tower of London, London
Traquair House, Borders
Wilton House, Wiltshire
Woburn Abbey, Bedfordshire

Comlongon Castle

THE EMERALD ISLE

Dunmanus Bay *(Irish Tourist Board)*

Back in Medieval Ireland a nobleman's standing was measured not simply by the might of his conquests or the gaudy grandeur of his possessions, but more simply, by his abilities as a host. A quickness to welcome friends and strangers alike and extend his arms and his home in hospitality was the measure of his true worth. Tradition is something that dies hard in Ireland.

Ireland, above all else, is a land of people, not the hordes who crowd the city streets but those instead who have retained the art of a gentler life, looking to share a conversation, a song, a little laughter, and perhaps a drink or two. The welcome is spontaneous; as they say here, there's no such thing as a stranger, only a friend you have yet to meet, and the unwitting visitor could well find himself dragged into an impromptu singing session amidst the warmth and cheers of an Irish pub.

From the moment you set foot on the 'Emerald Isle' you will realise that there is more than a little magic in the air; something vibrant in the light that has streamed for centuries across this

land where there are truly forty shades of green.

Time is all that you will find lacking in your visit to Ireland; almost everything else is in abundance. There is golf to be played on some of the finest tournament courses of the world; there are fish waiting to be hooked out of, or sailed over, some of the cleanest and clearest rivers, lakes and seas in Europe, and there is the horse-racing that runs deep in the veins of the people.

The walking and cycling in Ireland is some of the finest in the world, from rugged mountains and imposing valleys, to lush green fields, deep blue lakes and sandy beaches swathed in a kaleidoscope of colour. All this under the even-tempered weather of the balmy Gulf Stream, so mild you will find palm trees and southern exotics happily flourishing. Combine a walk with the most fascinating history and culture, passing under the ancient standing stones and earthen castles of the ancient Celts that have stood as monumental guards since way-

THE EMERALD ISLE

Ballynahinch *(Irish Tourist Board)*

before the Eastern pyramids were heaved into existence. Trinity College, Dublin, is the present resting place for the 8th/9th century 'Book of Kells', arguably the most beautiful book in the world, while 'The Book of the Dun Cow' still survives after almost 900 years to recount the Tain Bo Cualainge, the raid of Queen Maeve of Connacht to secure the legendary Brown Bull of Ulster. Some of the finest literature in the world finds its roots over 300 years before the birth of Christ and continues up through the centuries to produce three Nobel Prize winning authors. Pause to take a little history home; Donegal Tweed, Waterford Crystal and Limerick Lace.

After such exhilarating days there still remains the decision of where to spend the night; from caravans to cottages to castles; from river cruiser to horse-drawn caravan, the list is indeed too long. Thanks to unpolluted waters and lush all-year-round grazing, Irish meat and fish is outstanding, particularly when accompanied by fresh, locally-grown vegetables and herbs and served in the abundant helpings for which the island is so famous.

Travelling to Ireland is never a problem. There are direct flights to Dublin, Cork, Shannon, Knock, Galway, Farranfore, Waterford and Carrickfin, Co. Donegal; and car ferry ports at Dublin, Dun Laoghaire, Rosslare and Cork. For help with any aspect of your holiday, simply contact Bord Failte, the Irish Tourist Board, at the address below.

Ireland is a country rich in almost everything, but especially people. As they are so fond of saying, 'Cead Mile Failte' - a hundred thousand welcomes. Its the least you can expect from this most fascinating of kingdoms.

For further information please contact:-
Irish Tourist Board,
150 New Bond Street,
London W1Y OAQ,
Tel: (071) 493 3201 or Fax: (071) 493 9065

FOLLOWING THE FAIRWAYS

Golf was the boom sport of the 1980s and as a result, a number of hotel groups invested heavily in this lucrative market. The tough economic climate and some fairly poor management has sadly seen some of these projects go into liquidation, despite the continued growth of the sport. However, those hotels to survive will surely reap significant rewards in future years. One thing is certain, the 'golf bug' is spreading more quickly than ever. Furthermore, the success of British and European professionals ensures a high media exposure and therefore increasing interest in the sport.

There are in excess of two thousand golf courses in the British Isles and consequently many hotels are able to boast a location near to a golf course. However, many courses are private and unless you are organised in advance, play off a low handicap and are able to play midweek you may well find it very difficult to play some of these courses. It is therefore imperative to ascertain what the club's policy is in advance. It is also fair to say that some hotels who boast their own golf courses may not offer the most challenging of tests. Most golfers will be able to establish this over the telephone and need little advice on the subject. The great bonus of these courses, however, is that they are often in pleasant surroundings and are ideal for those just taking up the sport as they are often less daunting.

There are of course some hotels who boast championship golf courses and others who enjoy a prime location near some of the country's greatest links courses. A good number of hotels have excellent relationships with, or even shares in local golf courses. This ensures that hotel guests can play at pre-arranged times with no fuss.

Golf is by and large a fairly expensive sport to play and a golfing weekend can end up as being quite pricey. However, many hotels offer good discounts to guests who wish to play golf and will guarantee tee times. A considerable bonus at a time when demands far outstrips supply in many areas.

It is accepted that getting onto a golf course in the south of England can prove difficult. It is not unknown for enthusiasts to arrive before 4.00am at a course and still have to queue to tee off when the course opens. Away from the more densely populated south east and the larger towns finding a game of golf becomes easier and in parts of Great Britain you will find relatively uncluttered courses.

The Kingdom of Fife is the home of golf and St Andrews is its capital. There are many outstanding courses to be found in the region. The west coast of Ireland has also fashioned some of the world's most natural but demanding links courses.

Whether you are considering staying at the marvellous Turnberry Hotel and Spa or you are booking a weekend at one of Country Clubs' nine hotels with golf courses you will find Following the Fairways an invaluable source of information. With over 360 pages of details on where to play, when to play, and whom to contact, plus all manner of golfing information, it is the ideal companion for the novice and scratch golfer alike. To help you in your choice we have compiled a summary of some of the highly recommended courses and hotels within the book. Following the Fairways is available directly from Kensington West Productions or from any good book shop.

Outstanding Hotels with golf courses or with close connections with a local course.

Adare Manor, Adare
Alton Burn, Nairn
Ashford Castle, Cong
The Belfry, Wishaw
Belton Woods, Belton
Breadsall Priory, Morley
Briggens House, Stanstead Abbots
Buckland Tout Saints, Kingsbridge
Burghfield House, Dornoch
Cameron House, Alexandria
Carlyon Bay, St Austell
Castletown Golf Links, Derbyhaven
Chedington Court, Chedington
Chewton Glen, New Milton
Dale Hill, Ticehurst
Dalmahoy Hotel, Kirknewton
Dalmunzie House, Blairgowrie
The Dormy House, Ferndown
Dromoland Castle, Newmarket-on-Fergus
Forest of Arden, Meriden
Gleneagles, Auchterarder
Goodwood Park, Goodwood
Greywalls, Muirfield
Hanbury Manor, Thundridge
Highbullen, Chittlehamholt
Hintlesham Hall, Ipswich
Horsted Place, Little Horsted
The Hythe Imperial, Hythe
Kildare House, Straffan
Letham Grange, Colliston
Lostwithiel, Lower Polscoe
Meon Valley, Shedfield
Moore Place, Apsley Guise
Mottram Hall, Prestbury
Mount Juliet, Thomastown
Murrayshall, Scone
Puckrup Hall, Puckrup
Saunton Sands, Saunton
Selsdon Park, Sanderstead
Sprowston Manor, Norwich
St Andrews Golf Hotel, St Andrews
St Andrews Old Course Hotel, St Andrews
St Mellion, Saltash
St Pierre, Chepstow
Tewkesbury Park, Tewkesbury
Thurlestone Hotel, Thurlestone
Tudor Park, Bearsted
Ufford Park, Ufford
Waterford Castle, Ballinakill
Westerwood, Cumbernauld

TRAVELLING THE TURF

The thrills and spills of a day at the races are electrifying and heart stopping at the same time! Today, even in these recessionary times, racecourses are ploughing large sums of money into upgrading their facilities and ensuring that the visitor gets value for money. Mind you, in some cases this is not before time!

The introduction of Sunday racing is well overdue. However, it may be some time before it is established enough to justify planning a weekend away at the races. This is a great pity as it would provide a first class excuse for a day or two in the countryside in which so many of Britain's racecourses are located.

There are fifty nine racecourses in Britain with another twenty or more in Ireland where, incidentally, Sunday racing is approved and very popular. The racecourses vary hugely in their make up, from the vast stands of Epsom, Ascot and Newmarket to the more lowly but still delightful edifices that greet you at Fakenham, Cartmel or Bangor On Dee.

So a few days racing sounds like a good idea. Where would you start? There are a number of major festivals which are held throughout the year and although some are held at the weekend more often than not they take place midweek. This is a good excuse for escaping from the office to enjoy a day or two on the turf amidst bustling bars and boisterous bookies.

January is the mid-point of the National Hunt season and excellent meetings are held at Sandown Park, Cheltenham and Haydock Park. February offers some of the most ferocious weather of the year but if you're lucky, Newbury's Tote Gold Trophy may not be cancelled – a tremendous betting race. Once again, both Haydock and Sandown Park host first class fixtures. The focus for March is the Festival of National Hunt Racing held at one of Britain's foremost and most beautiful racecourses, Cheltenham. Those of you who have been to the festival and stayed in the Cotswolds will surely need no encouragement to return. Those who have not yet tried it must make a visit. The Cotswolds, despite the mantle of winter, positively vibrate with excitement as hotel dining rooms and country pubs buzz with the latest gossip from the turf.

In April, we see another major National Hunt event, The Grand National at Aintree. The Aintree Meeting starts on Thursday with the feature race on Saturday. This immensely challenging race always springs a few surprises.

April also sees the return of flat racing. Newmarket has a particularly strong calendar throughout the season. Headquarters, as it is known in racing circles, has a lot to offer. The town is alive from dawn to dusk and a long time after if a local horse has acquitted itself well. The choice of hotels is perhaps not as abundant as in the Cotswolds but the racing is spectacular. Other superb flat races over the summer are held at Chester, York, Sandown, Epsom and, of course, Ascot. The Derby currently takes place on the downs on a Wednesday but it is hoped that it may one day be run on a Saturday. The Royal meeting at Ascot provides four days of excellent racing. The 'Rollers' in the car park, the champagne and the pearls in the Members' are nothing to the equine riches which grace the turf. Tickets are still available for the Members' on the Friday but formal introductions are required. Fear not, you can still attend Ascot in the less celebrated enclosures where the viewing is sometimes better. Good luck which ever enclosure you choose – you will need it as the racing is extremely competitive.

Newmarket's July racecourse and Glorious Goodwood play host to two outstanding mid-week events in high summer with Ascot's Diamond Day and Sandown's Summer Eclipse providing the Saturday's entertainment.

Throughout the summer there are various evening meetings to take advantage of, so leave the office early and spend a Friday at the track. You might even earn a few extra bob!

Yorkshire has a number of racecourses of which York is the most famous. This historic city is ringed by delightful countryside offering some splendid hostelries. The August Festival is great fun and thoroughly recommended. In September, Doncaster, another classic Yorkshire course, hosts the St Leger. An historic meeting with a grand Saturday finale. Ascot also boasts a first class meeting with Newbury and Newmarket offering good October fixtures.

As the nights draw in the National Hunt game begins to start in earnest. The highlight of November is the Hennessy Gold Cup at Newbury. In December, Chepstow and Ascot host fine days and Boxing Day is one of racing's big days with a fistful of meetings, the highlight being Kempton's King George.

We have tended to focus our attention on the bigger meetings but excellent racing does take place at some of Britain's smaller courses; Devon and Exeter, Fakenham, Fontwell, Hexham, Kelso, Perth, Plumpton, Salisbury, Taunton, Thirsk, Warwick, Wetherby and Wincanton.

The Irish racing calendar is also brimful with events. The Curragh is the home of all the classics and is the focus of attention in the Spring and Summer but there are a number of courses which also command attention. Leopardstown is a tremendous track and Punchestown holds a festival of fun in April. Killarney and Tralee offer yet more good fixtures and Fairyhouse and Naas are also fine courses.

A day at the races in Britain and Ireland may not necessarily make you wealthier but it will help you to unwind and, as the saying goes; 'all men are equal on the turf, or six foot under' - Good Luck!

If you wish to know more about racing in Britain and Ireland and some of the excellent hostelries that lie close to the racecourses, please order a copy of Travelling The Turf from Kensington West Productions, or any good bookshop.

FISHING FORAYS

Fishing is the most popular participant sport in the country. Game fishing, however, is somewhat more exclusive and more elusive than course fishing.

Game fishing centres largely on salmon and trout fishing and will invariably take you to some of the most beautiful, unspoiled parts of Britain. Unfortunately, game fishing as a sport is almost as elusive as the catch, unless you are fortunate enough to have the 'right connections'. However, one way of fishing some of Britain's excellent waters is to contact a local hotel which owns a stretch of river with fishing rights, or at least can arrange some good fishing for you nearby.

We have included here a list of hotels who can do just that. They also have good facilities for the fishing fraternity; drying rooms and rod rooms and such like.

If you are looking for a sporting weekend away from it all we are confident in recommending any of the following hotels. If however, you require further information Fishing Forays, our guide to game fishing, offers literally hundreds of opportunities to ensure your finest catch. Fishing Forays is available from all good bookshops or from Kensington West Productions Ltd direct.

Altnaharra, Altnaharra
Arundell Arms, Lifton
Banchory Lodge, Banchory
Barnsdale Lodge, Oakham
Black Swan, Kirkby Stephen
Blackwater Lodge, Upper Ballyduff
Coopershill, Riverstown
Corsemalzie, Newton Stewart
Caragh Lodge, Caragh Lake
Carnarvon Arms, Dulverton
Culcreuch Castle, Fintry
Dunkeld House, Dunkeld

Downhill, Ballina
Dolmellynllyn, Dolgellau
Devonshire Arms, Bolton Abbey
Ednam House, Kelso
Enniscoe, Castlehill
Griffin Inn, Llyswen
Glyn Isa, Rowen
Gliffaes, Crickhowell
Glanrannell Park, Crugybar
Hornby Hall, Culgaith
Gleneagles, Auchterarder
Innishannon, Innishannon
Kinnaird, Dunkeld
Kenmore Hotel, Kenmore
Kildare Hotel, Straffan
Lake Country Hotel, Llangammarch Wells
Lake Vrynwy, Llandwyddyn
Lee Park, Romsey
Llangoed Hall, Llyswen
Longueville House, Mallow
Muckrach Lodge, Grantown-on-Spey
Mill End, Chagford
Newport House, Newport
Normanton Park, Oakham
Pale Hall, Llandderfel
Pennyhill Park, Bagshot
Roman Camp, Callander
Riverside, Ashford-in-the-Water
Royal Beacon, Exmouth
Sheen Falls, Kenmare
Sunlaws, Kelso
Ty Newydd, Hirwaun
Tillmouth Park, Cornhill-on-Tweed
Tyddyn Llan, Llandrillo
Ulbster Arms, Thurso
Whipper In, Oakham
Wood Hall, Linton

Welsh Waters, The Griffin Inn

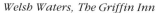

Gravetye Manor

ABBEY HOUSE HOTEL

This most impressive red sandstone building is a superb and slightly unusual example of the work of the eminent English architect, Sir Edwin Lutyens. It was completed in 1914 as a business guest house and, in its conversion to a graceful hotel of the very highest calibre, virtually all of the magnificently-proportioned rooms have adapted to their new role with minimal disturbance. There is an inherent grandeur and quiet dignity about the hotel equalled only by the fourteen acres of grounds, comprising a beautifully balanced mixture of formal gardens and wooded copses. Beyond these lies a splendid vista of mature woodland and meadow interspersed with established walkways which lead to the ruins of nearby Furness Abbey. In less than half-an-hour's drive you are in the centre of the English Lake District with all the historic and picturesque places of interest in and around Grizedale Forest.

Barrow-in-Furness lies on a peninsula with a road bridge to the Isle of Walney, and some tiny isolated islands in and around sheltered bays; Sailing craft complete the coastal picture. Inland excursions bring you to the tarns, fells and pikes of the Cumbrian Mountains.

Abbey House offers impeccable accommodation for business and holiday visitors alike, and the finest a la carte English and French cuisine of the Abbey Restaurant is available to residents and non-residents.

Excellent conference and banqueting facilities can be provided.

The Hotel is also an ideal stopover for those of you who wish to have that little flutter on the horses as it is within easy reach of the Cartmel Race Course near Grange-Over-Sands or Carlisle Race Course.

Abbey House Hotel
Abbey Road
Barrow in Furness
Cumbria LA13 OPA
Tel: (0229) 838282
Fax: (0229) 820403

ALLT-YR-YNYS

Allt-yr-Ynys, situated on wooded river banks in Herefordshire, and standing in an acre of well-established gardens, is an elegant country hotel with a fascinating history. Robert Cecil came to this beautiful spot in 1091, after the conquest of Glamorgan, and it is said that Elizabeth I was once a house guest here. The historical appeal of the hotel remains intact - Allt-yr-Ynys as it is today was built in 1550, and retains much fine craftsmanship of the period. Moulded ceilings, oak panelling and door pillars feature throughout the house, yet at the same time the hotel offers the very finest of modern comforts.

All the bedrooms are individually furnished - the Master Suite, for example, has a Jacobean fourposter, and each has an ensuite bathroom, telephone, colour television and radio. Ancient outbuildings have been converted to provide additional luxury accommodation.

Much attention is paid to personal service at the hotel - guest are warmly and genuinely welcomed and the staff do their utmost to meet the particular needs of every guest. The Chef is only too happy to prepare special dishes, and the hotel caters for weddings and functions of all kinds. Great care is taken with the quality and presentation of food, using only the finest cuts of meat and the freshest of vegetables and other ingredients.

Guest can enjoy the indoor heated swimming pool and jacuzzi at Allt-yr-Ynys, or perhaps the Clay Shooting Centre, ideal for corporate entertaining. Realising that nobody wants to be ankle-deep in mud in wet weather clothes and wellingtons, the stands and observation area are conveniently situated under one roof.

The setting is every bit as magnificent as the hotel. On the border between England and Wales, on the English side, the rolling wooded farmland of Herefordshire gives way to the Malvern Hills beyond. On the Welsh side the Fwddog Ridge dominates the landscape. Part of the Black Mountains, it runs north to Hay-on-Wye, all within the Brecon Beacons National Park. Houses and castles of historic interest abound in the area - just as a taster, the ancient castle at Chepstow, which looks down the River Wye, and Llanthony Abbey in the Black Mountains. If you are a keen golfer Allt-yr-Ynys is conveniently situated for Abergavenny, Monmouth, Chepstow and Hereford Golf Courses.

Allt-yr-Ynys is many things to many people: Conference Centre, country retreat, holiday hotel or activity holiday location. The common thread is the personal involvement of owners and staff - you as a guest will find that your interests are always paramount.

Allt-yr-Ynys
Walterstone
Herefordshire
Tel: (0873) 890307
Fax: (0873) 890539

ALTON BURN HOTEL

Alton Burn Hotel is an imposing building, originally constructed as a Preparatory School in 1901. It stands in it's own grounds over-looking the 17th Tee of the Nairn Golf Club, with glorious views across the course, Moray Firth with the Sutherland Hills in the background. The hotel has been owned and run by the Mac-Donald family since 1956, and is geared to the needs of the golfer and families in particular.

There are 25 rooms all with Private facilities, Colour T.V., Radio, Baby Listening and Tea & Coffee Makers.

Recreational facilities abound and one can have a relaxing round of putting on the green, or an exacting game of Tennis, followed by a session on the Practice Golf Area, finished off by a swim in the Heated Out-door Swimming Pool. There is also a Games Room with Pool Table and Table Tennis.

Nairn has a very fine Indoor Deck Level Swimming Pool, and Squash can be arranged from the Hotel, for the very energetic guest.

There are many fine courses in the area, and one cannot fail to mention Nairn Dunbar Golf Course – very popular venue for this year's Northern Open and only 2 miles from the Hotel. Forres, Grantown on Spey, Boat of Garten, Elgin, Lossiemouth, Inverness and Dornoch are all within easy driving distance of the Hotel. Inverness Airport is 8 miles from the Hotel and with prior notice, transport to the Hotel is easily arranged. It is possible therefore to be on the Nairn Courses within 2 hours of leaving Heathrow or Gatwick.

The A9 North now makes Nairn very accessible by car, with Edinburgh and Glasgow a comfortable 3 hours driving time. Within the surrounding area Cawdor and Brodie Castles, Loch Ness and the elusive Monster, Culloden Battlefield, Clava Stones are just a few of things to see. If you feel you are 'Over-golfed,' the Whisky Trail is also easily found and never forgotten!

So if you want to get away from it all, and enjoy good golf, good food and good company, there can be no better choice than Alton Burn Hotel, where we can cater for groups of up to 40.

Alton Burn Hotel
Nairn
Scotland

Tel: (0667) 53325

AMBERLEY CASTLE

When Bishop Luffa of Chichester began the building of Amberley Castle in the early 1100s he can hardly have foreseen that 900 years later his country retreat would have survived the ravages of the centuries as well as the destructive force of Oliver Cromwell's army.. Yet today, Amberley Castle stands majestic as if determined to endure as long as the softly undulating Sussex Downland landscape which is its setting.

For most of its long history, few were privileged enough to experience the peace that lies within the massive embrace of the ancient curtain wall. For Amberley Castle was a private residence, tenanted for the best part of half a millennium by wealthy and influential bishops.

Since 1989, however, the life of Amberley Castle is no longer an enigmatic secret. Owners Martin and Joy Cummings have hoisted the portcullis to welcome the world to share the splendour of their historic castle home. For Amberley Castle has been transformed by the Cummings into a country castle hotel offering its guests an incomparable blend of luxury, cuisine and service in the matchless surroundings of this magical building.

Each room, individually designed and deliciously decorated with jacuzzi bath en-suite, is named after a Sussex castle - and there are a few which have access by a stone spiral staircase to the battlements. Guests are never in doubt that this is a real castle.

The Queen's Room restaurant, a handsome barrel-vaulted room is so named for its 17th century mural depicting King Charles 11 and his queen, Catherine of Braganza, who visited Amberley Castle in the early 1680s.

Now it is the perfect setting for Castle Cuisine, the innovative inspiration of award-winning Head Chef, Nigel Boschetti. With Amberley Castle's rich fund of history as his prime source, Nigel has researched the culinary customs and dishes of our forebears and calling on his own creative talent, is deriving from them a repertoire of original recipes to delight the palate of today, but with more than a hint of England's gastronomic heritage.

It's hard to believe that so much tranquillity and seclusion can be so accessible from London, but you can be in Amberley in little more than an hour by main line train from Victoria or by road from Heathrow. Gatwick is a mere 40 minutes distant.

Yet Amberley, decidedly one of the most picturesque of Sussex downland villages is country - not suburb. With a wealth of breathtaking walks and an abundance of country pursuits on hand, it's perfect for blowing the cobwebs away or unwinding city tensions.

Amberley Castle
Amberley
Nr. Arundel
West Sussex BN18 9ND
Tel: (0798) 831992
Fax: (0798) 831998

THE ANCHOR HOTEL AND SHIP INN

A quiet and comfortable 19th century hotel by the water's edge of Porlock harbour, a small picturesque harbour set amidst Exmoor's magnificent scenery and dramatic coastline, within walking distance of the shingle beach and moor.

A visit to Exmoor is a visit to that fast vanishing old rural England and where time seems to run more slowly and you feel an atmosphere and charm unchanged for generations. Exmoor straddles the border of North Devon and West Somerset and is a paradise for the lover of beautiful scenery and open space. There are wonderful walks and rides every-where, sparkling rivers, sandy coves, picturesque harbours, ancient villages full of thatched cottages and Medieval churches - all will enchant you.

A visit to Dunster Castle or a trip to Combe Sydenham Hall, a stately home with a corn mill and deer park, should satisfy those in search of still more of Britain's heritage.

For those of you with a more active break in mind, the Minehead and West Somerset Golf Club is close by, a fairly flat windy course situated on the east side of Minehead. Game

fishing can also be found locally, the river East Lyn fishes particularly well, and a little further a field is the better known river Taw. If a day at the races is favoured then Taunton is the place to head for.

The Anchor Hotel and Ship Inn provides an ideal base from which to explore and enjoy the many delights of the Exmoor National Park and surrounding country side. The hotel's aim is to ensure that your stay is relaxed and enjoyable. The bedrooms are well appointed and you can chose between the cosy beamed rooms in the Ship Inn or the larger old fashioned rooms of the Anchor - some with excellent sea views.

The dining room looks directly out onto the water's edge. The cuisine is Anglo french using many local ingredients with Lobster Thermidor and Steak, Kidney and Oyster pie as specialities. Tasty home made bar food is also available at the 16th century Ship Inn.

Comfortable surroundings and attentive service will help you unwind and help persuade you to visit the hotel and Exmoor again.

The Anchor Hotel and Ship Inn
Exmoor National Park
Porlock Harbour
West Somerset
TA24 8PB
Tel: (0643) 862753
Fax: (0643) 862843

ARDFILLAYNE HOTEL

Nestling in what is arguably the most beautiful and unexploited area of Scotland, Ardfillayne is a rare find in today's world. Built in 1835 and commanding an enviable view over the Firth of Clyde from its own 16 acres of natural wooded gardens, it retains the charm and warmth of an era now all but lost. There is an almost ethereal quality of the past here, a captivating period charm enhanced by the informal elegance of its eminently Victorian atmosphere.

The drawing rooms reflect this gentler peace, with fine furniture objects d'art and a veritable treasure-trove of antiques perfectly complementing the affluent antiquity of such a house.

Carefully modernised, the seven intimate bedrooms are unique peaceful havens; all en suite, they are designed with your comfort in mind.

The fin de siecle ambience of Ardfillayne's Mackintosh in-spired dining room provides the magical setting for the famous Beverley's Restaurant. An atmosphere of sophistication per-vades, subtly aided by fresh flowers, candlelight, lace and crystal, and further enhancing the experience of such excep-tional food. Classic cuisine and traditional Scottish dishes are exquisitely prepared from the finest of fresh, local produce; game and fish caught from nearby land, loch and sea. All complemented by superb wines from one of Scotland's most exclusive cellars, and perfectly completed by old brandies, malts and vintage ports.

Ardfillayne is the example in this area that seems to have missed the march of time; nearby can still be found lochside hostelries, antiquated Drovers' Inns, and quiet walks through the peace and tranquillity that is uniquely the Forest Park of Argyll.

Ardfillayne Hotel
West Bay
Dunoon
Argyll
PA23 7QJ
Scotland
Tel: (0369) 2267
Fax: (0369) 2501

ARGYLL HOTEL

The beautiful island of Iona with its brilliant waters, white sands and clear light has inspired poets, painters and pilgrims for centuries. The Argyll Hotel, facing the sea with its lawn running down to the shore, is also designed to inspire its guests.

Built as an Inn in 1868, the hotel now has nineteen bedrooms, and a spacious dining room looking over the Sound of Iona to the hills of Mull and Erraid. The very special atmosphere is created by unrivalled hospitality and comfort. Original paintings, etchings and antique furniture are part of the ambience - even a 19th century landscape mural above the fireplace - in payment for the artist's hotel bill!

The hotel serves real home cooking, freshly prepared and using its own organically grown vegetables. Dishes include local produce such as wild Mull salmon, venison, Scottish lamb, Tobermory smoked trout and cheeses. Early morning teas, lunches and home baked afternoon teas are available upon request.

Only a quarter of a mile from the famous Iona Abbey which dates back to the eleventh century, the Argyll Hotel is an ideal place in which to enjoy the natural beauty and tranquillity of this sacred and remarkable island.

Argyll Hotel
Isle of Iona
Argyll
Tel: (06817) 334

ASHFORD CASTLE

An historic Irish castle, dating back to the 13th century, Ashford is now one of the finest hotels in the world.

Enter the main reception hall and the feeling of genuine history is matched only by the warmth of the welcome. Solid oak beams and wood panelling reflect a more formal age, but the most modern facilities and comforts are reassuring signs that Ashford is very much a hotel of today. And it's that same sense of elegant luxury which has entitled Ashford to host former US Presidents, European royalty and international celebrities.

For the past three years, Ashford Castle has been nominated 'Best Hotel In Ireland' by Egon Ronay. Experience the finest food and wine in the George V dining room or in the Connaught Room gourmet restaurant where the most fastidious palate is treated to the exquisite delights of French cuisine.

Standing on the shore of Lough Corrib, Ireland's second-largest lake, it's no surprise that Ashford offers its guests some of the most sporting salmon, trout, pike and perch fishing in the West of Ireland. But if golfing is more your bag, the hotel grounds comfortably accommodate Ashford's own 9-hole golf course - and golf clubs are available. For variety and an even stiffer challenge two additional courses are less than fifty miles away. From November 1st, shots of a different kind abound as hunters go in search of duck and pheasant; with unlimited rough shooting.

With its spacious grounds offering their own calming air of quiet it's no surprise that Ashford is consistently chosen by national and international corporations and organisations for conferences and management get-togethers.

Seven centuries since the first brick was laid, the setting, atmosphere and discreet luxury have made Ashford Castle more than a unique hotel. It's an experience.

Ashford Castle
Cong
Co. Mayo
Ireland
Tel: (010 353 92) 46003
Fax: (010 353 92) 46260

BANTRY HOUSE

Bantry House, overlooking Bantry Bay in Co.Cork, has one of the most beautiful settings anywhere in the British Isles. Owned by the White family since 1739, it was the seat of the 4 Earls of Bantry (1816-1891) and in 1945 was the first house in Ireland to be opened to the public on a full-time basis.

Bantry House contains furniture, paintings and other objets d'art collected mainly by Richard White, 2nd Earl of Bantry, on his extensive travels in Europe in the 19th century. He was also responsible for laying out the formal gardens. Now being restored, these were once rightly described as 'the Second Earl's first love'. With its Tea Room and Craft Shop, Bantry House is open all year. Admission to house and grounds is free to residents.

Both East and West Wings of Bantry House provide guest accommodation. In the East Wing are 4 double and 2 twin rooms, all with bathrooms en suite and direct-dial telephones.

The West Wing has a 2 room suite on the top floor; a further two twin rooms with a shared bathroom on the 1st floor are especially convenient for families with older children.

Facilities for residents include a sitting room, a billiard room and a balcony TV room overlooking the Italian Garden with its fountain, parterres and 'stairway to the sky'.

The Dining Room offers a full Irish Breakfast. It also has a wine license, and Dinner is available to residents by special arrangement or when enough people book.

Bantry House
Bantry
Co. Cork
Ireland
Tel: (010 353 27) 50047
Fax: (010 353 27) 50795

BARNSDALE LODGE HOTEL

Set in the heart of the ancient county of Rutland, amid unspoiled countryside, Barnsdale Lodge Hotel overlooks the ripply expanse of Rutland Water, Europe's largest man-made lake. Although the Hotel is housed within a restored 17th century farmhouse, the atmosphere and style distinctively echo the Edwardian era. This theme follows throughout, from the traditional high standards of courteous service to the furnishings - chaise longues and plump upholstered chairs. Traditional English cuisine and fine wines are served in the 3 Edwardian style dining rooms. The silver trolley of Prime Roast Beef is always available. Elevenses, buttery lunches, afternoon teas and suppers may be taken in the Bar, Drawing Rooms, or the Courtyard.

The 17 bedrooms (4 on the ground floor), each attractively furnished and with en suite facilities, colour TV, direct dial telephone, and self contained beverage unit, evoke a mood of relaxing comfort. Baby listening service and safe play area for younger visitors.

Residential (24 hour delegate rates) and day conference facilities available for up to 200 delegates with a full package of visual aids etc.

The Barn Suite (furnished as a luxury marquee) can accommodate up to 220 wedding reception guests with smaller suites available for up to 60.

Nearby places of interest include: Belton House, Rockingham Castle, Grantham with its famous church, Uppingham (Uppingham-in-Bloom), Oakham's famous 12th Century Castle with a unique collection of horse-shoes; Shakespeare at Tolethorpe Hall in the summer season; 1 hour passenger cruises on the 'Rutland Belle' from Whitwell Creek.

Barnsdale Lodge is situated on the north shore of Rutland Water where all manner of water sports are available as well as horse riding; a 350 acre Nature Reserve is within an easy drive; Clay Pigeon Shooting at competitive rates. See comprehensive details of Rutland Water's activities as described in the text of our sister hotel, Normanton Park.

Proprietors: Robert Reid and the Hon. Thomas Noel

Sister Hotel to Normanton Park.

Barnsdale Lodge Hotel
Exton Avenue
Oakham
Rutland LE15 8AH
Tel: (0572) 724678
Fax: (0572) 724961

BEECHLEAS

Situated in the pretty market town of Wimborne Minster, Beechleas, recently awarded 2 AA red stars and a rosette, is a truly wonderful place to stay when savouring the delights and treasures of Wessex and Dorset. Being Grade II listed this Georgian market town house hotel has been tastefully restored in keeping with the character of Georgian times, with all the rooms having luxurious en suite bathroom.

As well as elegantly furnished bedrooms with all the home comforts there are cosy beamed coach house bedrooms which create an ambience of the past but still allow the added comforts we enjoy.

In the colourful months of Autumn you can enjoy an open fire in the lovely dining room and in spring and summer the conservatory is a delight.

Sample gastronomical delights from the menu which is genuine English cooking with a little French influence, all cooked the traditional way in the Aga oven. The majority of food is made from naturally reared or grown produce, supplied by Hockeys Farm at Fordingbridge.

You shall certainly not be stuck for things to do and see. Exclusive Thomas Hardy country personal tours can be arranged by Range Rover with the luxury of a local guide. The walks in the Purbeck Hills or New Forest are wonderful as is the exploration of coastal coves. For the more active, sailing can be arranged by local seamen. Whatever you decide to do your stay at Beechleas will definitely make it memorable.

Beechleas
Poole Road
Wimborne Minster
Dorset BH21 1QA
Tel: (0202) 841684

BIGGIN HALL HOTEL

A thousand feet above sea level, amidst the wooded valleys, heather clad moorlands, timeless market towns and charming villages of the Peak District National Park, rests the Biggin Hall Hotel. As a Grade II listed building the renovations have taken nothing from the original character; in fact many of the stone mullioned leaded windows have only recently seen daylight again after their obliteration against the window taxes of the 1790s.

The rooms are spacious and furnished with fascinating antiques. In addition to the exclusive Master Suite there are three double bedrooms with en-suite facilities and two single rooms sharing an adjoining bathroom. Two sitting rooms provide guests with the choice of colour T.V. or magnificent open stone fireplace. Only thirty yards from the main house are two recently converted 18th-century stone buildings, now comprising of six self-contained 'studio' apartments and two 2-roomed suites, each with private bathrooms; along with amenities such as colour T.V. and tea making facilities, guests here also enjoy the facilities of the main house.

Dining is a special pleasure with open fire, excellent, traditional home-cooked food and a selection of carefully chosen fine wines. Much of the food is locally grown with the emphasis on free range wholefoods, prized for their delicious natural flavour.

The beauty of the Derbyshire Peak District is one of the splendours of England; from gentle rambles by quiet rivers to the challenges of fell-walking it has long had a special appeal to lovers of the outdoors in the off-season Autumn and Winter period.

Biggin Hall Hotel
Biggin
Buxton
Derbyshire
Tel: (0298) 84451
Fax: (0298) 84681

BILBROUGH MANOR

Whether you are enjoying the Sport at York's famous 'Champagne Course' or visiting our charming city and countryside at any time of year you will find Bilbrough manor your perfect House in the Country, complete with a butler to attend to your every need and a chef whose consummate flair has brought him major awards and an international reputation.

Standing in wooded grounds extending to 100 acres, the Manor was the ancestral home of the prominent Fairfax Family, the most famous of whom, General 'Black Tom' Fairfax, commander of Cromwell's New Model Army, is buried in the churchyard next door. The Manor House and grounds have been extensively refurbished to create one of the finest Country House Hotels in the North of England: few could believe the transformation that has been wrought by the resident proprietors, the Bell family and their team of craftsmen. Every aspect of the gracious stone mansion has been enhanced and the considerable new work involved was matched perfectly to the old to provide a setting of mellow panelling, warming fires and imaginative soft furnishings, ideally suited to comfortable relaxation, or indeed executive business meetings.

Accolades have been heaped on Bilbrough Manor from all directions; from appreciative guests, loath to leave the log fires and attentive butler, from the present Lord Fairfax and other dignita-

ries, and from the international Press, including Egon Ronay's Guide.

So what is Bilbrough's secret? It is evident that no expense has been spared in providing every comfort for visitors, who indeed are treated as family guests. Fixtures and fittings are of the highest quality, every bedroom is en suite and individually furnished with impeccable taste. The dining room is oak panelled and elegant, the public rooms sumptuous and magnificent, at the same time exuding an atmosphere of warmth and welcome.

Every comfort is catered for, encouraging guests to relax, unwind and enjoy to the full this taste of gracious country living. Bilbrough has the best of both worlds, only 3 miles West from the City of York but situated in an attractive conservation village and enjoying glorious views over the Vale of York.

With such surroundings and with such conscientious care for their guests' welfare, how could the Bells fail to make Bilbrough a resounding success.

The promise they saw has been fulfilled. Bilbrough Manor's reputation is only just beginning, but it will go on to be one of the legendary hotels in the land.

Bilbrough Manor
Bilbrough
Nr York YO2 3PH
Tel: (0937) 834002

BLACKHEATH HOUSE

Blackheath House is a fine old Rectory built by Frederick Harvey, the Earl of Bristol in 1791 for the Parish of Aghadowey. It is a listed building with an interesting history set in two acres of landscaped gardens.

Once the home of Archbishop William Alexander, whose wife Cecil the poetess wrote 'There is a green hill far away' and 'All things bright and beautiful'.

In Winter, residents can enjoy a glass of hot punch in the drawing room by a welcoming fire and in the Summer can have a cool drink in the gardens.

Each of the spacious bedrooms is individually styled for comfort with bathrooms, colour television and tea/coffee making facilities.

Blackheath House is situated in the beautiful countryside of Aghadowey, once the centre of flax growing for the linen industry, whose rivers are famous for salmon and trout. Shooting and fishing can be arranged and there are excellent equestrian facilities nearby.

Aghadowey is only 7 miles from Coleraine and 11 miles from the Causeway Coast with its magnificent coastline, sandy beaches, picturesque seaside resorts and eight golf courses. We have special rates with local Golf Courses and can arrange sea fishing.

There are many interesting places to visit in the area including the Giants Causeway, Carrick-a-Rede Rope Bridge, Dunluce Castle and Old Bushmills Distillery - the home of the oldest whiskey in the world.

MACDUFF'S RESTAURANT - The Restaurant situated in the cellars of the house is renowned for its excellent food, friendly service and warm and intimate atmosphere.

Macduff's offers Country House cooking at its best using freshly grown produce, local game, salmon and seafood.

From an extensive and interesting wine list you can choose a wine from the original wine vault.

Blackheath House
112, Killeague Road
Blackhill
Coleraine
Co. Londonderry BT51 4HH
Tel: (0265) 868433

THE BLACK LION

Situated on the green, in this fully restored 17th century coaching inn, you will find a family run hotel where nothing is too much trouble. A veritable home form home, famed for its Countryman restaurant.

Classically influenced, mouthwatering dishes are freshly made to your order by Stephen, who trained at the Dorchester Hotel. He uses fresh locally grown Suffolk produce, seasoned with herbs cultivated in his own garden. There are two menus at lunch and dinner to stimulate your tastebuds, and these are changed each month. To compliment this epicural delight, Janet his wife, can offer you a selection from 150 carefully chosen wines. Apart from her long standing interest in the subject, she has been awarded several higher certificates in wine, to give you expert guidance in making the perfect choice. After an agonising decision of which luscious dessert to choose, comes the cheeseboard. Expect to find at least 14 different cheeses, a speciality of the house. Retire from the intimate dining room to relax in the informal and delightful surroundings of either of the two lounges, equipped with books, magazines and games. Perhaps even a sip of liqueur from a selection of over 100.

And so to bed. From this vantage point, there are panoramic views of the hamlet of Long Melford and you can be forgiven for thinking that you have stepped back in time a couple of centuries. Each of the 10 spacious bedrooms are equipped with its own private bathroom, direct dial telephone, colour TV, radio and tea and coffee facilities. If you are lucky you could be sleeping soundly in one of the two four poster beds or the mahogany half tester. There is a family suite, and well behaved children are catered for. Dogs are accepted by appointment.

Long Melford is famous for its quaint architecture and a wealth of antique shops. A stones throw away are two country houses, 15th century Kentwell Hall, restored lovingly to its original state and National Trust Melford Hall, the family seat of the Hyde-Parkers, who are still in residence. Other places of interest nearby are the wool villages of Lavenham, historic Bury St Edmunds, winner of 'England in Bloom', Sudbury, the home of Gainsborough, horse racing at Newmarket, a preserved steam railway at Castle Headingham and Constable country.

The Black Lion Hotel and Countryman Restaurant is featured in all recognised guides and the Errington family wish you a warm and pleasant stay.

The Black Lion Hotel
The Green
Long Melford
Suffolk CO10 9DN
Tel: (0787) 312356

BLACKWATER LODGE HOTEL

Blackwater Lodge is a world-renowned retreat for anglers, nestling in a picturesque location overlooking the Munster Blackwater from the south bank. It caters especially for angling parties, with all requirements catered for including a tackle shop, drying room and facilities for in-house smoking, freezing or marinading of your catch, together with all the information and friendly advice you might need from the expert staff here.

The theme at Blackwater Lodge is definitely 'fishy' with the emphasis on catching salmon. There are information folders available on your allocated beat, how to get there and how to fish it, as well as angling videos to view in the lounge bar. You will fish on private beats which are rotated daily and average about three quarters of a mile in length. The Blackwater is considered to be Ireland's premier salmon river with the best fishing between Lismore and Mallow, of which some fourteen miles are preserved exclusively for your own use when you are fishing at Blackwater Lodge.

If you feel you need a diversion from all that salmon fishing, the Lodge is ideally situated for a variety of activities the beautiful, scenic drives through Blackwater Valley and the Knockmealdown and Galtree Mountains. The Blackwater estuary and Youghal's long sandy beaches are nearby too. Other facilities in the area include tennis, swimming and golf at Lismore and Fermoy. Riding and pony trekking can also be arranged at various locations in the surrounding area.

The Lodge has 21 bedrooms. Ten are in the main building the rest in annexes, ideal for small parties . There is a cosy A La Carte Restaurant and a spacious Fishermans Lounge Bar. The Lodge can also organise self-catering accommodation in cottages closeby, combined with rod reservations, ferry tickets and car hire if required.

Whether you are an experienced fisherman or just here with 'fishy' friends, you are assured a special break in this beautiful part of Ireland.

Blackwater Lodge Hotel
'The Complete Angler Centre'
Upper Ballyduff
Co Waterford
Ireland
Tel: (010 353 58) 60235
Fax: (010 353 58) 60162

BUCKLAND-TOUT-SAINTS HOTEL

1990 was the tri-centenary of the restoration of Buckland-Tout-Saints; William, Prince of Orange and Mary were then on the throne of England. Even in 1690 this grand Estate had been in existence 600 years before being extensively restored by Sir John Southcote. Now, located within 7 acres of beautiful parkland in the heart of the South Devon countryside, Buckland-Tout-Saints offers you a tradition that has grown out of the lavish Country House entertaining of bygone days, when the owner of a Country Estate would invite his guests down to be wined and dined and waited upon. Today, that feeling of being a privileged guest in a private house, in an atmosphere that is elegant yet informal, is something Buckland-Tout-Saints tries hard to preserve for you.

Only 20 miles from the City of Plymouth, and 30 minutes drive from the A38 dual-carriageway which links directly onto the M5 motorway at Exeter the Hotel is conveniently located. It offers many country house pursuits including croquet and its own Putting Green. Bird-watching, canoeing, clay-pigeon shooting, fishing, golf, horse riding, hot air-ballooning, sailing, squash, surfing, swimming, tennis and wind-surfing can all be arranged by the hotel with prior notice. The Dartmouth Golf and Country Club is close by, it is a beautiful course with a fine club house and many modern facilities, the hotel will be pleased to arrange your days golfing.

Plymouth attracts many major theatrical productions and tickets can be arranged - with prior notice - at the Theatre Royal.

Buckland-Tout-Saints Hotel
Goveton
Kingsbridge
Devon TQ7 2DS
Tel: (0548) 853055
Fax: (0548) 856261

CALCOT MANOR

If, in the course of your everyday life, you long for the peace of rolling hills, fields of flower-filled hedgerows, open log fires, delicious meals taken in friendly company and comforts to console even the most jaded, then the spirit of Calcot Manor has already invaded your life.

Originally part of Kingswood Abbey, founded by the Cistercians in 1158, this farmhouse and its beautiful stone barns and stables stands in one of the most unusual parts of England. Part of its estate includes a 14th century tithe-barn that is among the oldest in the country and yet further proof that time here really does stand still.

At Calcot you're in the very heart of the Cotswolds, nestling among one of the richest areas for the simple delights of touring and exploring; taking along, of course, a delicious hamper from the Manor. Staying at the hotel still leaves the choice of heated outdoor swimming pool fringed by evergreens and brilliant shrubbery, croquet on the lawn, or simply a sunny or shady retreat for reading, dreaming, or even working, before lunch in the light airy restaurant or on the terrace overlooking the lush green countryside.

Dinner is a civilised affair with a consistently surprising and delightful menu that makes full use of the fresh, local produce, prepared and presented by the highly covetable chef; the formal, but relaxed, atmosphere extends out for coffee and drinks on the terrace or elegant sitting rooms.

At the end of a long day the bedrooms at Calcot wait ready to welcome you; each one has private bathroom and its own unique character and decor echoing a particular aspect of the region. The Master Bedroom is particularly enticing, with its canopied and draped four-poster bed and whirlpool bath.

The area around Calcot has much to offer the sportsman. For the golfer two breathtakingly beautiful courses are mere minutes away and, of course, special arrangements can be made for guests, these include a two or three day golf package with green fees and tuition with a local professional. There is racing at nearby Bath, Cheltenham and Newbury, along with horse trials at Badminton and Gatcombe. Clay pigeon shooting is available in the hotel grounds, including tuition, while the fisherman has the choice of coarse in the local lakes or trout fishing in the chalk streams of the Wyle and Avon. The hotel can also arrange cycling, walking, watersports, ballooning and gliding, as well as offering help with the numerous Arts Festivals and theatres in the region, including the famous Theatre Royal at nearby Bath.

Calcot Manor also offers a variety of special-interest breaks, ranging from antiques and country gardens to a day with the resident chef; details are available on request.

Calcot Manor
Nr Tetbury
Gloucestershire GL8 8YJ
Tel: (0666) 890391
Fax: (0666) 890394

THE CASTLETOWN GOLF LINKS

Set on Fort Island with breathtaking views across the Irish Sea, the Castletown Golf Links Hotel's very own 18 hole Championship Golf Course offers you a challenging course with the finest facilities and service to match.

The Castletown Golf Links Hotel occupies pride of place in the centre of a wild and beautiful course with the first tee directly opposite the hotel's entrance.

The Airport is only five minutes away from The Hotel. From landing on the Island, you can be collected by our courtesy car, taken to The Hotel, checked in and be on the first tee within 20 minutes.

The course offers a challenge from the beginner to the more seasoned player. Holes such as the 8th - known as 'The Road' running parallel with the main shore line driveway leading to The Hotel, the 17th - christened 'The Gully', with a 200 yard drive across the Irish Sea, are so memorable, they will surely require a post-mortem afterwards in the 19th!

The Hotel itself has been refurbished and now all bedrooms and public areas offer elegance and a luxuriously high standard of comfort that will undoubtedly appeal to the most discerning traveller. Golfer or not, the complete enjoyment experience awaits you - indoor pool, saunas, snooker room and solariums are here to pamper you, or a walk around the course and the never ending countryside has to be given time out.

As the sun goes down over the Island's mountains, enjoy the fine wines and inspirational cuisine in one of our two restaurants. Whether you choose to dine in the main restaurant or L'Orangerie, you will be sure to delve into the very best cuisine - an experience all of its own, as the Islanders will recommend.

Afterwards - the choice is your own. Relax in one of our three bars, watch satellite TV, or let us whisk you away to our sister hotel in Douglas where you can dance the night away at Toff's Night Club, or enjoy the only immediate and complimentary membership Casino in Europe.

The Isle of Man and Castletown Golf Links Hotel and golf course, have to be seen to be believed.

The Castletown Golf Links Hotel
Deryhaven
Isle of Man
Tel: (0624) 822201
Fax: (0624) 824633

CHANNINGS

Walk through the quiet cobbled streets of Edinburgh's city centre, just a little way from the castle and push open the door of a row of five beautifully maintained Edwardian townhouses. These, together, make up Channings, a privately owned hotel with cosy, old-fashioned clublike atmosphere right in heart of historic Edinburgh. The style of Channings is rarely found today; a feeling of classic care from the peaceful, fire-lit lounges to any of the 45 individually designed guest rooms, several of which offer wonderful panoramic views over the Firth of Forth to the hills of Fife.

The Brasserie is one of the popular haunts of the city. A restaurant that prides itself on honest food and personable service. After dinner, the bar welcomes you with an interesting and highly tempting range of malt whiskies and the odd game of chess. In the warmer months, take your lunch outside where the hotel's terraced garden captures the heat of the sun.

The quiet, classical feel of the hotel makes it the ideal venue for a corporate dinner or small conference but it is more than homely enough for any private meeting too. Any such gathering can be held in one of seven different rooms, including the oak-panelled Library and the Kingsleigh Suite.

For a rewarding afternoon's browsing through local and not-so-local history, the hotel has an absorbing collection of antique prints, furniture, object d'art, periodicals and books, or wander through the streets of the Edinburgh itself and soak up the atmosphere and culture of this beautiful city.

Take a short trip into the surrounding countryside to the famous golf clubs of Scotland. It was at nearby Muirfield where the Honourable Company of Edinburgh Golfers was founded in 1744, on the southern tip of the Firth of Forth, the oldest golf club in history.

Channings
South Learmonth Gardens
Edinburgh
Scotland EH4 1EZ
Tel: 031-315 2226
Fax: 031-332 9631

THE CHELTENHAM PARK HOTEL

The Cheltenham Park Hotel is a beautiful Regency Manor House set in nine acres of landscaped gardens with a natural trout lake and waterfalls. The hotel has superb views over the Leckhampton Hills and the Lilleybrook Golf Course.

This luxury hotel was recently totally refurbished and extended to 154 luxuriously appointed bedrooms. These include the Presidential Suite and Executive Rooms which command superb views over the attractively landscaped gardens, with their meandering walkways, gentle waterfalls, romantic arbours and classically inspired gazebo.

The Lakeside Restaurant offers the best of modern English cuisine with a choice from either our Table d'Hote or our a la Carte menus, using only the freshest of produce. Your meal will be complemented with a selection of fine wines from our cellars.

There are two bars to choose from; the Tulip Bar with its marble fireplaces, original oak panelling and large patio overlooking the golf course, or the congenial Lakeside Bar with its terraces down to the lake.

The Cheltenham Park hotel is only two miles from the town centre and is therefore only a short drive from the Racecourse. Access to and from all parts of the country is quick and easy as Cheltenham Spa lies at the hub of the country's motorway/dual carriageway network with excellent rail and coach services as well as its own airport at Staverton.

The hotels location lends itself to ease of access to a wide range of attractions including the famous Pittville Pump Rooms in Cheltenham where the spa waters may be taken and the Gloucester Dockland areas which have recently undertaken major works to restore them to their former grandeur.

This beautiful hotel is right next door to the well known Lilleybrook Golf Course and only minutes away from Cotswold Hills Golf Course - a perfect golfing location. Alternatively a day at the races, a luxury break away from it all, or a peaceful environment for a business meeting, the Cheltenham Park Hotel is the ideal choice.

Cheltenham Park Hotel
Cirencester Road
Charlton Kings
Cheltenham GL53 8EA
Tel: (0242) 222021
Fax: (0242) 226935

CHEWTON GLEN

In verdant parkland on the southern edge of the New Forest stands a magnificent country house hotel. Chewton Glen and its combination of splendour, elegance and comfort affords the discerning visitor every amenity they could wish for. The public areas are beautiful decorated, such as the light, airy main sitting room looking out onto the garden and the cosy inner lounge with its marble fireplace.

Our suites and double bedrooms have bathrooms ensuite, colour television, direct dial telephone and radio. They are furnished with antiques, attractive painted furniture and luxurious fabrics.

Guests can stroll around the thirty acre grounds or play tennis, croquet, golf or alternatively bathe in the heated outdoor swimming pool or off the shingle beach nearby. The hotel has an indoor tennis centre, health club with indoor pool, and its own nine-hole golf course.

Once the appetite has been whetted, the Marryat Room, the Hotel's Michelin-rosetted restaurant offers sumptuous fare. Our distinguished modern only by the quality of the service.

To find us leave the A35 on the Walkford Road and once through Walkford turn left down Chewton Farm Road.

Your stay will be a pleasant one; we hope it will be a long one. Whether you have enjoyed a day at the races or a round of golf at one of the many nearby golf courses we know that Chewton Glen will make your day that extra special.

Chewton Glen
New Milton
Hampshire

Tel: (0425) 275341
Fax: (0425) 272310

COMLONGON CASTLE

Situated some 10 miles from Dumfries and 14 from Gretna this ancient castle was built by the Murrays and played its part in Border warfare. The present castle dates from 1450 and it has one of the most massive Keeps in Scotland with walls 13 feet (4 metres) thick. Adjoining the castle is a fine mansion of Scottish Baronial style built by the Earls of Mansfield.

The magnificent Great Hall is oak panelled with displays of weapons and armour. Bedrooms are en suite, some with whirlpool baths and 4 poster beds, including our 2 Bridal Chambers.

Surrounding the castle are 50 acres of gardens, woodlands and park. Currently new water gardens and a walled medieval herb garden are under renovation.

Each evening guests are given a unique candle-lit tour of the medieval Keep visiting vaulted cellars, Laird's chamber, dungeon with Pit and much more. The history of the castle is graphically told together with the story of our Ghost, the Green Lady who fell from the battlements in 1560.

After the tour guests may enjoy a dinner by candle light with a wide choice of Scottish fayre served in the oak panelled dining room.

Over the centuries many marriages have taken place in the castle as recorded by the many carved coats of arms or 'wedding stones'. The tradition has been revived since religious ceremonies are frequently conducted in the Laird's Chamber by a Minister of the Church of Scotland. Full details are given in our wedding brochure.

Comlongon Castle
Clarencefield
Dumfries
Scotland DG1 4NA
Tel: (038787) 283
Fax: (038787) 266

CONRAH COUNTRY HOUSE HOTEL

Resting in 22 acres of rolling landscaped grounds and woods the Conrah Country House Hotel is a delightful Mid Wales retreat. Tucked away at the end of a long rhododendron-lined driveway, only minutes from the Cambrian Coast, it commands magnificent views as far north as the Cader Idris mountain range.

Originally the Mansion House to the old Welsh 'Ffosrhydgaled Estate' it now takes pride of place amidst spectacular scenery as a first class hotel.

A crackling log fire often awaits guests in the Drawing Room for afternoon tea and Welsh cakes or pre-dinner drinks, while the quiet Writing Room allows for tranquillity with the vista of surrounding hills.

A drink can also be enjoyed in the Drinks Lounge before an evening of temptation in the Dining Room, where the Conrah chefs pride themselves on offering the finest of Modern Welsh and English dishes, especially with freshly caught salmon and succulent Welsh lamb; all accompanied by fresh vegetables, salads and herbs gathered from the hotel's own kitchen garden, along with the perfect wine from a carefully selected list. There is always an extensive choice for vegetarians, while on good days hampers are available for delicious picnics in the country.

All of the twenty bedrooms have en suite bath or shower rooms, colour television and tea and coffee making facilities.

For the golfing enthusiast details of the ideal mini break golfing packages are available on request. For a different sporting pursuit try tennis, sea fishing or pony trekking - all available locally, while table tennis and croquet are to be enjoyed in the hotel itself. The area abounds in sites of historic interest, along with museums, galleries and superb walking. On your return why not relax with a sauna and cool off with a swim in the private pool, heated as a matter of course, with the addition of roaring log fire in winter.

The Conrah Country House Hotel
Rhydgaled
Chancery
Aberystwyth
Dyfed SY3 4DF
Tel: (0970) 617941
Fax: (0970) 624546

COOPERSHILL

Coopershill is a fine example of a Georgian family mansion. Home to seven generations of the O'Hara family since it was built in 1774, it combines the spaciousness and elegance of an earlier age with the comfort and amenities of today. Five of the seven bedrooms have four poster or canopy beds and all have their own private bathrooms. The rooms retain their original regal dimensions and much of the furniture dates from the time that the house was built.

Guests can relax in front of a log fire in the large and comfortable drawing room. Dinner by candlelight with family silverware and crystal glass, a wide choice of wines and the personal attention of the hosts all add to the special Coopershill atmosphere.

Standing in the centre of a 500 acre estate of farm and woodland, separation from the outside world seems complete. There are many delightful walks and wildlife is abundant and undisturbed.

We have five 18 hole links courses within an hours drive of Coopershill; the up and coming Enniscrone course to the south, Bundoran and the Donegal course at Murvagh to the north, and the closest, Strandhill just 14 miles away. But perhaps the pick of them, the County Sligo Golf Club at Rosses Point, where the Home Internationals were played in 1991, is worth more than just one visit.

Long uncrowded beaches, spectacular mountains and hills for walking, lakes and megalithic monuments all add to make Sligo, which is Yeats' country, an ideal place to visit.

Coopershill is two miles from the village of Riverstown and 13 miles from Sligo town, signposted clearly from the Sligo to Dublin route N4.

We are served by two airports; Sligo Airport is 15 miles away with daily flights to Dublin; Knock Airport is 30 miles away with daily flights to Luton, North of London. Car hire is available at both Sligo and Knock.

Coopershill
Riverstown
Co. Sligo
Ireland
Tel: (010 353 71) 65108
Fax: (010 353 71) 65466

CORSEMALZIE HOUSE HOTEL

Corsemalzie House Hotel, a secluded country mansion is set in the heart of the picturesque countryside of the Machars (moors) of Wigtownshire, away from the rigours of city life. Relax in a setting which is hard to beat, the only noise to upset the tranquillity are the cries of the whaup (curlew) and the babbling burn. The seasonal changes create a different back-drop for the hotel, making Corsemalzie a delight to stay at whatever time of year is your preference.

The gastronome will find Corsemalzie has a great deal to offer, with dishes created using only the finest ingredients carefully and enthusiastically supervised by the proprietor Mr Peter McDougall. Fresh and local produce is used whenever possible.

This attention to detail is carried throughout the hotel with Mr and Mrs McDougall ensuring that your stay will not only be memorable for the cuisine but also for the little things that make the difference between a good hotel and a great hotel.

If you can drag yourself away from this comfort, the surrounding area has much to offer, with riding pony trekking and walking, some superb golf on your doorstep, a whole host of 9 hole courses, with 18 hole courses at Portpatrick, Glenluce where the hotel pays half your green fees, Stranraer and a little further afield at the famous Turnberry Links course.

For the game sportsmen, shooting and fishing are here in an abundance, Mr McDougall will personally organise and assist you shooting for pheasant, grouse, partridge, duck geese, snipe woodcock, rabbits and hares in the hotel grounds and neighbouring estates amounting to some 8,000 acres. The hotel has exclusive salmon and trout fishing rights on four and a half miles of the River Bladnoch and five miles on the River Tarff. Fishing can also be organised in the Mazie Burn. A gillie is available for most of the season to advise and assist wherever needed.

Corsemalzie House Hotel
Port William
Newton Stewart
Wigtownshire
Scotland DG8 9RL
Tel: (098 886) 254
Fax: (098 886) 213

THE COTTAGE IN THE WOOD HOTEL

The Cottage in the Wood Hotel and Restaurant has one of the finest views in Britain. Built into the hillside it is perched high on the Malvern Hills, like an eyrie. The magnificent vista below unfolds across 30 miles of the Severn Vale to Bredon Hill and beyond to the Cotswold Hills, which form the horizon.

The hotel consists of a cluster of three white painted buildings all sharing the view below, yet set in a wood stretching towards the hilltop.

You can walk directly from the hotel's own seven acres onto over 100 miles of paths and tracks that criss-cross the nine-mile range of the Malvern Hills.

The main hotel with eight bedrooms is housed in a Georgian Dower House together with the lounge bar, lounge and elegant dining room. In Beech Cottage, about 70 yards from the main hotel, are four peaceful 'cottagey' bedrooms whilst just beyond is the Coach House, restored to make eight further bedrooms, all front facing. And, as if to make up for being slightly smaller, with the most magnificent view of all.

John and Sue Pattin bought the hotel in 1987 and have lavished it with a lot of 'tender loving care' as John would tell you. He hates the regimented formality prevalent in the industry so he and his wife have set out to create a comfortable hotel with warmth and atmosphere which allows you to relax - whether for just a brief respite for a night or for several, whether on business or for pleasure. Before becoming an hotelier John was a frequent user of hotels so he is in a sense a self confessed

'poacher turned gamekeeper!' John added 'hotels mostly lack soul, so we have set out to be individual ... the antithesis of the chain hotel'.

The Cottage in the Wood has twenty bedrooms, all of differing sizes and decor, some with four posters. Most rooms face the front and the spectacular view. All are en-suite, of course, and have many little 'extras'. The hotel's restaurant is well known and widely regarded and one of John's loves, wine, is shown by a list of around 200 wines from Argentina to China. In addition there is a Boardroom facility for up to 14 delegates.

The Malvern Hills are themselves in an area of outstanding natural beauty. 'Rural civilisation' is how Sue sums it up. Malvern makes a superb touring base from which to see and do some of the many things in the area. There are no less than three cathedral cities - Worcester, Hereford and Gloucester - the Wye Valley, the Forest of Dean, Stratford and Shakespeare Country, the Cotswolds and the rural charm of Herefordshire and the Welsh Marches are all within easy reach. In addition there are some fine racecourses, including Cheltenham and immediately beneath the hotel, the Worcestershire Golf Course and the Three Counties Showground which stages events all year round from agricultural shows to car rallies to antique sales.

Special inclusive breaks are available for two nights or more, all seven days of the week and virtually all year round. Why start your break on a Friday? Miss the traffic and choose any other day.

The Cottage in the Wood Hotel
Holywell Road
Malvern Wells
Worcestershire WR14 4LG
Tel: (0684) 573487
Fax: (0684) 560662

CRABWALL MANOR

Crabwall Manor is one of the few hotels in Britain where you will feel totally at home as soon as you arrive. The moment you catch a glimpse of the distinctive turrets, rosy with the welcoming warmth of Cheshire brick, nestled against the backdrop of rich pastureland, the magic of Crabwall Manor begins to work on you.

Set in eleven acres of park and farmland, yet only two miles from Chester, the Manor was renovated and opened as a hotel in May 1987, but it still retains the original Tudor/Gothic castellated frontage dating back to the 16th century. The renovation has been so subtly and sympathetically carried out that it is impossible to distinguish the original from the new.

The menus at Crabwall Manor change weekly and offer only fresh seasonal produce. For lunch or dinner there is a table d'hote menu, complemented in the evening with an extensive a la carte menu. The kitchens have a reputation for creative, innovative modern British cooking, drawing on many interna-

tional influences. The wine list, consisting of some 500 wines, has been carefully assembled.

The decor at Crabwall Manor is timeless, the light airy lounges boasting subtle fabrics which are carried through into all the bedrooms. Crabwall has 42 twin or double bedrooms and 6 suites to choose from, each individually designed with special touches to make your stay even more memorable.

Crabwall Manor is within easy reach of the famous Grand National race course, the Oulton Park Motor Racing circuit, and some of the best golf courses in Britain. If you love country pursuits, you'll feel instantly at home. If you fancy your hand at any sport, the staff will cater to individual requirements with great pleasure.

Crabwall has been awarded 3 stars by the AA, 4 black stars by the RAC, 5 Crown highly commended ETB rating and is part of the 'Small Luxury Hotels of the World'.

Crabwall Manor
Parkgate Road
Mollington
Chester
CH1 6NE
Tel: (0244) 851666
Fax: (0244) 851400

CRAIGELLACHIE HOTEL

One of the most beautiful villages in Moray, Craigellachie, lies at the confluence of the Fiddich and Spey rivers in a picturesque setting equal only to the sumptuous and elegant Victorian hotel itself. Only one hour's drive from the airports of Aberdeen and Inverness, the Craigellachie is a haven of highland hospitality set in a spectacular countryside - unspoilt, wild and beautiful and ideal for all kinds of modern sporting activities.

According to the season you can play tennis, ski, ride horseback or mountain bike along forest and mountain trails and fish for salmon or brown trout.

And then there's the golf. The Craigellachie offers a unique opportunity to enjoy a holiday in the land where golf was born, with a choice of links, moor or parkland courses all within a short drive of the hotel. whatever your handicap, there's a course her to challenge your skill. We can arrange golf club hire and private tuition by professionals at selected clubs.

After sampling the variety of outdoor pursuits or one of the many golf courses in this beautiful part of Scotland, it's always a pleasure to return to the Craigellachie and sit beside the glowing embers of a real log fire in the hall or one of the comfortable lounges. An equally warm welcome will await you in the Quaich cocktail bar and when it's time to dine, the Ben Aigan Restaurant offers a tempting menu in the hearty tradition of the finest Scottish cuisine. Here, you can savour the delights of our culinary excellence (which, according to season, feature prime local produce from sea and countryside) and then linger over coffee in the drawing room before retiring to the comfort and luxury of one of 30 splendidly appointed bedrooms. Each has its own en suite bath/shower, direct-dial telephone, radio remote-control colour television and special hospitality features. And for your further enjoyment you can make use of our library, billiards room, exercise room, sauna, solarium and rod room.

Here, at the Craigellachie, all the amenities of an international class hotel have been tastefully incorporated to retain all the original charm of a delightful Scottish country house.

Craigellachie Hotel
Craigellachie
Speyside
Banffshire AB38 9SR
Scotland
Tel: (0340) 881204
Fax: (0340) 881253

CRINGLETIE HOUSE HOTEL

Cringletie is a distinguished mansion which has retained the warm atmosphere of a private country house. It is set well back from the Peebles/Edinburgh road (A703) in 28 acres of garden and woodland, in peaceful surroundings. Only 20 miles from Edinburgh, it is an excellent centre.

All rooms are tastefully decorated and furnished to a high standard of comfort, with colour televisions, direct dial telephones and en-suite facilities. There are magnificent views from all rooms. The restaurant has been consistently recommended since 1971.

Recommended by Johansen; Egon Ronay; The A.A.; The R.A.C.; Signpost; Ashley Courtenay and other guidebooks.

Cringletie House Hotel
Peebles EH45 8PL
Tel: (07213) 233
Fax: (07213) 244

TRAQUAIR HOUSE

CROSBY LODGE

Crosby Lodge was purchased by the Sedgwick family in 1970, and has been skilfully restored and converted into the romantically beautiful Country House Hotel it is today.

The front door opens into an enormous welcoming log fire, with an oak staircase leading up to the bedrooms. Each bedroom is decorated and designed individually, with en suite bathrooms. Various period pieces, such as half-tester beds, have been retained, whilst at the same time the hotel provides first class modern amenities. Crosby Lodge has an established reputation for excellence and the large spacious rooms, full of antiques and elegantly furnished, welcome guests with a comfortable and relaxed atmosphere. Overlooking tree-lined parkland, the delightful dining room, with its beamed ceiling, gleaming cutlery and long windows, is a haven for the connoisseur of good food and wine. Deliciously exciting menus feature authentic continental cuisine alongside the very best of traditional British fare. The four course Table d'hote menu has a vast choice and is complimented by a smaller A la carte menu providing such delights as steaks, scampi and Dover sole. The Crosby Lodge sweet trolley is renowned far and wide, and coffee and delicious home-made sweetmeats

can be taken in the charming lounge and cocktail bar. Chef Proprietor Michael Sedgwick produces exciting dishes using fresh, mainly local ingredients, ensuring everything is to the highest standard.

To the visitor, Crosby Lodge offers untold days of pleasure, with the Lake District and Scottish Lowlands so near at hand. Historic Hadrian's Wall, stunning Cumberland and Northumberland country and the ancient border city of Carlisle await the visitor; travelling further afield, yet returning to Crosby Lodge in the evening, one can reach Edinburgh, a city steeped in history and culture. For the golfer the hotel is ideal, with arrangements easily made on the new Riverside Course, only minutes away, or indeed on a variety of courses at Carlisle, Brampton, Penrith and Silloth.

Featured in the Egon Ronay, Michelin, with three AA stars and a British Tourist four crown hotel, Crosby Lodge is fully deserving of the praise it receives. With an emphasis on comfort, relaxation, good food, traditional courtesy and old-fashioned hospitality, Michael and Patricia Sedgwick, son James and staff will ensure that you have a memorable stay and every assistance with your arrangements.

Crosby Lodge
Country House Hotel and Restaurant
Crosby-On-Eden
Carlisle
Cumbria CA6 4QZ
Tel: (0228) 573618
Fax: (0228) 573428

FLOORS CASTLE

THE CROSS KEYS HOTEL

Why not have a break rather than just a day at Kelso Races. Spend a few days with us in the beautiful Scottish Borders and we bet that you'll go home feeling relaxed.

Other activities such as golf and fishing can be arranged and Edinburgh with its shops and theatres is only an hour's drive away.

Our welcoming family hotel offers comfortable en suite accommodation, good food and friendly service.

If all this wins your approval, why not send for more details to:-

For further details contact
B.M. Becattelli
The Cross Keys Hotel
The Square
Kelso TD5 7HL
Tel: (0573) 223303
Fax: (0573) 225792

3 star AA and RAC, 4 Crown STB

CULCREUCH CASTLE

Culcreuch Castle, the home of the Barons of Culcreuch since 1699 and before this the ancestral fortalice of the Galbraiths and indeed Clan Castle of the Galbraith chiefs for over three centuries (1320 to 1630), has now been restored and converted by its present owners into a most comfortable family-run country house hotel, intimately blending the elegance of bygone days with modern comforts and personal service in an atmosphere of friendly informal hospitality. The eight individually decorated and furnished bedrooms all have en suite facilities, colour television and tea and coffee making facilities. Most command uninterrupted and quite unsurpassed views over the 1600 acre parkland grounds, described by the National Trust for Scotland as a 'gem of outstanding beauty', and beyond a kaleidoscope of spectacular scenery of hills, moorlands, lochs, burns and woods comprising the Endrick valley and the Campsie Fells above.

All the public rooms are decorated in period style and furnished with antiques giving the aura and grace of a bygone age. Log fires create warmth and intimacy and the candlelit evening meals in the panelled dining room make for most romantic occasions, well complemented by freshly prepared local produce and a carefully selected wine cellar.

The Loch Lomond, Stirling & Trossachs area offers the visitor a wide and varied range of country activities, including golf, fishing, shooting, water sports, nature study and bird watching, historical research, or simply walking and exploring in stunningly beautiful countryside.

With over 40 golf courses within a 25 mile radius of the Castle, Culcreuch is a golfer's paradise. A special Golfing Brochure is available on request which gives details of the packages available at a large number of these venues.

Especially central for the racing circuit, Culcreuch particularly welcomes the racegoer and those with equestrian interests. Hamilton is only half an hour distant, Ayr an hour and a quarter and Edinburgh and Perth only 55 minutes away. For horse riding enthusiasts, special arrangements can be made with nearby Drumbae Riding Centre for professional instruction in flat or jumping. A special brochure is available on request.

Whether for either business or pleasure, Culcreuch is a most convenient centrally positioned base for visiting Edinburgh (55 minutes by motorway), Glasgow (35 minutes) and Stirling (25 minutes). For business clients there is no comparable venue for entertaining and the Castle specialises in offering its unique facilities for small meetings.

From Autumn to Spring, reduced terms for off-season breaks are offered, together with House Parties over the Christmas and New Year Holidays' and during these cooler months the log fires offer a cheerful welcome on your return from a day out in the Trossachs.

The location of Culcreuch is rural but not isolated, and with the fresh air of the countryside, the space, grace, comfort, good wholesome food and that unique warmth of friendship and hospitality offered from a family run home from home, a stay here is most conducive to shedding the cares and pressures of modern day life and utterly relaxing.

We look forward to your company. — The Haslam Family

Culcreuch Castle
Fintry
Stirlingshire G63 0LW
Tel: (036 086) 228
Fax: (0532) 390093
Telex: 557299

THE CULLEN BAY HOTEL

Set in its own grounds the Cullen Bay Hotel has magnificent views of Cullen Bay, with its long sweep of white sand, and Cullen Golf Course.

Within easy reach are numerous golf courses, and there are opportunities for bowling, fishing, pony-trekking, cycling and bird watching.

Other attractions close by include: the world's only Malt Whisky Trail; Scotland's Fishing Heritage Trail and the Castle Trail, taking in Fyvie, Cawdor and Brodie. There are many gardens and pretty villages to explore as well as coastal and woodland walks and places of interest such as Baxters of Speyside.

All 14 bedrooms have been upgraded and refurbished and now have en suite bathrooms with power showers, individu-ally controlled central heating, remote control colour television, radio, direct-dial telephone, hairdrier and tea and coffee tray.

The hotel's other facilities include the Cullen Bay Restaurant, overlooking the bay; the newly refurbished Verandah Restaurant and Bar with garden patio in the summer and log fire during the winter; a lounge with log fire; and a garden with children's play area. For conferences, dinner dances or weddings we can cater for up to one hundred and fifty guests in the Farskane Function Suite.

At the Cullen Bay you'll enjoy good food using local produce and can choose from an informal bar meal or high tea to a three course dinner from our a la carte menu. All this amidst a friendly atmosphere adds up to an unforgettable stay.

The Cullen Bay Hotel
Cullen
Buckie
Banffshire
AB56 2XA
Tel: (0542) 40432
Fax: (0542) 40900

CULLODEN HOUSE

Culloden House is a handsome Georgian mansion with a tradition of lavish hospitality stretching back hundreds of years. Among its famous visitors was Bonnie Prince Charlie who fought his last battles by the park walls. The house stands in forty acres of elegant lawns and parkland, enhanced by stately oaks and beech trees.

The resident proprietors, Ian and Marjory McKenzie, extend a warm welcome to all visitors to their hotel. Culloden House is decorated to the highest standard, particulary the comfortable drawing room, which is decorated with magnificent Adam-style plaster work.

Every bedroom is individually decorated and has redirect dial telephone, television, trouser press, bath and shower. Guests can chose from four-poster bedrooms, standard rooms, or rooms with a jacuzzi. The garden mansion also has non-smoking garden suites for those who wish. Dining is also a memorable experience at Culloden House; the emphasis in the Adam Dining room is on friendly and unobtrusive service, matched by the highest standards of cuisine. The wine cellars hold a superb range of wines from the great vineyards of the world, and there is a wide selection of aged malt whiskies.

Leisure facilities include a hard tennis court, sauna and solarium. There is much to visit in the area - golfing, fishing and shooting can be arranged and the Highlands, Loch Ness and Inverness are just waiting to be explored. Also nearby are Cawdor Castle, the Clava Cairns and Culloden Battlefield.

Situated three miles from the centre of Inverness, off the A96, Inverness - Nairn Road, Culloden House extends the best of Scottish hospitality to all its guests.

Culloden House
Inverness
Scotland
IV1 2NZ
Tel: (0463) 790461
Fax: (0463) 792181

DALE HILL HOTEL & GOLF CLUB

Unique comfort, style and location, together with superb facilities, can be found at the Dale Hill Hotel and Golf Club. This modern hotel is set in 300 spectacular acres, on an established, highly acclaimed parkland golf course. From the covered portico entrance, through to the open plan, two storey classic reception area, the warmth and charm of this hotel is already established. The Quedley Restaurant, from its unusual elevated situation, commands wonderful views and serves outstanding, award winning cuisine, together with a fine selection of wines. The highest standards of decor are apparent throughout the hotel, creating a stylish, sophisticated atmosphere. Each of the attractive 25 bedrooms are appointed with every facility required by the discerning guest, and most of the rooms enjoy breathtaking views. The Golf Course itself has been up-graded over the past few years, and you can enjoy unlimited golf during your stay at Dale Hill. Professionally coached golfing sessions can be arranged. The many amenities offered in the luxurious health complex are all appointed to very high standards, and for the ultimate in relaxation, massage and selected beauty treatments are available. Full conference facilities and technical equipment are ready for use, and support and advice provided, ensures the success of any meeting. This truly first class hotel is within easy reach of Tunbridge Wells and the stunning Sussex countryside where you will find historic medieval forts and castles. A stay at Dale Hill is highly recommended, whether on business or pleasure. Room and breakfast from £38.50.

Dale Hill Hotel & Golf Club
Ticehurst
Wadhurst
East Sussex TN5 7DQ
Tel: (0580) 200112
Fax: (0580) 201249

DALMUNZIE HOUSE

Dalmunzie House enjoys a glorious position in the mountains of the Scottish Highlands. The hotel stands in its own 6,000 acre mountain estate. It is owned and run by the Winton family who have been in the glen for a number of decades and have many years' experience looking after guests. Exacting attention to detail and unobtrusive service ensure a comfortable stay at all times.

As you would expect, the food at Dalmunzie House is fresh from the hills and lochs, cooked with flair and imagination to satisfy the most descerning palates.

Most of the bedrooms have ensuite facilities. Many are of individual character and all are centrally heated. Their charming decor, restful tranquility and beautiful arrangements of fresh flowers reflect the ambience found elsewhere at Dalmunzie.

Many activities can be pursued here. The hotel has its own private golf course, and in addition there is a tennis court and games room for the family complete with bar billiard table. River and loch fishing as well as shooting and stalking can all be easily arranged. Some of Scotland's finest mountains surround the hotel and for cross country and alpine skiers the Glenshee Ski Centre is only a few minutes' drive away.

For further information, contact:
Dalmunzie House Hotel
Spittal o'Glenshee
Blairgowrie
Perthshire
Scotland PH10 7QG
Tel: (0250) 885224
Fax: (0250) 885225

THE DEAN COURT HOTEL

Resting in the centre of this historic city, within the shadow of the magnificent York Minster, is this award winning hotel, offering guests the perfect setting for explorations into one of the most fascinating areas of England.

As the capital of the North and second city of the realm, it began its long and fascinating life around AD71 as a fortress to protect the Roman 9th Legion; the name itself is derived from the Viking Jorvik or Yorwik, and indeed this period of history has been superbly captured in the world-famous Jorvik Viking Museum. The city itself is still protected by ancient city walls, guarded by defensive bastions, working portcullis' and barbican at the Walmgate bar.

But it is not only the fascinating history which draws visitors to York and its surrounding area. Within three miles of the hotel are two fine golf courses; Fulford to the south and Strensall to the north. Fishermen are well catered for with the variety of well-stocked tributaries of the Ouse System; if you care for a flutter on the horses, York Racecourse is only a mile away. Add to these the wealth of antique and craft shops that fill the city streets, not to mention the fascinating crowded buildings of The Shambles, the delights of York really do seem never-ending.

After such a day's activity an aperitif in the Chapter bar will be a welcome relaxation before savouring the delights of the Dean Court Restaurant. Choose from Table d'hote and A la Carte menus; the excellent cuisine equalled only by the efficiency and warm, friendly hospitality of the staff. Take a break in the middle of the day for a lunchtime snack in the Dean Court Bar, or in the Conservatory for Afternoon Tea.

For a change of scenery allow the hotel to organise a tour for you to Castle Howard, the rolling North Yorkshire Moors or, a little further afield, windswept Bronte Country. However you choose to enjoy the splendour that is the ancient city of York, why not do so from the comfort and elegance of the Dean Court Hotel.

The Dean Court Hotel
Duncombe Place
York
Tel: (0904) 625082
Fax: (0904) 620305

THE DEVONSHIRE ARMS

Standing at Bolton Abbey is a traditional hotel in the Yorkshire Dales National Park. Set in the heart of one of the loveliest dales, Wharfedale, you will find the Devonshire.

This rather splendid hotel, originally a coaching inn, has been carefully restored and enlarged under the personal supervision of the Duchess of Devonshire, creating a hotel with much charm, character and sophistication.

The handsome lounges are superbly furnished with antiques and portraits from Chatsworth, the Derbyshire home of the Duke and Duchess of Devonshire. As the hotel's theme is of comfort and elegance you will enjoy relaxing in the Long Lounge, a friendly room of character furnished with sofas and antiques. You can relax in a friendly atmosphere surrounded by portraits from Chatsworth of the forebears of the present Duke. If you want a smaller more intimate room in which to

relax the Dog Lounge is ideal. Two portraits of favourite dogs of the Sixth Duke are the striking feature of the room, one being of an Italian greyhound and the other a rare tawny and black spaniel. If you feel like playing croquet, the lawn and nine hole putting green adjoin the newly planted Italian Garden. The Burlington restaurant has an intimate atmosphere which extends to the recently completed, Georgian style conservatory, where you will witness wonderful views. The exciting cuisine includes; table d'hote menu and an à la carte menu of international cuisine including local game in season. The decor of the comfortable bedrooms is outstanding, all of which include their own private facilities.

The Devonshire Arms Country House Hotel is an ideal base from which to explore and enjoy the Yorkshire Dales whilst still being close to the major conference centre of Harrogate.

The Devonshire Arms Country House Hotel
Bolton Abbey
Skipton
North Yorkshire BD23 6AJ
Tel: (0756) 710441
Fax: (0756) 710564

DOLMELYNLLYN HALL HOTEL

Dolmelynllyn Hall, or 'Dolly' as it is affectionately known, began its life back in the 16th century, it was enlarged in the 18th, rebuilt and enlarged again in the 19th and finally taken over in the last decade and turned into an hotel. Since then, it has been re-decorated, re-carpeted and re-furnished. It has retained the friendly atmosphere of a family home from a bygone age, an atmosphere which begins to penetrate even as one begins the trip up the gently winding, quarter mile, beech-lined drive to the house itself. There are 11 guest rooms, each with a different decorative theme and all well equipped. Each has an en-suite bathroom, colour TV and direct dial telephone.

The Dining Room is the centre of the house where five course dinners are served in an 'highly imaginative, traditional British' style. The menu changes daily and is complemented by a comprehensive wine list.

The Conservatory Bar, adjoining the Dining Room is tastefully well-stocked with bottles and flowering plants fighting for space. The elegant yet comfortable sitting room offers superb views down the valley through three large windows, there is also a library cum writing room.

Surrounding the hotel are three acres of terraced formal gardens, bounded by a swiftly running stream flowing into a small lake - part of the 1,200 acres of mountains, meadow and the Coed y Brenin Forest, all in the care of the National Trust. One can walk all day without seeing a car or crossing a road. Nearby there are castles, stately homes and all manner of other diversions.

Fishing here is excellent and the hotel offers twin bank fishing for salmon and sea trout over a stretch of some 12 miles on the Rivers Mawddach and Wnion. There is also lake fishing for wild brown and reared rainbow trout on the twin Creggenan Lakes and Lake Cynwch, all which is free for residents.

Dolmelynllyn Hall Hotel
Ganllwyd
Dolgellau
Gwynedd
Tel: (034) 140 273

DOWNHILL HOTEL

Far away from polluted air and water is the Downhill Hotel adjacent to the River Moy which is famous for its salmon fishing, attached to Lough Conn and flowing into Killala Bay provides an area rich in fresh and sea water fishing, coarse angling also available. We are in a position to organise a boat for your day trip be it on the lake, estuary or river (advance booking necessary). For that perfect game angling holiday come to the Moy and stay at the Downhill Hotel in the West of Ireland.

This Grade A hotel offers excellent cuisine, personal and friendly service and fine facilities. Bedrooms are luxurious with TV/video, satellite TV, radio, telephone, tea/coffee making facilities and trouser press. The Downhill is situated in beautiful grounds and offers Frogs Pavilion Piano Bar, split level restaurant with extensive menu, swimming pool, sauna, jacuzzi, gymnasium, squash, snooker room, sunbed and craft shop. If you are unable to escape from work the Downhill offers excellent conference facilities and is equipped to meet the most exact requirements.

The Downhill Hotel is conveniently located from Knock Airport and Sligo Airport both 35 miles away. In addition to excellent game angling guests may enjoy golf on one of the three championship courses close by, Enniscrone, Rossespoint and Westport. For those in search of a more peaceful break, a walk on one of the many beautiful sandy beaches or perhaps a scenic tour.

Downhill Hotel Limited
Ballina, Co Mayo
Ireland
Tel: (010 353 96) 21033
Fax: (010 353 96) 21338

132

DROMOLAND CASTLE

Once the seat of the O'Brien clan, Dromoland Castle has all the imposing stature you'd expect of the Kings of Munster. It stands proud on its own lakeside setting - a location that instantly highlights it as a very exceptional hotel indeed.

The warm red carpet in the expansive reception hall reflects the warmth of the Dromoland welcome - a genuine attitude further supported by a subtle combination of informality and efficiency.

The numerous lounges are of truly regal proportions, extremely comfortable with exquisite decor. A cosy bar and a relaxing snooker room are two additional options to help pass the evening hours.

The magnificence of the hotel is more than equalled by the quality of the French and indigenous cuisine. In 1990, the Earl of Thomond Room restaurant won an Egon Ronay star as 'Best Hotel Restaurant' in Ireland. With its expansive views, it's an ideal setting to while away some delightful hours accompanied by the finest of wines from one of the most extensive cellars in the country.

Golfing guests can enjoy the challenge of the hotel's own 18-hole golf course and for an even greater challenge the championship courses of Lahinch and Ballybunion are nearby.

Anglers are catered for with trout in the hotel's own lake and salmon and trout in the nearby Shannon. An hour away, the more adventurous can tackle some deep-sea angling on the West coast. hunting of a different kind starts on November 1st, for snipe, pheasant and duck.

With Shannon international airport only 8 miles away, it's not surprising that Dromoland has proved a very popular location for international conferences and seminars. Its prestigious reputation adds a unique status to any such event or management think-tank.

If the O'Briens of old returned to day, they could only but be impressed. The manicured lawns...the calm elegance...the finest in food and facilities. It's true what they say - there is only one Dromoland.

Dromoland Castle
Newmarket-on-Fergus
Co. Clare
Ireland
Tel: (010 353 61) 368144
Fax: (010 353 61) 363355

133

DUNKELD HOUSE HOTEL

A breathtaking location on the banks of the River Tay, 280 acres of grounds and a superb hotel offering a warm welcome to experienced anglers and novices alike.

Two miles of salmon fishing water offering the opportunity to fish from the bank or boat. Spinning and fly fishing available. Experienced ghillies who specialise in giving help and advice, not to mention catching fish!

Excellent trout fishing also available on our fishing beat or on a local loch. Make a day of it!

For an opportunity to catch a truly magnificent fish take advantage of our special 'Fishing Forays Package for 1992'.

A 3 day break to include 2 day's salmon fishing on the River Tay. From 1 May 1992 to August 1992. £240.00 per person to include dinner, bed and breakfast and all the fun that a 'Fishing foray' promises!

For more information or to make a booking please contact us on the number below:-

Dunkeld House Hotel
Dunkeld
Perthshire PH8 0HX
Tel: (0350) 727771
Fax: (0350) 728924

EASTWELL MANOR

Holding court over sixty-two acres of private grounds in the midst of a three-thousand acre estate Eastwell Manor Hotel offers a most appealing combination of luxurious surroundings, service second to none, and a cuisine that is the envy of the County. Quite simply it is the perfect setting in which to simply relax and enjoy yourself; to celebrate family occasions such as weddings and parties; or to rendez-vous with friends and colleagues for those important business meetings, conferences, seminars or re-unions.

Relaxing in the opulence of superb guest rooms and suites on a site whose history spans back almost a thousand years, you will soon come to understand how Eastwell has gained such a reputation for service and comfort. Whether your visit is in summer or winter there can be no doubting the rather special atmosphere that only a spacious Country Mansion can offer, making your stay an experience to remember.

On a sunny day there are terraces overlooking beautiful gardens, while in winter tranquil log-fired lounges are temptingly cosy. For the energetic the estate grounds and surrounding countryside offer numerous walking, jogging and riding routes; or perhaps make new friends over a game of tennis in the grounds or a round of golf at the adjacent Ashford Golf Club. Better still, take the opportunity to develop new skills; archery, fly-fishing, falconry, and clay-pigeon shooting can all be arranged. If that all sounds a bit too energetic how about a game in the beautiful oak-panelled snooker room, a little croquet or pitch-and-putt.

After such a day surrender body and soul to a relaxing hot bath, and later, to a mouthwatering selection of traditional or contemporary cuisine, impeccably served and accompanied by a choice of aperitifs, wines and liqueurs, guaranteed to satisfy the most discerning palate.

Eastwell Manor prides itself on its experience and expertise in organising conferences and corporate events of any kind. In addition to superb support facilities within secluded, richly panelled conference rooms, the hotel offers the finest cuisine, served as you wish, from buffet to luncheon to private dining. In addition to this, and on top of the various recreational facilities already mentioned, Eastwell Manor will be pleased to arrange a variety of events and entertainments for your friends and clients; from Hot Air Ballooning to Murder Mystery Dinners and Weekends; from Wine Tasting and Gourmet Evenings to Flights to Le Touquet or a day testing your driving skills at Brands Hatch.

Eastwell Park
Broughton Lees
Ashford
Kent TN25 4HR
Tel: (0233) 635751
Fax: (0233) 635530

EGERTON GREY COUNTRY HOUSE HOTEL

In a peaceful wooded valley, away from all main roads, rests the Egerton Country House Hotel. No other habitation or road can be seen from the hotel and residents are able to relax in surroundings of welcome seclusion. Egerton Grey began its life as a distinguished nineteenth-century rectory and private residence, opening as a hotel in the Spring of 1988. Ten miles from Cardiff it rests in seven acres of lush gardens, and looks down towards Porthkerry Park and down to the sea.

The original Cuban mahogany of the Dining Room recalls the days when it was the original billiards room, and both this and the oak-panelled Private Dining Room provide the perfect setting for the renowned cuisine, prepared with only the freshest ingredients. Relax afterwards in the Library, the magnificent Edwardian Drawing Room, or indeed in one of the ten exceedingly comfortable bedrooms, all with private facilities.

Within the hotel's grounds are a croquet lawn and an all-weather tennis court; whilst only a short stroll away towards the sea lies a delightful country park, complete with 18-hole 'pitch and putt' course. A little further afield are well-known golf courses, not to mention a fascinating array of historic sites; the Welsh Folk Museum, Castle Coch, Cardiff Castle and the magnificent formal gardens of Dyffryn House, to mention but a few.

Egerton Grey Country House Hotel
Porthkerry
Nr Cardiff
Glamorgan
Wales CF6 9BZ
Tel: (0446) 711666
Fax: (0446) 711690

ESSEBORNE MANOR

Esseborne Manor is set on the edge of the North Wessex Downs, high above the Bourne Valley in an area designated one of outstanding natural beauty.

Just eight miles from Newbury Racecourse, the hotel, which nestles in rich farmland off the A343, has been described as 'invitingly snug'.

Privately owned, with only twelve beautifully appointed bedrooms and an outstanding restaurant, Esseborne Manor has found favour with the important guide writers, and is a member of the prestigious hotel collection that make up the **Pride of Britain**.

The owners have a great deal of personal interest in racing, having shares in a filly trained in Cullompton by Gerald Cottrell. Bred in Canada, the filly who takes the name **Pride of Britain**, has shown great promise and won races on the flat in 1992 as a three year old.

Under a heading 'Racing from Esseborne Manor', the hotel produce a detailed pamphlet listing those many meetings in the year run at Newbury, Salisbury and Ascot. They also offer racing novices and enthusiasts alike some interesting packages.

1. **Fully escorted Racing Weekends with Foxhill Racing Promotions**, designed to give guests an insight to all aspects of racing with a guided tour of his yard by **Stan Mellor**, followed by an escorted day at the races with former ladies amateur champion jockey **Elain Mellor**. This package is ideal for those who know little or nothing about racing, but would like to learn. Elain completes the day by dining with guests.

2. For those who are familiar with Racing as a spectator, but who would like to learn more about training and daily routine, race days can be brought alive by arranged visits to the yards of **Oliver Sherwood and Kim Bailey in Upper Lambourn**.

Owner managed, nowhere in the area is more sympathetic to racegoers who will find Esseborne Manor an ideal place to relax after a wonderful day on the course.

For copies of the hotel brochure and details of the available packages write to:

Esseborne Manor
Hurstbourne Tarrant
Andover
Hants. SP11 0ER
Tel: (0264 76) 444
Fax: (0264 76) 473

FARLAM HALL HOTEL

Farlam Hall was opened in 1975 by the Ouinion and Stevenson families who over the years have managed to achieve and maintain consistently high standards of food, service and comfort. These standards have been recognised and rewarded by all the major guides and membership of Relais and Chateaux.

This old border house, dating in parts to the 17th Century, is set in mature gardens which can be seen from the elegant lounges and dining room, creating a relaxing and pleasing environment. The fine silver and crystal in the dining room complement the quality of the English Country House food produced by Barry Ouinion and his team of chefs.

The 13 individually decorated bedrooms vary in size and shape, some have jacuzzi baths, one an antique four poster bed, and there are 2 ground floor bedrooms.

This area offers a wealth of different attractions, - miles of unspoilt country for walking, 8 golf courses within 30 minutes of the hotel, and close by are Hadrians Wall, Lanercost Priory and Carlisle with the Castle, Cathedral and Museum. The Lake District, Scottish Borders and Yorkshire Dales provide an ideal days touring.

Dogs welcome. Winter and Spring Breaks. Directions, Farlam Hall is 2.5 miles east of Brampton on the A689, not in Farlam Village.

Price Guide (including dinner) Double/Twin £170-£200, Single £95-£100.

Closed Christmas.

Farlam Hall Hotel
Brampton
Cumbria
CA8 2NG
Tel: (06977) 46234
Fax: (06977) 46683

FINGALS AT OLD COOMBE MANOR FARM

The River Dart, one of the prettiest in England flows past the little unspoilt village of Dittisham in South Devon. Upstream it is about a mile wide, narrowing as it reaches the village allowing the ferryman to carry his passengers to the Torbay side. Nothing could be better than a summer's day spent visiting riverside pubs, picnicing, fishing, or simply enjoying its wildlife and tranquillity.

Resting in a valley set back from the river is Fingals, holding court over its beautifully landscaped garden, a perfect sun-trap where guests can be as energetic or relaxed as they wish. Old Coombe Manor, the site of this establishment, boasts a Queen Anne facade, although parts of the original house date back to the 16th and 17th centuries; the site itself is listed in the Domesday Book. Over the last ten years the building has been restored, renovated and extended using traditional methods by the owner Richard Johnston personally. The predominantly wood decor complements old country furniture and classical paintings to give an inviting, cosy feeling to the house.

Each of the nine bedrooms at Fingals is decorated with individual style and character; all have en-suite bathrooms and telephones; television sets are available on request. Children are always welcome and there is one family suite available, consisting of two interconnecting rooms. The hotel's sitting-room has a well-stocked library and an adjoining television-video room.

The latest addition is a magnificently structured, self-catering oak barn built in old wood building technique. Situated by the pool it is ideal for families who can enjoy the hotel restaurant and bar without abandoning their children. The facilities at Fingals ensure that you have plenty to occupy you when not exploring locally. The beautiful tiled pool with adjoining sauna and jacuzzi is half glazed for Summer fresh air but can be covered for the Autumn and Spring.

Snack lunches are available but the gastronomic highlight of the day is the superb four-course dinner, prepared with only the freshest ingredients and the best local produce. Dinner in the guests' dining room is served at one long table while a separate dining room is available should families wish to eat together in the evening or for guests planning a more intimate meal.

If you are looking for a hotel with reception desk, lobby and cocktail lounge with uniformed barman, then keep looking. Fingals is a unique and unconventional place. Staff dress informally, surnames are dispensed with and you are free to add your drinks to your bar tab any time of the day or night. if this sounds sloppy it is far from it. The staff are totally attentive, friendly and dedicated to the concept of this special feel-at-home atmosphere.

Fingals at Old Coombe Manor Farm
Dittisham
Dartmouth
TQ6 0JA
Tel: (080422) 398
Fax: (080422) 401

GARA ROCK HOTEL

The Gara Rock Hotel began its life as Rickham Coastguard Station, completed in 1847 as a direct result of a request from the Admiralty to Parliament. In 1909 this was disbanded and the building sold off to begin its career as a family hotel. Facing due south and surrounded by National Trust land the hotel overlooks scenery of breathtaking magnificence, and is justly proud of its long-standing reputation for hospitality. A wide array of special features for children, ranging from an Adventure Playground, Games Room and Pets Corner to specially staged entertainments such as a Magic Show and Children's Party, leaves adults free to work out in the gym and tennis court, relax in the solarium and sauna or cool off in the outdoor swimming pool. Alternatively, the secluded sandy beach is only a few minutes walk away, whilst the surrounding countryside waits to be explored; mountain bikes may be hired and boat / fishing trips are available in the summer months. However you spend the morning, make the afternoon special with the treat of a famous Devonshire Cream Tea.

The accommodation ranges from comfortable family rooms to family suites and spacious private flats, with spectacular coastal views from the south-facing rooms. Thirteen self-catering suites are also available within the grounds.

The oak panelled lounge with open fires provides the setting for a relaxing drink before choosing dinner from the imaginative Table d'hote and a la carte menu, including a local fish dish, and all served mainly with the produce of the hotel's own vegetable garden.

In the Spring and Autumn months the hotel provides the perfect retreat for walkers, bird-watchers, or simply those looking for peaceful comfort.

Gara Rock Hotel
East Portlemouth
Near Salcombe
South Devon
TQ8 8PH
Tel: (054884) 2342
Fax: (054884) 3033

THE GEAN HOUSE

The air of a dream seems to haunt this mansion house, set in 20 acres of parkland. The Gean House was commissioned in 1910 by Alexander Forrester-Paton, a leading industrialist, as a wedding present for his eldest son.

The Gean has since been caringly saved for the nation, restored to the grandeur of its halcyon days when conversations echoing in the vaulted ceiling of the Boardroom would breathe life into the serene opulence of this beautiful country home.

Luxuriously furnished, this architecturally important house has been decorated by resident directors Antony Mifsud and John Taylor. The luxury guest bedrooms retain an air of individuality with a dignified sense of a common heritage. The elegant reception hall has fine views of the nearby Ochil Hills - hillwalking, golf, horse riding and watersports on the beautiful Loch Lomond are but a stones throw away.

In the south facing walnut-panelled dining room, overlooking the ros parterre, guests may enjoy the stylish creative menus of Antony Mifsud whose reputation for fine contemporary continental cuisine and traditional Scottish country-house fare completes the cycle!

A rare discovery....

The Gean House
Gean Park
Alloa
Scotland FK10 2HS
Tel: (0259) 219275
Fax: (0259) 213827

GLANRANNELL PARK

Glanrannell Park lies in the valley of the river Cothi, the largest tributary of the Towy which flows six miles east of the hotel. Eight miles west runs the river Teifi which rises in the hills north of Tregarvon and meets the sea at Cardigan. These three rivers and numerous feeder streams are the basis of the sport available to the resident angler at Glanrannell.

Glanrannell Park Country house hotel, surrounded by lawns and overlooking a small private lake is set in twenty-three acres of parkland bounded on one side by the Annell, a trout stream from which the hotel gets its name. Arriving at Glanrannell Park you will be captivated by the setting of the hotel and the calm and serenity of the surrounding countryside.

The hotel has eight comfortable bedrooms with views over the lawns and paddocks of the estate, whilst the dining room overlooks the lake and adjoins a modern well-equipped kitchen. Local produce is used and our menu and service are in the best traditions of the country house.

Glanrannell Park provides an excellent base from which to explore this lovely part of Wales. Nearby are the Dolaucothi Roman gold mines at Pumpsaint, the 12th century Talley Abbey and Felin Newydd, a water mill still producing stone ground flour. The Brecon Beacons National Park is a short distance to the east and to the west are the sea cliffs, rocky coves and sandy beaches of Cardigan Bay and the Pembrokeshire Coast National Park. To the South is the expanse of Carmarthen Bay, sheltered by the Gower Peninsula, Britain's first designated area of outstanding natural beauty.

West Wales has an abundance of castles, woollen and flour mills, craft workshops, museums and many other places of interest besides its excellent fishing so there is always something for you to do and see.

At Glanrannell Park we take personal care of our guests and great pride in the relaxed, happy hotel that we run. The Welsh for 'welcome' is Croeso - which is what we provide.

Glanrannell Park
Country House Hotel
Crugybar
Llanwrda
Dyfed SA19 8SA
Tel: (0558) 685230
Fax: (0558) 685784

Glenfeochan Gardens

GLENFEOCHAN HOUSE AND GARDENS

Glenfeochan House is a listed, turreted, Victorian Country Mansion at the head of Loch Feochan, built in 1875 and set amidst a 350 acre Estate of Hills, Lochs, Rivers and Pasture. The House is surrounded by a mature 6 acre Garden (open to the Public) with a 1½ acre Walled Garden with herbaceous borders, vegetables fruit and Herb beds.

The house has recently been carefully restored with family antiques and beautiful fabrics. All the main rooms have high ceilings with original ornate plasterwork. The intricately carved American Pine staircase with beautifully Pargeted canopy lead Guests to three large comfortable bedrooms with ensuite bathrooms. The views over the Garden and Parkland through to Loch Feochan are spectacular. This is a really peaceful setting for a holiday.

The Victorian Arboretum is "One of the Great Gardens of the Highlands". Many rare shrubs and trees, some planted in 1840, make a wonderful canopy for the tender Rhododendrons and other rare shrubs including a large Embothrium and Davidia which abounds with "White Handkerchiefs" in the Summer.

Carpets of Snowdrops, Daffodils and Bluebells herald the Spring. Many tender Acers love this sheltered garden. The Herbaceous Borders are a blaze of colour in the summer and provide many of the flowers for the house. The walled garden has one of the old Victorian heated walls. This gives shelter to a huge Magnolia, Eucryphia and a Ginkgo. All the vegetables for the house are grown here. There is a large greenhouse entirely for white and yellow peaches and nectarines. Salmon and Sea Trout fishing on the River Nell and wonderful bird and otter watching make Glenfeochan a unique place to stay.

Glenfeochan House and Gardens
Kilmore
Oban
Argyllshire PA34 4QR
Tel: (063 177) 273

GLIFFAES COUNTRY HOUSE

A thoroughly charming Victorian country house hotel, Gliffaes boasts fine gardens and parkland, situated in the National Park yet only one mile off the main A40 road. It offers peace and tranquillity as well as being easily accessible.

The house, which faces due south, stands in its own 29 acres in the beautiful valley of the River Usk, midway between the Brecon Beacons and the Black Mountains. Built in 1885 as a private residence, it has been ideally adapted to provide spacious comfort in the country house tradition. There are 22 bedrooms with private bathrooms or showers and all are individual in decor and furnishings, including three in the converted lodge.

The downstairs rooms include a large, comfortable, panelled sitting-room which leads into an elegant regency style drawing-room. From here, french windows open into a large conservatory with double doors on to the terrace. The dining-room and comfortable bar also open on to the terrace, with the glorious views of the surrounding hills and River Usk one hundred and fifty feet below. The billiard room has a full sized table and provides an additional sitting-room with something of a club atmosphere.

Breakfast is served from a sideboard, lunch is a cold buffet with soup and a hot dish. Dinner is either table d'hote or a la carte. In fact, country house standards of the old order are carefully maintained by the resident owners; the Brabner family have held sway here since 1948.

External facilities include fishing for salmon and trout in the part of the Usk which the hotel overlooks, tennis, bowls, putting and croquet. There is an extensive range of short walks in the vicinity and a nearby riding and pony trekking establishment where horses and ponies can be hired.

The hotel is justly proud of its in-house cooking and remains open from the middle of March to the end of the year.

Gliffaes Country House Hotel
Crickhowell
Powys
Wales NP8 1RH
Tel: (0874) 730371 Fax: (0874) 730463

GLYN ISA COUNTRY HOUSE HOTEL

Originally built as the home of a local country landowner back in the seventeenth century the Glyn Isa has been developed over the years into one of the finest Country House Hotels in Wales. Resting just outside the ancient town of Conwy, the Glyn Isa really is one of the most perfect locations for enjoying North Wales.

The hotel's name has remained surprisingly relevant throughout its lifetime. Literally translated it means 'The Lower Valley' and guests here find themselves truly surrounded by natural sweeping countryside, rolling lawns and an intricate series of unique Victorian secret gardens, each one different from the rest and some containing highly regarded specimen trees.

Deep in the rolling vistas of the Conwy Valley there is much to see. Edward Plantaganet's finest fortress, the dramatic Conwy Castle, still stands out against the skyline; Llandudno, the Victorian 'Jewel in the Crown', is just nearby. Not far away are some of the finest gardens in the world, the seventy acres of Bodnant Gardens, while traditional Welsh weaving is a fascinating sight at the Trefriw Woollen Mills. If you are feeling a little more energetic, there is the stunning Snowdonia National Park, with its breathtaking views, pure rushing rivers and peaceful mountain lakes. Wales is, of course, perfect for walking, climbing, birdwatching, pony-trekking, golfing, cycling, sailing, water-skiing or simply traditional seaside fun.

Naturally, if all this sounds a bit much, simply take a drink, a book or a newspaper into one of the secret gardens, sit in the sun and reflect on all the activity you simply don't have to do. If fishing is your preferred relaxation then a mere 100 yards away is a well stocked trout lake / fishery; offering, as it does, special discounts to hotel guests, it is sure to provide you with hours of contemplative tranquillity. Stocking mainly Rainbow Trout - the biggest so far being 13½ pounds - it doubles as a smokehouse, preparing local eels, mackerel and trout, as well as Scottish Salmon brought down especially.

However you spend your day the Heron Restaurant is sure to be a welcome sight; its wide choice of imaginative meals are prepared with the freshest of local ingredients, including those locally caught trout. In the warmer months, meals can be served on the front lawn where the beautiful setting adds a special touch. Afternoon tea with the famous Welsh tea bread - Bara Brith - is a must.

Each bedroom at Glyn Isa is individually decorated, incorporating into each a unique charm and character; all have beverage making facilities and television, while for that extra special occasion why not order a candlelit dinner or refreshing breakfast in your room.

Glyn Isa Country House Hotel
Rowen
Nr Conwy
Gwynedd
N. Wales LL32 8TP
Tel: (0492) 650242

THE GRIFFIN INN

Dating back to the fifteenth century, The Griffin Inn is believed to be one of the oldest sporting inns in Wales. That tradition endures today, under the ownership and management of the Stockton family. A keen fisherman himself, Richard Stockton aims to ensure that visitors to The Griffin are able to enjoy a rewarding variety of game fishing.

The Griffin Inn is able to offer excellent salmon fishing along some twenty miles of the lower, middle and upper Wye. There is also superb trout fishing - both for wild brown river fish, and for rainbows in a nearby well-stocked private pool.

Recently, The Griffin embarked on a complementary new enterprise - Griffin Field Sports, incorporating a world-class fishing and shooting school under the personal direction of one of Britain's foremost exponents of both arts: Crawford Little. Throughout the season, the Crawford Little School of Country Sports offers a variety of residential courses in salmon and trout fishing - structured for complete beginners, competent enthusiasts and accomplished sportsmen and women.

The courses range from a broad introduction to fly-fishing, to specialised tuition in the most sophisticated salmon fishing techniques - including Roll and Spey-casting. From basics such as the selection of tackle, to the finer points of salmon line and fly control, all the courses have been carefully devised by Crawford Little to encourage the development of fishing skills - at every level. The School's facilities also include private tuition on a half-day or daily basis - mainly for those wanting to improve a particular aspect of their fly-fishing.

The Griffin itself exudes all the warmth and welcome to be expected of a hostelry where enthusiasm for country pursuits is shared by all the Stockton family, regulars and visitors alike.

Game fishing is very much a theme of The Griffin - the attractive cottage style bedrooms are all named after famous fishing flies, while the bar features a fascinating collection of cased flies, fish and maps of the River Wye.

The unspoilt Fisherman's Bar of The Griffin deserves special mention. Dominated by a huge inglenook fireplace and decorated with traditional simplicity, it has a timeless charm - a haven in which to enjoy good ale, good food and good company, where conversation naturally tends to turn to country matters, in particular, game fishing and shooting.

The Griffin has a well-established and far-reaching reputation for serving outstanding meals - country-style cooking at its best, always prepared from fresh local produce. The Inn's sporting interests are, not surprisingly, reflected in the menu. Depending on the season, it will generally include fresh salmon, river trout or game, invariably well prepared and attractively presented in either the restaurant or bar.

There is residential accommodation for sixteen guests, a comfortable residents' lounge with separate TV room and an attractive dining room. A free house - and incidentally the first 'Logis' in Wales - The Griffin Inn is on the A470 Builth Wells road, 9 miles from Brecon and 7 miles from Hay-on-Wye.

Further details are available from: Richard & Di Stockton:

The Griffin Inn
Llyswen
Brecon
Powys ID3 OUR
Tel: (0874) 754241

HAMBLETON HALL

Hambleton Hall is set in a part of Britain whose natural advantages remain remarkably unspoilt and undiscovered, and yet it is only 100 miles north of London.

The grassy bumps and stone-built market towns may remind you of the Cotswolds but you will find fewer souvenir shops and traffic jams.

Arriving through a corridor of laurels, yews, hollies and fine cedars, you find a substantial, much gabled, stone, Victorian house. But it is inside the house that its chief glories are apparent. Facing south from its hilltop site the hotel's principal rooms have spectacular views over the gardens, the Rutland landscape and Rutland Water, a 500 acre man-made lake of surprising beauty.

The decoration and furnishings impart an immediate sense of comfort and a welcome that is immensely stylish, without a trace of stuffiness or excessive formality.

An oak-panelled hall, a cosy bar and a 'glam', spacious drawing-room lead to a magnificent dining-room. Each of these rooms seems the right size for the house party of 25-30 which the hotel's 15 bedrooms can accommodate.

Upstairs, the same attention to detail is apparent. Down pillows, Egyptian cotton sheets and the softest merino wool blankets ensure a good night's rest, while charming chintzy decorations in the English country house idiom achieve the same combination of comfort and elegance.

Hambleton is particularly well known for its food and wines. The culinary style seems to combine the presentational flair of the best modern cooking, with a fundamental respect for top ingredients and authentic flavours. Brian Baker, who took over as head chef from Nicholas Gill in 1986, uses local pike and trout, herbs and salads from the garden and the prodigious range of game available in season to help create a menu that is always unusual, without being fussy or over-complicated. The wine list won Egon Ronay's Cellar of the Year award in 1986.

Tim and Stefa Hart established Hambleton Hall in the early '80's and still play an active part, with the day to day management of the hotel in the capable hands of Jeffrey Crockett, General Manager. It is the welcome and efficient service produced by Mr. Crockett and his team, as much as anything which keeps Hambleton in the front rank of British country house hotels.

Hambleton Hall,
Hambleton,
Oakham,
Rutland LE15 8TH.
Tel: (0572) 756991 Telex: 342888 Hamble
Fax: (0572) 724721

HANBURY MANOR

Hanbury Manor, recently awarded a much sought after 5 star rating by the AA, is a country house experience to be savoured. A lovingly restored mansion with 96 bedrooms and 10 conference suites, turn-of-the-century charm blends with every modern comfort and service that is always friendly and courteous.

The beautiful 200 acre estate provides a vast array of amenities, including a championship golf course, tennis, squash, snooker and a fully equipped Health Club.

The perfect place to relax or to combine business with pleasure, Hanbury Manor is easily accessible, only 25 miles north of London. The elegantly appointed bedrooms spoil the most discerning traveller, whilst fine dining is available in three enticingly different restaurants including the gourmet Zodiac Restaurant and the casual Vardon Grill.

One of many highlights of a stay at Hanbury Manor will undoubtedly be the magnificent 18 hole golf course, created out of rolling Hertfordshire countryside by Jack Nicklaus II, of Golden Bear Associates. The course measures a testing 7011 yards from the championship tees, with a number of strategically placed bunkers and several picturesque water hazards providing a series of challenges for all levels of players.

The contrasting nature of the Downfield nine - beautifully sculpted out of existing meadowland and an old quarry site - and the inward half - set in breathtaking parkland with mature trees - provides a remarkable variety of panoramic scenery that make for a whole series of spectacular memories. The careful design and conditioning of the course makes Hanbury Manor one of the most beautifully manicured layouts anywhere in Britain.

Whether toning-up or winding down, Hanbury provides the perfect environment for relaxing after a game on the championship standard golf course. Indoors or out, the variety of freely accessible leisure activities are numerous, making Hanbury Manor a genuine resort property. The centrepiece of the magnificently equipped leisure facilities is undoubtedly the 17m x 7m swimming pool where a warm welcome is tendered to all aquaphiles, under a stunning Romanesque canopy. Steam rooms, Swedish sauna, and a jacuzzi are offered as wonderful wet alternatives and vie with the Hanbury Beauty Studio and sumptuous gymnasium for guests' attention.

Hanbury Manor has set out to offer guests a level of facilities and service that re-define traditional standards. Whether as a hotel guest, or as a member of our Golf and Leisure Sections, Hanbury Manor is quite simply an experience not to be missed.

Hanbury Manor
Thundridge
Nr Ware
Hertfordshire SG12 0SD
Tel: (0920) 487722
Fax: (0920) 487692y

HATTON COURT

Nestling in the hills of Upton St. Leonards, and set in 37 acres of beautifully maintained gardens this historic old Cotswold Manor is only 3 miles from the historic city of Gloucester. Hatton Court combines standards of comfort and sophistication with existing 17th century charm and character.

All the individually furnished bedrooms have superb ensuite bathrooms, many with luxurious jacuzzi, as well as colour television, in-house video, radio, direct dial telephone, trouser press and hairdryer.

Hatton Court's restaurant, with its exceptional panoramic views across the Severn Valley to the Malvern Hills, provides a superb setting in which to enjoy culinary excellence. The Chef, a student of some of the great chefs of France and England, cooks in the modern French style, creating dishes that are at once a feast to the eye and a pleasure to the palate. The superb cooking is complemented by an extensive wine

selection housed in the unique 'Wine-Shop'.

Executive meetings or private functions can be arranged, always with an exacting attention to detail.

The surrounding area provides a wealth of interesting places to visit, such as Gloucester, Bath and Stratford upon Avon, as well as many fine country houses and gardens and unspoilt Cotswold villages. Sporting facilities for riding, golf and dry skiing (to name but 3 examples) are available only minutes from the hotel. The hotel has the added facility of a small Residential Health Suite which includes a Sauna, Work Out and Relaxation Area Solarium and Jacuzzi.

Unsurpassed service and a warm personal welcome ensure a wonderfully enjoyable stay in the splendid surroundings of Hatton Court.

Hatton Court
Upton St. Leonards
Gloucester
GL4 8DE
Tel: (0452) 617412
Fax: (0452) 612945

HAWKSTONE PARK HOTEL

Even a fairly detailed map is unlikely to show Weston-under-Redcastle, but ask a golfer for the location and it is possible he will direct you there blindfolded! The Hawkstone Park Hotel, where Sandy Lyle learned his game, sits in an exquisite 300-acre estate and is more than just a golfers' paradise. It features one fine eighteen-hole golf course and one 9 hole golf course. The Hawkstone Course is over fifty years old, set in wooded, undulating parkland which includes several antiquities, such as the thirteenth-century Red Castle, and is bordered on one side by the beautiful Hawk lake.

The hotel, situated just a chip shot from the course, is steeped in history. It was built as an elegant and spacious hostelry in 1790 and was then known as the Hawkstone Inn. It has been developed into a really superb hotel complex which provides a catalogue of sporting and leisure facilities, including a tennis court, a croquet lawn, an open-air swimming pool, a sauna, a solarium and a trimnasium.

Where better to reflect on a round or two of golf than in the tastefully designed restaurant, which offers traditional English cuisine? Hawkstone's renown has spread far and wide and many visitors arrive expecting that the wealth of facilities at Hawkstone Park will impress them most.

However, it is the pleasantness and efficiency of the staff which really linger longest in the mind. Kevin Brazier, Company Operations Executive, proudly declares that the hotel's motto is 'client loving care' and this approach is apparent throughout the hotel. You will find Hawkstone Park fourteen miles north of Shrewsbury, off the A49 road.

Hawkstone Park Hotel
Weston under Redcastle
Shrewsbury
Shropshire SY4 5UY
Tel: (0939) 200611
Fax: (0939) 200311

HAYTON HALL HOTEL

Hayton Hall is an historic deluxe castle/mansion in its own 70 acre private estate between the Scottish Borders and Wordsworth's Lake District. Hadrian's Wall passes close by, and the picturesque Eden Valley stretches Southwards.

The hotel is approached along a half mile driveway wending through the estates woodland, where wild deer roam. The grounds were reputedly landscaped by Capability Brown, including three stocked ornamental lakes, and Italianate fountain and rose garden.

The interior includes warm timber panelling, rich antique furnishings, and welcoming open fires in the entrance hall, drawing and dining rooms. The feeling throughout is of a country home, and the high level of service is both friendly and personalised.

Candle-lit dining is offered in the elegant Oakroom overlooking the rose gardens, where the highest level of cuisine is under the personal direction of one of Britain's Master Chefs. Alternatively there is the hotels informal family restaurant in the courtyard.

Bedrooms, suites, and Bridal Boudoir are lavishly equipped, decorated and furnished to 4 star deluxe standard, and all have en suite bathrooms, some with private spa baths.

Clay pigeon shooting, archery, croquet, jogging, and fishing are on site, and golf, horse riding, salmon & trout fishing are nearby.

Hayton Hall Hotel
Nr Wetheral
Carlisle
Cumbria
Tel: (0228) 70651
Fax: (0228) 70010

HIGHBULLEN

Highbullen is a splendid Victorian Gothic mansion complete with parkland, carriageways, home farm and outbuildings. The house was designed and built by William Moore of Exeter in 1879 near the site of old 17th century farmhouses known as Whitehall and Mountjoy. He and his family lived there until 1923. In more recent times cannon balls were discovered nearby, suggesting the site was the scene of a skirmish in Commonwealth days.

The hotel stands on high ground between the Mole and Taw Valleys in wooded seclusion, yet with fine views over surrounding country. A spectacular 9 hole golf course is set in the 60 acres of parkland.

An indoor swimming pool now occupies the old coach-house and the home farm and outbuildings have been discreetly converted into guest rooms.

Rowcliffes, 300 yards down from the home farm, has five more bedrooms with its own heated open-air pool and lovely views. There is also a self-contained 2 bedroom cottage.

The adjoining property, Whitehall, set in a country style garden is 200 yards away and has five elegant bedrooms and its own sitting room.

All thirty seven bedrooms, 12 of which are in the House, are centrally heated, and have their own private bathrooms.

The extensive cellars are now the social and gastronomic heart of the hotel, with the bar opening onto a pretty courtyard. The restaurant has appeared in all the reputable guides for over 25 years. Light lunches are available in the bar or courtyard every day.

The breakfast room opens out from the restaurant and has a magnificent view of the valley. Both the breakfast room and the restaurant are non-smoking areas.

Life at Highbullen is informal and relaxed. We tend to clear breakfast soon after 10 am and not take orders for dinner after 9 pm but, that apart, there are no rules.

Whatever the season, it's a perfect place for doing nothing, with many quiet hideaways - the drawing room, conservatory and library inside and many secluded corners in the grounds. But if you incline to a more active leisure style you can sample the heated outdoor pool, the squash court, the 9 hole par 31 golf course, the hard tennis court or the indoor court, which is floodlit and has an Escotennis carpeted surface.

More gentle pursuits are croquet and billiards, sauna, spa bath, sunbed, steamroom, table tennis and indoor putting green. Massage and hairdressing are available by arrangement. There is a comprehensively stocked golf and sports shop.

Highbullen Hotel
Chittlehamholt
Umberleigh
North Devon EX37 9HD
Tel: (0769) 540561
Fax: (0769) 540492

HINTLESHAM HALL

Hintlesham Hall, originally built in the 1570's, with a stunning Georgian facade offers the best in country house elegance and charm. Gracious living, good food and wine, attentive service and tranquil relaxation greet every guest to the hotel.

The Hall is set in over 170 acres of rolling Suffolk countryside some of which is devoted to a beautiful 18-hole championship full-length golf course, and has 33 luxurious bedrooms and suites, of different shapes and sizes, some with four poster beds. Thoughtful attention to detail pervades the hotel, and this includes the restaurant. Head Chef, Alan Ford, believes good food starts with good produce. French truffles, Scottish salmon, Cornish Scallops and Suffolk lobsters are just some of the enticements on the menu which changes seasonally. There is an award-winning 300 bin wine list which ranges the world from France to Australia.

All moods are reflected in Hintlesham's fine reception rooms - the intimate book-lined Library, the tranquil spacious Garden room and the cool entrance Arcade. The Hall is just 45 minutes drive from Newmarket and is an ideal base from which to explore East Anglia, be it the medieval wool villages of Lavenham and Kersey, Long Melford and Woodbridge with their wealth of antique shops or Dedham and Flatford Mill famous for their Constable associations. The cathedral city of Norwich and the University colleges of Cambridge are also close by. However, perhaps most importantly, Hintlesham Hall is the perfect retreat for those who wish to go nowhere at all.

Hintlesham Hall
Hintlesham
Suffolk IP8 3NS
Tel: Hintlesham (047 387) 334
Fax: Hintlesham (047 387) 463

HOLNE CHASE HOTEL

Your hosts at Holne Chase, now in their 22nd year at the Hotel, have an excellent knowledge of local facilities - particularly:-

GOLF: Kenneth Bromage has compiled a list of no fewer than 15 courses within a hour of the Hotel, plus three others of International Standing within about 90 minutes. Other courses, recently built but said to be good, he has not listed because he has not yet played over them.

Small golfing parties staying at the Hotel will find flexibility in meal times to help them plan their golfing tour.

HORSE RACING: Newton Abbot is England's most Westerly race course, National Hunt meeting run from early August through to late May. Frequently, meetings at Newton Abbot are followed/preceded by meetings at Devon and Exeter Racecourse. Holne Chase is handy for both.

FISHING: The Dart is, arguably, one of Britain's loveliest rivers. Certainly, it is a challenge to the ardent fly fisherman. Holne Chase has a single bank beat of about a mile, which is available to residents at no extra charge.

Holne Chase became an hotel in 1934. The surrounding woodlands were partly laid out as Arboretum in 1878 and so afford many interesting walks taking in an old mine shaft (c.1790), an iron age fortified camp and early 20th c. charcoal burners hearths.

The woodlands abound with wildlife including roe and red deer, badger, fox, rabbit and otter. Buzzard, heron, kingfisher and even a flight of shellduck which have colonised a stretch of the river.

The Bromage family took the hotel in 1972 and have been working on it ever since. All 14 bedrooms have bath and/or shower en suite. The Hotel is classified 4 Crown 'Highly Commended' by the English Tourist Board and has won many awards over the years, both in the kitchen and in the cellar. The Head Chef is an expert Mycologist which helps add extra variety to the late summer menus.

Holne Chase is an exceptional place in which to relax. Deep, comfy sofas and armchairs, a well stocked library, blazing fires on winter evenings make relaxation easy. Dartmoor itself is wonderful walking country and guided walks can be arranged at all times of the year. We can also arrange riding from some of the best stables on Dartmoor all within 20-30 minutes from the hotel. Expert tuition is available.

Holne Chase is 3 miles north of the Ashburton. To find the hotel, take the Two Bridges/Princetown turning off the A38 and follow the road for approximately 3 miles. The hotel turning is on the right, just after the road crosses the River Dart.

Holne Chase Hotel & Restaurant
Nr Ashburton
Devon
TQ13 7NS
Tel: (03643) 471
Fax: (03643) 453

HORNBY HALL

This seventeenth century farmhouse is situated just off the A66, 3 miles south-east of Penrith on the river Eamont.

The house has recently been refurbished and furnished with antiques in keeping with the period of the red sandstone building.

There are two en-suite double bedrooms and three twin rooms. Up the original spiral staircase are two small single rooms. The sandstone flagged main hall is used as a dining room. Dinner must be pre-booked as meals are freshly cooked from local produce. Set menus Monday to Thursday, choice of menu on Friday and Saturday. There is a residential table licence. Splendid packed lunches are available. We have an excellent drying/boot room for all those wet clothes and boots! Dogs are not allowed in the main house, but may sleep in here. In addition, a self-catering flat is available which sleeps four.

The two mile stretch of fishing on the right bank of the Eamont produces good dry fly fishing. The Brown Trout season starts on 15th March, closing end September. The Salmon season opens on 16th January until 14th October. The best Salmon fishing is usually at the end of the season.

A wealth of other country pursuits are available in the area, from walking in the Pennine fells to sailing in the Lake District. Fishing and shooting parties can be arranged.

Why not enjoy the privacy of your own house party at Hornby Hall by taking the whole house?

Tourist Board - Highly Recommended (2 crowns)

RAC - listed. Highly Commended.

Hornby Hall
Brougham
Penrith
Cumbria CA10 2AR
Tel: (0768) 89114

EAST SUSSEX NATIONAL GOLF CLUB AND HORSTED PLACE

Occupying a majestic setting in twenty three acres of land-scaped Sussex countryside, Horsted Place offers an enviable combination of modern facilities in a delightful and elegant form. Individually decorated suites, a magnificently appointed main dining room, two private dining rooms, executive meeting and conference libraries, a heated indoor swimming pool, a tennis court and helicopter landing area are all designed to more than cater for the needs of the modern traveller. Rated as one of the best hotels in the British Isles by the Guide Michelin and also renowned for its culinary prowess, Horsted Place provides unequalled standards of service and facilities for visitors, golfers and the business community. Over one thousand acres of rolling countryside surrounding Horsted Place have now been transformed into two golf courses which have quickly become established as two of Britain's finest inland challenges. If quality is the cornerstone of excellence, East Sussex National sets a standard that will not easily be equalled. American course designer Robert E. Cupp, has coaxed out of the beautiful Sussex countryside two layouts that offer a stern competitive challenge, as well as some

memorably beautiful holes. The East course features gallery mounding for the benefit of spectators, the area of the eighteenth green alone being able to accommodate up to 30,000 spectators. The West course, meanwhile, is like the East over 7,000 yards from the gold tees and features nine holes where water comes perilously into play. The special qualities of the courses have been recognised by top players on the PGA European Tour resulting in the East course being chosen to host the 1993 GA European Open. The momentous challenge posed by both courses is made slightly less awesome by the provision of a three hole Teaching Academy and fabulous practice facilities.

Visitors to East Sussex National and Horsted Place are immediately struck by both a glorious setting and an attention to detail that result in an ambience of all-round excellence. Every visit is guaranteed to become a memorable encounter-contact the numbers below for your own taste of a unique leisure experience.

East Sussex National Golf Club and Horsted Place
Little Horsted
Uckfield
East Sussex, TN22 5TS
Tel: (hotel) (0825) 750581
Tel: (golf) (0825) 841217
Fax: (hotel) (0825) 750459
Fax: (golf) (0825) 841282

HUTTON COURT

For most golfers, a great golfing break involves not just the game, but also the 'base camp': a place to relax and enjoy good company, food and drink before the triumphs and frustrations of tomorrow's game.

Gleneagles springs to mind; but what of the West Country, and what about non-golfing companions or days off the course? The championship links of Burnham & Berrow in Somerset is less than twenty minutes from the manor of Hutton, itself just five miles off the M5, two and a half hours by car or train from London.

With a history going back before the Norman Conquest, Hutton Court is now a hotel and restaurant in the classic country house style. You sleep in bedrooms dating from the 17th century, with modern comforts added, and dine in the great hall of the 1450s. Local meat, fish, game and venison of the region are specialities. Cuisine befits the best British tradition, substantial yet refined, and matched by over a hundred wines from a dozen countries, ranging from house wines to classics like Cheval Blanc and Petrus.

The key to the place is its relaxed atmosphere, and service that

makes you a personal house guest rather than a paying customer with a room number. Serious golfers can not only play Burnham and Berrow, but three other courses within twenty minutes drive. The area offers much more than golf, however. The cathedral cities of Wells, Bath with its splendid shopping and Bristol are all in easy reach. You can walk or ride on the Mendips, explore Cheddar, Wookey, Glastonbury and the Somerset levels, or potter around antique shops and old country pubs.

You can fish the trout lakes of Blagdon and Chew, and there is sea angling on the Bristol Channel. Naturalists watch buzzards, sparrow hawks or even the odd peregrine or goshawk in and around the hotel grounds, which foxes and badgers visit.

At Hutton Court, we'll do everything to ensure you get the most from your stay, whether you're a glutton for action or just want a lazy few days. Special rates are available for individual or party breaks, and we'll tailor food and drink to your requirements, from packed lunches to full-scale banquets. Ring us for information: we promise you a warm West Country welcome.

Hutton Court,
Church Lane,
Hutton,
Avon BS24 9SN

Telephone: Bleadon (0934) 814343

THE INN AT WHITEWELL

Originally built as a manor house for the keeper of the King's deer in the 14th century, the Inn at Whitewell still belongs to the Royal family as part of the Duchy of Lancaster. As a result, it still retains its associations with field sports and grouse and pheasant shooting can be arranged in season. The Inn also has fishing rights to five miles of both banks of the River Hodder where you can fish for salmon and trout.

You will often find fresh fish on the menu, including local smoked salmon and game in season, black pudding and a foot long Cumberland sausage. The wine list is extensive and claims to be one of the best lists for a pub in the country as the proprietors are also wine-shippers.

Interestingly, the Inn has an art gallery where you can by works by artists from all over the country. You can also buy locally made shirts and shooting stockings, for which they have Royal customers, and hand lasted shoes. Despite all this, the Inn maintains a country pub atmosphere with carved stone fireplaces, oak beams, wood-panelling, oak settles and a baby grand in the corner of the lounge.

The setting is quite stunning. The Inn is set in three acres of beautiful grounds and looks straight across to the Trough of Bowland. In fine weather, you can sit outside at wooden tables, high above the river, and enjoy the peace and beauty of the country.

Shooting and horse riding can be arranged and Browsholme Hall and Clitheroe Castle are nearby. For the golfer, the splendid inland course of Clitheroe Golf Club is closeby. Situated on the edge of the Forest of Bowland amidst superb countryside the course looks across to Pendle Hill - a delightful setting. A short drive away lies Lancaster Golf and Country Club and the county of Lancashire is home to the famous Royals; Lytham and Birkdale, both within easy reach of the inn.

The Inn At Whitewell
Forest of Bowland
Clitheroe
Lancashire BB7 3AT
Tel: (02008) 222

INNISHANNON HOUSE HOTEL

One of the most exclusive hotels in the country, the Innishannon effortlessly lives up to its reputation as "the most romantic hotel in Ireland". Dating back to 1720 when it began its varied life as a substantial farmer's residence, it grew up beside an ancient ford, the first point at which the Bandon River could be crossed, and an important commercial centre in medieval times.

Conal and Vera O'Sullivan, the owners/managers like to see their hotel as 'A restaurant with Rooms', and have gone to quite enormous efforts to ensure that the food is of a superlative quality. Only fresh herbs and vegetables from surrounding farms are used, along with local meat and game. Seafood such as brill, turbot, salmon and Dublin Bay prawns are served on the same day as they are landed in nearby Kinsale. An excellent selection of carefully chosen wines complements superb cuisine, served in a dining-room as elegant as the food itself.

The hotel also boasts a lounge bar, cosy snug, and ballroom catering for special occasions such as weddings, thoughtfully self-contained for privacy.

All of the bedrooms offer the modern amenities of colour television, direct-dial telephone cum clock/radio with extension in the bathroom. All bedrooms are, of course, ensuite and have been individually decorated and furnished with traditional woods, chintzes and a selection from the O'Sullivan's exten-sive collection of original paintings and prints, which also brighten the walls of the public rooms.

For the avid angler, the Innishannon offers a tremendous opportunity to fish for salmon and sea trout from the hotel lawns, comprising both banks of the river, or on the quarter-mile stretch of the Brinny River where the hotel holds exclusive rights. Permits can also be obtained for fishing other stretches. Deep sea angling can be arranged by the hotel for those with an interest in those waters.

It would be presumptious of me to try to describe the beauty of the surrounding countryside, when poets such as Edmund Spenser have already done so, but perhaps a small poem by local girl Alice Taylor, "Return to Innishannon", best captures visitors' sentiments:

"I have lived my life
far from here
But I have taken
This little place
In the walled garden
Of my heart
To rekindle
My tranquillity."

Innishannon House Hotel
Innishannon
Ireland
Tel: (010 353 21) 775121
Fax: (010 353 21) 775609

THE INTERNATIONAL HOTEL

The International Hotel is one of Killarney's most prominent and centrally situated hotels, convenient for touring, shopping and entertainment. Kerry airport is only 10 miles away.

This 90 bedroom first class hotel offers all rooms with private bath/shower en suite, centrally heated, telephone, TV, video and radio.

The Hotel has been recently modernised and improved without sacrificing its unique atmosphere and Irish charm. The Restaurant, Grill Bar and speciality Seafood Restaurant all offer very good food, using only the freshest local produce, superbly cooked and served in a truly relaxing atmosphere. The Bars and Lounges have an air of friendly informality, combined with efficient and personal service - the ideal rendezvous.

Its praise's sung by many travellers, the Lakeside Fells of Killarney. 'Beauty's Home' cast a spell on all those who visit the region and who often return year after year.

Killarney is the perfect place for a golfing holiday. It offers the visitor the finest facilities for golf with Killarney, the host of the 1991/92 Carroll's Irish Open and the Curtis Cup 1996, only five minutes from the Hotel. 'The beauty of the setting has few peers. All golfers should take a pilgrimage to his enchanting place'. The hotel offers concessionary green fees to the guest Monday to Friday.

Killarney also has excellent fishing in the lakes and rivers and pony trekking through the beautiful 25,000 acre National Park at Muckross.

There is so much to see and do in Killarney, and what better place to base yourself than the charming International Hotel, for a warm welcome and a truly relaxing stay and seven championship courses to choose from within 50 miles.

The International Hotel
Best Western
Killarney
Ireland
Tel: (010 353 64) 31816
Fax: (010 353 64) 31837

JERVAULX HALL

Set amidst the beautiful scenery of the Yorkshire dales and standing adjacent to one of England's most resplendant ruins, Jervaulx Abbey, there could be no better or more unique place from which to tour the surrounding countryside than this friendly and well run hotel.

Bought in 1979, the idea was to create a splendid hotel from this imposing country house. Eight acres of delightful gardens and mature woodlands surround the house which lies midway between the quaint market towns of Masham and Middleham.

It is essentially a quiet and peaceful hotel in which to relax and enjoy beautiful surroundings. The gardens are a delight and can be explored. Over 120 species of wild flowers have been recorded in a single season in the grounds of Jervaulx. The Abbey, founded in 1156 by the monks who gave Wensleydale Cheese its name, is also well worth visiting - its walls are a spectacular riot of marjoram and wall flowers.

The original character of the house interior has been preserved.

The hotel has ten double bedrooms, bathrooms en suite. One bedroom is situated on the ground floor with its own doorway opening on to the garden, making it particularly suitable for the elderly or disabled, or guests with dogs.

The hotel also offers a residential and table licence. Fresh vegetables and soft fruits, local lamb and game are offered on the menu when in season. The hotel's balanced menu and good wines will thus add to the enjoyment of one's stay at Jervaulx. Having lingered a while in the superb setting of Jervaulx it might be as well to get out and about to sample the rest of the area. Castle Howard, Harewood House, Fountains Abbey, York, Harrogate, Richmond and Ripon are all places that should not be missed.

With all of Yorkshire's eleven racecourses conveniently near and the A1 only 20 minutes away, this haven of peace and tranquility is a splendid place to ponder after a day's racing or golf.

Jervaulx Hall Hotel
Jervaulx
Nr Masham
Ripon HG4 4PH
North Yorkshire
Tel: (0677) 60235

THE JOHNSTOUNBURN HOUSE HOTEL

Scotland is the home of golf, and Johnstounburn offers the golfer an opportunity of staying in one of Scotland's original homes. The earliest reference to the estate goes back to 1260, and the house dates to certainly the early 17th century. Since those distant days, Johnstounburn has been cared for and enhanced by influential Scottish families - Borthwick, Broun and Usher - with most of the building on the estate having been effected in the nineteenth century.

The house sits proudly, surrounded by spacious lawns, gardens and unspoilt countryside overlooking the Lammermuir hills. The eleven bedrooms in the main house are rich in individuality and have been decorated to achieve the standard of comfort required by discerning travellers. Each has a private bathroom (only one is not ensuite), colour television and direct dial telephone. A further nine bedrooms were added when the coach house (circa 1840), some 300 yards through the gardens, was converted in 1986.

The 'Piece De Resistance' is the dining room with ornate hand carved wood panelling from floor to ceiling, created in the mid eighteenth century. After a sumptuous meal from the table d'hote menu featuring the finest fresh local produce, and served by candlelight in traditional style, you can retire to the Cedar lounge and enjoy your coffee in front of an open hearth. Or, if the night is kind, you can stroll in the gardens and experience the tranquillity of the surrounds.

The famous golf courses of East Lothian - Muirfield, Gullane, North Berwick, Dunbar - are all within thirty minutes drive. There are more than a dozen courses from which to choose. For those not playing (or just taking the day off), Edinburgh City centre is thirty minutes away. To the south lies the beautiful Border region, with many historic castles, houses and gardens scattered about its rolling hills.

Johnstounburn offers comfort and friendly hospitality in a truly outstanding setting, with fine food carefully presented. Most of all, here you have the opportunity to savour the tradition of Scotland in a house that feels like home.

Johnstounburn House
Humbie
Nr. Edinburgh
East Lothian EH36 5PL
Tel: (087533) 696
Fax: (087533) 626

KILDARE HOTEL AND COUNTRY CLUB

The fifteenth of July 1991 saw the official opening of the Kildare Hotel and Country Club, widely acclaimed as Ireland's premier resort development and a five star complex to rival the very best that Europe can offer.

The Kildare Hotel and Country Club has been developed at a cost of £27.5 million by the Jefferson Smurfit Group plc. Ireland's first world class hotel and sporting facility encompasses an 18 hole championship golf course designed by Arnold Palmer, salmon and trout fishing, indoor and outdoor tennis, exercise, swimming and croquet.

The entire project was created in less than three years and involved the complete renovation of the existing Straffan House. A new wing was added in the style of the existing house, establishing in the process 45 bedroom hotel, whose exacting standards have few equals.

The bedrooms and suites are complemented by exquisitely appointed self-contained apartments and a magnificent three bedroomed lodge in the grounds. Meetings and private dining take place in the 'Tower' and 'River' rooms, where work can happily be combined with play by taking advantage of the wide range of leisure and recreational activities.

The Kildare Country Club, now fast becoming known simply as the 'K' Club, is a multi-facility sporting paradise. Members, hotel guests and visitors alike can enjoy the Championship golf course, river and lake fishing, indoor and outdoor fishing, squash, exercise rooms, swimming pool, beauty treatment room, sauna and solarium.

The golf course, designed by Arnold Palmer and his expert team, has already received excellent reviews and is scheduled to host many national and international tournaments. Covering 177 acres of prime Co. Kildare woodland, the course has a championship length of 6,456 metres and a testing par of 72 (four par fives, four par threes and ten par fours).

Among eighteen exquisitely and imaginatively sculpted holes, particularly outstanding memories could stem from the monster par five seventh, the water-clad eighth or the spectacular par three seventeenth. Every hole, however, has its own challenge and its own beauty. In the words of Arnold Palmer himself, reflecting proudly on his work whilst standing on the terrace of the elevated clubhouse sited behind the eighteenth green: "We could draw for 100 years and not come up with as good a vision".

The Kildare Hotel and Country Club
Straffan
Co. Kildare
Ireland
Tel: (010 353) 1 6273333
Fax: (010 353) 1 6273312

KINLOCH CASTLE

One of Scotland's most remarkable hotels, Kinloch Castle, is situated on an island nature reserve of spectacular wildness and beauty. The hotel offers guests the opportunity to experience living history in the Edwardian castle rooms, whose character and contents have altered little since the turn of the century.

Kinloch Castle was built in 1901 as a sumptuous shooting lodge for Sir George Bullough, a wealthy Lancashire industrialist who used Rum as a sporting estate. No expense or extravagance was spared in either the building or furnishing of the castle, which was sold to the nation along with the island in 1957.

The castle is now owned by Scottish Natural Heritage and is run as a unique hotel with the majority of the original fittings and furnishings intact.

Guests are invited to step back in time to savour a luxurious Edwardian lifestyle. Highlights of an invariably memorable stay include the wonderful reception rooms, with their evocative period detail, and baths equipped with seven controls, ranging from wave, plunge and sitz to the startling jet.

Meals at Kinloch Castle are no less impressive, with breakfast

and dinner served at the original dining table from the Bulloughs' ocean-going yacht 'Rhouma'. After dinner drinks can be savoured whilst listening to the sounds of the orchestrion, a mechanical organ reputedly built for Queen Victoria.

There can be few better settings for a hotel of distinction than the Isle of Rum. A private sporting estate for many years, it is now owned and managed by Scottish Natural Heritage as a National Nature Reserve which the public are welcome to visit. The island is roughly diamond shaped and is about 8 miles in length and breadth. It is renowned for its wild flowers, birds, red deer, wild goats, Rum ponies and highland cattle, with nature trails laid out in the area around Loch Scresort and Kinloch Glen. Angling can also be arranged for sea trout through the Reserve Office.

Visitors to Rum and this outstanding hotel should make their way by car or train to Mallaig, from where the Small Isles Ferry service runs throughout the year. The journey to reach Kinloch Castle is matched in its magnificence only by the quality of the hotel itself and its magical setting. Visitors to one of the country's most sumptuous and unique retreats are inevitably entranced and vow to return, time and time again.

Kinloch Castle
Isle of Rum
Scotland
PH43 4RR
Tel: (0687) 2037

KINNAIRD ESTATE

Mrs Constance Ward invites you to Kinnaird, a splendid country house dating in part from 1770, set in its own estate with lovely views over the Tay valley. With glorious gardens, open fires, a genuinely warm welcome and bedrooms of great charm and comfort, Kinnaird is a delightful spot for a relaxing break and is ideally situated for visiting the many beauty spots and places of interest in Perthshire.

Kinnaird owns over 2.5 miles of high quality fishing on the Tay and employs two full time ghillies. The Lower Kinnaird Beat is renowned for its fishing in September and October and consists of seven attractive pools, while the Upper Kinnaird Beat is a spring beat with an increasing annual catch. The three hill lochs provide fishing for brown trout and pike amongst some of Perthshire's most scenic surroundings.

In addition the estate offers a variety of other sporting including superb pheasant shooting for groups of eight guns, duck flighting and roe stalking.

Less taxing perhaps are the lovely walks that are available from a gentle stroll round the garden to longer walks on the hill and moor. The outdoor tennis court and a croquet lawn provide entertainment for summer afternoons, although should the weather prove inclement, the cedar panelled sitting room provides a selection of amusements including bridge, backgammon, billiards or simply good conversation.

The award-winning restaurant, directed by Chef John Webber, offers modern cuisine of the highest standard; There is an extensive and detailed wine list partnered with a comprehensive selection of Malt Whisky. Both dining rooms enjoy magnificent views, while the former drawing room features exquisite painted panels of figures and landscapes. These superb surroundings provide a stunning setting for a menu of carefully chosen dishes, imaginatively prepared and beautifully presented. In addition to table reservations, private luncheons, dinners and meetings may be reserved. Lunch and dinner are always available for both resident and non-resident guests and booking is appreciated.

On the Kinnaird Estate as well as the hotel there are at present 5 Country Cottages available for let, for more information on fishing and reservations please telephone (0796) 482440.

Kinnaird
Kinnaird Estate
By Dunkeld
Perthshire PH8 0LB
Tel: (0796) 482440
Fax: (0796) 482289

LADYBURN

Ladyburn, the home of David and Jane Hepburn, lies in the heart of 'the most beautiful valley in Ayrshire' on the edge of the magnificent estate of Kilkerran surrounded by the most intriguing pattern of woods and fields. Ladyburn was acquired in the late 17th century by the Fergussons of Kilkerran and remained in their hands until the death of Francis, widow of Sir James Fergusson.

Visitors are welcomed to Ladyburn by the friendly atmosphere of gracious living enjoyed by former generations of Hepburns. The house is furnished with antiques inherited by the family. All the bedrooms are different, each with its own character and style of furniture and furnishings.

The cuisine is traditional using only local fresh produce, much of which is grown in the gardens, and is prepared and cooked by Jane.

For those who are 'Travelling the Turf', Ladyburn is situated only 12 miles from Ayr, site of Scotland's foremost racecourse, with over 30 fixtures organised normally, incorporating a full programme for both the Flat and National Hunt. Fishing and shooting can also be arranged. Set in the heart of Robert Burns country, other places to visit would be Culzean Castle and Country Park, Crossragnel Abbey and, further afield is Loch Lomond and the Trossachs.

Staying at Ladyburn is being a guest in a beautiful country house where the welcome and attention given by David and Jane Hepburn is reminiscent of a bygone era.

Ladyburn
By Maybole
Ayrshire
KA19 7SG
Tel: (06554) 585
AA★★   Fax: (06554) 580   RAC ★★★

THE LAKE COUNTRY HOUSE

The Lake is a riverside country house set in 50 acres of beautiful grounds with sweeping lawns, woods, riverside walks and a large well stocked lake. The hotel offers spacious and luxurious accommodation, enhanced by log fires and antiques. Excellent imaginative food, prepared from fresh local produce, is served in the elegant dining room, accompanied by one of the finest wine lists in Wales. The Lake has been awarded the Restaurant of the Year by Johansens for 1991 and has also received a Rosette for food from the AA for the last two years. The Lake offers all that is best in country house hospitality and satisfied guests return again and again.

For the golf enthusiast there are four full size courses in close proximity, with Builth Wells Course only 10 minutes away, an attractive parkland course of 5386 yards, par 66, the hotel can organise concessionary tickets here.

It is a fisherman's paradise with a lake covering 2 1/2 acres, within the grounds and a 4 1/2 mile stretch of the River Irfon

running through the extensive parkland of the hotel. The trout in the river are mostly wild fish and run up to 5lb, with some larger. Our water is divided into six beats, a maximum of two rods being allowed on each. **The Wye** provides good trout fishing, specimens up to and over 1lb are not uncommon. The number of rods per beat is restricted. **The Irfon** is likely to produce salmon almost anytime in the season, but really comes into its own in the latter part. There are also a number of Welsh Water Authorities Reservoirs within easy reach. Our gillie is on hand to give fishing instruction at a very reasonable charge.

The region is well known to birdwatchers and is an ideal centre for walkers and also a haven for wildlife, including badgers and red kite. There are spectacular drives in all directions. Clay pigeon shooting and horse riding are available. AA and RAC 3 Stars and Merit Award. Children welcome. Dogs by arrangement.

The Lake Country House
Llangammarch Wells
Powys
Wales LD4 4BS
Tel: (05912) 202/474
Fax: (05912) 457

LAKE VYRNWY HOTEL

In 1881 The Corporation of Liverpool began work on a huge masonry dam in the Vyrnwy Valley, to provide fresh water supplies for the city. The hotel began its life at the same time, finally completed in 1890. Built of local stone in the style of the old manor houses that make this part of Wales and the Border Counties so famous, it rests 900 feet above sea level. The lake was first stocked with fish in 1889 with 400 000 Loch Leven trout. The official first day of fishing was in March 1891, and sporting traditions are maintained to this day.

Lake Vyrnwy is a unique country house and sporting hotel; looking out over the unspoilt countryside, it holds court over mist-topped mountains, heather-clad moorlands, leafy forests and rolling meadows; its character constantly changing as each individual season frames and re-focuses its colours and shapes. The strong lines of classic Victorian architecture exude all the confidence of the period, while its interior echoes the welcome assurance of antiquity. Private ownership allows the hotel to maintain its individuality and loving attention to detail. Public rooms are quiet and restful; from the steady tick of the grandfather clock and crackling winter log fire in the sitting room, complete with an elegant Bechstein grand piano, to the luxurious club atmosphere, surrounded by fisherman's trophies, in the heart of the hotel.

All of the 38 bedrooms have ensuite spacious bathrooms; some, for that extra special luxury, have a jacuzzi. All have direct-dial telephones, radio, remote control colour televisions, hairdryers, indeed everything for your comfort and convenience. All that is left for you is to decide between a cosy cottage atmosphere, the privacy of a suite, perhaps a private balcony, or even a four-poster for those romantic nights. Larger and interconnecting rooms are available and especially suitable for families.

In the dining room light and elegant dishes contrast with traditional. The award-winning restaurant's luncheon and dinner menus change regularly but are always freshly prepared in the hotel's kitchens; everything in fact, from marmalades at breakfast to the petits fours after dinner, even a range of preserves, chutneys and mustards. The seasonal vegetables and herbs are picked fresh from the kitchen gardens.

In such surroundings there can never be a dull moment; anything from a simple walk along one of the nature trails, a gentle cycle around the lake shores or maybe an exhilarating sail. Above all there is peace and solitude and freedom on this 24,000 acre estate.

Lake Vyrnwy Hotel
Llanwddyn
Montgomeryshire
Mid Wales SY10 0LY
Tel: (0691) 73692
Fax: (0691) 73259

LANGAR HALL

This charming small country House Hotel & Restaurant in the village of Langar, 12 miles S.E. of Nottingham is set in quiet seclusion overlooking the Vale of Belvoir and ancient trees in the park. It is the family home of Imogen Skirving and although it is fully staffed and managed as an hotel the atmosphere is still that of having the run of someone's country house.

There are three superb double rooms in the front of the house (including two four-posters) & four comfortable double rooms in the wing. (Three of the rooms have adjacent single rooms). There are a further two rooms in the recently converted stable including one named after Desert Orchid. All the bedrooms have ensuite bathrooms/shower, direct dial telephone, tea making facilities, clock radio and lovely views over the garden & parkland.

Head chef Frank Vallat runs the kitchen with the help of two talented under chefs. The emphasis is on fresh ingredients cooked to order and served with sauces. His style of food is an individual expression of his taste & talents combined with the experience gained from working in star restaurants and are slanted towards customers coming for a special night out & to cheer the traveller at the end of a tiring day.

The Butler, Crispin Harris (actor/playwrite/musician) runs a popular restaurant and sometimes plays the piano. On the last Friday of the month he produces after dinner theatre: 1/2 hour plays written or adapted for the dining room & performed by 'Scoundrels' a local professional theatre company. This makes an amusing evening without interfering with the 'serious' appreciation of the food.

The wine list is written & chosen by James Seely author of 'Great Bordeaux Wines' and 'The Loire Valley & it's wine'.

Langar Hall makes an ideal venue for private meetings & conferences (Max 25).

Children and Dogs welcome by arrangement.

Whole house bookings taken for private parties/weddings.

Langar Hall
Langar
Nottinghamshire
NG13 9HG
Tel: (0949) 60559
Fax: (0949) 61045

LEE PARK LODGE

Lee Park Lodge is a converted farm house on the famous Broadlands Estate, situated at the Southern end of the Test Valley close to the River Test. It has been luxuriously and tastefully refurbished to provide comfortable reception rooms and eight twin bedded bedrooms, all with bathroom en suite and direct dial telephones.

Our imaginative cuisine will satisfy the most discerning of palates and ample use is being made of fresh local produce, fish and game. Our talented cooks prepare tastefully presented dishes as a feast to the eye and such is the faith of some of our clients that the choice of the menu is often left to them.

The Lodge is ideally situated for a great many sporting activities, fishing being one of the favourites. During the April - October season it is possible to fish on the waters that Prince Charles has known and loved ever since he was a young boy, whilst staying in first class accommodation close by. Lee Park Lodge offers superb fly fishing for trout for up to six rods on its own beats on the world famous River Test - full outfits of rods, flies and nets are available for an extra charge.

A residential fishing package at the Lodge includes accommodation, all meals, fishing with a ghillie service available and use of a hospitality marquee on the river bank for relaxation and weather protection. A picnic lunch will be prepared each morning and brought over to you wherever you are fishing so the only thing you have to think about is the fishing.

It is not necessary to stay at the Lodge in order to 'sample its many delights'; a day fishing package can also be arranged consisting of three course lunch and a buffet supper at the Lodge, fishing with ghillie service and use of the hospitality marquee.

For a relaxing break filled with all the comforts of home yet the service of a first class hotel, Lee Park Lodge has successfully combined the two to provide the perfect holiday for the keen fisherman.

Lee Park Lodge
Broadlands
Romsey
Hampshire
SO51 9ZD
Tel: (0703) 734087
Fax: (0703) 740409

LETHAM GRANGE HOTEL AND GOLF COURSES

In the heartland of golf lies the superb new Letham Grange Hotel and Golf Courses. The magnificent Victorian Mansion nestles with the panoramic Letham Grange Estate. The Mansion has been restored to its former glory as a top quality, 3 star hotel with 20 bedrooms, offering a style and standard of living which is both traditional and sumptuous.

36 Holes of magnificent golf! Widely acclaimed as one of the premier courses in Scotland, the Old Course provides a blend of tree lined parkland and open rolling fairways. With water playing a major role, the Course is both scenic and dramatic. The New Course, although slightly shorter - and without the water hazards, offers golfers a more relaxed and less arduous round. However, it can be deceptive!

For further information on special golfing breaks, or a day's golf

Letham Grange Hotel
Colliston
by Arbroath
DD11 4RL
Tel: (0241) 89 373
Fax: (0241) 89 414

171

LINDEN HALL

Linden Hall, a magnificent Georgian Country House, is situated in 450 acres of splendid park and woodland, in mid-Northumberland. Grand and elegant without being stuffy or formal, Linden Hall offers an escape to tranquil comfort in a warm and friendly atmosphere. Carefully restored to recapture the style of the original Georgian mansion, preserving its Tuscan portico, magnificent staircase and classical lines, Linden Hall fully justifies its Grade II listing as a building of architectural importance.

Splendid log fires roaring on a chilly winter's evening, antique-filled rooms and the hotel's very own country pub, converted from an old granary, are combined with more modern comforts: a sauna and solarium, fully equipped bedrooms, including private bathrooms and shower, colour TV, direct dial telephone, baby listening service, and much more. The Dobson Restaurant offers a delightful menu in graceful surroundings with panoramic views over the croquet lawn to the rugged Northumberland coastline.

Talking of croquet, the satisfying thud of mallet on wooden ball is just one activity to be indulged in at Linden Hall. There is also a putting green and tennis court, and coarse fishing is available from the hotel's lake. In addition, guests can join a party for clay pigeon shooting with expert tuition and supervision provided by the Estates manager and his team. Prepare to take your aim! The hotel also has excellent golfing facilities in the area and can make arrangements for guest at the links courses of Foxton Hall, Bamburgh Castle and Dunstanburgh Castle. If the weather is inclement, the indoor games area includes a snooker table.

Situated in the peace of some of England's most stunning countryside, there is a wide variety of things to do within a reasonable distance of Linden Hall. Northumberland boasts fabulous beaches, salmon and trout fishing, busy market towns and sleepy villages, and a history of Roman forts and Norman castles. Wallington Hall and Cragside, both National Trust properties, are close to hand, as is Dunstanburgh Castle and the towns of Morpeth and Bamburgh. You may want to take a boat trip to the Farne Islands; cross the causeway at Holy Island or perhaps visit the open-air museum at Beamish.

An ideal setting for a weekend away, a longer stay, or special occasions like weddings, dinner parties, conferences or seminars, Linden Hall offers rural seclusion, luxury and quite exceptional service.

Linden Hall Hotel
Longhorsley
Morpeth
Northumberland NE65 8XF
Tel: (0670) 516611
Fax: (0670) 88544

LLANGOED HALL

On this site, fourteen hundred years ago, the Welsh Parliament stood; at least according to legend. Inspired by this, the celebrated architect, Sir Clough Williams-Ellis transformed the largely Jacobean mansion he found here into the great country house it is today. Llangoed Hall was completed in 1918 although parts of the South facing wing, including the panelled library date, from 1632. Inside it is the Laura Ashley genius that is most striking, that ability of interpreting the past to bring comfort and beauty to the present.

The intention of Sir Bernard Ashley, when he decided to convert the hall, was never that of the usual hotelier. Having decided to return to the idea of entertaining guests, rather than patrons, he worked hard to re-create the style and atmosphere of what it once was, a great Edwardian country house where visitors could stay and enjoy the way of life it once stood for. Thoughtful luxuries abound, personal touches make all the difference; fresh fruit; a decanter of sherry or mineral water ready to pour; plenty of books in the bedrooms fleecy robes and luxurious oils in the bathrooms a tray of famous Welsh afternoon tea of scones and home-made jam, shortbread and cream-filled meringues and local Bara Brith served in the Morning Room to welcome you on arrival.

The dining room is handsome with yellow and cornflower blue, a perfect complement to the menu of one the finest young chefs in Britain; always insisting on fresh local produce; Welsh lamb, Wye salmon and traditional laverbread; vegetables and herbs collected from the hotel's own gardens. All to be enjoyed with a choice from some of the 300 superb wines assembled from the greatest wine regions of the world.

For the sportsman, three superb golf courses are within easy driving distance; all 18-hole with breathtaking scenery. In addition to the hotel's own all-weather tennis court and croquet lawn guests may fish for salmon and trout on the Upper Wye and River Irfon. The countryside, rich in wildlife, offers a variety of rough shooting and bird-watching. Riding can be easily arranged and the magnificent Brecon Beacons have much to offer both the serious and casual walker; not to mention the fascinating surrounding countryside, from Wordsworth's beloved Tintern Abbey to the ancient castles of Raglan and Caerphilly.

Conference facilities are, naturally, extensive, with a variety of rooms available, from the panelled, book-lined library to separate dining room, the Flower Room. For all guests a chauffeur-driven car is available for day-to-day touring or collection from rail and air terminals, and helicopters may use the south lawn by prior arrangement.

Llangoed Hall
Llyswen
Brecon
Powys
Wales
LD3 0YP
Tel: (0874) 754525
Fax: (0874) 754545

LOCKERBIE MANOR COUNTRY HOTEL

Set amidst 78 acres of tranquil park and woodland, Lockerbie Country Manor is a haven of peace and relaxation, yet it is situated only a mile off the A74. Built in 1814 for Sir William Douglas and Dame Grace Johnstone, whose great-grandson, the Marquis of Queensbury, formulated the present day boxing rules, it became the smart country hotel it is today in 1920.

Guests can enjoy the traditions of a bygone era at Lockerbie Manor. The long tree-lined driveway gives a taste of the luxury that lies ahead. Both of the public lounges are furnished in authentic period style with an Adam fireplace amidst period furniture and walls lined with oil paintings. The atmosphere exudes warmth and hospitality; a home away from home for the traveller.

All the 29 bedrooms are individually decorated with private bathrooms, colour T.V. and every comfort. There are three four-poster bedded suites, with front-facing views over the fields and surrounding countryside. The Queensbury Dining Room, with its wood panelled wall, ornate chandeliers and magnificent views, is the ideal setting for a delectable meal. The cuisine is of an international nature, where Eastern flavours and cooking subtly blend with Western recipes.

Golfers will love the courses in the area, offering challenges of varying degrees of difficulty. Lockerbie, Dumfries, Lochmaben, Powfoot and Moffat are all near by. If shooting is more your scene, there are numerous large estates around Lockerbie offering facilities. For the fisherman, the Rivers Annan, Milk, Cree, Blanock and Penkiln all beckon. Within the space of a short drive you can visit the beautiful Galloway coast, Drumlanrigg Castle, Maxwellton House in Monaive, Threave Gardens and Castle near Castle Douglas, and Thomas Carlyle's birthplace at Ecclefechan.

Lockerbie Manor Country Hotel
Boreland Road
Lockerbie
Dumfries and Galloway
DG11 2RG
Tel: (05762) 2610
Fax: (05762) 3046

LONGUEVILLE HOUSE

Longueville is set in the centre of a 500 acre private wooded estate, overlooking one of the most beautiful river valleys in Ireland, the Blackwater - itself forming the Estate's southern boundary, famous as one of Ireland's foremost salmon and trout rivers.

Longueville is three miles on the Killarney road ex Mallow; Killarney itself in the heart of scenic Kerry being less than one hour away. Cork airport is 24 miles distant and Shannon airport is 54 miles away. Guests can make day trips to the Dingle and Beara Peninsulas. Blarney, Kinsale and the Vee Gap are all less than one hour's drive. For stay-at-homes, Longueville offers three miles of game fishing on the famous Blackwater river. There is horse-riding at nearby stables and golf at a dozen courses closeby including Premier Championship courses at Killarney, Ballybunion and Tralee.

A games room with full sized billiard table is in the basement. The estate is quiet and peaceful for walking or jogging with idyllic paths through wooded ways and water meadows.

Built in 1720, Longueville is the ancestral home of your hosts. Their aim is to maintain the friendly atmosphere of a home rather than a hotel. The centre block and two wings were added in 1800 and the Turner Curvilinear Conservatory was added in 1862.

Inside, Longueville offers many beautiful ceilings, doors and items of antique furniture in the public rooms and bedrooms - but in the latter, whether it be antique or otherwise, the acme of comfort is the bed. All bedrooms have en suite bathroom, colour television, radio and direct dial telephone.

The aim of Longueville's hosts is to have guests relax and feel completely at home in the comfort of their beautiful house, a classic Georgian country house. Central to all this is the kitchen, the heart of Longueville, over which the O'Callaghans' son William, a French-trained chef, presides. In here three lovingly prepared meals a day are made, using only the fresh produce of the estate's river, farm and gardens.

To match the superb food, Longueville's cellar includes over 150 wines, both from the Old and New World. The family's interest in wine has led them to plant their own three acre vineyard - unique in Ireland - produced in years of favourable climate.

Longueville House & Presidents' Restaurant
Mallow
Co Cork
Republic of Ireland
Tel: (010 353 22) 47156/47306
Fax: (010 353 22) 47459

LOSTWITHIEL HOTEL, GOLF AND COUNTRY CLUB

In an idyllic setting among the wooded hills which look down on the beautiful valley of the river Fowey, Lostwithiel Hotel, Golf and Country Club is unique.

A hotel of great charm and character, Lostwithiel offers outstanding service and comfort in a memorable setting in the heart of Cornwall. Old Cornish buildings, mellowed stone, beamed ceilings - these are all part of the rural tranquillity that awaits guests.

The spacious and individually designed bedrooms each have colour TV, direct dial telephone, tea and coffee making facilities and luxurious bathrooms. Imaginative and interesting menus emphasise fresh local produce and the wine list is impressive.

All guests have Golf and Leisure Club membership during their stay, with excellent facilities which include two all-weather tennis courts, and a superb indoor heated swimming pool. Keen anglers can enjoy excellent trout and salmon fishing. The hotel grounds sweep down to the banks of the river Fowey.

The variety of leisure facilities makes for very successful corporate days. In addition to well equipped conference rooms and banqueting facilities, activities can include golf, fishing, swimming, tennis, clay pigeon shooting, even hot air ballooning.

The 18 hole golf course is one of the most interesting and varied in Cornwall. Designed to take full advantage of the natural features of the landscape, it combines two very distinctive areas of hillside and valley. All along the challenging and interesting front nine there are magnificent views down the valley while the back nine with its lakes and streams go through leafy parkland, flanked by the waters of the Fowey. Exceptional all year round practice facilities include a foodlit driving range with undercover and grass bays, two-tier putting green and practice bunkers. What more could you ask for?

For those of you who don't know Cornwall, you will discover that Lostwithiel is a perfect base for discovering its breathtakingly beautiful coastline, quiet inland villages, ancient towns and historic houses. You can explore the haunting landscape of Bodmin, Llanhydrock House in its fascinating Edwardian timewarp or the catherdral city of Truro.

Lostwithiel Hotel, Golf and Country Club
Lower Polscoe
Lostwithiel
Cornwall Pl2 0HQ
Tel: (0208) 873550
Fax: (0208) 873479

LOWER SLAUGHTER MANOR

A Manor House has stood on this site for over a thousand years. In 1443 Syon Abbey took over the buildings to establish a nunnery, and they remained as such until Henry VIII, fighting the legality of abandoning his marriage with Catherine of Aragon, broke England's ties with Papal Rome and dissolved the monasteries. The land was seized by the Crown and finally granted to Sir George Whitmore, High Sheriff of Gloucestershire, by James I in 1603. The house was largely re-built in the 1650s by his son, Richard, who directed a then-famous stonemason, Valentine Strong, to build a house on the site for 'the sum of two hundred pounds in lawful English money'. The present house retains the essential details of that original, despite a number of extensions and alterations.

Situated on the edge of one of the Cotswolds prettiest villages The Manor is a haven of tranquillity. The picturesque walled garden is the setting for a dovecote featured in the Domesday Book; while public rooms are elegant with fine paintings, antiques and blazing log fires in the winter. The sumptuous bedrooms are airy and spacious and, despite providing every modern comfort and convenience, have lost none of their centuries-old charm.

Besides the obvious attractions of the surrounding countryside there are plenty of ways to awaken an appetite within the Manor; from indoor heated swimming pool and sauna to all weather tennis court, putting green and croquet lawn. Afterwards relax in the restaurant to be tempted by an array of traditional country house cuisine prepared with fresh, locally grown produce and herbs from the garden; complemented by a choice wine from the fine cellars.

Lower Slaughter Manor prides itself on offering guests something a little more personal than the average hotel; a welcome more akin to the family guests of a country house in days gone by. With such experienced staff and the option of a self-contained suite, the Manor proves itself the perfect venue for the conference, as well as the ideal break.

Lower Slaughter Manor
Lower Slaughter
Gloucestershire GL54 2HP
Tel: (0451) 820456
Fax: (0451) 822150

LUCKNAM PARK

Lucknam Park is a magnificent country house, situated six miles from the Georgian City of Bath, set in extensive parkland of two hundred and eighty acres. A focus of fine society and gracious living for over 250 years, Lucknam Park now recreates, as a luxurious hotel, the elegance and style of an era long ago.

Guests approach the hotel along a mile-long beech-lined avenue, leading to the house and its honey-toned stonework. Wide lawns, abundant fresh flowers and an aura of quiet and calm promise a very individual welcome. Whether you are a traveller, a gourmet or simply a romantic, guests will find at Lucknam Park an elegance and tranquillity born out of a sense of everything being right and well ordered.

The eleven suites and thirty-one bedrooms are furnished with a delicate sense of historical context, but also with the luxury and facilities demanded of a first class country-house hotel. Individually designed, with generous space and splendid views, each one enjoys the comfort and charming service which help to make Lucknam Park an extra special hotel.

The award-winning restaurant (recently receiving its first Michelin Star) is set with exquisite porcelain, silver and glass, reflecting the sumptuous but discreet atmosphere and service. Our highly acclaimed Head Chef, Michael Womersley, provides a frequently changing menu of Modern English cuisine using only the freshest ingredients. Wine can be chosen from an impressive list of over 350 wines and our Sommelier is delighted to assist and advise on the perfect choice.

For relaxing and unwinding the Leisure Spa facilities at Lucknam Park are second to none, providing a superb balance between gentle exercise and total pampering. In the style of a Roman Villa and set within the walls of the old garden the Leisure Spa opens up another world: indoor swimming pool and jacuzzi, saunas and steam room, a fully equipped gymnasium, snooker room, beauty salon and tennis courts are all of the highest standards.

The Beauty Salon offers all Clarins Beauty products and treatments. These treatments range from '6 minute' makeovers, using the new Le Maquillage range to full Paris Method massages, known as the 'Rolls Royce' of treatments.

Guided tours with personal guide can be arranged to explore the splendours of the glorious City of Bath and surrounding countryside. The delightful villages of Castle Combe, Lacock and the stately homes of Bowood House and Corsham Court are all close by. Many other activities are available too. Take your pick from Hot Air Ballooning, Golf, Motor Racing, Horse Riding, Clay Pigeon Shooting, Fishing, Archery and Boating. The magnificent Theatre Royal in Bath even holds private seats for guests at Lucknam Park.

Lucknam Park epitomises a country house hotel at its best. The hotel is less than two hours drive from London and guests can be sure that their memories of Lucknam Park will stay with them for a long time to come.

Lucknam Park
Colerne
Wiltshire SN14 8AZ
Tel: (0225) 724777
Fax: (0225) 743536

LYGON ARMS

For over 450 years, the picturesque village of Broadway has been the home of the Lygon Arms. Set in delightful Cotswold countryside, the Inn offers charming, olde worlde accommodation and combines a quality of service with a warm and friendly atmosphere.

In our restaurant, The Great Hall, you can relax and enjoy fine English cuisine, complimented by our extensive selection of wines. Adjacent to the Inn, Goblets Wine Bar provides the cosy setting for a delicious meal in front of a roaring fire.

For the horse racing enthusiast, Cheltenham, Stratford upon Avon, Warwick and Worcester race courses are all within easy reach of the Lygon Arms. We are always delighted to arrange a picnic hamper to make your 'day at the races' a day to remember.

For conferences, seminars, meetings or dinner, The Lygon Arms is the perfect venue. Our comprehensive range of facilities boast the very latest in communications technology, together with comfortable, well equipped and spacious meeting rooms.

The Lygon Arms
High Street
Broadway
Worcestershire WR12 7DU

Tel: (0386) 852255
Telex: 338260
Fax: (0386) 858611

HOTEL MAES-Y-NEUADD

Maes-y-Neuadd, an ancient Welsh Manor House, built between 1350 and 1720, was home to the Nanney Wynn family for several centuries. Since 1981 it has been owned and personally run by the Slatter and Horsfall families.

The hotel setting is superb, Maes-y-Neuadd - "The Mansion in the meadow" stands in eight acres of landscaped lawns, orchards and paddock on a wooded mountain side high above the waters of Tremadog Bay, perfect for exhilarating walks.

All modern comforts have been blended into this historic house, with its inglenook fireplace, decorated plaster work and oak beams. Each bedroom is imaginatively designed and furnished, each with its own very individual style, and many have fabulous views of the mountains or Tremadoc Bay and the distant Lleyn Peninsular. Some have antiques collected over the years, and others contain examples of the very best work of some of our contemporary crafts people.

A Boardroom facility has been created for the small, important meeting and clay pigeon shooting, riding, golf and gun dog demonstrations can be arranged.

Snowdonia's grandeur is right on the doorstep, with some of the most stunning scenery in Britain. Harlech, with its mighty Castle and famous Golf Links if but 3 miles away. There are beautiful beaches, the Italianate village of Portmerion, world famous slate caverns and many of the great little trains of Wales, all within easy reach.

Hotel Maes-y-Neuadd
Talsarnau
Nr. Harlech
Gwynedd
North Wales
LL47 6YA
Tel: (0766) 780200
Fax: (0766) 780211

THE MAGHERABUOY HOUSE HOTEL

On the Causeway Coast in Northern Ireland, stone walls blend into green fields and sweeping cliffs roll towards the sea. This is also natural golfing country, and it is difficult to find anywhere that surpasses this natural coastal setting or a hotel that offers such a delightful base for exploring surrounding golf courses. Stand on the steps of the Magherabuoy House Hotel and you can breathe in the fresh salt air of the Atlantic Ocean.

The Magherabuoy House Hotel incorporates the period home of the former Minister of Home Affairs and has been carefully restored and extended, providing modern comforts in a majestic setting. Opulence is the key note, the elegant reception area creating a warm, sophisticated atmosphere, reflecting the standard and quality of service throughout. There are 38 luxurious bedrooms, all with private bathrooms, colour T.V. and tea and coffee making facilities. Guests can enjoy delicious a la carte meals in the Lanyon Room after a day on the golf course.

The jewel in the crown is undoubtedly the famous fairways of the championship course of Royal Portrush. Barely five minutes from the hotel, the links of Portrush set a challenge to players of every standard. There are three excellent courses: the Dunluce Course on which the Championships are played; the Valley Course on which the Ladies mainly play and the nine hole pitch and putt course at the end of the links nearest the town known as the Skerries. Throughout the years more than forty national championships, British and Irish, have been decided on these links.

Exhilarating rounds of golf in a stunning setting are available at five other courses in the area. The recently improved Portstewart can offer a challenge almost on a par with Royal Portrush; and Rathmore, Castlerock, Bushfoot, and Ballycastle all provide varied and testing golf.

The Hotel is situated only an hour's drive from the airport and docks, and guests can be collected from the airport in the hotel's own courtesy transport. For a really unusual golfing holiday you can be assured of a warm welcome.

The Magherabuoy House Hotel
41 Magheraboy Road
Portrush BT56 8NX
Tel: (0265) 823507
Fax: (0265) 824687

181

LE MANOIR AUX QUAT'SAISONS

Le Manoir aux Quat'Saisons is situated in 27 acres of gardens and parkland in the Oxfordshire village of Great Milton. Easily accessible from London or Birmingham via the M40 motorway, this internationally acclaimed country house hotel and restaurant is one of only nine establishments in the World to be awarded the Relais & Chateaux Gold and Red shields. This is their highest classification and confirms the overall standard of excellence and hospitality at this magnificent 15th century Cotswold manor house.

There are nineteen elegant bedrooms at Le Manoir aux Quat'Saisons. Each one has been individually designed and captures the atmosphere of warmth and friendliness by the use of beautiful fabrics and antique furnishings. Many of the luxurious bathrooms feature whirlpool baths or steam showers. In the converted stable block, most of the bedrooms have a private terrace overlooking the gardens and orchard. Even the medieval dovecote has been transformed into a romantic suite.

Chef/Patron Raymond Blanc is one of the World's finest chefs and Le Manoir is widely acknowledged as Britain's finest restaurant. The extensive vegetable and herb gardens in the grounds provide the kitchen with a great variety of produce. An extensive wine list, the work of Restaurant Director, Alain Desenclos, complements Raymond Blanc's cuisine.

Before or after your meal, a stroll through the gardens at Le Manoir is a delight. Colourful herbaceous borders line the paths, the water gardens and lake attract wildlife and, in the private swimming pool garden, residents can relax, sip a cool drink and soak up the sun. More energetic guests can enjoy a game of tennis.

Private lunch or dinner parties can be held in the Cromwell Room where up to 46 guests can enjoy the specially priced party menus created by Raymond Blanc.

Le Manoir aux Quat'Saisons - a unique combination of exceptional cuisine and comfort.

Le Manoir aux Quat'Saisons
Great Milton
Oxford
OX9 7PD
Tel: (0844) 278881
Fax: (0844) 278847

THE MANOR HOUSE

Time stands still in the Bybrook valley at the southern tip of the Cotswolds. Renowned as one of the prettiest villages in England, picturesque Castle Combe nestles in this delightful wooded valley where nothing has changed for the past 200 years. Rough-hewn limestone cottages, ancient market cross and a packbridge over the Bybrook, described in 1458 as 'the great town bridge', are the epitome of a peaceful English village.

Certainly there can be no lovelier approach to any village than the narrow lane winding its way down to Castle Combe through a green tunnel of interlocking branches.

To the enchantment of this hidden village, the Manor House lends an extra fairy tale dimension. Steeped in history, with parts of the house dating back to the 14th century and added to by the Jacobeans in 1664, it is the quintessential English manor. A symphony of chimneys, mullioned windows and creeper covered walls and inside welcoming log fires and inviting sofas.

There is rich wood panelling, and gleaming glass and silver in the candlelit 'Bybrook' restaurant. There are bedrooms tucked away in romantic attics, or boasting an Elizabethan fireplace and triple aspect views. They are all luxurious, some with four poster beds, others with Victorian style bathrooms. All the rooms in the main house have been restored and refurbished during the past two years to an exceptional degree, revealing hidden beams, stonework and a grain drying kiln.

Croquet, tennis and a heated outside swimming pool are all available for guests, with trout fishing on the one mile stretch of the Bybrook flowing through the 26 acres of gardens and parkland.

The Manor House is surrounded by countryside designated as an area of outstanding natural beauty. There are suggested walks through neighbouring woodland, or for the more energetic there are cycles to hire for visits to the many delightful nearby Cotswold villages.

Set in 200 acres of wooded valley and downland, an exceptional new golf course has been created. Castle Combe Golf Club, dominated by ancient oak and beech woods is only two minutes driving distance from the Manor House.

Guests staying at the Manor House are welcomed at the Golf Club and the 6,200 yard, par 71 course, designed by Peter Allis, will provide interesting and challenging golf for the average golfer and good player alike.

Although lost in the heart of the Cotswold countryside, access is not difficult. The M4 motorway is only 15 minutes away and the journey from London by road takes but 1 hour, 40 minutes. The intersection with the M5 is only 20 minutes away, linking the Midlands, the North and South West for ease of access.

The Manor House
Castle Combe
Chippenham
Wiltshire
SN14 7HR
Tel: (0249) 782206
Fax: (0249) 782159

MICHAELS NOOK HOTEL

A gracious, stone-built Lakeland home, with a wealth of mahogany woodwork, Michaels Nook is quietly tucked away overlooking the Grasmere valley and surrounded by well-kept lawns and beautiful trees. It was opened as a hotel over twenty years ago by owner Reg Gifford, a respected antique dealer, and furnishings, enhanced by an abundance of flowers and plants, reflect his appreciation of English furniture, antique rugs, prints and porcelain. The Hotel retains the mellowness of the private home, and a hint of pleasing eccentricity, accentuated by the presence of a Great Dane and some exotic cats.

There are twelve, lovely, individually-designed bedrooms, all with en suite bathrooms, and two magnificent suites. Each room has colour television and direct dial telephone, and is provided with many thoughtful extra touches, such as fresh flowers, fruit, and mineral water. Full room service is available.

In the Restaurant, polished tables gleam, set with fine crystal and porcelain, and only the best fresh ingredients are used for dishes memorable for their delicate flavour and artistic presentation. Different choices are offered each day. A very extensive

Wine List offers selections from all the best wine-producing areas, and makes for fascinating reading, as well as excellent drinking. The panelled Oak Room, with handsome stone fireplace and gilt furnishings, hosts Director and Senior Manager meetings and private celebrations.

Spectacular excursions, by car or on foot, start from the doorstep of this delightful house, and encompass some of Britain's most impressive scenery. Dove Cottage, Wordsworth's home during his most creative period, is close at hand, and Beatrix Potter's farm at Sawrey only a short drive away.

The Hotel itself has three acres of landscaped grounds, and a further ten acres of woodland and wild fell, plus a speciality rhododendron garden covering four acres of nearby hillside. Guests are also welcome to make use of the heated swimming pool, and other health facilities of The Wordsworth Hotel, less than a mile away, and under the same ownership. Both Hotels offer special arrangements with Keswick Golf Club, and enjoy a close proximity to some of the excellent northern links courses.

Michaels Nook
Grasmere
Ambleside
Cumbria LA22 9RP
Tel: (05394) 35496
Fax: (05394) 35765

MILL END HOTEL

The River Teign flows through some of the most beautiful and unspoilt countryside in Devon. The fishing the Teign has to offer is varied. Between Chagford bridge and Steppes Bridge the angler can fish for moorland trout. Salmon and Sea trout begin to appear in the Upper Teign waters from about April, with greater numbers becoming available from the middle of June until the end of the season on 30th September. The hotel can arrange fishing for its guests on about fourteen miles of brown trout water and six miles of salmon and sea trout water.

The Mill End Hotel is a superb base for fishing. Immediately adjacent to the hotel are 600 yards of private bank and four pools for salmon and sea trout. Fernworthy and Hennock reservoirs, stocked with rainbow trout, are within easy driving distance. Mr Roddie Rae, a local expert and Upper Teign water bailiff, is available to tutor the inexperienced or act as a ghillie to skilled fishermen.

The Mill End hotel was formally a flour mill and its wheel still turns in the peaceful courtyard. Converted in 1929 the hotel has an atmosphere of a comfortable private house. All rooms have a private bathroom, telephone, colour television, hairdryer and other practical comforts.

To complete your day a superb dinner with fresh ingredients, carefully prepared on the premises the day you eat them - is the Mill End promise. An award winning cheese selection includes several local favourites as well as many from France. There are over a hundred wines listed and an interesting selection of Cognacs and Malt Whiskys.

For the non-fisherman Mill End is ideally situated for exploring Dartmoor. There is an excellent 18 hole golf course near by and opportunities to ride and shoot. There are many delightful walks on Dartmoor and National Trust properties to explore.

Mill End Hotel
Sandy Park, Chagford
Devon TQ13 8JN
Tel: (0647) 432282
Fax: (0647) 433106

THE MILLERS HOUSE HOTEL

Nestled in the heart of the Yorkshire Dales the elegant Georgian Millers House makes an ideal base from which to explore Herriot Country whether by car or on foot. We offer guided walking tours, pony trekking or hot air ballooning for the more adventurous. There are four good golf courses nearby, local fishing permits and equipment can be arranged.

Breathtaking views across Coverdale and Wensleydale with a backdrop of Middleham Castle and racehorses from the many local racing stables, exercising over the Low Moor. Guests on our Racing Breaks then visit a Training stables and enjoy a day at the Races - Members' badges, Timeform cards and a tour of the course included.

Our reputation for excellent food and wine makes our Gourmet Wine weekends popular. We sample a range of wines before dinner on Friday and Saturday with a professional speaker from the wine trade plus a fabulous 6 course banquet complementing the wines.

Luxury Christmas and New Year Breaks plus bargain rates in Autumn and Spring and for House Parties.

The Miller's House Hotel
Market Place
Middleham in Wensleydale
North Yorkshire
DL8 4NR
Tel: (0969) 22630
Fax: (0969) 23570

MOORE PLACE

When Francis Moore built his elegant Georgian mansion in the tranquil Bedfordshire village of Aspley Guise in 1786 he could never have imagined it would be such a focal point for hospitality 200 years later. Thoughtfully renovated and extended, the original house now has a Victorian style conservatory restaurant, and a collection of new bedrooms which create a courtyard effect, featuring a rock garden and water cascade. The hotel's attractive day rooms – including an airy, glass roofed reception and relaxing bar-lounge – are decorated and furnished in handsome period style.

The 54 prettily decorated bedrooms all have ensuite bathrooms, direct dial telephone, colour television, tea and coffee making facilities and hairdryer.

There are 3 private function rooms in this charming Georgian house, where banquets and conferences are well provided for. The rooms are traditionally decorated, yet equipped with full audio-visual facilities.

The highly acclaimed restaurant is an outstanding success. Accomplished cooking in the modern mode can be enjoyed in the beautiful, picture windowed restaurant. Excellent cuisine is complemented by a good selection of fine wines. Moore Place is surrounded by interesting places to visit, such as the Duke of Bedford's Woburn Abbey, Dunstable Downs and Whipsnade Zoo. Woburn golf course is also nearby.

Moore Place,
Aspley Guise,
Nr Woburn, Beds MK17 8DW
Tel: (0908) 282000
Fax: (0908) 281888

MOORLAND HOTEL

The Moorland Hotel, Haytor, stands in one of the most beautiful and majestic parts of the British Isles. Set amid a delightful aspect of moors, and nestling within a copse of firs at the southern foot of Haytor rocks, the hotel commands spectacular views across the rolling Devon countryside towards Teignmouth, Torbay and South Hams.

Set within the Dartmoor National Park, the moor offers a wide range of outdoor activities, including walking, riding, fishing and golf. The Moorland Hotel is the ideal place to relax and unwind after such exertions, a haven of comfort and hospitality.

The bedrooms in the hotel are designed to ensure a high degree of comfort for guests. All rooms have en suite facilities, colour television, direct dial telephone and hot drinks for the discerning visitor. For a real treat, two of the rooms have a traditional four poster bed, whilst all rooms command stunning views of gardens and moors, most with panoramic sea views in the distance.

Guests can enjoy the cosy, hunting lodge atmosphere of the Moorland Pine Bar or the elegance and style of the Agatha Christie lounge, named after the famous author who completed her first detective novel 'The Mysterious Affair at Styles' whilst staying at the Moorland Hotel, and found the hotel an ideal retreat as she recalls in her autobiography.

The restaurant offers varied table d'hote and a la carte menus, with an emphasis on fresh seasonal produce. The patio restaurant is ideal for bar meals, coffee or perhaps a cream tea.

Another delight of the Moorland Hotel is the self contained appartments, which provide a comfortable location for an 'away from it all' holiday. Each includes a comfortably furnished lounge with colour television and direct dial telephone, fully equipped kitchen and bathroom, with linen, heating and electricity provided.

There is much for guests to see and visit in the vicinity. The town of Bovey Tracey is close by, Widecombe in the Moor is another popular attraction, and Exeter, Newton Abbot and Plymouth are within easy reach. Alternatively, if guests prefer to keep the pace of their holiday at a more leisurely tempo, Haytor itself, a craggy outcrop of granite rocks, is virtually on the doorstep, and the village of Haytor is worth exploring, with its pretty hamlet of cottages, village post office and inn.

Whether you wish to use the hotel as a base for exploring or prefer just to relax in the hotel and its delightful gardens, you are assured of a warm welcome and precious memories of Devon hospitality.

The Moorland Hotel
Haytor
Dartmoor
South Devon
TQ13 9XT

Tel: (0364) 661407

MOUNT FALCON CASTLE

Resting in its one hundred acre estate, is the historic country mansion of Mount Falcon. Originally built in 1876 by John Fredrick Knox, it overlooks the Moy Valley towards the changing hues of the heathery slopes of the Ox mountains in the distance.

The owner, Constance Aldridge, plays the part of hostess to her visitors who quickly realise that, in keeping with the tradition of the house, they will experience the friendliness and attention given to a personal guest rather than simply another booking. Here, you can relax beside a log fire in the tranquillity of gracious rooms filled with antique furniture and fresh flowers picked from the gardens.

The superb menu is traditional country house cuisine. Frequently acclaimed in international good food guides, it includes local ingredients, fresh produce from the estate as well as fresh rod-caught salmon from the Mount Falcon Fishery on the River Moy. The delicious food is accompanied by a comprehensive selection of fine wines. After dinner, coffee and drinks are served in the Drawing Room where guests can engage in conversation or make plans for the following day.

There are ten bedrooms all enjoying views of the estate. All the bedrooms have private bathrooms as well as all the amenities you would expect of a good hotel.

Mount Falcon is the ideal base from which to explore the magnificent countryside of County Mayo. Beautiful beaches, rugged coastline, lakes and mountains are all on the doorstep as are fascinating sites of ancient Celtic history.

For the golfer, the first class 18 hole course of Enniscrone is only ten miles away and Ballina has a good 9 hole course. Horse riding is available in the area and the lively old fashioned town of Ballina is worth a visit.

For the serious fisherman, Mount Falcon has excellent facilities having catered for generations of county sportsmen. The River Moy is Ireland's most prolific salmon river and 3 miles away the large limestone loughs, Conn and Cullen provide some of the finest fishing for wild brown trout in Europe.

In the winter months, the castle can arrange excellent rough shooting for woodcock and snipe.

Mount Falcon Castle
Ballina
Co. Mayo
Ireland
Tel: (096) 21172
Fax: (096) 21172

MOUNT JULIET

This magnificently restored 18th century house stands proudly on nearly 1,500 acres of unspoiled parkland and offers every possible comfort naturally beautiful surroundings. This beguiling combination of old and new cannot fail to leave an indelible mark on even the most discerning of guests.

The hotel is well suited for prestigious conferences - a perfect 'out of town' venue, supported by all the necessary modern facilities plus superb hospitality and a wide range of sporting and recreational facilities.

For the golfer, Mount Juliet boasts its own 18 hole golf course designed by Jack Nicklaus. His great talent, combined with the magnificent rolling expanses of the estate, has resulted in a first class parkland course. The 7,000 yard championship layout, set on some 180 acres, offers variety and a challenge to golfers of all standards. From water to specimen trees to vigilant bunkers, each hole has its own unique features.

Top class professional tuition is on hand at all times. In addition, there is the unique 3 hole teaching academy offering players the opportunity to improve every aspect of their game. The Clubhouse is unique too, an interesting blend of leisure facilities combined with the charm and character of old estate buildings.

The estate also has an equestrian centre with fully qualified instructors which caters for all levels from beginners to serious cross-country riders. The experienced angler, can fish both the River Nore and King's River, while instruction for novices is provided at the Fishing Academy. Clay Pigeon shooting and a driven shoot are also available on the estate as are tennis and croquet whilst for the less energetic, the estate's enormous woodlands and gardens are ideal for walking, cycling or bird watching .

Dining here is a delight. The Lady Helen is recognised as one of Ireland's most distinguished restaurants, while the Old Kitchen offers relaxed dining in more informal surroundings. Each of the 32 en-suite bedrooms has its own unique ambience. Overnight guests can choose between Presidential Suites, deluxe mini-suites and superior rooms.

Whether it is for business or pleasure, there are few places to rival Mount Juliet.

Mount Juliet
Thomastown
Country Kilkenny
Ireland
Hotel Tel: (056) 24455 Fax: (056) 24522
Golf Tel: (056) 24725 Fax: (056) 24828

THE MOUNT ROYALE HOTEL

The hotel is the result of the tasteful blending of two beautiful William IV detatched houses. The proprietors, Richard and Christine Oxtoby, have spent a good deal of effort on restoring the former glory of these buildings and their efforts have been well rewarded.

Any traveller having an interest in English history must surely rank the fascinating city of York at least alongside London. The capital of the north and second city of the realm, it began its long and fascinating life around AD71 as a fortress to protect the Roman 9th Legion. The marauding Vikings gave the city its name, derived from Jorvik or Yorwik. This period of history has been magnificently captured in the Jorvik Viking Centre, one of the most entertaining museums in the country. The Minster or Cathedral is the largest medieval structure in Britain. There has been a Minster on the site since the 7th century, the present one is the fourth and was started about 1220, taking 250 years to complete. The city is still protected by ancient city walls, guarded by defensive bastions, working portcullis' and barbican

at the Walmgate bar.

Wander around the Micklegate bar, where traitors' severed heads were displayed or visit the National Rail Museum.

Staying in York involves mixing with some of the most fascinating sights in the world. Relaxing afterwards in the intimate cocktail bar of the Mount Royale, or enjoying a delicious meal in the restaurant overlooking the delightful garden, enhances the whole experience. Enjoying the gracious beauty of the hotel, the style and antiquity of much of the furnishings, or slipping into the secluded heated swimming pool is the perfect way to pamper the body as well as the mind.

The hotel is ideal for the small conference or private dinner party, and is only a short drive from the rolling Yorkshire Dales. The perfect base, offering peace and tranquility, practically in the heart of this wonderful city.

Mount Royale Hotel
The Mount
York YO2 2DA
Tel: (0904) 628856
Fax: (0904) 611171

MUCKRACH LODGE HOTEL

This former Shooting Lodge set in 10 secluded acres overlooking the Dulnain River offers high standards of comfort and service. Privately owned and run by Captain Roy and Pat Watson they invite you to enjoy Highland hospitality, excellent cuisine in the Conservatory Restaurant and log fires in the Cocktail Bar and Lounge. The outstanding menus place a strong emphasis on a 'Taste of Scotland' using local produce wherever possible, with some European influence, complimented by a well balanced wine list featuring wines from around the globe. There are 8 en suite bedrooms individually furnished and 3 suites, 2 of which are in the Steading Annexe, just a short walk from the Hotel. The Dulnain Suite in the Steading is completely fitted out for the disabled.

Muchrach Lodge is ideally situated for all types of activities, including Cairngorm hillwalking, skiing, fishing on the River Spey or just complete relaxation. The Hotel has private fishing a short drive away on the River Findhorn.

The hotel is situated 12 miles north of Aviemore on the A938 between Dulnain Bridge and Carrbridge and is open all year except November.

Price Band: High Season £39 - £47. Low Season £30 - £40. Price per person in shared twin/double room with private facilities and full Scottish breakfast.

Muckrach Lodge Hotel
Dulnain Bridge
Grantown on Spey
Morayshire PH26 3LY
Tel: (047985) 257
Fax: (047985) 325

MURRAYSHALL COUNTRY HOUSE HOTEL

The Murrayshall Country House Hotel and Golf Course is only 4 miles from Perth, set in 300 acres of parkland. Deer stroll the wooded hillside, pheasants and peacocks call from the greens. The natural beauty and splashes of colour in the garden are complemented by the mellow stone of the main house with its crow stepped gables.

The hotel, completely refurbished, is elegantly furnished in a traditional style but with the use of the wonderful fabric designs available today. The bedrooms all have en suite facilities, self dial telephone and colour television.

The aptly named Old Masters Restaurant has walls hung with Dutch Masters and table settings befitting the artistry of master chef, Bruce Sangster. The restaurant has received various culinary accolades. Vegetables and herbs from the hotels walled garden and an abundance of local produce form the basis of the menus which have a Scottish flavour with a hint of modern French cuisine. A well balanced wine list is complemented by the finest of rare malt whiskies.

The 6420 yard, 18 hole, par 73 course is interspersed with magnificent specimen trees lining the fairways, water hazards and white sanded bunkers to offer a challenge to all golfers. Buggies and sets of clubs are available for hire. Neil Mackintosh, our resident professional, is pleased to give tuition, from half an hour to a weeks course. Perth is ideally situated for Scotland's courses. Golfers can relax in the newly refurbished club house which overlooks the course and provides informal dining.

Other sporting activities include tennis, croquet and bowls. However, situated only a few miles from the famous Salmon Waters of the River Tay, even closer to Perth Race Course, Murrayshall is uniquely placed to make it an attractive venue for whatever might bring you to this area of Scotland.

Private dining and conference facilities are available in both the hotel and club house. Conference organisers, requiring the best of service and attention for their senior delegates, will find Murrayshall the ideal conference haven.

Murrayshall is one of three group golf courses, the other two are Westerwood and Fernfell. Westerwood Golf Course was designed by Seve Ballesteros and Dave Thomas and is located at Cumbernauld, near Glasgow. Fernfell Golf and Country Club is located just out of Cranleigh, 8 miles from Guildford in Surrey. Corporate golf packages are offered at all three courses with the opportunity to place your company name and logo on a tee and to reserve the course for your company golf day. Golf Societies and Green Fee Payers are welcome.

Murrayshall Country House Hotel and Golf Course
Scone
Perthshire
PH2 7PH
Tel: (0738) 51171
Fax: (0738) 52595

NEWPORT HOUSE

Adjoining the town of Newport and overlooking the tidal river and quay the impressive country mansion of Newport House stands guard over the centuries of history that form the backbone to its grounds and the surrounding countryside. Once the home of a branch of the O'Donel family, descended from the famous fighting Earls of Tir Connell and cousins to 'Red Hugh' of Irish history, it is now a superb example of a lovingly maintained Georgian Mansion House.

Encircled by mountains, lakes and streams, Newport is within easy reach of some of Ireland's most beautiful rivers. Renowned as an angling centre, it holds private salmon and sea-trout fishing rights to 8 miles of the Newport River; and the prolific waters of the stunning Lough Beltra West are close by. Less than twenty minutes drive from the hotel are Lakes Mask and Corrib, while the nearby Loughs Feeagh and Furnace are the site of the Salmon Research Trust of Ireland.

The discerning golfer has the pleasure of the 18-hole championship course at Westport as well as the more relaxed 9-hole course near Mulrany.

Outdoor activities are numerous amidst the breath-taking scenery of County Mayo. Riding is easily arranged or try swimming and diving on wide and often empty beaches, while hanggliding is a relatively new sport gaining popularity from the local Achill Cliffs. One of the best recreations though is simply walking across the ever changing panorama of mountain, forest and sea.

Warmth and friendliness fill this beautiful hotel in a country already famed for its hospitality. The house is furnished with a tasteful collection of fine antiques and paintings and the elegant bedrooms are individually decorated. Food is taken seriously, with much of the produce collected fresh from the fishery, gardens and farm. Home-smoked salmon and fresh sea-food are specialites, and all the dishes are complemented by a carefully chosen and extensive wine list.

Many of the staff have been long in the service of the estate, up to forty years in one case. Combine this with the solid background of the house and there is a rare feeling of continuity and maturity so rare in modern hotels today.

Newport House
Co. Mayo
Ireland
Tel: (010 353 98) 41222
Fax: (010 353 98) 41613

NORMANTON PARK HOTEL

Normanton Park Hotel is situated on the south shore of Rutland Water, one of the country's leading water sports and leisure centres offering sailing, canoeing and wind surfing for those with experience and with tuition for beginners; fishing from the shore or hire boat. More gentle pursuits of kite flying, bird watching (350 acre Nature Reserve with hides), cycling (26 miles of cycling around purpose built off-road tracks). Alternatively, many lovely walks through Rutland's pretty villages and along the shoreline of the Water.

The Hotel is a restored Georgian Coach House, Grade II listed, and stands in 4 acres of parkland with one of the country's oldest Cedar of Lebanon trees. The elegant Orangery restaurant, as well as serving the finest of traditional English menus, using fresh local produce, affords magnificent views over the Water, shimmering and glistening just 50 yards across the lawn. Fine cuisine is complemented by a wine list offering something to satisfy everyone's palate. Should a formal meal not be required, the stylish galleried Sailing Bar offers light lunches and suppers, cream teas; cafetieres of coffee and speciality low-cholesterol icecream yoghurts available all day long.

Normanton Park welcomes disabled guests; 4 bedrooms have wheelchair access, as have all the public rooms on the ground floor. 8 rooms are directly accessible from the original courtyard at ground level. Ample car parking on site. The hotel's facilities offer a comprehensive package of traditional elegance combined with modern amenities. 14 en suite bedrooms, single, double, and family, are all tastefully furnished, with colour TV, direct dial telephone and a self-contained beverage unit.

Normanton Park Hotel is an ideal setting for picturesque wedding receptions, family celebrations etc.

Residential (24 hour delegate rate) and day conferences are catered for in the quiet and undisturbed surroundings of our Waterside Room with comprehensive visual aid facilities.

Nearby places of interest include: Burghley House, Belvoir Castle, Oakham - the historic county town of Rutland, Stamford - the country's first conservation area; Peterborough, Ely and Lincoln Cathedrals.

Proprietors: Daniel and Jane Hales and Robert Reid.

Sister hotel to Barnsdale Lodge.

Normanton Park Hotel
Normanton Park Road
Rutland Water South Shore
Oakham
Rutland LE15 8RP
Tel: (0780) 720315
Fax: (0780) 721086

PALE HALL

Built in 1870 for a wealthy railway engineer, Pale Hall has recently been converted to a luxurious and exquisite hotel. It has however, retained all its finest original Victorian features.

The most interesting of all these must surely be the original barn and adjoining bedroom used by Queen Victoria during her stay at Pale Hall for a short time after Prince Albert's death. Then there is the 'boudoir', a beautiful interior boasts a magnificent hand painted dome ceiling and the Corwen Bar where one can see the unusual bar made from the marble firplaces that have been removed from the bedrooms.

Each of the seventeen bedrooms are individually designed and finished to compliment their own particular features. It is this fine attention to detail that makes Pale Hall so interestingly unique. Despite its strong historical identity, however, it still provides all the home comforts of the present day subtly blended into this fine regal setting.

The restaurant and its cuisine is also of an exceptionally high standard. Interestingly, breakfast and morning coffee is served in the Bala Kitchen, which is still enhanced by its original cooking range from the late nineteenth century.

From the building and its grounds, spectacular views can be enjoyed. Here you can walk in solitude, sail serene waters, shoot, fish or enjoy a round of golf. Whatever your interests the Welsh hospitality will ensure a relaxing visit.

Pale Hall
Llandderfel
Nr Bala
Gwynedd
Tel: (06783) 285

PARK FARM HOTEL

Park Farm Hotel occupies a tranquil and secluded location in beautifully landscaped grounds situated just five miles south of the city of Norwich. The bedrooms are luxuriously decorated and equipped with every convenience. For those wishing to pamper themselves 'Executive' rooms are available providing even more comfort, including the added luxury of four-poster beds and jacuzzi baths. Our superb leisure complex to suit all ages has been carefully incorporated onto the original Georgian house to include an indoor 50 by 25 ft heated swimming pool, sauna, steam room, solarium, jacuzzi, gymnasium and work-out room. Croquet and Putting on the front lawns. Outdoor hard tennis court.

The Georgian restaurant can accommodate up to sixty covers in comfortable surroundings. We are renowned for our high standard of cuisine and service from a large selection of menus,

complemented by an excellent selection of wines from our cellar. The close involvement of the owners in the day to day management of Park Farm Hotel ensures its continuing popularity.

The hotel is perfectly located for exploring the Norfolk countryside, the Norfolk Broads and the east coast. Nearby Norwich is an interesting historic city with a bustling market centre, castle museum and a lovely Cathedral.

Directions: For those in a hurry there is a light aircraft landing strip and a helipad in the grounds. For a more conventional mode of transport Park Farm Hotel is 8 miles from Norwich Airport, 6 miles from Norwich railway station, and 5 miles from Norwich Bus Station. We are situated just off the main A11 on the B1172.

Park Farm Hotel
Hethersett
Norwich
NR9 3DL
Tel: (0603) 810264
Fax: (0603) 812104

PARK HOTEL KENMARE

Welcome to a hotel of unrivalled charm, elegance and splendour. Welcome to the Park Hotel Kenmare. Step over the threshold and take a step back in time. Surrender to the gracious living of a forgotten age. Allow us to attend to your every need, let your senses succumb to the allure of our hospitality, commitment and dedication to service. From the moment you arrive we are ever-mindful of your individual desires and are unwavering in our resolve to fulfil them to your satisfaction.

Treat your eye to antiques from all over Ireland and Europe which create the magnificent furnishings in our guests bedrooms and the classical elegance of our dining room. Treat your palate to our innovative culinary delights from a cuisine judged among the highest in the land.

Spend your nights at the Park Hotel Kenmare, in comfort and splendour. Spend the day in outdoor pursuits of croquet, walking, tennis, golf or fishing - so rich and varied is the terrain of the Emerald Isle.

Based at Park Hotel Kenmare, you can choose to play golf at

Killarney's 36 holes - it's famous courses of Mahony's Point and the newer Killeen sited on the shore of the Lakes of Killarney - or at Waterville - one of the largest courses in Europe and one of the greatest golfing tests.

A little further afield is Ballybunion, a glorious links course on the Atlantic shore regarded as one of the world's best. Closer to home, adjacent to the hotel is an executive 9 hole course, ideal for our guests.

If fishing is more your line you are spoilt for choice. In the Rivers Waterville and Comeragh and lakes Currane and Caragh you can fish for trout and salmon in one of Ireland's most beautiful regions. In the stretch of water around Bearon Island, an angler can catch ray, conger, flatfish and dogfish. As this could entail boat-fishing the Park Hotel Kenmare would prepare your packed lunch.

The Park Hotel Kenmare bids you an eternal welcome.

Park Hotel Kenmare
Kenmare
Co Kerry
Ireland
Tel: (010 353 64) 41200
Fax: (010 353 64) 41402

PARK HOUSE HOTEL

Park house has been run by the O'Briens for nearly 45 years and still retains the distinctive atmosphere of a private country house, where all guests receive unparalleled hospitality and maximum comfort. All the amenities of an English country house are available, yet the hotel is just fifty-two miles from London.

Set in nine acres of garden, Park House is a blend of 16th century manor and late Victorian mansion. The large and elegant public rooms include a drawing room lined with books and ornaments and a long dining room with polished tables. Great pride is taken in the nutritious and satisfying food served for the guests' delight.

All the bedrooms are individually furnished, overlooking the gardens and grass tennis courts, and include private bath-rooms, colour television and radio telephones. In addition there is a fully-serviced cottage annexe with a sitting-room, double bedroom, dressing-room and bathroom adjoining Park House.

For racegoers who can tear themselves away from the delights of the hotel, Goodwood Racecourse is only six miles away, and golfers are amply served by the range of first-class golf courses in the locality. Indeed guests can even practise at their leisure on the hotel's own 9-hole pitch and putt course. Cowdray Park in Midhurst is the centre of English polo and the famous Chichester Festival Theatre is within easy reach.

This gem of a hotel cannot be recommended too highly for a week-end away, but guests may find that this is simply not long enough!

Park House Hotel
Bepton
Midhurst
Sussex GU29 OJB
Tel: (0730) 812880
Fax: (0730) 815643

PENALLY ABBEY

Penally Abbey is an eleven bedroom, gothic style, stone built mansion, situated in an elevated position, adjacent to the church, on the village green in the picturesque floral village of Penally, two miles from Tenby.

Penally is, quite simply, one of Pembrokeshire's loveliest country houses. Elegant but not imposing, its very name conjures up an air of tranquillity where time stands still and the emphasis is on relaxation.

For our active guests, every season brings with it a variety of outdoor pursuits. Spring and Autumn are the perfect time for horse-riding, sailing, or playing golf. Summer brings surfing and swimming and Eisteddfods, pageants, concerts and county shows galore. In winter you can walk the coastal park in appreciation of Pembrokeshire's incomparable, savagely beautiful coastline.

Whatever the weather Penally Abbey is a haven of comfort and cheerful ambience, with crackling log fires and the warmest of welcomes.

Set in five acres of gardens and woodland, Penally Abbey boasts its own flemish chimney wishing well and ruined chapel, the last surviving link with its monastic past.

The elegant lounge and dining room overlook the gardens and terrace and enjoy spectacular sea views across the golf course and Camarthen Bay.

Dinner is a candle-lit affair with mouthwatering dishes of fresh seasonal delicacies, complemented by excellent wines from our cellar. Vegetarian and special diets are cared for. Each meal is a celebration especially prepared for you.

The bedrooms are perfect for that special occasion, anniversary or honeymoon. Exquisitely furnished and decorated with antiques and period furniture, many have four poster beds. All are centrally heated, have en suite bathrooms, tea and coffee-making facilities, telephones, colour television and hairdriers. Whether in the main building or in the adjoining converted coach house you will be delighted with their old world charm.

Penally Abbey
Penally
Pembrokeshire
Tel: (0834) 843033
Fax: (0834) 844714

PENRHOS COURT

Penrhos Court stands on the hill between Lyonshall and the ancient border town of Kington. The earliest part is a cruck hall built around 1280, when Edward the First took Kington away from the Welsh. Sometime about the year 1400 a post & truss, timber-frame house was butted onto the East-side and again in 1590 there was another major addition to complete the house as it stands today. Barns and stables have since been added to form a courtyard, adapting Penrhos over the ages to meet the demands of the times.

In recent years Penrhos has once again evolved to survive. During 1974 a restaurant was started in the cowbyre. This quickly gained a local reputation, won national awards and received acclaim in the food guides. Since opening, this business has provided a stable background to the project of re-building the whole complex of derelict buildings.

Daphne Lambert is the leader of this justly renowned kitchen. Using only the finest of raw ingredients, home-grown herbs and vegetables she turns her craft into an art.

Although her main aim is to run a high-standard, 20th-century restaurant, Daphne has quite naturally turned her attention to the food and cooking of the medieval ages. She has made a deep study of the subject and runs six or seven special medieval banquets each year on the dates of their original holidays; Mid-summer, Michaelmas, Martinmas etc. Using medieval recipes and traditional entertainment, each banquet is full of interesting flavours and variety, enormous fun and spectacular to behold, producing an event no doubt very close to some of the special feasts that were perhaps held at Penrhos some 600 or 700 years ago. Her knowledge and enthusiasm mixed with the practical creativity that a chef has with food and cooking, has helped to dispel the ridicule that some historians have put on medieval food.

Now as the repair of Penrhos Court reaches its completion there emerges one of the most delightful hotels you could hope to find anywhere, catering for all sorts of special events and countryside holidays.

Penrhos Court Hotel and Restaurant
Kington
Herefordshire
HR5 3LH
Tel: (0544) 230720
Fax: (0544) 230754

PETTY FRANCE HOTEL

Petty France Hotel is a privately owned country hotel located at the southern end of the Cotswolds on the A46 just 5 miles north of the M4 junction 18. The main hotel building was built in the 18th century as a dower house for the Beaufort estate and has 8 large bedrooms. Most of these individually decorated rooms have a view of the extensive gardens. There are a further 12 bedrooms across the courtyard in what were formerly stables and these have all been recently refurbished. These stables were part of an earlier coaching inn which Jane Austen mentions in Northanger Abbey. The grounds cover 4.5 acres of which more than half are in lawns and gardens to be enjoyed by our guests.

The Dining Room is very special. It is housed in the main building in three interconnected rooms of elegant proportions with high ceilings and large bay windows. Original fireplaces have been kept and the rooms have recently been redecorated in light shades of peach. The imaginative menu which features the best of French and English cooking prepared from truly fresh ingredients is attractively presented by an interested and caring kitchen and dining room staff. Drinks before dinner and coffee after dinner are served in our large lounges which also retain the atmosphere of the original house.

The location of the Petty France makes it an excellent base for touring the Cotswolds and visiting the nearby cities of Bath and Bristol. The castle of Berkeley which dates back to Norman times is close by as are the National Trust properties of Dyrham Park, Lacock Abbey and village, Snowshill and Sudeley. Day trips to south Wales, including Chepstow Castle and Tintern Abbey, are within easy reach. Badminton House, the setting for the famous international horse trials, is only two miles away.

Petty France Hotel
Dunkirk
Badminton
Avon GL9 1AF
Tel: (0454) 238361
Fax: (0454) 238768

PETWOOD HOUSE

Petwood House was built at the turn of the century for Lady Weigall, only child of Sir Blundell Maple, the great furniture store magnate during the 1800s. Lady Weigall built her country mansion in the area of her favourite wood and called it 'Petwood'. Maple craftsmen were responsible for the carving and building of the superb Oak staircase and oak panelling. A great deal of the furniture was also originally Maple made and a few of these items can still be seen around the Hotel today. Sir Archibald Weigall (who was Conservative MP for Horncastle, Lincolnshire) and his wife entertained numerous visitors at Petwood, including King George V and the future King George VI, while Queen Victoria's grand daughters the Princesses Alice and Marie Louise were guests for a considerable time.

Petwood became a hotel in 1933 and thrived as such until World War II, when the Royal Air Force requisitioned the building as an Officers' Mess for many squadrons, including the famous 617 Squadron - The Dambusters. Today the hotel still welcomes many World War II veterans.

Luxuriously refurbished, Petwood House stands in 30 acres of secluded gardens and woodland, ideally situated for quiet breaks, conferences, weddings and special events. All 46 bedrooms are elegantly furnished and include en-suite bath-

room, colour television, telephone, radio, hair dryer, trouser press and tea/coffee making facilities. The 'Talking Oak' Drawing Room is open through the day for light snacks and traditional afternoon teas and the 'Squadron Bar' contains fascinating memorabilia of its former occupants. The restaurant is highly recommended, offering the very best in traditional and imaginative cuisine, complemented by its well-stocked cellars of wines, ports and liqueurs. Altogether Petwood House offers a high standard of comfort and hospitality, with management and staff dedicated to making your stay a pleasurable one.

The Hotel also boasts a full size snooker table, an 18 hole putting green and croquet and boules. Residents are also entitled to use The Bainland Park Leisure Centre, located just one and a half miles away which has an 18 hole golf course, Bowls, Sauna, crazy golf, multi-gym, sunbed spa bath and swimming pool. Altogether a superb range of facilities.

The cathedral city of Lincoln is some eighteen miles away and of course for keen golfers the famous Woodhall Spa Golf Course is on the doorstep, often described as the ultimate golfing oasis.

Petwood House
Woodhall Spa
Lincolnshire LN10 6QF
Tel: (0526) 52411
Fax: (0526) 53473

PLAS PENHELIG COUNTRY HOUSE HOTEL & RESTAURANT

In the tranquil beauty of the Welsh hillside, the secluded grounds of the Plas Penhelig offer peace amidst peace. Surrounded by seven acres of award winning landscaped gardens and enjoying glorious views across the Dovey estuary and Cardigan Bay, the hotel has an air of welcome about it, comfortable armchairs, open log fires and friendly staff give a charming atmosphere.

The beauty of the gardens can be seen from the delightful terrace, inviting the visitor to take a stroll of gentle exploration. For the more energetic, there is a manicured putting green and perfectly maintained croquet lawn.

Inside, the oak-panelled entrance hall and lounge provide a relaxing setting for afternoon coffee or tea, whilst the dining room is a world unto itself. Decorated with beautifully arranged flowers collected from the hotel gardens, the restaurant prides itself on its fresh, locally-produced fare. Fresh fruit, seasonal vegetables and crisp salads are a speciality, carefully grown in the hotel's own greenhouses, orchards and walled kitchen garden, and used to creatively complement both the imaginative and more traditional daily menus that the chef presents. For a lighter lunch or snack, smaller meals may be taken in the cocktail bar or beneath a sun-shade out on the terrace, to the accompaniment of a cool, refreshing drink.

The area around the hotel provides a wealth of relaxation. Sailing is a popular pursuit and walking around the natural beauty of the surrounding countryside is wonderfully satisfying and you will be refreshed still further by the pure Welsh air. For the golfer, the hotel has arranged reduced fees at the Aberdovey Golf Club.

The Plas Penhelig has 12 rooms, all with bath or shower ensuite, colour television, radio and self-dialling telephones. The staff have experience at accommodating meetings, seminars or small private parties and are renowned for the extra care and attention devoted to these successful receptions.

Plas Penhelig
Country House Hotel and Restaurant
Aberdovey
Gwynedd LL35 0NA
Tel: (0654) 767 676
Fax: (0654) 767 783

THE PRIORY HOTEL

The Priory has long been regarded as one of Britain's finest country house hotels. Built in 1835 of Bath stone, the hotel is located on the Western edge of Bath adjoining Victoria Park.

The hotel has 21 tastefully appointed bedrooms, each with its own individual style of decor, which are enhanced by their antique furniture and superb works of art. Most of the rooms have views over the beautiful garden.

The Priory Restaurant has long been acclaimed internationally and has consistently received awards from the main guide books. The cuisine is predominantly French but features national and local classical dishes. Each of the rooms in the Restaurant focuses on the garden and may be used separately or as a whole depending on the clients requirements.

Organisations looking for a prestigious location for senior management meetings or seminars will find The Priory an ideal venue. Its high reputation, peaceful location in idyllic surroundings make it very conducive for work or for pleasure. Recreation facilities include a heated outdoor swimming pool and a croquet lawn.

The World Heritage City of Bath offers a multitude of interesting attractions from its wonderful architecture to a wide choice of museums, art galleries and the world famous Roman Baths. There are numerous golf courses within easy distance and Bath race course, which has eight meetings a year, is only minutes away.

Bath is well served by transportation, by train from London in 1¼ hours, Heathrow in 1½ hours and Bristol airport is 40 minutes.

The Priory House Hotel
Weston Road
Bath
Avon BA1 2XT
Tel: (0225) 331922
Fax: (0225) 448276

PUCKRUP HALL

Standing in just over one hundred acres of lawns and rolling parkland between the Cotswold and Malvern Hills, Puckrup Hall is a grand Regency house offering the ideal location for a touring base, quiet break or management retreat. To the north are Worcester and Great Malvern, while to the east the Vale of Evesham lads to Shakespeare country. Just to the west of the hotel the great river Severn meanders for three miles to Tewkesbury and its magnificent Abbey.

The emphasis at Puckrup Hall is on a relaxing and luxurious stay. There is a remarkable air of light and spaciousness throughout the hotel, perhaps influenced by the design and decor of the delightful Orangery and Conservatory. Leading off from the elegant hallway is the Worcester Room, a beautifully proportioned meeting or dining room for up to 16 guests and an integral part of the original house. The magnificent Ballroom is second to none and can cater for up to 200 people for private dining or company entertaining.

Each of Puckrup Hall's delightful, well appointed en suite bedrooms is individual, both in shape and interior design. This is reflected in that each of the twelve double or twin bedrooms is given a name, after the month of the year, while the four suites, including two with four poster beds, are named after the four seasons, with interior designs to catch the colours of the year.

The gourmet will certainly not be disappointed with the cuisine at the hotel. Dining in an atmosphere of soft intimate colours, be prepared for imaginative menus which are changed daily and a much acclaimed a la carte menu which changes with each season, emphasising the freshness and quality of the best from the Vale of Evesham and the finest produce available at the time.

For a memorable stay in an idyllic country setting, Tewkesbury Hall is hard to beat. The hotel is just two miles north of Tewkesbury Centre on the A38 and only a few minutes from junction 8 of the M5, via junction 1 of the M50, making it easily accessible from Birmingham, Bristol and South Wales.

Puckrup Hall
Puckrup
Tewkesbury
Gloucestershire GL20 6EL

Tel: Tewkesbury (0684) 296200   Fax: (0684) 850788

RAEMOIR

The Raemoir House Hotel located sixteen and a half miles South West of Aberdeen, is delightfully situated in spacious grounds, liberally wooded and sheltered from the northerly winds by the Hill of Fare which rises some 1,500 feet behind the house.

The main mansion was built in the 18th century and extended at later dates. Immediately to the rear of the mansion in Ha' Hoose adjudged to be the finest example of this type of building in existence, and which has now been officially included in the list of buildings of special architectural and historic interest.

There are 24 principal bedrooms and suites with private bathrooms, including a 400 year old 4 poster in the Old English Wing. A great many of these rooms face south, with fine views of the the surrounding countryside. The furnishings are in a style in keeping with the house, many of the rooms having valuable tapestried walls. The hotel is centrally heated throughout, fully licensed and open all the year round. There is spacious parking around the hotel and a private helipad is also available. Small conferences, seminars and dinner parties can be held in the lovely oval Ballroom and elegant panelled morning room suites.

3,500 acres of low ground shooting adjoins the hotel and fishing, shooting and stalking are available by arrangement. There is a 9 hole pitch and putt course and all weather tennis court and many beautiful walks may be taken in the wooded grounds of the hotel. Several golf courses are within easy reach including an 18 hole golf course situated nearby at Banchory. The family run Raemoir Hotel offers ideal conditions for a restful holiday in the luxurious surroundings of a country house with good food, perfect service and the personal attention of the resident Directors.

Raemoir House
Banchory
Kincardineshire

Tel: 03302 4884   Fax: 03302 2171

RATHSALLAGH HOUSE

Converted from Queen Anne stables which burnt to the ground in 1798 this large comfortable farmhouse is situated in 500 acres of peaceful parkland surrounded by some of the most beautiful countryside of Eastern Ireland.

The addition of full modern amenities has done nothing to spoil the traditional splendour of the house where welcoming log fires combine with full central heating to ensure your comfort. The delightful bedrooms are individually decorated with care and attention; all are large and luxurious and offer en suite bathrooms with enormous bath towels.

The atmosphere is happy and relaxed in this hotel with its huge variety of diversions; choose from Tennis, Golf Driving Range, Golf Practice Holes, Putting, Archery, Croquet, Clay Pigeon Shooting with C.P.S.A Club Coach and snooker, or simply take a stroll around the award winning two-acre walled garden. Either way treat yourself to a sauna afterwards, then cool off with a dip in the indoor swimming pool.

For the racing enthusiast the hotel is ideally situated for the Irish National Stud, along with Curragh, Punchestown and Naas Racecourses, and Goffs Sales Paddock.

For a change deer-stalking can be arranged, while your host, Joe O'Flynn, is master of the local hunt and can arrange fox-hunting in season. Besides the outstanding natural beauty of the surrounding area there is also a variety of historic sites well worth a visit, not least of these being Glendalough and Russborough House.

At the end of such a day, the real log fire of the restaurant provides a pleasing welcome. The cooking is superb with the emphasis on fresh, local produce, while the too-tempting sweet trolley fairly groans with luscious offerings.

Naturally Rathsallagh is fully able to cater for business meetings and offers, amongst other things, a fully-quipped purpose-built Conference Room and Helipad.

Rathsallagh Country House and Restaurant
Dunlavin
Co. Wicklow
Ireland
Tel: (010 353 45) 53112
Fax: (010 353 45) 53343

HAREWOOD HOUSE

RAVEN HALL COUNTRY HOUSE HOTEL & GOLF COURSE

Standing dramatically 600 feet up on the southern most tip of Robin Hoods Bay, Raven Hall is set in 100 acres of award-winning landscaped gardens and battlements, on the site of an old Roman fortress. This 18th century country house captures the most unique, breath-taking panoramic views across towards the smugglers haunt.

Raven Hall has been referred to as 'Yorkshire's best kept golf secret' possessing its own 9 hole, cliff top golf course, free to hotel residents and open to non-residents, providing a challenge to even the keenest golfer.

For the golfer who wishes to try out other golf courses, within a radius of 20 miles there are five 18 hole courses one of which is the championship course at Ganton.

Apart from our golf course the hotel can offer numerous other sports and leisure facilities including: tennis, outdoor swimming pool, croquet, giant chess, crown bowls, putting, table tennis, full size snooker table and a Health and Beauty Salon with sauna.

Renowned for its excellent Yorkshire cuisine, provided since 1970 by Don Holmes, and the special warmth of the Gridley family's hospitality since 1961, the hotel has 53 en-suite bedrooms - all with spectacular views. Included in these are eight bedrooms situated on the third floor and named 'The Cottage'. These rooms capture the style of the traditional English country cottage complete with wooden beams and individual names.

Raven Hall is situated 12 miles north of the Victorian seaside resort of Scarborough: 15 miles south of the Historic Fishing Town of Whitby and it is only an hour away from the famous Medieval walled City of York.

Ideally sited for golfers, walkers and traditional family holidays - "Raven Hall is where coast and country meet...just waiting to be discovered."

Raven Hall Hotel
Ravenscar
Scarborough
North Yorkshire
YO13 0ET
Tel: (0723) 870353
Fax: (0723) 870072

RESCOBIE HOTEL AND RESTAURANT

Rescobie is a 1920s country house set in two acres of grounds on the edge of the old village of Leslie, which adjoins the new industrial town of Glenrothes. The house, whose gardens contain a functional herb garden and a wild flower meadow, was converted in the 70s and 80s to a fully licensed hotel; all of its ten individually decorated bedrooms now have private bath or shower, direct dial telephone, colour television, radio/alarm, room bar, etc. The furnishings are comfortable, old village photographs adorn the walls of the bar and in cooler months a log fire burns in the lounge.

Perfectly positioned for golfers in the heart of an area rich in golf courses - St Andrews, Dalmahoy, Carnoustie and Gleneagles to name but a few - Rescobie is only half an hour's drive away from Perth and Dundee and forty five minutes from the centre of Edinburgh.

The owners take great pains to run the hotel as a traditional country house. There is no formal reception area; guests will find a bell in the hall and other public rooms to summon waitresses, who are dressed smartly but informally in tartan skirt and blouse in preference to the customary black and white. The owners, Tony and Wendy Hughes-Lewis, make a point of meeting all of their guests, and if Wendy does not actually welcome you into hotel one of them will meet you later on.

There are four full-time chefs, which is a large brigade for a small hotel, but they make by hand what most other catering establishments buy in. In addition to producing stocks, soups and sauces, the chefs make all of the sweets and petits fours, roll their own pasta and even cut their own chips. Tony himself makes marmalade with Seville oranges in the spring and jellies with crab apples and elderberries in the Autunm, and tends the herb garden, where the chefs can be seen in the summer gathering their daily requirements.

The effort the owners make to preserve the atmosphere of a country house is reflected in their personal attention to the well-being of their guests, the conduct of their staff and the quality of their cuisine. Such high standards are expected in a four star establishment; to find them at two star level makes the Rescobie Hotel a rare find and excellent value for money.

The Rescobie Hotel and Restaurant
Valley Drive
Leslie
Fife
KY6 3BQ
Tel: (0592) 742143
Fax: (0592) 620231

RIVERSIDE COUNTRY HOUSE HOTEL

Between the famous towns of Buxton and Bakewell is Ashford-in-the-Water, a delightful, seventeenth century stone-built village that rests in a limestone ravine on the banks of the River Wye in the Peak District National Park. The Peak District has long been recognised, particularly by energetic romantics, as one of England's most outstanding areas of natural beauty.

Just below the beautiful Sheepwash bridge is the Riverside Country House Hotel, dating back to 1630 with its impressive ivy-clad Georgian facade and mature gardens it was originally constructed as a grace and favour house of the Chatsworth estate.

Each of its fifteen rooms has been individually designed and furnished to create its own distinctive personality. Several are four-posters or have half-tester drapes and many have soft furnishings hand-crafted by the owner, Sue Taylor. The hosts' personal touch can be seen in the many thoughtful extras, while the unobtrusive modern amenities include colour television, radio, direct-dial telephone, and tea and coffee making facilities.

The Head Chef, Jeremy Buckingham, has long been recognised as one of the best in the area. Using game in season from nearby Chatsworth and freshly caught fish from the Wye and Derwent he produces outstanding cuisine, complemented by an impressive and extensive wine list, and served at polished antique mahogany tables set with fine silver and cut crystal. Everything is freshly cooked on the premises, including the hotel's own bread, biscuits, sweets and chocolates.

Some of the best walking country in England is to be found in the Derbyshire Dales. Not far from the hotel is Chatsworth House, the magnificent seventeenth century stately home of the Duke and Duchess of Devonshire with spectacular gardens by Jeremy Paxton. Haddon Hall, also nearby, is one of the most complete and authentic medieval manors in England, with battlements, towers and turrets, exquisite tapestries and carvings, as well as its noted terraced rose-garden. Good fishing is to be found along the River Wye and the Derwent, rods can be arranged on either river via the hotel, and knowledgable staff are more than happy to chat and help organise any activities their guests would like to try.

Riverside Country House Hotel
Ashford-in-the-Water
Bakewell
Derbyshire
DE4 1QF
Tel: (0629) 814275
Fax: (0629) 812873

ROCK GLEN HOTEL

A converted shooting lodge first built in 1815, the Rock Glen is now a 29 bedroomed cosy first class Grade A Hotel, nestling in the heart of Connemara.

Lush pasture rolls from the door of this 18th century former shooting lodge and down to the shore of the narrow bay where Connemara's mountain range, the Twelve Bens, drift in and out of the clouds.

Family run, the Hotel is renowned for its exceptional cuisine. An extensive five course menu with a wide variety of meat, shellfish, salmon, trout and lobster, all fresh and available locally, is personally supervised by John Roche, the owner. There is a fine selection of wines to complement the fine food.

The bar is cosy where plump armchairs out-number bar stools and a turf fire glows all year round. Guests can enjoy a pleasant evening of musical entertainment with our resident pianist. Spontaneous sing-songs occur regularly, and you are invited to join in. Coffee is served in the drawing room where you can relax and enjoy the conversation and our cosy sun lounge can be a delight to all even on the dullest day.

AMENITIES

The superb full size snooker table is guaranteed to give pleas-ure to all. Clay pigeon shooting can be arranged by request. The all-weather floodlit tennis court is in excellent condition and is free to residents. The bedrooms, 15 of which are on the ground floor, are all individually and comfortably decorated and have private bathroom, radio and television, trouser press, hairdryer, and direct dial telephone.

LOCAL AMENITIES

The hotel is ideally situated for the golf enthusiast. Connemara's 18 hole championship course is in a spectacular setting on the coast, with the Twelve Bens in the background. It is just a 15 minute drive from the Hotel. Lessons are available on request, golf clubs and caddy cars can be hired also at the club.

For the non-golfer the area is perfect for walking, hill climbing, river, lake and deep-sea fishing. Miles of sandy beaches for the swimmer and pony trekking (Clifden is famous for its Connemara ponies) can all be arranged at the reception desk.

John and Evangeline Roche, their family and staff look forward to welcoming you to the Rock Glen where you may recall the pleasures of a leisurely and more sedate way of life, then return home refreshed, rested and fit.

Rock Glen Country House Hotel
Clifden
County Galway
Ireland
Tel: (010 353 95) 21035
Fax: (010 353 95) 21737

THE ROMAN CAMP

The Roman Camp Hotel sits on the North Bank of the River Tieth amongst twenty acres of mature and secluded gardens, which nestle by the picturesque village of Callandar, the Gateway to the Trossachs and the Highlands of Scotland.

The House was originally built as a Hunting Lodge for the Dukes of Perth in 1625 and was given its name from the conspicuous earth mounds, believed to be the site of a Roman Fort, which are visible across the meadow to the east of the walled garden.

The building has grown over many years as each consecutive family has added their own embellishments to this lovely home. The most obvious of these are the towers, one of which contains a tiny Chapel.

Today under the guidance of Eric and Marion Brown the traditional country house atmosphere still evokes its alluring charm. As you enter you will notice the abundance of freshly cut flowers, their scent lingering in the air, and be greeted to this peaceful retreat by great log fires.

Our Library and Drawing Room are of grand proportions, with an atmosphere of warmth and relaxation and are places to enjoy and reflect on the days sport, especially after dinner in

the company of friends and a fine malt.

The tapestry hung Dining Room is crowned by a richly painted 16th century style ceiling. Here dinner is served at candle lit tables, laid with fine silver and crystal, while you choose from menus of local game and fish, prepared by our chef and accompanied by vegetables and herbs from our own gardens.

Each of our bedrooms has its own distinctive style and character, and is equipped with all the little thoughtful extras to make your stay as comfortable as possible.

At the Roman Camp Country House you are within easy reach of many Championship and picturesque Golf Courses, and we are able to arrange and book tee times at the local course, only two minutes walk from the hotel.

We have three-quarters of a mile of river running through our gardens, enablng guests to fish complementary for Wild Brown Trout and Salmon on our private beat. There is also the opportunity for the hotel to arrange fishing on the many lochs and other private beats surrounding Callander.

We hope that you will be able to make the Roman Camp your favourite country retreat.

The Roman Camp Country House Hotel
Callander
Scotland FK17 8BG
Tel: (0877) 30003
Fax: (0877) 31533

ROOKERY HALL HOTEL, NANTWICH

Rookery Hall is a magnificent Georgian Country House Hotel which offers the highest standards in service and surroundings. Situated in 200 acres of Cheshire countryside, Rookery Hall is easily reached from the M6 and is well placed for racing in Chester, Haydock, Aintree and Bangor on Dee.

Rookery Hall has 45 individually-designed bedrooms, all with luxurious bathrooms. The bedrooms have a complimentary decanter of sherry, fresh fruit and flowers, home-made biscuits and sweets and all those added little extras that make Rookery Hall so special.

Our wood panelled restaurant is the perfect setting and over-looks our Victorian Fountain. The food is exceptional and is listed in the world's good food guides, and the wine list is exemplary. We have several private dining rooms which will cater for small intimate dinners for four, up to larger occasions for 65.

Our wonderful grounds lend themselves to country pursuits and we can offer clay pigeon shooting and falconry in addition to croquet, tennis, hot air ballooning and many other adventurous activities.

Rookery Hall rightly deserves its RAC Blue Ribbon Award and will make your visit a truly special occasion.

Rookery Hall
Worleston
Near Nantwich
Cheshire CW5 6DQ
Tel: (0270) 610016/626866
Fax: (0270) 626027

ROOKHURST GEORGIAN COUNTRY HOUSE HOTEL

This beautiful Georgian Country House Hotel set in its own grounds combines the very best of traditional hospitality with a setting of utter peace and tranquillity. Rookhurst is set amidst stunning Dales scenery in the heart of Herriot country. The views across the garden and the charm of the place have not been eroded by time, and the proprietor, Iris Van der Steen, welcomes guests as her friends.

All bedrooms are individually furnished, including such luxuries as brass or mahogany four-poster beds, and all have en-suite facilities. The public rooms are filled with antiques, and the cuisine is of the traditional, home-cooked variety. Guests can enjoy fresh, locally-grown produce in a candle-lit setting, or the cosiness of the sitting room and bar complete with wood-burning stove. The Victorian dining-room faces east and on sunny mornings shafts of light pierce through the large stone mullion windows.

As well as providing the ideal base from which to explore Herriot country - the Yorkshire Dales are a must for serious walkers and strollers alike - the hotel is perfect for exploring treats such as Bolton Castle, where Mary Queen of Scots was imprisoned for a while. Also on long list of attractions is Middleham, once home to Richard II, Skipton Castle, Jervaulx Abbey, Bowes Museum near Barnard Castle, and the White Scar caves.

Guest are welcome to sample the peace and quiet of Rookhurst for a short break, or to luxuriate in a longer stay.

Rookhurst Georgian Country House
Gayle
Hawes
North Yorkshire DL8 3RT
Tel: (0969) 667454

215

ROYAL BEACON HOTEL

Situated in Exmouth, the oldest seaside resort in Devon, the Royal Beacon has long been established as a premier hotel. An elegant building, it was originally a Georgian posting house. The early traditions of hospitality, good fare and comfort have continued throughout the years, adapting, evolving and modernising to meet the expectations of today's sophisticated guests.

The quiet location is magnificent, facing south and looking down across our own gardens immediately to the beach, the sea and the Devon coastline.

Beautiful surroundings and comfortable furnishings are not everything - our staff create the real atmosphere. Courtesy, friendliness and professionalism are a matter of pride for them all.

The lounge and bar are spacious and there is a superb snooker room for the enthusiast ... and outside there's Devon! The perfect place for windsurfing, bird-watching, fishing, walking, visiting the theatre or playing a round of golf. Exmouth is an ideal centre from which to explore an area rich in natural and man-made beauty from the estuary's flocks of sea birds and the beautiful flower and tree displays at Bicton Gardens to the colour and excitement of Exeter Maritime Museum or the splendour of Exeter Cathedral.

End the day at the hotel's exceptional Fennels Restaurant which reflects the Victorian period in its charm and elegance. Traditional Devon cream teas are served in the afternoon and in the evening you are invited to choose from our thoughtfully planned table d'hotel or extensive a la carte menu complemented by fine wines.

Retire for the night to one of the Royal Beacon's superbly appointed, spacious rooms, many of which enjoy sea views. All have en suite facilities and colour television, radio, direct line telephone, tea and coffee making facilities, hair drier and trouser press. Each room has its own distinctive style and individuality.

Royal Beacon Hotel
The Beacon
Exmouth
Devon
EX8 2AF
Tel: (0395) 264886/265269
Fax: (0395) 268890

RUFFLETS

St Andrews certainly needs no introduction as a golfing mecca. This is a town where records show that the game was played as long ago as 1547. The people of St Andrews have always enjoyed welcoming visitors in the warm and friendly manner that has been part of the true Scottish hospitality for generations, and Rufflets Hotel is one of the finest upholders of this tradition.

Built in 1924, and designed by the Dundee architect Donald Mills, this turreted mansion house, set in ten acres of award-winning gardens, has been privately owned and personally managed by the same family since 1952. Under the personal supervision of owner Ann Russell and general manager Peter Aretz, the excellent reputation of Rufflets has grown both nationally and internationally. Welcoming open fires in winter, friendly and personal service and excellent home cooking, make it an idyllic retreat, just one hour's drive north from Edinburgh.

Spacious and attractively furnished in contemporary country house style, the hotel has twenty-one tastefully and individually decorated bedrooms with ensuite bathrooms, colour television, direct dial telephone, and tea and coffee making facilities. The Garden Restaurant has gained an AA Rosette and an RAC merit award for the past two years; cooking is light with an emphasis on fresh Scottish produce, and many of the vegetables, fruits and herbs are chosen from the hotel's own flourishing kitchen garden.

Guests to Rufflets will find much to enjoy in the historic town of St Andrews, its combination of Medieval, Victorian and Edwardian streets forming one of the most attractive towns in Britain. The Castle, Cathedral, University and Harbour, theatres, museums, art galleries, the fun of the Lammas Fair, the traditions of the Highland Games ... and golf of course.

At Rufflets, guests can enjoy the rich blend that St Andrews has to offer, and a warm welcome second to none.

Rufflets Country House Hotel
Strathkinness Low Road
St Andrews
Fife KY16 9TX
Tel: (0334) 72594
Fax: (0334) 78703

RUNNYMEDE HOTEL

Set in 12 acres of landscaped gardens on the very banks of the Thames, the Runnymede combines modern facilities with old fashioned service and courtesy. Built on the site of the 17th Century Anglers Rest Inn, it has a special atmosphere that makes it an attractive and pleasant place to stay.

For weekend breaks, private meetings or simply to relax, the Runnymede offers 172 air-conditioned bedrooms, many of which have fine river views and feature refinements such as satellite television, in-house movies, hairdryer and trouser press, towelling bathrobe, together with a mini bar and tea and coffee making facilities.

Guests can enjoy a drink on the terrace overlooking the bustling Bell Weir lock or a view of the lush banks of the river whilst dining in the River Room Restaurant - with an enviable reputation for excellent food and immaculate service. A La

Carte and Table d'Hote menus are available for lunch and dinner, and for a leisurely outing, special riverboat cruises with on-board lunch or dinner parties prepared by the Chef are available by arrangement.

In August 1992 the Runnymede Hotel opened a luxurious health and fitness spa with a 18m x 9m pool, jacuzzi, gymnasium, hair and beauty salon, dance studio, steam, sauna and solarium and a full sized snooker room. There is also a croquet and putting lawn.

For those with a sporting inclination, the famous golf courses of Wentworth, Sunningdale and Foxhills are a few minutes drive away, while racegoers will find the Runnymede an ideal base: Ascot, Kempton Park, Sandown Park, Windsor and Epsom are all in close proximity.

Runnymede Hotel
Windsor Road
Egham
Surrey TW20 0AG
Tel: (0784) 436171
Fax: (0784) 436340

SELSDON PARK

Set high in the rolling hills of the Surrey countryside Selsdon Park combines the ancient virtues of hospitality and courtesy with the modern attributes of efficiency and friendliness.

The estate was purchased by the present owner's father and converted into an hotel in 1925. Additions were made during the thirties, and again in the eighties to include a modern courtyard wing and a tropical leisure complex. The hotel now has 170 bedrooms and suites and a considerable range of conference and banqueting rooms.

An outstanding asset to Selsdon Park is the 18 hole championship golf course laid out in 1929 by five-times British Open Champion, J H Taylor. Originally cut out of the thick forest which clothed this part of the Surrey Hills, the course has been extended over the years, but the layout remains substantially as it was sixty years ago. Covering 6402 yards, this course is not perhaps for the novice, although it provides a stimulating challenge to low and high handicappers alike.

A round or two on this interesting course prepares the golfer to sample the pleasures of luncheon or dinner in the Restaurant, or the more informal cuisine of the Phoenix Brasserie and Grill which is open from Monday to Friday The traditional Bar Lounge, warmed in winter by crackling logs, provides old world comfort while the contemporary atmosphere of the Phoenix Bar makes it an ideal place to sample the wide range of cocktails available.

Golfing weekends here are a delight, and there is plenty to occupy the time of a non-golfing partner. There is a heated outdoor swimming pool (open from May to September), a jogging trail, two hard tennis courts and two grass courts (floodlit as necessary), boules pitch and croquet lawn. A large billiard room containing four full sized snooker tables remains open for the use of resident guests until 1 am. Horse riding can be organised at a stables nearby. The architect-designed Leisure Complex contains a well-equipped gymnasium and squash courts, providing opportunities for vigorous exercise, while the tropical swimming pool, sunbeds, steambath, sauna and jacuzzi provide less strenuous pleasures.

Selsdon Park Hotel has an almost unbeatable combination of sporting and leisure facilities to offer the golfer and non-golfer alike, together with all the amenities of a 4-star hotel.

Selsdon Park Hotel
Sanderstead
South Croydon
Surrey CR2 8YA
Tel: 081-657 8811
Fax: 081-651 6171

SHARROW BAY COUNTRY HOUSE HOTEL

Evidence of our heritage surrounds the Sharrow Bay and the beauty of its location has been brought inside where antiques and soft furnishings, together with fresh flowers and the aroma of the cooking, create the feeling of established comfort associated with our country houses.

Nestling beneath Barton Fell, Sharrow Bay Country House Hotel - which is reputed to be the first 'Country House' hotel to be created in Great Britain - is on the shore of Lake Ullswater, the waves actually lapping the terrace wall of soft grey stone.

The views - of lake, woods and mountains - are legendary, constantly changing and as inspirational today as they were for the poets who are part of the history of this area. There are twelve acres of gardens and woodlands and half a mile of lake shore (complete with a private jetty) where guests can wander in total peace. The bedrooms are as one would expect; luxuriously cosy and full of porcelain, pictures, antique furniture, books and games.

In the main hotel there are twelve bedrooms, eight with private bathroom. There is also a garden cottage and a charming Quaker cottage in the village of Tirril, four miles from the hotel. The Edwardian gatehouse at the entrance to the hotel, has an additional room and three superb suites - ideal, as are many of the rooms, for honeymoons.

In addition, the hotel has a converted Elizabethan farmhouse, a mile and a quarter further along the lake from the main house. Bank House is approached by a sweeping drive which takes one up onto the fell-side where the views are unbelievable. All of the seven bedrooms look down on Ullswater and the superb refectory breakfast room has breathtaking views. Guests join those at the main house for dinner but this is the only time they need leave the tranquil surroundings.

Because guests are genuinely cared for, comfort is the key word associated with Sharrow. There are two lounges in Bank House, as there are in the main house, where soft sofas jostle for space with antique chairs and freshly cut flowers and numerous lights make even grey days light. It is an oasis where one can escape from the world and one's own problems.

The cuisine has become internationally renowned and the emphasis is on traditional British dishes, created with imagination and served with graciousness and care by the excellent staff, some of whom have been at Sharrow for over twenty five years. 1992 will see the commencement of Sharrow's 44th season under the present proprietors.

A haven for those who wish to relax completely in peaceful surroundings, guests will find echoes of the Italian lakes, and will understand why Sharrow was given an award by the AA for having the best view of any hotel in the United Kingdom. In the immediate vicinity, guests can enjoy boating, fishing, and of course walking or climbing. Alternatively, the market town of Penrith lies seven miles to the east - a friendly little town full of atmosphere and ideal for shopping. On the outskirts of the town there is a fine golf course with wide views of the Fells. The area also offers a variety of places of archaeological interest which can be visited, such as Hadrian's Wall east of Carlisle, or Long Meg stone circle near Penrith.

Just six miles from the M6 motorway, and with modern high speed electric train links from Carlisle to London and the North, Sharrow Bay, with its delightful atmosphere and outstanding vistas, is a rare treat.

Sharrow Bay Country House Hotel
Lake Ullswater
Pooley Bridge
Penrith CA10 2LZ
Tel: (07684) 86301
Fax: (07684) 86349

SHEEN FALLS LODGE

Discover the charming village of Kenmare along the coastal peninsula of Ireland's South West and you will come upon the luxurious Sheen Falls Lodge.

The Lodge nestles against a background of hazy mountain panoramas and overlooks the Falls of the Sheen River as they tumble dramatically into the Kenmare Estuary.

Sheen Falls Lodge is all you could possibly dream of in a gracious country hotel as it stands amid 300 acres of lawn, semi tropical gardens restored to their 17th century glory, green pastures and forests. Fishing rights on a 15 mile stretch of the Sheen River, famed for salmon and sea trout, are available in season to guests.

We invite you to golf on any of six golf courses within a 40 mile radius of the hotel, one of which is Killarney which hosted the 1991 Carrolls Irish Open. Alternatively Kenmare golf course only a short distance from the Lodge, offers a charming nine hole along the bay.

Other facilites include a conference centre, health and fitness centre, horseriding along wooded trails, tennis and croquet.

Sheen Falls Lodge
Kenmare
Co. Kerry
Ireland
Tel: 010 353 64 41600
Fax: 010 353 64 41386

SHRIGLEY HALL

Shrigley Hall is a four star Regency Style Country House Hotel set in the 262 acre estate of Shrigley Park in one of the most beautiful parts of Cheshire.

The estate was the seat of the Downes family for over five centuries and was bought by William Turner the High Sherriff of Cheshire in 1821. He built the present hall in 1825 which was desighed by Thomas Emmett. Shrigley Hall was passed by marriage into the Lowther family until 1929, when it was sold to the Salesian order of missionaries, with whom Shrigley remained until the 1980's. Guests can now enjoy it as a hotel of remarkable splendour and luxury.

The hotel has been restored to its original grandeur, with many of the Neo Classical features of the original architecture retained. The sumptuous Oakridge Restaurant offers a superb choice of dining with the finest cuisine and service, and guests can relax in the individually designed bedrooms, many having magnificent views over the estate and the Cheshire Plains. For those who prefer a more informal atmosphere, meals can also be enjoyed in the relaxing Wine Bar and Leisure Club.

The former church building now houses the Country Club, offering truly magnificent facilities in luxurious surroundings. Guests can take advantage of a glorious indoor heated swimming pool, squash, tennis, snooker, gymnasium, saunas, solarium, steam room and beauty therapy. For the golfer, a round of golf can become a very special experience. The rolling landscape of the course and the spectacular views of Cheshire and the Peak District can be admired whilst enjoying the challenges of the hotel's own 18 hole golf course, designed by the internatioally renowned golf architect Donald Steel.

Guests to Shrigley Hall of an active persuasion can take in the many other activies and attractions on offer nearby, such as walking, sailing, climbing and riding. If guests come together as a large party,activities can be arranged, including clay pideon shooting, skirmish, archery, hot air ballooning and many others.

For a Country Club atmosphere and a refreshing break away from the stresses of every day life, Shrigley Hall provides the perfect answer.

Shrigley Hall
Shrigley Park
Pott Shrigley
Nr. Macclesfield
Cheshire SK10 5SB

Tel: (0625) 575757   Fax: (0625) 573323

SLIEVE DONARD HOTEL

The Slieve Donard Hotel is located in Newcastle, Co Down, just 45 minutes south of Belfast.

Magnificently situated at the foot of the beautiful Mountains of Mourne, the Slieve Donard Hotel stands in 6 acres of private grounds which extend to an extensive golden strand. Originally a luxurious railway hotel, the Slieve Donard is now owned by the Hastings Hotels Group and offers Grade 'A' accommodation and excellent facilities. It is the most popular hotel in the province for a conference, wedding or holiday break.

Each of its 120 luxury bedrooms are beautifully appointed with all the modern facilities you would expect from a top international hotel.

The Slieve Donard Hotel is the first choice for golfers who play at the world famous Royal County Down Golf Club. It is only 2 minutes through a beautiful hedged, arched walk to the course. Other courses close at hand are Kilkeel, Ardglass and Warrenpoint. The Slieve Donard warmly welcomes all golfers and can arrange starting times with local courses, including Royal County Down.

Within the hotel, the Elysium Health and Leisure Club is a must for all visitors, with tennis, swimming in the luxurious indoor pool, putting on the lawn, or a relaxing sauna or jacuzzi. The Chaplin's Bar and the Percy French, an informal pub/restaurant in the grounds of the hotel, are also popular venues.

The Slieve Donard at Newcastle is truly one of Ireland's great holiday hotels. Newcastle is a splendid centre for golfers and also for fishermen. Newcastle is the gateway to the Mourne Mountains and Tollymore Forest Park, providing excellent walking on clearly marked trails. Pony-trekking is also popular. Everyone visiting the Slieve Donard is given a very warm welcome and customers often comment on the friendliness and efficiency of the service. The Oak Restaurant is renowned for its gourmet food and fine wines.

The Slieve Donard is a member of Hastings Hotels, the leading chain of hotels in Northern Ireland. This is a further guarantee of its excellence. Newcastle - 'Where the Mountains of Mourne sweep down to the sea' - Percy French.

Slieve Donard Hotel
Downs Road
Newcastle
Co. Down BT33 0AH
Tel: (03967) 23681
Fax: (03967) 24830

SLIEVE RUSSELL

The Slieve Russell Hotel Golf and Country Club opened it's doors on the 1st August 1990. The hotel is situated on 300 acres of parkland landscape and encompasses gardens and two natural lakes in the grounds covering 50 acres.

Each of the 150 bedrooms is furnished with impeccable taste and great attention has been given to guest comfort. The deluxe rooms offer the added luxury of an Airbath. The Suites are spacious and luxurious, many offer a fine view of the Golf Course.

There are two restaurants; the elegant Conall Cearnach Restaurant serves the finest of Irish Cuisine. The Brackley restaurant, the less formal of the two, specialises in traditional Irish and French dishes. Both restaurants offer a comprehensive Wine List to complement your menu choice.

Guests have a choice of three bars in which to enjoy a drink in relaxed surroundings. The Kells bar, the public bar, is decorated on the theme of the Book of Kells and features a handmade copy of that famous tome. The Pike bar, the residents bar, is the perfect place to idle way your time busily doing nothing or why not have your favourite tipple in the Conservatory.

The Slieve Russell is the perfect Conference Venue with meeting rooms suitable for 4-800. A comprehensive range of audio-visual equipment is available to conference groups.

Leisure facilities include Leisure Pool (20m), Saunas, Steamroom, Jacuzzi, Fitness Suite, Solarium, Tennis and Squash Courts, Health and Beauty Salon.

The 18-hole championship standard golf course opened in August 1992. The unique style of the course fits and complements the typical Cavan drumlin and valley landscape, with gently tumbling fairways and contoured greens.

The superb golf Clubhouse is an added bonus and includes a golf shop, restaurant and bar. An excellent feature is the marvellous view which extends over most of the course.

The Slieve Russell Hotel
Golf & Country Club
Ballyconnell
Co. Cavan
Tel: (010 353 49) 26444
Fax: (010 353 49) 26474

SOPWELL HOUSE

Once the country home of Lord Mountbatten, Sopwell House Hotel's gracious Georgian elegance summons images of gracious living. A sanctuary of peace and tranquillity set amidst 11 acres of picturesque gardens, where our warmest welcome awaits you.

Romantic whispers linger in our magnificent gardens, reputedly the setting of the King of Greece's proposal to Princess Alice. Unwind in the Music Room Lounge with a traditional afternoon tea or browse through our Library's well-stocked bookcase and settle down to a leisurely read before retiring, to prepare for the evening.

The country style permeates the tasteful furnishing and individual decor of each guest room. Every facility has been included, from satellite T.V to trouser press, to assure you of a comfortable stay.

Dining amongst mature magnolia trees in our Magnolia Conservatory Restaurant, the crisp, pink linen bedecked tables and festoon blinds echo the floral leafy setting. Savour our acclaimed cuisine - awarded two AA rosettes - imaginatively created using only the finest seasonal produce. A wide selection of fine wines, many from the New World, ensure the perfect accompaniment to complement each course.

For light, healthy eating, our Brasserie offers a delicious choice of cuisine to appease even the heartiest of appetites.

Natural light floods into each meeting room in our purpose-built £2 million conference centre. Self-contained with a separate entrance and reception, 400 delegates may be accommodated theatre-style in the St Albans suite, whilst 20 Directors 'brainstorm' undisturbed in the Lady Edwina.

The perfect stage and setting for romance and celebration - whether a grand summer wedding or ball spilling out on to the terrace overlooking the gardens, ablaze with colour, or an intimate champagne dinner party to celebrate an anniversary with some close friends. An atmosphere of charm and discretion pervades to ensure a very special occasion.

The jewel of our crown - the health and country club, is a sanctuary dedicated entirely to your relaxation, health and fitness.

Swim in the crystal clear waters of our ozone purified pool. Laze in the bubbling waters of the revitalising spa. Indulge in the benefits of deep heat in the sauna or steam room.

Our beauty therapists are waiting to pamper and cossett you with aromatherapy massages and facials, body wraps or manicure.

And if our gymnasium beckons, fully qualified instructors will supervise your workout, fitness assessment or lifestyle evaluation - the choice is yours.

When choosing a weekend away, whether for health and relaxation or for complete gourmet indulgence, Sopwell House offers the perfect venue. Breaks include Stressbuster, The New You, Fitness, Romance and Rejuvenation and special programmes for Easter and Christmas.

Sopwell House Hotel and Country Club
Cottonmill Lane
Sopwell
St Albans
Hertfordshire AL1 2HQ
Tel: (0727) 864477
Fax: (0727) 44741

SOUTH LODGE HOTEL

One of the best kept secrets in West Sussex, South Lodge Hotel captures the essence of Victorian style and elegance, with an atmosphere of warmth and hospitality, hidden amongst 90 acres of beautiful gardens and parkland, with views over the rolling South Downs.

Built in 1883, this grey stoned mansion, strewn with wisteria, was once the home of the Godman family; Fredrick Ducane Godman, a keen botanist and explorer, collected hundreds of rare shrubs and trees and an outstanding variety of rhododendron and camellia, which today make the gardens at the hotel such a delight.

Dining at South Lodge is always a special occasion. In the elegant wood panelled dining room guests enjoy innovative menus created by top chef Anthony Tobin, featuring local meat, game and fish, with herbs and soft fruits grown in the hotels own walled garden.

Each of the 39 bedrooms and suites is perfectly appointed. All are individually decorated in the true country house style, sympathetically incorporating all the modern amenities one expects to find at a first class hotel.

South Lodge, situated in Lower Beeding, near Horsham, West Sussex, is only a short drive from the challenging 18 hole, par 73 Mannings Heath Golf Club, where hotel guests enjoy special privileges. The hotel will reserve tees at the course for guests during their stay.

Other activities at the hotel include tennis, coarse fishing, putting, croquet or petanque, and horse riding can be arranged at the local stables.

South Lodge is also an ideal base to explore the countryside and wealth of English heritage that Sussex has to offer, with many fine National Trust houses and exquisite gardens to discover. The Georgian costal town of Brighton, with its famous lanes, is only 30 minutes away, and both Petworth and Arundel are within easy distance.

South Lodge Hotel
Lower Beeding
Near Horsham
West Sussex
Tel: (0403) 891711
Fax: (0403) 891766

THE SPREAD EAGLE

The Spread Eagle at Midhurst has been welcoming guests since it was built as a tavern in 1430 and throughout its well documented history as a famous coaching inn.

Now in private ownership, the hotel has been sympathetically renovated, extended and unobtrusively modernised.

Traditional Sussex Christmas puddings compete with the copperware in decorating a lovely restaurant which features a large inglenook fireplace and dark oak beams.

With the emphasis on quality and seasonal produce, the menus are varied and the talented chefs offer both classic and innovative cooking. Making your choice from the well-devised and extensive wine list is an enjoyable challenge.

The oldest part of the Spread Eagle had medieval foundations and a timber-framed structure. The 1650 part of the hotel is built of red brick, now painted with stone angle dressings. And there are plain architraves to the windows.

There is some fine oak panelling in the southern-most rooms and in the Oak Room's panelling a cupboard conceals one of the original windows bricked up in 1805 to avoid window tax.

The lounge bar with its polished ships timbers formed part of the original Spread Eagle Tavern and has been at the heart of Midhurst life since the 15th century.

Log fires welcome guests in colder months and summer drinks can be enjoyed in the walled courtyard, flanked by climbing roses and clematis.

Above the lounge bar, in the King Edward VII room, huge Queen-Post roof trusses dominate affairs and are high on the list of hotel's features.

Careful thought has been given to the individual furnishings and fabrics in each of the 37 bedrooms, all of which have bathrooms, colour televisions and direct-dial telephones.

Two family suites are available in the hotel's adjoining Market House. And the perfect setting for those with something very special to celebrate is the Queen Elizabeth I four-poster suite.

Tudor bread ovens, a wig powder closet and a series of Flemish stained-glass windows are just some of the characteristics making for a rare atmosphere at the Spread Eagle.

The Spread Eagle Hotel
South Street
Midhurst
West Sussex GU29 9NH
Tel: (0730) 816911
Fax: (0730) 815668

ST. ANDREWS GOLF HOTEL

St. Andrews Golf Hotel is a tastefully modernised Victorian House situated on the cliffs above St. Andrews Bay, some 200 yards from the 18th tee of the 'Old Course'.

There are 23 bedrooms all with private bath and shower, and all furnished individually to a high degree of comfort, with telephone, radio, T.V., tea/coffee maker, trouser press and hair-dryer. A nice touch is the fresh flowers and welcoming fruit basket.

There is a quiet front lounge for residents and a most interesting golfer's cocktail bar featuring pictures and photographs of Open Champions past and present. This gives onto a small south facing patio garden.

With a separate entrance is 'Ma Bell's' Bar and day time restaurant, popular with students and visitors alike. Tasty food, hot and cold and reasonably priced is served from noon to 6.00 pm. A main attraction is the selection of more than 80 bottled beers from all over the world, and no fewer than 14 on draught, including cask-conditioned ales.

The central feature of the hotel is the candle-lit oak-panelled restaurant with its magnificent sea view. A la carte and table d'hote menus both feature the best of local produce – fish, shell-fish, beef, lamb, game and vegetables – conjured into delightful dishes by chef Adam Harrow. The food is well complemented by an interesting and comprehensive list of wines selected personally by owner, Brian Hughes.

Golf of course, is the speciality of the hotel, and you can find either prepared golf packages and golf weeks or have something tailored to your particular requirements, using any of the thirty or so courses within 45 minutes of St. Andrews.

St. Andrews Golf Hotel
40 The Scores
St. Andrews
KY16 9AS
Tel: (0334) 72611
Fax: (0334) 72188

ST ANDREWS OLD COURSE HOTEL

If you are a golfer, then welcome home, for St Andrews is known to every Golfer Worldwide quite simply as 'The home of Golf' and it is certainly the ambition of every player to play here at least once, as a pinnacle to their career, whether they be amateur or professional.

The St Andrew's Old Course hotel, formerly the Old Course Golf and Country Club, is adjacent to the famous 17th 'Road Hole' on the Old Course.

Although being seen as the Mecca for Golf by many, the hotel is now very much a luxury resort offering guests a whole host of alternative activities and facilities to make your stay everlasting memorable.

Each bedroom or suite offers luxurious en-suite marble bathrooms many with balconies which look out over the Old Course, the town and St Andrews Bay.

Stewards will arrange your golf outings, organising your transportation, club rental or club storage, and for those who need a quick reminder, the hotel has a golf professional who is available for lessons.

For the sport minded you can also organise shooting, with a clay pigeon shoot just 15 minutes away 'atop' a hill overlooking the sea and the mountains. Fly fishing for salmon on the Tay can

also be included in a package, but prior notification is recommended.

For the golfing widow or for those who are just here to relax, the spa at St Andrews offers guests the opportunity to pamper both 'body and soul'. From the invigorating whirlpool, the lap pool, the latest technology in the fitness room, steam rooms and sunbeds, to a whole variety of massages, hairdressing, facials and body treatments all carried out by a team of fully qualified therapists.

St Andrews is situated amidst some marvellous countryside. For the historically minded, Glamis Castle, Scone Palace and Stirling Castle are all within easy reach. St Andrew's town is in itself well worth spending a couple of hours walking around, being Scotland's oldest University town it is reminiscent in many ways to Oxford and Cambridge.

The evenings can be spent in the magnificent luxury of the hotel with marvellous cuisine in the restaurant supplied by Chef Billy Campbell who was inspired by the world renowned Anton Mosimann.

St Andrews is also a superb location to organise banquets and corporate events. Whatever your reason for travelling to St Andrews, it will be permanently etched in your memories.

St Andrews Old Course Hotel
St Andrews
Scotland
Tel (0334) 74371
Fax (0334) 77668

STOCKS HOTEL AND CLUB

Stocks, an historically elegant country house hotel located in the heart of the Chiltern Hills, dates back to 1176 and was the former home of entrepreneur Victor Lownes, who turned the house into a training school for his 'Bunny Girls'. The house is situated amidst twenty acres of parkland, surrounded by 10,000 acres of National Trust Estate. Stocks however, is not only a peaceful house for unwinding and enjoying the delightful relaxing atmosphere and excellent cuisine, but also offers sporting and leisure facilities that are second to none.

Construction of an 18 hole championship golf course started in May 1992. The course will be 7185 yards long and has been skilfully designed to blend with the layout of the already established parkland, using the natural features and many of the existing fine old trees. The work has been timed to take advantage of the summer growing season and it is anticipated that the course will be available for some limited play by advance members in the Autumn of 1993. The official opening will be in Spring 1994.

For companies who require corporate entertainment or hospitality days, hot air ballooning, clay pigeon or laser shooting and off-the-road driving events, are all available. One can take advantage of the riding and livery stables, four tennis courts

(one floodlit), gymnasium or squash court, croquet, table tennis, volley ball, cricket, five a side football and heated outdoor swimming pool (May to October). However, if you prefer more gentle pursuits, there is also the country's largest jacuzzi or a snooker table to while away an hour or so.

The bedrooms are most luxurious and are beautifully furnished and equipped with all amenities including such niceties as towelling robes.

The Tapestry Restaurant is inviting with its crisp linen, features a seasonal a La Carte menu and a table d'hote menu (changes daily), making good use of fresh ingredients and offers an exceptional cheese-board to finish. Here you can sample some of the finest cuisine in the Home Counties. The Tapestry Restaurant is open daily for lunch and dinner. breakfast is served in the Conservatory with wonderful views of the Chilterns.

There is also a terrace, situated beside the swimming pool, where lunch or afternoon tea can be served on warm summer days. A visit to Stocks is thoroughly recommended whether on business or pleasure; you will find the staff are pleasant and helpful. Your 'Home from Home' in the country.

Stocks Country House Hotel
Stocks Road
Aldbury
Nr Tring
Hertfordshire HP23 5RX
Tel: (044285) 341
Fax: (044285) 253

SUMMER LODGE

Summer Lodge, so aptly named, is set in the rural peace and charm of Thomas Hardy's Dorset.

This Georgian dower house, once owned by the Earls of Ilchester whose magnificent estate is close by, sits in a walled garden which comes complete with croquet, a swimming pool and tennis courts. Now a luxurious hotel, owners Nigel and Margaret Corbett offer guests a real home from home and a genuinely friendly welcome in this unspoilt area of outstanding beauty.

The seventeen comfortable and attractive bedrooms all with pretty bathrooms have views over the gardens or over the village to the meadowlands beyond. Log fires and arrangements of fresh flowers throughout the house create a homely atmosphere.

Delicious dinners, fresh local produce, superb English breakfasts and afternoon Dorset cream teas reflect the Corbett's love of good food, generous hospitality and the skill of Roger Jones the Head Chef and Tim Ford, the Second Chef. A list of over 700 wines rounds off the culinary offerings. It is not surprising that Summer Lodge is now a member of the highly prestigious Relais et Chateaux hotel chain.

This is truly an idyllic corner of England, with quaint villages, ancient hillforts and towns like Sherborne and Dorchester close by and the coastline just a few miles away. The setting brings to life Tess of the d'Urbevilles and all the other novels and poetry of Thomas Hardy. Many National Trust properties and gardens in the locality are open to the public, and there are stables, golf courses and trout lakes nearby. Summer Lodge is the ideal base from which to tour these places or to discover delights of your own.

The turning to Evershot leaves the A37 half way between Dorchester and Yeovil. Once in the village turn left into Summer Lane and the hotel entrance is 150 yards on the right.

Summer Lodge
Summer Lane
Evershot
Dorset DT2 0JR
Tel: (0935) 83424
Fax: (0935) 83005

SUNLAWS HOUSE

Sunlaws House stands in the heart of Scotland's beautiful Border country, in 200 acres of gardens and mature parkland along the banks of the Teviot, three miles from the historic town of Kelso.There has been a house on the same site at Sunlaws for nearly 500 years and from its beginnings it has always been a Scottish family house – and that, to all intents and purposes, is how it will stay!

Sunlaws has a place in history, from the faint echoes of ancient strife when English armies of the 15th and 16th centuries came marauding through Roxburghshire and the Borders, to the Jacobite rebellion of 1745. Indeed Prince Charles Edward Stuart is reputed to have stayed on November 5th 1745 and to have planted a white rose bush in the grounds.

Sunlaws hope that their guests will find that in the intervening year there have been some welcome changes. Its owner, the Duke of Roxburghe, has carefully converted Sunlaws into the small, welcoming but unpretentious hotel of comfort and character that it is.

There are 22 bedrooms, which include the splendid Bowmont Suite and six delightful rooms in the stable courtyard, all furnished with care to His Graces' own taste and all with private bathroom or shower, colour television, radio and direct-dial telephone. Disabled guests too are provided with the amenities they need.

The spacious public rooms are furnished with the same care and elegance, which adds to the overall atmosphere of warmth and welcome with log fires burning in the main and inner hall, drawing room, library bar and dining room, throughout the winter and on cold summer evenings.

Flowers and plants, from the gardens and the conservatory, will be found all over the house; herbs too are grown for the kitchen and will be found in many of the traditional dishes that are prepared for the dining room. Not only is Sunlaws right in the heart of Scotland's beautiful Border Country, it is also the perfect centre for a host of holiday activities. Sporting and cultural interests are well served, too.

Salmon and trout fishing, and a complete range of shooting are available at the Hotel, with golf, horse-riding, racing and fox hunting all nearby.

Sunlaws is the perfect location for touring the Borders, with great country houses including Abbotsford, the home of Sir Walter Scott, and a number of abbeys and museums all within easy reach.

Sunlaws House Hotel
Kelso
Roxburghshire
Scotland
Tel: (05735) 331 Fax: (05735) 611

THE THREE SWANS HOTEL

It was on the evening of June 13th 1645, that Charles I, on his way through Market Harborough, called in at The Three Swans for pre-battle refreshments before proceeding to the field at Naseby where his Cavaliers met defeat by Cromwell's Roundheads.

Whether The Three Swans' hospitality had any effect on the outcome of the Civil War battle is not recorded.

A later royal visitor was the Duke of Windsor, then Prince of Wales, who was taken to The Three Swans after breaking his collar bone in a fall on the hunting field.

When a hotel has been around for over five hundred years, it will have built up quite an impressive guest list and a wealth of dramatic stories could be told about the visitors, famous and infamous, who have sought hospitality under its roof. Many such stories were recounted by the hotel's most famous owner, the somewhat eccentric John Fothergill, in his book, 'My Three Inns'.

Today the beautiful wrought-iron sign depicting Three Swans is still prominent outside the ancient coaching inn on Market Harborough's gracefully curving High Street. The outward appearance of The Three Swans has changed little since the sixteenth century, but step inside and evidence of a very tasteful refurbishment programme will soon be apparent.

Guests staying at The Three Swans experience the atmosphere of a centuries old coaching inn coupled with the benefits of the most modern of facilities. All 36 bedrooms are en suite with remote control colour T.V., radio, tea / coffee making facilities, trouser press, hairdryers etc. If it is possible to add a little old fashioned romance to your stay at the hotel why not try a touch of grandeur of days gone by and try sleeping in one of our real oak Four Poster beds.

The Swans' restaurant, such an elegant dining room. The craftsmanship and dedication of Head Chef, Richard Payne, and his team will be evident throughout the meal. His creativity and imaginative menus have earned him a much deserved reputation for excellent cuisine throughout the country.

Our Swans' Nest conservatory serves a selection of meals throughout the day. A favourite meeting place for morning coffees and traditional afternoon teas. Al Fresco dining during the summer months in our delightful courtyard area.

There are many places of interest nearby, Rockingham Castle, Althorpe House (family home of the Princess of Wales), Rutland Water, Warwick, Stratford, to name but a few.

However short or long your stay with us we ensure it will be a memorable one.

The Three Swans Hotel
High Street
Market Harborough
Leicestershire LE16 7NJ
Tel: (0858) 466644
Fax: (0858) 433101

TILLMOUTH PARK HOTEL

Comment:

Spring runs on the Tweed are increasing and with the Tweed nets off, summer fishing offers an exciting new dimension. Latest catch records prove the point. Spring is up 48%, summer is up 112%, August is up 93%.

The Autumn fishing is superb, many heavy fish have been taken - best 43lbs by Lady Burnett. In 1990 there was one of 30lb with many over 25lb. The best September day saw 28 fish into the hotel, the best October day 14, the best November day 12. In 1990 rods staying at the hotel took 619 fish. The best individual rod daily take in 1990, 10 fish, best 19lb.

The hotel offers fine cuisine, classic bedrooms and a service to cover all angling requirements.

I rate it as one of Britain's top angling hotels.
Maynard Atkinson
Angling Correspondent to the leading sporting journals.

The Unique Tweed Package for Salmon and Sea Trout:
A Three Star Hotel with fishing, boat and Ghillie.

If you are considering fishing the Tweed, we are possibly the only place able to offer this package.

A traditional Country House Hotel, set in lovely grounds, with good fresh food, friendly service and five miles of the Tweed for you to have the experience of a lifetime.

Some of our senior fishers have been coming for 32 years. Perhaps you might like to join them.

You will be a most welcome guest.

Tillmouth Park Hotel
Cornhill-On-Tweed
Northumberland TD12 4UU
Tel: (0890) 2255

THE TOWER

Set in Hampshire farmland between the New Forest and the Solent, The Tower offers some of the most select and unusual accommodation in the south of England. Stretching 200 feet above the barrow on which it was built over a hundred years ago, the listed building has magnificent views of the surrounding countryside.

Set on five floors, the accommodation is outstanding. The en-suite bedrooms each take up a separate floor, and are reached by an enclosed spiral staircase. Retaining the elegance of a bygone era, each bedroom has its own individual character, complete with modern comforts such as satellite TV and direct dial telephone with ansaphone. Exquisite Table d' Hote menus are served by candle light.

An all weather tennis court is available in the grounds and the 20 metre indoor pool tempts guests after a hot day exploring the surrounding countryside and sights. Nearby, Bucklers Hart and Lymington provide much to sample and see. Winchester Cathedral, Salisbury and Stonehenge are within an hour's drive. Ancient Beaulieu with its famous motor museum is also close to hand. For keen golfers, the area may need no introduction, and for the uninitiated offers many treats, such as the courses at Lymington and Brockenhrust.

Other activities in the area include yacht charter, sailing courses, even aircraft hire. The New Forest offers miles of secluded trails over varied terrains, full of wildlife and surrounded by superb views - rambling maps can be provided and cycle and car hire are nearby.

All in all, your visit to The Tower at Sway is sure to be a pleasant, memorable and unique experience.

The Tower
Sway
Hants. SO4 16DE
Tel: (0590) 682117
Fax: (0590) 683785

TOWERS HOTEL

The Towers is a family run, Grade A Hotel, situated on the famous ring of Kerry. The Hotel offers its visitors a friendly homely atmosphere and a genuine Irish hospitality.

Dining in our restaurant is a treat and is recognised as one of Ireland's most distinguished restaurants, offering the best in seafood and shellfish delicacies.

Residents at the Towers enjoy beautifully appointed bedrooms, with central heating, T.V., direct dial telephone and private bathroom. Old Bar with open turf fire and cocktail bar with baby grand piano.

For the golfer we are situated in one of the best spots in Ireland - Dooks 18 hole Golf Links is 3 miles away. There are championship courses at Waterville, Ballybunion and Killarney with the scenic Tralee and Dingle courses all within easy reach.

For the non-golfer the surrounding countryside provides a wealth of things to do and see, sightseeing, mountaineering, salmon and trout fishing - on rivers and lakes - boat and Ghillie can also be arranged. Ideal for a walk is a lovely uncrowded four mile long beach. Horse riding can be arranged, either trekking through 25,000 acres at the National Park at Killarney or a gallop on the beach at Rossbeigh.

Kerry Airport is only 30 minutes drive away, Cork or Shannon Airports are approximately 2 hours drive.

Towers Hotel
Glenbeigh
Co. Kerry
Ireland
Tel: (010 353 66) 68212
Fax: (010 353 66) 68260

TREARDDUR BAY HOTEL

The Isle of Anglesey has long been popular as a peaceful retreat and the Trearddur Bay Hotel, with its magnificent location, has proved to be one of its most prized assets. Step outside the hotel and the bay beckons with scenic walks, miles of golden sandy beaches and the ideal haven for watersports.

Few hotels are able to offer guests such striking, varied accommodation; but then few hotels boast such panoramic views from so many rooms. There are 31 rooms, nine being studio suites, including the four-poster 'Shearwater'; with authentic oak beams and all the facilities of a first class hotel every one of them provides the perfect home away from home.

Before dinner why not enjoy a cocktail or your favourite aperitif in a quiet corner of the bar before settling down to the superb cuisine of the restaurant to savour a meal chosen from table d'hote and a la carte menus. Besides the breathtaking views another advantage of the hotel's location is the sheer range of fresh, locally caught seafood that is so readily available, accompanied, perhaps, by a fine wine from the extensive cellars.

There are many activities available to guests at Trearddur Bay, form the heated indoor swimming pool to pool in the games room; while outside the whole of the Isle awaits with a range of sports, including tennis and golf, to the fascinating historical sites of Beaumaris Castle and Bryn Celli Ddu.

Naturally a hotel of such stature offers the finest in conference and function facilities where nothing is too much trouble.

Trearddur Bay Hotel
Holyhead
Isle of Anglesey
North Wales
Tel: (0407) 860301
Fax: (0407) 861181

TURNBERRY HOTEL GOLF COURSES & SPA

Voted Britain's 5 Star Hotel of the Year in 1990, and perhaps best known for its two championship links golf courses, Turnberry is located on the west coast of Scotland, set in 360 acres overlooking the islands of Arran and Ailsa Craig.

The two golf courses, owned and managed by the hotel, make it a year round Mecca for golfers and the Ailsa Course will again host the British Open in 1994. A superb new Clubhouse will open in Spring 1993.

The new Turnberry Spa and Leisure is an additional amenity for our guests. The leisure facilities include a 20 metre deck level pool, poolside spa bath and bio-sauna, 2 squash courts, cardiovascular and muscular gymnasium and planned aqua and floor aerobics. The nine treatment rooms offer a complete range of treatments, including aromatherapy and hydro-therapy.

Nearby are riding stables, and fishing, rough shooting, clay pigeon shooting can be arranged. Culzean Castle, Robert Burns country and the Burrell Collection are also of interest in the area.

The hotel was built at the turn of the century and the tradition of elegance and comfort is retained in the bedrooms. At Turnberry, living is indeed comfortable and relaxed; every bedroom has its individual character.

The Turnberry Restaurant, under the direction of Executive Chef, Stewart Cameron, specialises in an alliance of traditional Scottish and French cooking. Entertainment is provided each evening by resident musicians and the atmosphere is very much that of the grand Country House.

The Bay at Turnberry Restaurant enjoys spectacular views of Turnberry Bay towards Arran and Ailsa Craig. The focus is on a lighter style of cooking both at lunch and dinner, in an informal setting.

Whilst staying at Turnberry, guests will enjoy warm hospitality, the constant concern and those little formalities and gracious touches that make all the difference. Perhaps it is because of this that so many guests and their families choose to return year after year.

Turnberry Hotel, Golf Courses and Spa
Ayrshire
Scotland KA26 9LT
Tel: (0655) 31000
Fax: (0655) 31706

TY NEWYDD

Rich in history the Ty Newydd Country Hotel and Restaurant stands proudly on the site of the ancient farm from which it derives its name. The present Ty Newydd was built by William Llewellyn, the uncle of the famous Olympic champion, Sir Harry Llewellyn, who was a frequent visitor to the house. Today Ty Newydd offers itself as the perfect country retreat, retaining its historic aura while providing all the modern comforts and amenities that the modern guest has come to expect. This, combined with tranquil surroundings and fine cuisine really do make it the ideal location for that relaxing break.

Comfort, quality and excellence of service are the priorities here, where the aim of everyone is to make your stay a relaxing and pleasurable experience. In the original wing of the house all the bedrooms have been individually designed and decorated to the highest standard of luxury with antique furniture complemented by beautiful soft fabrics. The new wing has been furnished more simply with fine reproduction furniture, but still with the same careful attention to quality. All of the thirty bedrooms have superb en suite bathrooms, direct dial telephones and remote control television with satellite channels.

The sophisticated but relaxed atmosphere of the elegant restaurant is the perfect venue in which to sample the cooking of the resident chef who uses only the freshest ingredients to create memorable cuisine.

The area surrounding Ty Newydd is that of breathtaking splendour. Situated, as it is, at the foothills of the Brecon Beacons it boasts much of the stunning scenery for which Wales is so famous. Within five minutes of the hotel you can enjoy fishing, golf or just long, invigorating country walks.

Since the Ty Newydd is only a few miles from London, with excellent road links to the Midlands or M4 it is ideal as the venue for nationwide companies looking to meet in such a secluded, peaceful setting. The main function room can double up as a large conference room, while smaller rooms, ideal for seminars and small meetings, are available. On sunny days the conservatory bar may be used as a private dining room or meeting room.

With such facilities in such a setting the Ty Newydd is naturally perfect for a wedding reception, with beautiful grounds providing the ideal backdrop for wonderful photographs.

Ty Newydd Country Hotel
Penderyn Road
Hirwaun
Mid Glamorgan CF44 95X
Tel: (0685) 813433
Fax: (0685) 813139

TYDDYN LLAN

Smooth lawns surround this Georgian House of stone, setting up the resonance of a quiet oasis among mountains, rivers and the great outdoors. Inside all is light and elegance.

A cosy bar, often the centre of fishing exploits, looks into our much acclaimed Restaurant. The food, prepared with skill and imagination from fresh ingredients of the highest quality, will add to your feeling of satisfaction and physical well being at the end of an exhilarating day. Run as a very high quality country house, the Hotel is friendly, informal and always ready to help with any of your plans or requests. We take pleasure in providing a haven for guests wanting a peaceful holiday in style and comfort.

We have 4 miles of private fishing on the River Dee. This beautiful stretch of water has many named holding pools, where some excellent salmon have been caught, either on lure or fly.

The river is also known for its trout, but mostly as superb grayling water, with an enormous head of this wonderful fish. The grayling, caught on wet or dry fly, is a great fighter and very good to eat. Average weight is 1lb to 2lb.

As a natural unspoilt river, surrounded by the most breathtaking scenery, the fisherman will encounter a large variety of indigenous wildlife that will add greatly to the pleasure of the day.

Fly fishing lessons can be arranged by the Hotel with experienced Ghillies, whose expert tuition and personal knowledge of the local waters is invaluable. They will also give lessons in the art of tying your own fly or act as Ghillie to Hotel guests requiring their special knowledge.

Rod licences can be obtained at the Hotel.

Tyddyn Llan
Country House Hotel & Restaurant
Llandrillo
Near Corwen
Clwyd
Tel: (049 084) 264
Fax: (049 084) 264

ULBSTER ARMS HOTEL

Anglers are beginning to re-discover the delights of brown trout fishing on the remote hill lochs of the northern Highlands. Apart from the natural beauty of their setting and the peace which surrounds them, they provide both fish and fishing of a quality far higher than many people today realise. Examples of the best of them are the hill lochs managed by Thurso Fisheries Limited for the Ulbster Arms Hotel, which has boats on these lochs and can arrange permits for others in the area.

The Hotel is the centre for fishing the River Thurso, one of Scotland's finest fly only salmon rivers, having both a Spring and Autumn run.

As well as fishing, many other outdoor pursuits can be undertaken using the hotel as a base; Birdwatching, Photography, Rambling, Painting and Geology, to name but a few, can all provide the visitor with the relaxation or stimulus that is desired.

The Hotel also arranges shooting and stalking over a wide variety of moors.

Caithness is renowned for its resident and visiting sea birds and waders, and fully equipped boats can be chartered for Sea Angling in the Pentland Firth. There are also many sites of archaeological interest in the area and exploring the castles, cairns, standing stones and old buildings can fill fascinating hours.

Ulbster Arms Hotel
Halkirk
Caithness
KW12 6XY
Tel/Fax: (084783) 206/641

Comlifoot Pool   (Ulbster Arms)

241

WAREN HOUSE HOTEL

The North East Coast offers few hotels of distinction but Waren House, the first English Tourist Board 4 crown Highly Commended Hotel in Northumbria, and recently voted favourite 'Best Northumberland Hotel' for 1992, is setting the standards for the discerning adult traveller.

A haven for ornithologists, the hotel is set in six acres of gardens and wooded grounds on the edge of Budle Bay Bird Sanctuary, with magnificent views over the sea to Holy Island. Throughout the hotel the furnishings, mostly antiques, and the immaculate and well chosen decor, exude a warm and friendly atmosphere. The rooms and suites all have colour television, sherry, hot drinks, trouser press, hairdryer, lovely bathrooms and a host of extras to make you feel at home. The resident owners Anita and Peter Laverack have created a haven of peace and tranquillity from which to explore the magnificent Castles and Heritage coastline.

Seated in the beautiful candlelit dining room, surrounded by family pictures and portraits, guests can select dishes chosen from Anita's ever changing menu and the 200+ bin wine list. Smoking is not permitted in any of the hotel rooms except the library.

The Farne Islands are just a boat trip away, while Bamburgh, Alnwick and Dunstanburgh Castles are nearby. There are seven golf courses within half an hours drive. The hotel is open all year.

There are advance signs on the A1 from both North and South so take the B1342 to Waren Mill, the hotel (floodlit at night) is two miles from Bamburgh.

Waren House Hotel
Waren Mill
Belford
Northumberland
NE70 7EE
Tel: (06684) 581
Fax: (06684) 484

242

WATERFORD CASTLE

Built around the time of the Norman Invasion, Waterford Castle Hotel stands in splendid isolation on its own island off the south-east coast of Ireland.

The Island's private ferry provides the only access to the Hotel. Once there, guests will find rooms of supreme elegance and luxury and enjoy exceptional cuisine in the oak-panelled majesty of the Great Dining Room.

With Tramore, Gowran Park, Clonmel and Wexford all within easy reach, enthusiasts will not have to travel far to sample the special charm of racing in Ireland. All provide a mixture of Flat and National Hunt sport.

Moreover, major fixtures at the Curragh, Leopardstown and Fairyhouse are all no more than an hour and a half's drive from the Island.

The Castle boasts its own leisure club which offers tennis, an indoor heated swimming pool, gymnasium and sauna, while horse riding and clay pigeon shooting can also be arranged.

In April, Waterford Castle Golf Course will be ready for play. Designers Des Smyth and Declan Branigan have used the natural undulations to fashion Ireland's first island course.

The Castle may be private, but it is not remote. Ryanair fly direct from Stansted to Waterford Airport, itself only ten minutes' drive from the Castle.

For tranquility and luxury coupled with a range of sporting activities, there is nothing quite like the Isle of Waterford Castle.

Waterford Castle - the Isle of the Castle
For further information and bookings, contact:
Geraldine Fitzgerald
Tel: (010 353 517) 8203
Fax: (010 353 517) 9316

WENTBRIDGE HOUSE

Dating from 1700 and set in 15 acres of grounds in the beautiful Went Valley, Wentbridge House has become established as one of the finest hotels in West Yorkshire.

The Fleur de Lys restaurant enjoys an excellent reputation for its high standard of cuisine. It has an international ambience, heightened by efficient and friendly service. The comprehensive and discerning wine list has been carefully complied by the Master Sommelier.

The hotel has 12 individually furnished bedrooms including the spacious Oak Room with its four-poster bed, antiques and Persian rugs. All rooms have full private facilities and direct-dial telephones.

The fine Georgian building surrounded by superb lawns and century old trees, provides a relaxing and tranquil setting for guests to enjoy a country wedding or a private dinner.

The Tudor Room is a small intimate dining room with oak beams and panelling and is a popular choice for private parties.

The Crystal Suite provides an ideal setting for country weddings, private dinner dances and conferences. It can accommodate up to 120 persons and the suite still retains the warmth and atmosphere endeared in a country hotel.

Wentbridge House is ideally located for racing enthusiasts, being close to York, Doncaster, Ripon, Wetherby, Beverley, Catterick, Thirsk and the local race course at Pontefract.

Easily accessible by road, the hotel fronts the 'Old' A1 11 miles north of Doncaster. The A1 is only ½ mile away, the M62 just 4 miles north and is within easy reach of the M18 and M1 motorways.

Wentbridge House
Wentbridge
Nr. Pontefract
West Yorkshire WF8 3JJ
Tel: (0977) 620444
Fax: (0977) 620148

THE WEST ARMS HOTEL

The West Arms Hotel nestles in the Ceiriog Valley, surely one of the loveliest in Wales.

Surrounded by sheep-studded hills and forest there is little to disturb the tranquillity of this setting: peace and relaxation for which the West Arms is widely renowned.

Whilst across the valley floor the fast flowing Ceiriog tumbles through lush meadows, where hardy Welsh black cattle graze and pheasant strut to the water's edge.

There is no 'best time' to visit: each season presents its particular delight, from the wonderful colours of the fern-hung hillside in spring and autumn, through balmy summer days into crisp winters evenings around a log fire.

A charming Country Inn, it is over 400 years old and the visitor is immediately aware of the warmth and character of by-gone years that pervade - slate-flagged floors, vast inglenooks and timberwork abound, all set off by period furnishings.

This period quality extends into the bedrooms, spacious and comfortable and all with private bathrooms. There are two large suites with lounge and TV, ideal for family occupation.

We are justly proud of our delightful restaurant where you can enjoy Chef's freshly prepared dishes and fine wines and there is a good selection of cognacs and liqueurs from which to choose with after-dinner coffee - in the lounge or simply around a crackling fire.

No matter what brings you to the West Arms, hospitality is assured by the proprietors and their staff, ever on hand to give their personal friendly service.

The West Arms Hotel
Llanarmon Dyffryn Ceiriog
Nr. Llangollen
Clwyd LL20 7LD
Tel: (0691) 76665
Fax: (0691) 76622

WESTERWOOD HOTEL, GOLF & COUNTRY CLUB

Westerwood Hotel, Golf and Country Club is located in Cumbernauld 13 miles from Glasgow City Centre. Its location on the A80 makes Westerwood within easy access of the key road networks and both Glasgow and Edinburgh Airports.

The hotel has 47 bedrooms, comprising of standard and executive rooms and both one and two bedroomed suites. All rooms are furnished in a traditional style with modern fabrics, many of which have scenic views over the golf course to the Campsie Hills.

Dining at Westerwood offers a choice of a light snack, an informal meal in our Club House overlooking the course or an a la carte menu in the Old Masters Restaurant where a pianist plays nightly.

Set in ideal golfing country the 18 hole par 73 course designed by Seve Ballesteros and Dave Thomas offers an exciting challenge to all golfers. The most spectacular hole is the 15th aptly named the Waterfall, set against a 40 foot rock face.

Each hole meanders through the silver birches, firs, heaths and heathers which are natural to this area of countryside, each offering a different and exciting challenge to every class of golfer.

Standing on the first tee, the player sees the fairway sweep away to the left and two very well struck shots will be required to reach the well guarded green tucked away amongst the trees. This sets the scene for the round and before the majestic 18th is reached there are another 16 golfing delights to savour. These include the difficult 4th with its two water hazards, Seve's trap, the 6th with Seve's cunningly placed bunker in front of the green, the tantalising 9th with its small undulating green, the 15th aptly named the waterfall - a fabulous par 3 and finally the 18th, possibly one of the finest finishing holes in golf.

The round is over, but not the memories. These will linger with you for many a day and entice you back to once again tackle this superb test of golf.

Westerwood is one of a group of three courses, the other two are Murrayshall and Fernfell. Murrayshall is at Scone, Perth and boasts a Country House Hotel with award winning cuisine. Fernfell Golf and Country Club is located just out of Cranleigh, 8 miles from Guildford, Surrey. For details of these courses please refer to their entries in this guide. Corporate golf packages are offered at all three courses with the opportunity to place your company name and logo on a tee, and reserve the course for your company golf day. Golf societies and Green Fee Players are welcome.

Westerwood Hotel
Golf and Country Club
St Andrews Drive
Cumbernauld
Glasgow
G68 OEW
Tel: (0236) 457171
Fax: (0236) 738478
Pro-shop (0236) 725281

WESTON MANOR HOTEL

Weston Manor Hotel, the ancestral home of the 11th century Earls of Abingdon and once the house of Henry VIII, nestles in 13 acres of beautiful gardens and has been sympathetically restored to its original splendour.

What better welcome could there be than the Weston Manor welcome - a huge roaring fire, friendly, helpful and efficient staff intent on making your stay as pleasurable as possible.

Many of the manor's 37 charming bedrooms retain antique furniture and have garden views, private bathrooms and charming surroundings.

Surrounded by the beauty of the Cotswolds, this is an ideal retreat for those wishing to visit some of Oxford's 650 historic buildings, visit the birthplace of William Shakespeare in Stratford-upon-Avon or the home of the Duke of Marlborough and birth place of Sir Winston Churchill at Blenheim Palace.

After a hard day exploring the Cotswolds what better way to relax than by having afternoon tea on the croquet lawn or beside the outdoor heated swimming pool. For those who still have the energy the squash court is available free of charge and we can always arrange horse riding, clay pigeon shooting and golf nearby, for those who require it.

Weston Manor is able to boast the magnificent baronial hall where delectable cuisine and classic wines are on offer, always making this a memorable occasion.

Weston Manor Hotel
Weston-on-the-Green
Oxfordshire
OX6 8QL
Tel: (0869) 50621
Fax: (0869) 50901

WHITECHAPEL MANOR

In a hurried and increasingly impersonal world Whitechapel Manor is a quiet tribute to calm, solitude, and peace. From the moment that you arrive you will be absorbed by its pure enchantment.

Whitechapel, as you will discover, is set in terraced walled gardens of lawn and clipped yew hedges surrounded by meadow and woodland.

Listed Grade 1, it is quintessentially English. The entrance hall displays a perfect Jacobean carved oak screen and throughout the rest of the house the William and Mary plasterwork and panelling, complete with painted overmantels, is remarkable for its beauty and lusty country character.

The Great Hall is where you are welcome to relax with a magazine and afternoon tea, which might include home-made Devon honey cake or freshly baked scones with raspberry jam and local clotted cream. It is also here, by a fragrant fire, that you can enjoy canapes and pre-dinner drinks while choosing from the evenings menu. The cuisine at Whitechapel Manor has won international recognition and many British Awards. It is Devon's only Michelin starred hotel restaurant. You may begin your dinner with sauteed Cornish scallops with a basil and tomato sauce or roasted quail with broad beans and a rhubarb sauce. Options on the main course include fillet of Devon beef with wild morels and a Madeira sauce or sauteed breast of Gressingham duck with a confit of turnip and coriander. Desserts are a speciality - strawberry millefeuille with a strawberry coulis or warm apple tart with caramel ice cream. The cuisine is complemented by a carefully selected list of wines, liqueurs and digestifs.

You may wish to stay in one of our large bedrooms overlooking the gardens or a smaller cosy room looking out over trees and bank, all are beautifully appointed with a great deal of thought for your comfort and respite. A superb country breakfast awaits. Crisp lightly smoked bacon, herb sausages and home-made chutneys. Eggs? scrambled, poached, boiled, pan fried or omelletes. Or oak smoked kippers if you prefer. You also have home-made breads, croissants and brioche with our own blackcurrant jam or orange marmalade.

After breakfast our guests go their different ways, some to enjoy the surrounding area, some to unwind in our gardens followed by a relaxing lunch and other to return refreshed to the real world. Our visitors book is a silent testimony to the many delights of Whitechapel Manor, many guest promise to return - you will notice that several names do appear more than once - a promise many guests keep.

Whitechapel Manor is the ideal base to explore the National Park of Exmoor, the numerous gardens, picturesque villages and National Trust properties. If golfing is one of your favoured pastimes then there is a choice of 8 courses within 40 minutes to choose from including the championship courses at Saunton Sands and England's oldest links course at Westward Ho! If you are interested in a golfing holiday a golfing package is available on request.

Special breaks are available throughout the year.

Whitechapel Manor
South Molton
North Devon EX36 3EG
Tel: (0769) 573377
Fax: (0769) 573797

WOOD HALL

Wood Hall will be a delight to guests who admire a true country house hotel. Remote and tranquil yet easily accessible by rail, air or car, Wood Hall offers a wonderful location for the businessman or holidaymaker needing a base from which to explore Victorian Harrogate, the Yorkshire Dales and the ancient city of York.

Set in over 100 acres of rolling Yorkshire parkland and bounded by a mile of the River Wharfe, Wood Hall was an ecumenical college before being lovingly transformed into one of England's finest country house hotels. Built of old stone from the estate, it is a Georgian mansion with a Jacobean addition and a new six bedroom courtyard wing. With a panoramic approach of valley and farmland giving way to a sweep of parkland, the guest is greeted with a breathtaking view from the terrace, and the warmest of welcomes at the hotel.

Leading from the grand entrance hall are Wood Hall's three principal public rooms. The elegant dining room with beautiful dark wood furniture offers the ideal setting for a perfect meal, while the emphasis in the Drawing Room is on sumptuous soft furnishings and relaxation. Finally the oak panelled bar combines the essence of a smoking room and gentleman's club, yet still retains all the elements of a country house.

Each of the 22 luxury bedrooms has been individually furnished, some with private sitting rooms. Most offer spectacular views some over the valley of the River Wharfe or into the park and woodland. No two rooms are the same, both in size and furnishings, but all are equipped to the highest standards.

Harewood House, home of the Earl and Countess of Harewood is only a few minutes drive from Wood Hall. Croquet, coarse fishing and shooting can be arranged in the extensive grounds and for the racegoer, Wetherby and York racecourses beckon. Wood Hall is truly a delight that has to be experienced to be believed.

Wood Hall
Linton
Near Wetherby
West Yorkshire LS22 4JA

Tel: (0937) 587271 Fax: (0937) 584353

THE WOODHOUSE HOTEL

The Woodhouse is a privately run hotel and restaurant offering a personal service tailored to the needs of their guests.

In the heart of the Warwickshire countryside, the hotel is ideally placed to use as a base from which to explore historic Warwick, or more contemporary Coventry.

All 17 rooms are well equipped with tea/coffee making facilities, colour television and telephone, residents are invited to make use of extensive gardens, open air heated swimming pool and all weather tennis courts. Its location also makes it a useful focal point for forays into the racing world at Warwick, Stratford and Cheltenham.

A superb range of cuisine is prepared by the owner, Swiss trained master chef Desmond Grundy and his team and served in one of 3 uniquely located restaurants.

The Orchard Room has panoramic views and the style and elegance you would expect from a 1st class restaurant. The menu is varied, the food excellent and the quality of service unsurpassed.

The Walnut Tree Room looks out onto an ancient Walnut Tree that has watched the progress of the building across many generations. The ambience is relaxed and friendly. The Menu, featuring the renowned Woodhouse Buffet, is designed for informal meals, which may also be enjoyed on the Patio overlooking the gardens during summer months.

The Barn is an attractive conversion from an 18th century building and is the place for private parties. Its mellow brickwork, timbered roof and original Minstrels Gallery create a perfect atmosphere. Its quiet location, complete privacy and separate seating areas also make the Barn a versatile venue for Conferences and Promotions.

Whether it's to relax after a hard days racing, enjoy an excursion into Britain's heartland, or just to enjoy yourself, the Woodhouse Hotel can cater for you in a tranquil environment providing excellent service.

The Woodhouse Hotel
Leamington Road
Princethorpe
Nr Rugby
Warwickshire
Tel: (0926) 632303/632131

THE WORDSWORTH HOTEL

In the very heart of English Lakeland, and the centre of one of its loveliest villages, The Wordsworth combines the sophistication of a first-class Hotel with the magnificence of the surrounding countryside. Situated in two acres of landscaped grounds next to the churchyard where William Wordsworth is buried, its name honours the memory of the area's most famous son. The scenery that so inspired the Lake Poets can be enjoyed from the peaceful lounges, furnished with fine antiques , or in the Conservatory and Cocktail Bar with the aid of a favourite aperitif or specially mixed drink.

The Hotel has 35 most attractive and comfortable bedrooms, each with private bathroom, colour TV, radio, direct-dial telephone, and intercom. Some rooms have romantic four-poster beds (a honeymoon package is offered) and there are two suites. 24-hour room service is available. The facilities of the Coleridge Room are ideal for private functions of up to 100 guests, and a marquee on the lawns is not uncommon for larger parties, especially summer weddings.

The Prelude Restaurant, named after Wordsworth's famous autobiographical poem, is the place to enjoy the best of the seasonal produce skilfully prepared by the Chef and his team. The accompanying Wine List combines familiar favourites with some pleasantly surprising 'finds', and a fine selection of claret and burgundies. The Hotel's own pub - 'The Dove and Olive Branch' -is a friendly meeting place for a traditional beer or tasty snack, and has recently received accolades from The Good Pub Guide and national newspapers.

For the energetic and those wishing to pamper themselves, the Wordsworth has an indoor heated swimming pool, opening onto a sun-trap terrace, a jacuzzi, mini-gym, sauna and solarium. In the area, the sports-minded can indulge in clay shooting, fishing and all manner of water sports.

For the golfer, the Hotel can arrange free rounds from Monday to Friday at Keswick Golf Club - par 71 - in a delightful valley setting amidst spectacular mountain scenery. It is also within easy reach of several excellent links courses, such as Silloth, as well as the famous championship courses at Royal Lytham and Royal Birkdale. The Hotel Management will do whatever it can to assist with arrangements at these courses.

The Wordsworth Hotel
Grasmere
Ambleside
Cumbria LA22 9SW
Tel: (05394) 35592
Fax: (05394) 35765

THE WORSLEY ARMS HOTEL

The Worsley Arms Hotel, an attractive stone-built Georgian Coaching Inn, is situated in the heart of Hovingham near York, and has a history stretching back to Roman times. The Hotel is overlooking the village green and surrounded by delightful gardens. Having been built in 1841 by Sir William Worsley, the first Baronet, it is still owned and run by the Worsley family whose home, Hovingham Hall, stands nearby in wooded parkland amidst beautiful rolling countryside.

Elegant traditional furnishings and open log fires give the Worsley Arms the welcoming and restful atmosphere of a pleasant and comfortable country house. The graceful and spacious sitting rooms are havens of peace and tranquillity and are the ideal place in which to relax over morning coffee, full afternoon tea or an aperitif. There is also a congenial bar where residents can meet both local people and other guests.

The Worsley Arms Hotel often plays host to private shooting parties, and with 500 acres of picturesque nature trails and jogging paths, created entirely by Sir Marcus Worsley, it is an ideal place for an enjoyable picnic. Executive Chef William

Dillon, is happy to provide picnic hampers and champagne for guests. William, who was trained in Geneva, offers an exquisite and imaginative menu in the Hotel's Wyvern Restaurant. With its eighteenth century paintings, delightful decor and a host of fresh flowers, the emphasis is on delicacy of preparation, with intriguing combinations of flavour and texture in the food that it serves. Specializing in local game from the Estate, when in season, the carefully selected wine list has to offer quality and fine variety.

The Chef's own herb garden is recognized in his cooking of fine fresh herbs.

Situated on the edge of the Howardian Hills, close to the Yorkshire Dales, the Wolds and the North Yorkshire Moors National Park, the Worsley Arms Hotel and Hovingham Hall are within easy driving distance from the City of York, Castle Howard and other Heritage and National Trust properties, and offers a warm and friendly personal welcome to its guests. Staff will ensure that your stay in the heart of Yorkshire is both restful and memorable.

The Worsley Arms Hotel
Hovingham
York YO6 4LA
Tel: (0653) 628234
Fax: (0653) 628130

THE HIDDEN IRELAND

For accommodation in Private Country Houses, the Hidden Ireland is a unique organisation offering the more adventurous visitor a chance to sample Irish country life at its very best, in a way not usually experienced by the ordinary tourist.

Tourist Board approved, our houses are most definitely not hotels, guesthouses or the average B & B. They are all houses of architectural character and merit with owners to match who are prepared to share them and their way of life with those who appreciate such things. A warm welcome, family atmosphere and decanter of sherry on a tray might be some of the replacements for the reception desk, bar and residents' lounges of more impersonal establishments. Bearing this in mind, it is a good idea to inform your hosts of your time of arrival - otherwise they could well be in the depths of the garden or elsewhere. It would also be appreciated if you would advise your hosts if you cannot take up a reservation.

For the sportsmen there is access to the very best hunting, fishing, shooting and golf. For family holidays they provide tranquil havens where there are enough activities for all. But perhaps the greatest attraction is the ambience of being a guest at a country house party. There is an air of exclusivity and privacy; you will meet the people who actually live in the house and are a fund of local knowledge. The group include great houses designed by important architects, lived in and visited over the years by world famous figures; among our houses there are those that have belonged to the same family for 300 years or more, those that are haunted and those with outstanding gardens.

Prices vary considerably and on the whole reflect the type of house in which you wish to stay. From the charm of a small family run shooting lodge to the special ambience of the great ancestral house, all offer value for money, and above all, a truly Irish way of life. The price for bed & breakfast is per person sharing. If a single room is required a supplement may be payable.

Many of the properties are very suitable for small conferences or family groups and can be taken on an exclusive basis. Special rates can be arranged.

We will be happy to arrange itineraries and self drive or chauffeur driven cars.

Kensington Hall
Grove Park
Dublin 6
Ireland
Tel: (010 353 1) 686463
Fax: (010 353 1) 686578

A SELECTION OF HOTEL CHAINS AND CONSORTIA

Best Western
Tel: 081-547 1515
Fax: 081-546 1638

Clipper Hotels
Tel: (0202) 687777
Fax: (0202) 683404

Consort Hotels
Tel: (0904) 620137
Fax: (0904) 611320

Copthorne Hotels
Tel: (0342) 714971
Fax: (0342) 717353

Country Club Hotels
Tel: (0582) 396969
Fax: (0582) 400024

Crystal Holidays
Tel: 081-390 8513
Fax: 081-390 6378

De Vere Hotels
Tel: (0925) 265050
Fax: (0925) 601264

Doyle Group
Tel: (010 353 1) 605222
Fax: (010 353 1) 608496

Edwardian Hotels
Tel: 081-564 8888
Fax: 081-759 8422

Elegant Ireland
Tel: (010 353 1) 751665
Fax: (010 353 1) 751012

Forte
Tel: (0345) 404040

H H Group Ltd
Tel: (0342) 844400
Fax: (0342) 844566

Hamdden:
Tel: (0222) 813322
Fax: (0222) 811329

Hastings Hotels
Tel: (0232) 745251
Fax: (0232) 748152

Hilton International (UK)
Tel: (0923) 246464
Fax: (0923) 815519

Holiday Inn
Tel: 071-586 7551
Fax: 071-722 5483

Hospitality Hotels Of Cornwall
Tel: (0872) 553655
Fax: (0872) 553774

Irish Country Houses & Restaurants
   Association
Tel: (010 353 46) 23416
Fax: (010 353 46) 23292

Jarvis
Tel: 071-225 1831
Fax: 071-589 8193

Lansbury Hotels
Tel: (0582) 400158
Fax: (0582) 400024

Leading Hotels Of The World
Tel: 071-936 5000
Fax: 071-353 1904

Marriot Hotels
Tel: 071-434 2299
Fax: 071-287 0271

Mount Charlotte Thistle Hotels
Tel: 071-937 8033
Fax: 071-938 3658

Novotel
Tel: 071-724 1000
Fax: 081-748 9116

Poste Hotels
Tel: (0780) 782223
Fax: (0780) 783031

Premier House
Tel: (0925) 413416
Fax: (0925) 52501

Pride Of Britain
Tel: (0264) 76444
Fax: (0264) 76473

Queens Moat Houses Plc
Tel: (0708) 730522
Fax: (0708) 762691

Rank Hotels
Tel: 081-569 7211
Fax: 081-569 7109

Relais et Chateaux
Tel: 071-491 2516
Fax: 071-409 2557

Resort Hotels
Tel: (0273) 676717
Fax: (0273) 606675

Sarova Hotels
Tel: 071-589 6000
Fax: 071-225 3476

Scotland's Commended Country
   Hotels & Inns
Tel: (0349) 64040
Fax: (0349) 64044

Sheraton Hotels
Tel: 071-731 0315
Fax: 071-731 0532

Shire Inns
Tel: (0282) 414141
Fax: (0282) 415322

Small Luxury Hotels Of The World
Tel: 081-877 9477
Fax: 081-877 9500

Stakis Hotels
Tel: 041-221 0000
Fax: 041-304 1111

Swallow Hotels
Tel: 091-5294666
Fax: 091-5295062

Thames Valley Hotels
Tel: (0452) 611233
Fax: (0452) 612945

The Hidden Ireland
Tel: (010 353 1) 686463
Fax: (010 353 1) 686578

Welsh Rarebits
Tel: (0686) 668030
Fax: (0686) 668029

Wolsey Lodges
Tel: (0449) 741771

INDEX OF THE KENSINGTON COLLECTION

INDEX OF THE KENSINGTON COLLECTION